THE CURRICULUM LEADER:

**A Comprehensive Guide for the
Curriculum Decision Maker**

THE CURRICULUM LEADER:
A Comprehensive Guide for the Curriculum Decision Maker

STUART B. ERVAY
Emporia State University

CAROL S. ROACH
The Curriculum Leadership Institute

The Curriculum Leadership Insitute
Emporia, Kansas

ISBN 0-15-505167-9

CONTENTS

PREFACE

There are two disclaimers we must make about the proper use of this book. First, it is not designed to be used as a college text for graduate or undergraduate courses that emphasize theoretical discussions about curriculum design and implementation. Second, it is not designed as a reference book for those who have particular problems in the development of their school's curriculum. There are many books on the market today that provide overviews of theory, or give specific advice to those needing to troubleshoot or solve immediate difficulties.

This book is written to *The Curriculum Leader* —— in the field or enrolled in a college class—who is looking for a systemic and holistic method for restructuring public school curriculum. It is essentially a how to do it manual that contains step-by-step procedures created out of an intensive research and development program started in 1982. Everything written in this manual was created by or with field practitioners, and is a product of "what works" research. The procedures we mention are used in hundreds of school districts around the nation, and at least one state department of education uses them as recommended school improvement techniques. That state is also preparing accreditation standards which fit those techniques.

In order to unify the procedures we advocate, they are collectively discussed in this book as being a *model* for restructuring public school academic programs, a model we call **Accountability Based Curriculum (ABC)**. Throughout the book we will refer to the ABC Model not as dogma but as a guide which is proving effective over time. Because of that, there are certain principles associated with the ABC Model that readers of this book should either agree with now, or be willing to tentatively accept pending the presentation of evidence. Read each of the following principles and ask yourself, "Do I agree with this, or find it intriguing enough to investigate further?" If the answer to either question is "yes," you should find this book to be one of the most helpful how-to-do-it manuals for educational improvement you've ever used.

Principle 1

Accountability is defined as allegiance to a cooperatively developed and implemented mission. This definition of accountability is a significant departure from previous perspectives, since it rejects top-down management as being a primary means for insuring responsible teacher behaviors. Instead, it upholds the need for all professional educators and lay leaders (board members) to be accountable to a clearly written and meaningful mission statement. It is especially important for teachers to recognize this statement as an opportunity to become more professionally assertive.

Principle 2

Curriculum is designed and implemented at the local level, and validated according to state, regional and national priorities. For a variety of reasons, it is important that *local educators* initiate and maintain curriculum improvements. The most important of those reasons is that teachers, who are ultimately asked to implement a curriculum, must possess initial and continuous authority to make professional decisions. While that individual and collective authority must always be subject to review by policy makers and stakeholders, it is necessary for teachers to feel professionally assertive enough to implement day to day changes in the classroom on their own volition. Also, they must accept the need to validate their decisions in terms of recommendations by learned societies and others responsible for the systematic examination of curricular effectiveness.

Principle 3

Parents, patrons and board members are fundamentally involved in the establishment and maintenance of policies and basic procedures that drive curriculum development and use. Community members must be actively involved in all matters pertaining to establishing policy and procedures for curriculum development and maintenance, primarily through membership on curriculum coordinating councils and building level site councils (or advisory committees). It is a local option as to whether lay representatives also serve on subject area committees; however, if the decision is to include lay persons, it is imperative that the district have predetermined criteria for selecting who will serve. All new curriculums developed by subject area committees must be subject to intense and continuous review by boards of education and curriculum coordinating councils.

Principle 4

Teachers, professional support staff, and administrators cooperate in the design and implementation of curriculum. Fragmentation of organizational functions has too long been a characteristic of public schools. School reform initiatives make it more necessary than ever for teachers of all grades, all subjects, and all buildings to work together on the design and implementation of curriculum and instruction. Just as necessary is the need for regular classroom teachers to work closely with special educators, media specialists, counselors, psychologists and other professional support persons. And perhaps the key to this new level of collegiality is the administrator who is ready and willing to work elbow to elbow with other educators in districts and buildings to remake schools into places that insure quality learning for students.

Principle 5

Public school curriculum is created out of broad social and market needs, with an emphasis on the kind of student growth that is compatible with those needs. The primary purpose of public schools in this nation is often hard to define because there are too many agendas and too many assumptions. Some educators automatically assume that public schools are meant to prepare students for college and vocational/technical schools. Others, depending on the location and socioeconomic level of the neighborhood in which the school is located, assume that most students will take entry level jobs after dropping out, or graduating from high school. Still others almost disregard the society in which students will move as adults, and claim that education is to insure that students have the kind of self esteem and academic abilities which will ready them for any future situation. In some ways all of those perspectives are correct, but they are neither blended nor focused enough to be very helpful to students. We need to merge those varied perspectives and help students focus on an adult future that is both authentic and visionary.....and based on the realities of a rapidly changing society.

Principle 6

Real curriculum improvement occurs only when it is approached as a systemic and very long-term endeavor. A major problem with past school reform efforts is that virtually no one believed procedural and fundamental organizational changes required much effort, nor that extended periods of time were needed to make those changes. Today we are indeed fortunate that such a quick fix mentality is no longer the norm, but putting into effect what is accepted in theory is still easier said than done. Human beings tend to forget what original intentions were after two or three years, making allegiance to change hard to stabilize. Only when a well understood change model is used, and constantly reinforced, will original intentions bear fruit over time. Our Accountability Based Curriculum model builds on that concept, and is dependent on a district's willingness to "stick with it" for the duration.

Principle 7

Faculty development is strongly related to curriculum development, and curriculum development requires a substantial commitment from policy makers in terms of time and money. All of us in education are very realistic when it comes to the availability of money for doing anything more than what is absolutely necessary, so to establish a principle like this is not taken lightly. But if the public really wants improvement in the schools, it isn't going to be done without a price tag. An important way to look at the issue is that— to get more bang for the buck—initiatives must be done right the first time, sustained over an extended period, and proven effective in terms of quality student learning, improved faculty effectiveness and morale, and a high level of acceptance among students, parents, and patrons.

Principle 8

Curriculum development, administrative management, and accreditation processes are mutually supportive. A traditional perspective on curriculum among those who administer schools, and those who design and conduct accreditation programs, is that curriculum is an almost incidental part of the school's organization. Virtually all districts have elaborate policies covering everything from personnel administration to facility maintenance, but rarely does one find similar attention given to the administration of curriculum and instruction. A primary reason for that condition is that most school administrators are neither well trained in curriculum, nor are they held specifically accountable by boards of education for the design, implementation, and evaluation of curriculum and instruction. At state levels, and among learned societies and accrediting organizations, that notion is beginning to change....putting administrators in the position of having to work on curriculum and instruction as never before.

If elements of these principles sound familiar, it is because we have associated our "what works" findings with a theory base that comes primarily from the research and writing of three people: Ralph Tyler, Benjamin Bloom, and William Edwards Deming. Throughout this book we make liberal use of the concepts those men either created, identified or underscored during the high point of their professional lives from the 1930s through the 1980s.

To make this book a true manual (defined by Webster as *a handy book of facts, instructions, etc. for use as a guide*) we provide a set of sequential processes to be used by a district's curriculum leader as thoroughly as possible. Those processes are:

- a review of the ABC model's primary points, and the logic, field research, and theories which undergird them.

- the creation of strong academic program governance procedures and documents.

- the establishment of a strong link between academic program governance and the implementation of a results based curriculum.

- the development and maintenance of instructional programs that are focused on the kind of student learning considered essential——and authentic——by stakeholders.

Just four components—1. using sound theory to support good practice, 2. building a firm foundation through academic program governance, 3. using processes that link academic program governance to curriculum design and implementation, and 4. creating and monitoring instructional programs that are based on an essential and focused curriculum—constitute the Accountability Based Curriculum Model. In the next section of this book is a schematic of the step by step processes that can guide *The Curriculum Leader* into using the model effectively.

We are indebted to many educational innovators and field practitioners who have made significant contributions to the book. Specifically, we thank Gerritt Bleeker, Toni Bowling, Clarice Faltus, Linda Willis Fisher, James A. Hannon, R. Scott Irwin, Dan Lumley, Jeannine Schaull, Connie S. Schrock and Kaye Tague.

The following pages depict the Accountability Based Curriculum Model in schematic form. Everything done in the course of your school district improvement project should be based on the processes and steps shown in this schematic.

One way of making sense of the schematic is to place yourself in the position of someone given the responsibility for starting a K - 12 school district from scratch. For the purpose of this scenario, we'll assume the only requirement placed on you is that *a school district be created that prepares young people to become happy and productive citizens in the society they will enter as adults.* To accomplish that goal, it is clear that students should possess certain skills and generalized areas of knowledge. Therefore those selected as teachers should already possess the skills and knowledge areas you want students to demonstrate, as well as the ability to effectively teach young people. It seems logical, then, that the first order of business is to choose teachers who:

- understand what the school district is intended to do,
- have the education and background that reflect society's priorities, and
- can design and implement the kind of curriculum and instruction which match those priorities.

Teachers who meet those criteria are not easy to find because our present system of higher education does not usually sponsor teacher preparation programs that make clear what the mission of public schooling is — or ought to be — in terms of society's evolving priorities. Another problem is that teachers are rarely trained in their preservice preparation programs to be curriculum decision makers . Those problems notwithstanding, we will assume that you were successful in finding a quality teaching staff and are able to give them training in the theory base you intend to use. That theory base, found in the schematic under the section entitled **Theories That Support Practice**, comes from three important researchers: William Edwards Deming, Ralph Tyler, and Benjamin Bloom.

The second order of business is to create a process for building and maintaining the school's curriculum. In your new school it is important that the curriculum stay focused on real societal needs, and that teachers <u>continuously</u> view curriculum and instruction as being authentic and dynamic media for promoting student growth. To do that, you need a model for academic program governance that fully and regularly involves teachers, administrators and professional support people in curriculum development and management. That model, found in the schematic under the section entitled **Academic Program Governance**, is sequential, comprehensive, and inclusive... characteristics of a *systemic* method for doing business in any human organization.

Third — because you want to create a strong link among curriculum development, management, and implementation — you identify organizational processes to insure that each written curriculum is aligned with district and school mission statements, and other perspectives developed by the community and educators associated with academic program governance. For example, decisions made by a curriculum coordinating council should have a direct influence on those subject area committees given the responsibility for the preparation of curriculum documents. It is essential that the taught curriculum corresponds with the written curriculum, and that student learning is evaluated on the basis of that curriculum. It is here that the term "design down" takes on real meaning, because your teachers have broken down the district's mission into subject missions (traditional or thematic), and have — in turn — created: (1) course or grade level purpose statements, (2) units of instruction written in terms of student outcomes, and (3) task analyses that tell how each outcome will be taught and evaluated. Those elements are found in the schematic under the section entitled **Linkages Between Governance and Curricular Implementation**.

Finally, it is necessary that teachers understand the critical elements associated with the disciplines taught, especially those having to do with the priorities held by the market place, society in general, and the learned societies. Those areas of concern lead naturally to the creation of: (1) clearer definitions of mastery, (2) better techniques of instruction that lead to student mastery, (3) improved methods for recording and maintaining records of student progress, and (4) more precise ways of reporting student progress to parents. The element that describes some of those steps is found in the schematic under the section entitled **Linkages Between Curriculum and Instructional Practice**.

Although few of you will start your own school district, our recommended processes associated with restructuring are close to that way of doing things. Therefore, restructuring schools requires a new way to:
- select and train teachers *[Rationale That Supports Practice]*,
- involve teachers and other educators in the decision making mainstream *[Academic Program Governance]*,
- connect curriculum management with curriculum implementation *[Linkages*

Between Governance and Curricular Implementation], and

- insure that intended and taught curriculums are essentially the same *[Linkages Between Curriculum and Instructional Practice].*

Understanding these basic characteristics of the model will help you more effectively use the rest of this manual as you systematically design and implement restructuring activities. Use the schematic as a road map, and subsequent sections of the manual as descriptions of what there is to do along the way!

THEORIES THAT SUPPORT PRACTICE

Organizational Management

William Edwards Deming: Since William Edwards Deming came on the American scene in the mid 1980s, his organizational and management philosophies have become gospel-like for business and industry. School leaders began looking at Total Quality Management [a derivative of Deming's theories] a few years later, and are now trying to use that management model. Some view "TQM" as being a corruption of Deming's real message, because many managers would rather use the pieces of his philosophy that serve their own needs, rather than exercise the self and organizational discipline required to institutionalize all aspects of the model. For the record, the Curriculum Leadership Institute has used Deming's philosophy since 1986. THINK OF DEMING'S MODEL AS A CATALYST FOR SCHOOL IMPROVEMENT, OR A TECHNIQUE WHICH CAN SO CHANGE THE WAY SCHOOLS FUNCTION THAT QUALITY STUDENT LEARNING IS ASSURED OVER TIME. Deming is a strong believer in *constancy of purpose, commitment to quality, elemental rather than mass inspection, motivation of employees through encouragement and not fear, improved communication between staff areas, continuous training programs, taking action when it counts, long-range planning, and local development of solutions.*

Curriculum

Ralph Tyler: Tyler's work is usually said to be derived from the progressive era of school reform, but he synthesized its basic principles better than anyone else as a consequence of serving as research director for the Eight Year Study. His *Basic Principles for Curriculum and Instruction* was taken from the Eight Year Study, and became a syllabus for a course he taught at the University of Chicago. Tyler's principles actually begin with four very simple but essential questions that every educator should ask:

1. What educational purposes should the school seek to attain?
2. What educational experiences can be provided that are likely to attain these purposes?
3. How can these educational experiences be effectively organized?
4. How can we determine whether these purposes are being attained?

Tyler's philosophy is often reduced to indicators that are easy to translate into action:

1. identifying objectives,
2. selecting means for the attainment of these objectives,
3. organizing these means, and
4. evaluating the outcomes.

Instruction

Benjamin Bloom: While Benjamin Bloom did much more than develop his Taxonomy, it is that contribution for which he is best known. Bloom merged learning theory with the technical aspects of instruction, thereby giving more contemporary writers (like Madeline Hunter) specific ideas for helping teachers design and deliver lessons. Also, most undergraduate teacher education students have been taught Bloom's domains: cognitive, affective, and psychomotor. Within his cognitive domain are the famous six educational objectives that relate to these intellectual qualities: (1) knowledge, (2) comprehension, (3) application, (4) analysis, (5) synthesis, and (6) evaluation. We will make extensive use of Bloom's six educational objectives under the cognitive domain when we discuss linkages between curriculum and instructional practice. We believe the linkages are clear: Deming's *constancy of organizational purpose* to Tyler's *design-down format of curriculum design,* to Bloom's *precise instructional planning.*

ACADEMIC PROGRAM GOVERNANCE

CHOOSE A MODEL

School leaders and educators commit to an academic program improvement model, and a developmental period lasting three to five years.

BOARD AND EDUCATORS
MEET...LISTEN...DECIDE

This is an improvement plan designed to effectively deal with external accreditation and assessment of student learning.

CHOOSE A COORDINATOR

Academic program governance is given strong leadership and a priority spot on the district's agenda.

DISTRICT CURRICULUM
COORDINATOR

Note that external assessment and accreditation measures do not drive reform and restructuring, but are more easily met because the district becomes proactive rather than reactive.

PREPARE AN ACTION PLAN

An action plan is prepared based on the improvement model to which the district has committed.

COORDINATOR PREPARES MULTI-FACETED ACTION PLAN

CHOOSE A STEERING COMMITTEE

Steering Committee is appointed by the superintendent, and is representative of all district educators.

STEERING COMMITTEE IS A TEMPORARY BODY OF DISTRICT EDUCATORS

STUDY AND ADOPT ACTION PLAN

Action plan is studied and discussed by all district educators and approved by the board.

COORDINATOR AND STEERING COMMITTEE LEAD THE ACTION PLAN REVIEW

PREPARE BYLAWS

Be It resolved

Steering Committee receives training in the model and creates bylaws to clarify purposes, authority and relationships.

BYLAWS ARE APPROVED BY SUPERINTENDENT AND BOARD

This is a systems approach that emphasizes much attention to detail, yet it is easy to manage once it becomes part of a district culture.

CHOOSE A CURRICULUM COUNCIL

Curriculum Coordinating Council (CCC) is selected according to the guidelines of the model and provisions of the new bylaws.

COUNCIL IS REPRESENTATIVE OF DISTRICT EDUCATORS

A mission is a vision, and a way of thinking and acting. But it must start as a printed document.

INITIATE DISCUSSION OF VISION/MISSION

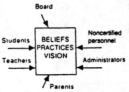

Council begins work on a comprehensive district mission statement to which all district personnel (including board members) will be held accountable.

EVERYONE GIVES ALLEGIANCE TO A WORKING MISSION (PROCESS MORE THAN PRODUCT)

INITIATE PROCESS OF ADOPTING MISSION

Council sponsors activities that lead to mission statement acceptance by general consensus of all district personnel.

CONSENSUS IS GENERAL ACCEPTANCE; NO VOTES EXCEPT FOR BOARD ADOPTION

INSTITUTIONALIZE MISSION

Mission statement is "institutionalized" through staff development and regular inclusion in deliberations of decision making bodies.

MISSION LEADS TO PERSONAL BELIEFS AND PROFESSIONAL PRACTICES

DEVELOP LONG RANGE PLAN

Council develops comprehensive plan which includes curriculum, resource selection, process for implementation, validation and evaluation. The long range plan is usually five to seven years in length.

CHOOSE SUBJECT AREA COMMITTEES

Council begins executing long range plan via appointment of Subject Area Committees (SAC), use of staff development strategies and possible use of consultants.

TRAINING IS HIGHLY FOCUSED, AND MEETINGS ARE CRISP AND ACTION ORIENTED USING SPECIFIC MODELS.

The Council continues to meet in order to:

INSURE INTERNAL COMMUNICATION

Council continues to monitor and lead improvement program; cooperates with a professional development council or inservice director to assure a coordinated and coherent training program; learns how to theorize via connections to state and national improvement models and concepts.

COMMUNICATION SHOULD BE ACTIVE IN ALL IMPROVEMENT FUNCTIONS

MAKE INNOVATION INCLUSIVE

Implementation requires considerable staff development, primarily to assure an understanding of results based concepts and implications behind mastery learning, alignment of purposes with site-based strategies and appropriate assessment.

CORRALLING CONCEPTS AND PRACTICES WITHIN A SCHOOL IMPROVEMENT PERIMETER IS BOTH POSSIBLE AND ESSENTIAL

CAREFULLY MONITOR PROGRESS

Council carefully monitors progress to be certain that organizational short-circuiting and teacher burnout are avoided.

TRYING TO DO TOO MUCH TOO SOON IS A MAJOR PROBLEM IN ALL ORGANIZATIONS

WORK WITH BUILDING ADMINISTRATORS/TEAMS

Building administrators are more important than ever, because they must work with the day-to-day challenges teachers face as they try to implement new concepts.

ADMINISTRATIVE LEADERSHIP BECOMES MORE INTERACTIVE, NURTURING AND FACILITATIVE

MAKE EXTERNAL MANDATES WORK FOR YOU

EXTERNAL MANDATES

↓

EDUCATIONAL TRANSFORMER (COUNCIL) → DISTRICT IMPROVEMENT PLAN/ACTIONS

Council reviews and acts on all matters pertaining to externally mandated assessment and accreditation. It organizes actions to assure that any required CRT's and data collection/disaggregation procedures are systematically merged with the total improvement plan.

MANY DISTRICTS DO NOT HAVE TRANSFORMERS THAT CAN CONVERT EXTERNAL PRESSURE INTO POSITIVE ACTION

LINKAGES BETWEEN GOVERNANCE AND CURRICULAR IMPLEMENTATION

Step 1

SAC CREATES ACTION AGENDA

The Subject Area Committee (SAC) meets and lays out an action agenda.

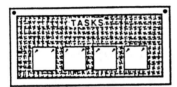

TASKS NEED TO BE SEQUENTIAL OR HIGHLY COMPATIBLE

Step 2

SAC COLLECTS INFORMATION

As an initial task, the SAC gathers information about curriculum that is currently taught.

INFORMATION COMES FROM QUESTIONNAIRES AND INTERVIEWS WITH TEACHERS

Step 3

SAC ANALYZES CURRICULUM

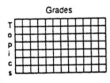

As a follow-up task, the SAC analyzes currently taught curriculum, makes decisions about what is most essential, and decides on appropriate scope and sequence. Alignment with external mandates and assessments is also reviewed.

INFORMATION MUST BE LOGICALLY ORGANIZED FOR PRECISE STUDY

Step 4

SAC CREATES FOCUS AREAS / INDICATORS

ALL TOPICS COVERED

CENTRAL FOCUS OF COURSE OR GRADE LEVEL; PRIMARY INDICATORS UNDER EACH FOCUS AREA

Most K-12 curriculums are characterized by a topical scope and sequence (elementary) and isolated topics (secondary). Topics must become more focused by creating focus areas and indicators.

Step 5

SAC CREATES SUBJECT MISSION

Then the SAC writes a subject mission statement that causes everyone to know why the subject is being taught in this district.

MISSION ALIGNMENT WITH DISTRICT MISSION IS CRITICAL

District Mission
↓
Subject Mission

These stages are quite time-consuming and will require training and practice.

Step 6

SAC CONVERTS FOCUS AREAS TO PURPOSES

Subject Mission
↓
Course/Grade Purposes

The SAC converts course and grade level focus areas into properly written course and grade level purposes.

ALIGNMENT OF PURPOSES WITH SUBJECT MISSION IS IMPORTANT

Step 7

SAC CONVERTS INDICATORS TO OUTCOMES

Course/Grade Purposes
↓
High Achievement Outcomes

The SAC converts indicators into properly written high achievement outcomes.

ALIGNMENT AND USE OF BLOOM'S TAXONOMY ARE VERY IMPORTANT

High achievement outcomes number between 5 to 15 per subject and grade level; those will be translated into units of instruction that will include many learning strands.

Step 8

SAC CREATES TASK ANALYSIS GUIDES

The SAC prepares suggested learning tasks, instructional methods and assessment processes, criteria for mastery, and extensions.

ALIGNMENT HERE IS EVEN MORE IMPORTANT

High Achievement Outcomes
↓
Student Learning Tasks
↓
Instructional Methods
↓
Assessment Processes
↓
Mastery Criteria
↓
Extensions

Step 9

RESULTS BASED CURRICULUM DOCUMENT PREPARED

SAC completes an outcome based curriculum for training and ongoing use by teachers.

DOCUMENT INCLUDES ITEMS SHOWN IN STEPS 5, 6, 7, AND 8

Step 10

RESULTS BASED CURRICULUM DOCUMENT APPROVED

Council and Board approve new curriculum.

APPROVAL IS GIVEN AFTER THERE IS FULL UNDERSTANDING OF ITS CONTENT

Step 11

FACULTY DEVELOPMENT IS INITIATED

Training is conducted by the SAC for the staff involved in teaching the new curriculum.

PRINCIPLES TAUGHT ARE IN STEPS 5 THROUGH 8

Step 12

EXTERNAL VALIDATION EXERCISE IS INITIATED

It is important that the new curriculum meet external expectations to the degree possible.

Step 13

INTERNAL VALIDATION EXERCISE IS INITIATED

The subject area committee is responsible for making certain the new curriculum can be effectively used by teachers.

Step 14

SAC MAKES ADJUSTMENTS TO DOCUMENT

Adjustments to the curriculum are made in accordance with teacher feedback and validation findings.

TEACHERS REPORT PROBLEMS WITH THE NEW CURRICULUM, AS WELL AS ITS EFFECTIVENESS WITH INSTRUCTION AND STUDENT LEARNING

Step 15

SAC IDENTIFIES RESOURCES

Resources are selected that are compatible with the locally prepared, high achievement curriculum.

 Magazines

 Films

Books Videos

Field Trips

 Computer Software

 Speakers

Step 16

SAC PREPARES EVALUATION PROCESS

A process is created whereby evaluation is continuous to assure on-going effectiveness.

PROGRAM EFFECTIVENESS

STUDENT LEARNING

LINKAGES BETWEEN CURRICULUM AND INSTRUCTIONAL PRACTICE

MASTERY IS DEFINED

Teachers and other district educators must continually discuss this. Too many superficial assumptions have been made, so mastery should be considered a qualitative result as well as a quantitative outcome.

The Curriculum Coordinating Council (CCC) is primarily responsible for defining mastery in its generic form, and for helping teachers understand it.

The CCC is responsible for creating opportunities for correctives and enrichments that are conducted outside the classroom.

EXTENSIONS ARE CREATED

Opportunities to master previously unlearned outcomes (correctives), and extended learning opportunities (enrichments), must be planned for in each classroom. These extensions need to be planned for each outcome specific tutorial and peer teaching situation, as well as for summer school classes.

STUDENT PROGRESS REPORTS MODIFIED

Methods of reporting progress to parents should reflect insistence that students master skills and knowledge areas at acceptable levels.

The CCC is responsible for slowly changing reporting processes, so that teachers, students and parents are comfortable with new processes.

Colleges and universities must no longer dictate public school curriculum. There are many other post-secondary imperatives to consider.

SCHOLARSHIP IS BETTER DEFINED AND ACTED ON

Schools have responsibilities that go beyond college preparation. Traditional higher education is only another form of post-secondary education.

PART I:
RATIONALE FOR THE ABC MODEL

Educational practitioners need a sound theoretical base or rationale for what they do for two simple reasons: *it makes it possible to explain to others why a particular practice works,* and *it keeps practice from derailing because of pressures having to do with expediency.* Using a rationale to explain something to others is more than just a useful public relations tool; it demonstrates that an action is being taken because careful prior analysis of human behaviors and organizational dynamics tells us that certain conditions occur over and over again, and that specific interventions seem to work in modifying those conditions. And using a rationale as a kind of theoretical gyroscope is essential for keeping change-oriented practice stable and on-track for long periods of time.

A problem we've discovered in connecting theory to practice is that there is far too much of each. Maybe it's insensitive to say that educational theorists are a dime a dozen, or that practitioner actions are as varied as the limits of human whimsy, but we don't think that observation is incorrect. All educators have seen too many flimsy bandwagons, some of which they have jumped on (voluntarily or involuntarily), going down the street to nowhere. Consequently we have focused our theory-base on the research and writings of three people who are generally recognized as being the clearest thinkers of the Twentieth Century in the areas of organizational management, curriculum development, and instructional practice.

The three people we turn to for theoretical guidance should not be considered gurus, any more than those currently on the consultant and speaker circuit. They are merely men who had an ability to ask the right questions and find the right answers. We know the rightness of their questions and answers because continuous research, development, and practice have proven their theories correct... over and over again. As with Einstein's theory of the universe, it is hard to argue with perspectives that evidence verifies after each examination.

MANAGING THE ACADEMIC PROGRAM

Rethinking the Curriculum Development and Management Process
— William Edwards Deming —

When we first started using the principles established and used by William Edwards Deming, he was not well known in this country. In 1987 we found that his *Fourteen Principles,* as described in Mary Walton's **The Deming Management Method** (G. P. Putnam's, 1986), could serve as the theoretical foundation for the work we had been doing in the field since 1982. We had already concluded that the most significant curriculum problem in schools and colleges was the lack of good ways to manage academic programs. Like Deming, who identified the reasons why American industry did not consistently produce quality goods and services, we concluded that quality student learning doesn't occur because school management strategies are not properly focused and applied on what is most important to the survival of the organization.

Although some educators do not accept business related analogies, it became increasingly clear to us that the management strategies used in American industry, and those used in American education, were and are amazingly similar. The organizational structure of American business, with its board of trustees, chief executive officer, management teams, supervisors, line workers, and assembly line processes, serves as a template for public school districts. It fits beautifully over a district's table of organization, with its board of education, superintendent, building principals, supervisors and department heads, teachers, and classrooms. That template also fits when it comes to decision making techniques, line and staff relationships, and supervisory techniques.

Of Deming's Fourteen Points and Seven Deadly Diseases, we believe that eleven principles are especially pertinent to the Accountability Based Curriculum Model. Each of those points is discussed below.

Constancy of Purpose

Like the proponents of effective schools strategies, we support the collegial development and use of mission statements to stimulate Deming's "constancy of purpose" — as well as an increased sense of accountability among all the district's educators. Our model includes other strategies to insure a constancy of purpose long after the initiating leaders have left: key decision making bodies, guidelines or bylaws under which those bodies function, systems for long range planning, implementation, and evaluation. Time consuming but steady processes for academic program development and maintenance stimulate commitment to quality as an operational philosophy. Some curriculum theorists refer to this principle as a "climate" or "culture" in which quality is understood as both a deeply felt dedication *and* a precise perception of what it is in terms of processes and outcomes.

Commitment to Quality / Less Dependence on Mass Testing

Though we're realists when it comes to the public's preferred technique for evaluating school effectiveness, we believe that mass testing rarely if ever insures quality. While some curriculum theorists speak approvingly of teaching to standardized norm or criterion referenced tests administered outside the confines of the course or classroom, we believe that only well prepared teachers who have given allegiance to the school's curriculum, effectively teach it, and continually evaluate student learning, can insure quality programs and pupil growth. Though mass testing continues to be a much admired method in the quest for quality, there is more than enough evidence to demonstrate its fundamental inadequacies.

Elimination of Fear

Educational leaders might accept Deming's admonition against using fear as a technique to motivate employees — but not a topic to be discussed in a book on curriculum. We believe it is an appropriate topic because the primary thesis of this book is that curricular accountability should not be a function of arbitrary administrative expectation but rather a function of how well educators fulfill a mission — one they have developed and/or readily accept. Unilateral administrative expectations of teachers may be appropriate with regard to basic logistical matters such as daily attendance, preparation of reports, and participation in meetings and special functions. Motivation toward better teaching behaviors cannot be achieved by setting and enforcing such arbitrary expectations, nor can curriculum articulation be strengthened through such methods. In this book we either openly discuss or allude to the concept of collegial decision making, and suggest evaluation techniques which are based on mission related goals. In our opinion, teachers who fear the consequences of not meeting expectations in curriculum and instruction will short circuit student learning.

Reducing Poor Communication

Improving communication is another important consideration, particularly between or among an organization's natural divisions. The Accountability Based Curriculum Model is designed as a K - 12 or district level procedure, not merely a strategy to be used within one of the district's buildings. The primary organization must be the district, and curricular articulation — no matter how large that district — should be comprehensive enough to cover all buildings and all grade levels. Horizontal (building/department) and vertical (grade level) curricular alignment require the kind of attention to communication that is offered in this book, the kind that breaks down the tendency for secondary, middle and elementary educators to view each other as alien creatures performing alien functions.

Better Continuing Education of the Faculty and Staff

Staff development programs in some districts tend to be eclectic (a little of this and a little of that), focused on whatever is trendy, and based on the guidance of professional consultants, speakers, and authors. Though much of that staff development activity is helpful, it is rarely based on the school's stated mission and system for accomplishing it. Moreover, many of those activities incorporate inadequate techniques for follow-up or institutionalizing recommended practices. In our model we advocate the use of staff development programs that improve the teacher's professional stature within the organization, cause effective implementation of the district's prescribed curriculum, and better insure student learning of academic "essentials." We agree with Deming that the education and training of everyone in the organization ought to be continuous; that it should not rely on two or three inservice days a year.

Taking Action Where it Counts

Deming's point about executives "taking action where it counts" is just as important in schools as it is in industry. Throughout this book we stress the significance of making decisions and acting on them. Too often educational leaders are uncertain as to which model to use and hesitate to make decisions or assertively act on them after they are made. Almost every seasoned educator can relate maddening experiences with confusion, indecision, and inaction —— the three purveyors of educational stagnation. Workable models help defeat that condition, as does the confidence that comes with collegial decisions made by intelligent practitioners from throughout the organization. That kind of confidence results in bold action backed by enough long term commitment to see the project through.

Evaluation by Merit / Performance

Industrial leaders are sometimes dubious about Deming's argument that evaluation by performance and merit rating should be eliminated. The issue is reversed in public schools where performance and merit ratings are seldom used for pay purposes, with many taxpayers and administrators promoting the implementation of such plans. Interestingly, there is evidence to support Deming's position that such ratings tend to promote fear and serve to demean subordinates. The Accountability Based Curriculum Model does not advocate merit pay, but woven throughout the governance system is a kind of career ladder approach that suggests greater pay and recognition to those serving on various committees or in certain other functions. In principle, we agree that extra pay based on meritorious performance is a bad idea — but we do advocate extra pay for those teacher-leaders chosen to assume roles outside the context of their day-to-day work.

Reducing Management Mobility

Another ideal expressed by Deming is the reduction of executive mobility. Though we agree with that goal, it is clear that nothing will completely slow the turnover of administrators and board members. So the question is less one of how we slow the turnover rate of key district leaders, and more a matter of how we maintain and strengthen the model even after key leaders have left. As can be seen in this book, one proven technique is full implementation of the Accountability Based Curriculum Model — as the model insists on broad teacher involvement and leadership. In essence, new board members and administrative leaders are actually taught the model by those they are hired to lead. The model becomes part of a district "culture" that asks prospective administrators to accept the existing operational agenda, and to encourage change only after becoming a member of the existing culture.

Long Range Planning

One aspect of that culture is long range planning, because it clarifies agendas for future action without setting them in concrete. Deming points out that an industry can fall victim to lethargic behaviors which diminish quality and even threaten its survival, unless it constructs a vision of the future and acts on it. No plan must be an inviolable blueprint that discourages modification, but it should be capable of providing both stability and manageable change. The model's long-range plan for schools pertains to development of curriculum documents, implementation, validation, resource selection and evaluation.

Develop Solutions, Not Examples to Follow

The adage used by many educators that "there is no sense in re-inventing the wheel" may be exaggerated. True, there is no reason to duplicate effort in basic day to day functions, but when it comes to planning academic programs there is no substitute for local solutions — even if it means a little wheel reinvention. Full acceptance of a district mission statement, scope and sequence chart or any other document or process, is contingent on how much local preparation has gone into its creation. In this book we regularly talk about *process* as being equal to or even more significant than *product*. Products can be ignored but processes become habit and a source of commitment.

Avoid Excuses

As indicated in the previous paragraph, problem solving and program building should be employed to create better products and processes no matter how much the district is the same or different than others. Unfortunately, there are those districts that opt to do nothing or use ineffective strategies because they view their status as being so dramatically different that an "alien" model wouldn't work. As consultants we've heard excuses such as these:

The district is too small/large to use this model.

The teacher union would create barriers to anything we attempted.

Students are already doing well on standardized examinations, so if the curriculum isn't broken, why fix it?

The superintendent / board of education would see the model as interference with their prerogatives.

Teachers are so hostile to curriculum work after that last fiasco that we'd better leave well enough alone.

Building principals would see the model as interference with their prerogatives.

The district is so (geographically/demographically/culturally) (diverse/different) that a district managed model would not work.

Those kinds of excuses are rarely valid if care is given to the implementation of our model or one similar to it. Many projects fail because of inadequate planning and a notion that the timeline must be both fixed and brief. Policy makers almost subconsciously sabotage projects by imposing procedural restrictions and unnecessary deadlines. No excuse is valid if policy makers realize that academic program development is not at all like procedures and timelines associated with the construction of facilities, purchase of equipment, and the hiring of personnel. Academic program planning takes lots of time, patience, and a willingness to adjust procedures as appropriate.

The points made by Deming are recognized as being significant in the execution of the Accountability Based Curriculum Model, and are compatible with principles established by our best known curriculum theorists. Our experience in using the Deming philosophy with public schools is that its application causes:

- improved collegiality among all educators in the district
- a clearer sense of what schooling is for among educators, students and parents
- greater satisfaction by faculty, administrators, and board of education members
- an increase in professional conviction and leadership among faculty members

- acceptance of the notion that educational improvement need not be cyclical or faddish — that it can be systematically built on sensible and long lasting principles

A problem with reducing anything to a few basic principles is that under them is an array of challenges associated with implementation. Implementation is the responsibility of local educational leaders who need both comprehensive training and an effective support system. Local leaders need to be trained so that they, in turn, can train their colleagues; their support systems should not be limited to those who originated the model, but should include other practitioners who have been successful in implementing it.

Training and support are needed in developing and instituting a workable mission statement, and for making certain that every element of the Accountability Based Curriculum Model becomes inherently part of the district's improvement program. There are right and wrong ways to develop and use a mission statement, organize and institute a governance system, establish techniques for educator decision making, prepare curriculum documents, use outside consultants, organize an evaluation technique, and build a communication network.

RESULTS BASED CURRICULUM

Curriculum Development as a Process for Improving Professional Practice, Accountability and Quality Control
— Ralph Tyler —

Most professions give their practitioners opportunities to do more than work at their publicly or privately defined function. Professions, in general, afford practitioners opportunities to perform their craft at levels above and beyond day to day duties and responsibilities.

Many professions offer practitioners opportunities to decide what the craft will be (product or service design), standards of minimum professional performance, the intended impact of the product and/or service, and the way it is practiced on a daily basis. The education profession has provided few opportunities for either administrators or teachers to be involved in defining the products or proceedings of the profession.

Curriculum development, particularly as it was conceived by Ralph Tyler, provides opportunities for professional educators to work with their peers and discuss the what, why and how of education, schooling, and teaching. Without opportunities for professional involvement in determining the product and service, educators are not true professionals. Without opportunities for involvement in curriculum development, educators have no influence in products other than on that aspect of the curriculum which is practiced in their individual classrooms.

Tyler, more than any other curriculum theorist in the Twentieth Century, believed that deciding the content of curriculum means understanding the needs of learners in terms of the society in which they live and the subject being taught. The people working in schools who best undrstand those learner needs are teachers, so Tyler believed that teachers who together have established a solid philosophy can best initiate decisions about curricular content. That kind of involvement makes school become a dynamic and living institution.

Today, few district educators — even those identified as leaders — sense any real opportunity to be involved in curriculum development. Most administrators are prepared and given opportunities to work with budgets, transportation, food service, facilities, personnel and other such aspects of organizational management, and are held specifically accountable for those areas. However, we do not enjoy the same success in our leadership of curriculum and instruction, as we have great difficulty in deciding *who* is responsible for *what* outcomes and means. Inability to decide these basic issues leaves curriculum accountability weak in comparison to areas like budget and transportation.

In its simplest form, accountability means meeting collegially determined expectations. These expectations answer questions about who, what and how. In school districts where there are no specified expectations based on a clear mission statement, accountability can not and does not exist.

In most districts the design and maintenance of curriculum are responsibilities of virtually everyone and — as a result — no one. Teachers independently control classrooms and are greatly influenced by multitudes of often competing conditions: student and parent attitudes, student abilities, and perceptions of teachers and principals. In addition, textbook content and quality are major influencing factors in the teacher's ability to control content and quality in classrooms. Further, everyone — from publishers to practitioners to community leaders — dictates curriculum without assuming responsibility for anything other than that which serves their special interests.

Curriculum influenced by everyone is not readily definable. The result is a hodge-podge curriculum composed of eclectic subjects loosely held together by common use of textbooks and basic, traditional educational practices. It tends to be a curriculum best characterized as a kind of *trivial pursuit.* Moreover, the curriculum is so filled with academic odds and ends that it is like a river which is a mile wide and only an inch deep.

With everyone in charge, operating within loose-knit and indefinable programs, no one is especially responsible, and academic programs lack purpose and structural unity. The situation is further compounded by liberalizing curriculum to meet individual expectations and interests to the point that administrators, teachers and students are doing their own thing... under that infamous condition known as the "hidden curriculum."

The strongest measure of accountability is accountability for outcomes. Schools exist to promote student learning, so accountability for curriculum in schools should focus on defining and achieving learning outcomes; but, due to a lack of effective methods for accomplishing that focus, schools resort to extensive emphasis on instructional process. For example, teachers are subjected to massive doses of inservice on "how-to's" of instruction: how to develop set, provide checks for understanding, and bring closure, to name just a few. While no one argues that these instructional processes aren't essential to effective teaching, they do not replace the need to determine the outcomes of learning before deciding how teaching should be conducted.

The danger of "process accountability" is that process does not always guarantee student learning. Two teachers may follow similar directions, such as in using appropriate questioning techniques, and end up with completely different kinds of student learning. The use of identical processes (teaching techniques) does not guarantee that students will learn specified content; in fact, research indicates that no one teaching technique is best for all students. On the other hand, unanimity with regard to outcomes (curriculum content) is absolutely essential. Curriculum development models that are designed for accountability provide systems for clearly defining outcomes by answering the critical question, "What are the outcomes of the teaching and learning process?" Once the critical outcome questions are answered, it becomes much less difficult to deal with operational questions of "how?" and "who?"

Traditions of local control and professional autonomy have caused educators to move cautiously in building systems of accountability for academic programs. We resist curriculum accountability because the outcomes of our programs are poorly defined, we favor autonomy over control, and we lack mechanisms for balancing specified outcomes and individual autonomy.

Accountabilty based models maintain vital balances between specification of outcomes and individual autonomy — by design rather than default. In the absence of a design for accountability, we are forced to accept default as an alternative. The lack of a design that results in specification of student learning outcomes causes us to to limit our acceptance of responsibility to process (monitoring teaching techniques). Accepting responsibility for process without specification of outcomes requires that we assume responsibiliity for whatever happens. In an accountability based system, autonomy is best achieved when there is acceptance of the responsibility for achieving specified outcomes for the teaching/learning process. Teacher creativity and decision-making are enhanced when outcomes are specified. Professional autonomy, or power, is maximized when two opportunities are provided:

- professionals have opportunities to influence ultimate decisions about outcomes, and
- professionals have opportunities for full decision making authority in areas of operations, i.e., decisions about "how" and "who."

Accountability based curriculum development and maintenance models have many distinct advantages over other models in that they:

- specify leadership responsibilites in curriculum development processes,
- define the concepts and practices of curriculum development that leaders will use so that accountability for outcomes is possible,
- build in accountability and empower all participants of the educational process,
- delineate roles and functions in such a way that professional accountability is a reality,
- improve professional communications and coordination,
- make it possible for professional educators to develop a real sense of mission and ownership in appropriate decision making processes, and
- develop school climate supportive of improved conditions for quality teaching and learning.

RESULTS BASED INSTRUCTION

**Linking Curriculum Development Processes to Quality
Instruction and Student Learning
— Benjamin Bloom —**

As discussed in the previous section, the successful implementation of any process requires that leaders and practitioners be able to conceptualize a curricular design in which student learning is the intended outcome. Without that ability to see the big picture and how processes fit within it, educators risk the possibility of negatively impacting student learning. Adjustments in process should only be made when those modifications are compatible with a curricular design that is well understood by all. Therefore, it is essential that practitioners think of effective curriculum development and instructional planning as much more than mechanical processes — they must be more akin to cognitive habits and well ingrained mental disciplines.

Benjamin Bloom has been the leading proponent of comprehensive methods for designing and executing instruction... taken from a curriculum that is both coherent and thoroughly integrated into the thinking of the teachers who use it. His taxonomies (cognitive, affective and psychomotor) have long been used to define the different aspects of human behavior and growth. Although most teachers have been taught these taxonomies in their undergraduate and graduate programs, they rarely use them in actual day-to-day instruction. When the taxonomies are used daily, it is possible for teachers to better design, teach and measure their instructional objectives (outcomes). It gives teachers and students a common language that focuses on what students should know and be able to do.

Professional practice, curriculum development and instructional planning are enhanced when three conditions are present:

- there is accurate conceptualization and general consensus on the major constructs of curriculum development,
- leadership has the ability to conceptualize, develop, implement and evaluate effective curriculum design, and
- there is is leadership emerging from clearly defined and delineated individual and team roles.

Curriculum leadership begins with conceptualization of basic theories and fundamental constructs. Accurately defined, theories and constructs provide foundations for building and professional practice of curriculum design.

For those theories and constructs to be integrated into the thinking of a professional staff, there must be a systematically applied common language to facilitate accurate communication, a clear definition of roles and responsibilities so that each participant understands indiviudal and collective tasks, a step by step process that provides a road map for everyone to follow, and the best possible interactive leadership... the kind that inspries others to respond dynamically as fully functioning participants in the process.

Although we know that some teaching in classrooms is guided by prescribed instructional programs (curriculum guides), we also know that some teaching may not be supported or constrained by either a district curriculum or a prescribed instructional program (such as those found in text-related materials). Such teaching is conducted by teachers who are neither compelled to deviate from prescribed programs nor restrained from doing so. The following example may help clarify actual interrelationships among the functions of curriculum, teaching and learning.

The art teacher lectures her class about general behavior in school assemblies, emphasizing the virtues of self control and individual responsibility. Her lecture is appropriate as a response to incidents of student misbehavior, as most school curriculum designs include either explicit or implicit statements about good citizenship. However, there is no instructional plan (curriculum guide) that directs a teacher of art to teach students about citizenship. Hence, teaching about citizenship is not part of the planned program of instruction but permissible in the total activities of teachers because of the curriculum goal to produce "good citizens."

In reality there will never be a pure interrelationship that both supports and constrains the sequential functions of curriculum, teaching and learning. However, current disparities and haphazard relationships can certainly be improved upon and, in fact, must be improved if schools are to be both efficient and effective in helping students learn. It is imperative that mechanisms are devised and implemented to integrate relationships among curriculum, teaching and learning.

It is not a question whether schools will have curriculum or not. Curriculum exists as it is practiced, either as expressed or implied. Curriculum can be determined *a priori* or by inference: an *a priori* curriculum is based on that mission which is explicit, announced in advance, and clearly evident in practice. A mission can also be determined by inference: trained observers are able to infer intentions and purposes from observed actions of individuals within organizations and from effects (responses) of those actions upon clients (students). However, an inferred mission, if achieved at all, is almost always achieved by chance or default. Though all schools have a curriculum, and therefore a mission, it is our belief that an a priori curriculum design is much better than one based on inference or default.

To Bloom, as with Deming and Tyler, nothing in schools should be done by chance, inference or default. All educators should know exactly what they are doing, what they are teaching, and what the learning expectations are of students. Nothing should be left to assumption, and very little should be consigned to the so-called hidden curriculum. Unfortunately, too many educational programs offered today are of the default type, a condition which needs immediate attention.

DISTINGUISHING BETWEEN EDUCATIONAL AND MANAGERIAL FUNCTIONS

Separating Professional Decision Making Processes From Decision Making That Is Purely Administrative

In addition to supporting and constraining functions, curriculum has educational and management functions. The educational or professional function of curriculum is to define those skills, knowledge, and attitudes that are to result from systematically applied teaching. A well defined curriculum identifies those things to be included because there exists compelling reasons to do so. The management or administrative function of curriculum refers to the organization of resources necessary to accomplish educational purposes. Educational and management plans, as components of curriculum design, include numerous characteristics: They must:

- be written and formally organized;
- identify plans for activities;
- identify intentions, specifically:
    - what learning students are to master,
    - the means of evaluation to be used to assess learning,
    - criteria that guide student admissions to specific academic programs,
    - materials and equipment to be used, and
    - qualities required of teachers;
- include intentions deliberately chosen to promote learning;
- articulate relationships among different elements (objectives, content, and evaluation) integrating them into a unified and coherent whole; and
- be a system.

Curriculum design is a management tool for identifying and controlling results, e.g., pupil learnings. It is also a plan that specifies what is to be done and what is needed to enhance the probability that defined purposes are attained.

Educational plans state affirmatively "of all things we could teach in schools, these are the things we are going to teach." Or, stated in learner outcomes, "of all things students could learn, these are the things they will learn." Educational plans serve similar functions to financial budgets. Financial budgets identify those functions for which organizations intend to spend money because they have been determined to be more important than other functions that were not, but could have been, included. It is the same for educational plans of curriculum design — they establish our academic priorities.

In the absence of educational plans, worthy outcomes in terms of benefits to students are left to chance. Worthwhile outcomes are achieved by accident or default but not by intention or design. Rational and responsive organizations cannot leave to chance those purposes for which they are responsible, and expect to survive very long. The educational plan of curriculum design focuses on the learning process, as well as programs, services, courses and subjects necessary to carry out that process. The educational plan spells out "why" as well as "how."

Another component of curriculum design is the management plan. Management plans spell out all of the ways in which the school will organize itself to accomplish the education plan. Management plans include policies, budgets, schedules, monitoring, supervision, and evaluation. Through the use of both education and management plans, curriculum design results in structuring the school enterprise in ways that define directions and destinations, establish road maps to reach destinations, and organize for support of the trip. Curriculum design is a systematic structuring of schools around purpose, goals and activities. Here is a visualization of that process:

BOARD OF EDUCATION

MANAGEMENT PLAN - EDUCATIONAL PLAN
    [Administrative Team]   [Curriculum Council]

Policies	Philosophiy
Budgets	Purposes/Mission
Schedules	Curriculum Content
Monitoring	Curriculum Management
Supervision	Instructional Management
General Evaluation	Curricular Evaluation

High Schools   Middle Schools   Elementary Schools

Many organizations use a system like the one shown above, in which administrative (managerial) and professional (educational) functions are dealt with separately. The clearest example of that organizational structure can be found in hospitals, wherein there is a board of directors, administrator, and chief of staff. The board is responsible for everything that happens in the organization; its administrator executes the board's wishes with regard to day to day management concerns, and the chief of staff oversees the work of professional persons providing patient care. In a hospital the managerial function exists to support the professional function. For doctors to provide good care, the managers must be certain that facilities are adequate, supplies are abundant, and all other logistical matters are more than merely sufficient. Interaction between the managerial staff and professional staff occurs as necessary, when problems arise or when new plans for serving patient needs require administrative decisions.

In education the managerial and professional functions are intertwined, a condition which tends to diminish the weight of professional decision making. For example, boards of education spend more than 95% of their meeting time on the logistics of running a school disrict. Since administrators — particularly superintendents — serve boards, they too are placed in the position of giving more attention to managerial concerns than those having to do with the quality of student learning. And because of that organizational characteristic, managerial decisions tend to supercede those that are professional in nature. That is why allocations for curriculum and faculty development are often secondary to expenditures on athletic uniforms, equipment replacement, and facility upgrades.

Members of boards of education, when they are fundamentally involved in discussions about curriculum and instruction, have a greater inclination to allocate budgets that directly impact the quality of student learning. Those same boards will be even more persuaded to develop budgets with different priorities if they can actually see — and understand — the curriculum, and know it is being taught.

In summary, curriculum is the foundation for building teaching and learning, and is the boundary that differentiates what schools do from all the things they could do. A curriculum design includes management plans and educational plans; the first explains the "whys" and "hows," and the second spells out procedures for planning, preparing and presenting learning experiences for students that are congruent within the instructional program of schools, and within the boundaries of the curriculum. Teaching also includes the setting of outcomes, directed teaching, and evaluation of the results. Learning is what learners do in response to teaching, and is fundamentally a responsive behavior ultimately leading to a measureable change in what the student knows, is able to do, or feels. Because learning is a responsive behavior, teaching is not a function of dispensing knowledge, developing skills, or professing attitudes and values. Instead it is the development of teaching-learning relationships that create a student responsiveness to the material being taught.

Conceptualizing also includes the ability to understand procedures necessary to actually develop and maintain a strong academic program. Many who understand curricular theories have difficulty in the day to day execution of those theories. Consequently, many pages of this book are devoted to academic program governance: the programs, services and activities designed to accomplish curricular development and maintenance. More specifically, academic program governance includes philosophy, mission, courses, curriculum content, management and evaluation, and instructional management. In short, it is everything that is done to achieve the intended outcomes found in the overall curriculum design.

REFERENCES

Books About William Edwards Deming

Mann, Nancy R. (1989). The keys to excellence: the story of the Deming philosophy. (3rd ed.). Los Angeles: Prestwick Books.

Rosander, A.C. (1991). Deming's 14 points applied to services. New York: Marcel Dekker, Inc; Milwaukee, WI: ASQC Quality Press.

Walton, Mary. (1986). The Deming management method. New York: G.P. Putnam's.

Walton, Mary. (1990). Deming management at work. New York: G. P. Putnam's.

Articles About William Edwards Deming

Blankstein, A.M. (1993, February). *Applying the Deming corporate philosophy to restructuring.* The Education Digest, pp. 28-32.

Brandt, R. S. (1992, November). *On Deming and school quality: a conversation with Enid Brown.* Educational Leadership, pp. 28-31.

Clayton, K. (1991, March). *Wanted: caring, courteous, joyful bosses (total quality management).* Vocational Education Journal, pp. 7.

Collins, A. (1990, May/June). *Quality control as a model for education: It would improve our output.* English Education, pp. 470-471.

Dinklocker, C. (1992, November). *Our Deming users' group.* Educational Leadership, p. 32.

Holt, M. (1993, January). *The educational consequences of W. Edwards Deming.* Phi Delta Kappan, pp. 382-388.

Korschgen, A.J., and Rounds, D. (1992, May). *Quality management in career services, a'la Deming.* Journal of Career Planning Employment, pp. 47-50.

Richie, M.L. (1992). *Total quality management and media services: the Deming method.* Technology Trends, pp. 14-16.

Schmoker, M., and Wilson, R.B. (1993, January). *Transforming schools through total quality education.* Phi Delta Kappan, pp. 389-395.

Total quality schools. (1992, March). Educational Leadership, pp. 66-80.

Latest Books by Ralph W. Tyler

Tyler, Ralph. (1974). Crucial issues in testing. Berkeley, CA: McCutchan Publishing Corporation.

Tyler, Ralph. (1978). From youth to constructive adult life: the role of the public school. Berkeley, CA: McCutchan Publishing Corporation.

Tyler, Ralph. (1976). Prospects for research and development in education. Berkeley, CA: McCutchan Publishing Corporation.

Latest Articles By Or About Ralph W. Tyler

Antonelli, G.A. (1972, July). *Ralph W. Tyler and the curriculum arena.* The Journal of General Education. pp. 123-131.

Fishbein, J.M. (1973, September). *Father of behavioral objectives criticizes them;* interview. Phi Delta Kappan, pp. 55-57.

Fogarty, J.S. (1976, March). *Tyler rationale: support and criticism.* Educational Technology, pp. 28-32.

Klein, M.F. (1976, May). *Tyler and Goodlad speak on American education: a critique.* Educational Leadership, pp. 65-70.

Tyler, Ralph. (1975, September). *Reconstructing the total educational environment.* Phi Delta Kappan, pp. 12-13.

Tyler, Ralph. (1975, March). *Universal education in the United States: milestone influences on the past and future.* Viewpoints, pp. 1-108.

Tyler, Ralph. (1972, December). *What if school doesn't have an oil well?* Compact, pp. 31-32.

Tyler, Ralph. (1974, January). *Where learning happens.* The National Elementary Principal, pp. 38-42.

Tyrell, R.W. (1974, November). *Appraisal of the Tyler rationale.* School Review, pp. 151-162.

Latest Books By Benjamin Bloom

Bloom, Benjamin. (1981). All our children learning: a primer for parents, teachers, and other educators. New York: McGraw-Hill.

Bloom, Benjamin. (1981). Evaluation to improve learning. New York: McGraw-Hill.

Bloom, Benjamin. (1976). Human characteristics and school learning. New York: McGraw-Hill.

Latest Articles By Or About Benjamin Bloom

Apt, L., (1973, April). *Behavioral objectives and history.* Intellect, pp. 445-447.

Bloom, Benjamin. (1972, May). *Innocence in education.* School Review, pp. 333-352.

Bloom, Benjamin. (1959). *Appraising reading progress under different patterns of grouping.* Conference on Reading, Pittsburgh University, pp. 180-184.

Bloom, Benjamin. (1957, June). *Changes in the states on the tests of general educational development from 1943 to 1955.* School Review, pp. 204-221.

Bloom, Benjamin. (1956, March). *The 1955 normative study of the tests of general educational development.* School Review, pp. 110-124.

Bloom, Benjamin. (1956, February). *Development and application of tests of educational achievement.* Review of Educational Research, pp. 72-88.

Supplemental Texts

Burden, Paul. and Byrd, David. (1994). Methods for Effective Teaching. Allyn and Bacon.

English, Fenwick (Ed.). (1983). Fundamental Curriculum Decisions. ASCD.

Glatthorn, Allen A. (1987). Curriculum Leadership. Scott, Foresman and Company.

McNeil, John D. (1990). Curriculum: A Comprehensive Introduction. Scott, Foresman and Little Brown.

Oliva, Peter. (1982). Developing the Curriculum. Little, Brown.

Oliver, Albert I. (1977). Curriculum Improvement: a Guide to Problems, Principles, and Process. Harper and Row.

Ornstein Allan C. and Hunkins, Francis P. (1988). Curriculum: Foundations, Principles, and Issues. Prentice Hall, Inc.

Saylor, J. Galen and Alexander, William M. (1974). Planning Curriculum for Schools. Holt, Rinehart and Winston, Inc.

Schubert, William H. (1986). Curriculum: perspective, paradigm, and possibility. Macmillan.

PART II:
ESTABLISHING ACADEMIC
PROGRAM GOVERNANCE

Academic program governance is not a difficult concept, but it is often the point at which many curriculum development and maintenance projects fail. Failure occurs because those responsible for implementing the process don't recognize the need for initiating and continuing a clear and on-going governance system. Most readers of this book can cite circumstances in which failure occurred because a key leader left, poor communication caused insurmountable confusion, participants in the process divided into camps, or credibility was diminished because a proposed practice didn't work. No model can guarantee that one or more of those conditions won't arise, but the more systematic the governance component of the model, the better chance it will work at the outset, survive those conditions, and continue over a long period of time.

CHOOSING THE SCHOOL IMPROVEMENT MODEL

There are a number of considerations when a district begins its search for a viable improvement model. The first and probably most important consideration is to find a model that defines accountability in a way that creates positive, dynamic and stimulating results. Our accountability based model focuses on a working mission statement, one that begins with a serious yet informal dialogue among change agents in a district. That diaglogue is described in this section.

The Search for Accountability

Educational accountability is a term that is broadly used but rarely understood in an operational sense. No one can argue with the need for accountability among employees or professional persons in any field of endeavor. However, it is often not clear as to what or whom that accountability should be directed. Vocations other than education can define accountability in fairly specific terms. A lawyer serves a client's legal interests and a doctor is responsible for a patient's health. Business people serve their organization and the profit motive. Blue collar and office workers are expected to fulfill their functions at a level established by employers. Standards of performance in all those roles can be precise enough for someone to create and administer a means of measurement, whether done formally or informally.

Teacher Accountability

The act of teaching tends to elude the kind of performance clarity used in other fields. The problem with holding public school teachers accountable is that they are asked to meet three different goals: (1) the current learning requirements of students, (2) the academic and professional aspirations parents have for their children, and (3) social and business needs expressed by the community, state and nation. Moreover, the breadth and depth of that accountability includes many subjects, academic skills, social perspectives and supervisory techniques. Accountability to such a diverse body of clients, outcomes, and supervisory structures is like being accountable to nothing. Teachers can efficiently serve only one master or one directive; beyond that they tend to invent their own priorities and agendas, thereby short-circuiting any imperatives created by the leaders of a school district or building.

Reform by Clutter-Cutting

Reform movements in American education traditionally attempt to simplify the conditions of accountability by cutting through the clutter. The most common approach is to focus on student learning, which is a vague phrase meant to satisfy the greatest number of clients, outcomes, and supervisory expectations. Beyond the fact that it serves many constituencies, the student learning goal is probably the best way to resolve the problem, as student learning is certainly the most logical product of the school's efforts.

Accountability à la Student Learning

Numerous questions arise when student learning is the targeted outcome of accountability. Common questions include: *"What should be learned at each grade level?" "What criterion should be applied for determining mastery of that learning?"* and *"What are the most appropriate techniques for assessing student learning?"* There is a great temptation for educational theorists or supervisors to answer those questions and impose their solutions on classroom teachers. As a matter of fact, that is the procedure most commonly used — usually with poor results. Sometimes the authors of textbooks answer the questions, with the expectation that teachers will use those texts to drive their curriculum. Sometimes district curriculum directors bring many educators together in a process designed to create curriculum guides out of district-level goals, hoping that the educators elected to help write those guides will encourage colleagues to use them. At other times building principals unilaterally assume the authority to develop and direct academic programs exclusive of priorities applied in other buildings or in the district as a whole.

Top-Down Doesn't Work

When theorists or supervisors use arbitrary techniques to establish curricular content and design, and impose plans on classroom teachers who played no role in the creative process, accountability becomes less a function of teaching behaviors and more a function of supervisory effectiveness and "product evaluation" via formal, summative assessment. In other words, leaders "front-load" the system with high expectations and check the effectiveness of this system after it has had a chance to work. The problem, of course, is that very little attention is given to the routine day-to-day functioning of the system itself. Quality goes in with the assumption that quality will come out, an assumption only infrequently supported by a good understanding of how well the system is really working.

Systems Accountability Does Work

Obviously, more needs to be done to help our schools and the teachers working within them to be systematically accountable for student learning. To accomplish that objective a number of premises must be accepted: (1) district teachers and support staff, who are sensitive to community perspectives, must be given an opportunity to create the district's educational mission as it applies to all grade levels; (2) a majority of district educators should be given an opportunity to design and execute the curriculum which is based on essential principles found in the district's mission statement; and (3) district educators should design and execute an evaluation system that is coherent, continuous, and a true reflection of actual student growth.

Accountability = Mission

Educational accountability is present when the majority of a district's educators participate in the collegial development and implementation of a workable mission statement. Mission statement construction and use is discussed later, but it must be pointed out here that motives, conditions and goals for preparing a mission statement must be clear in the minds of all district educators before work is begun on the statement itself. Laying that foundation is a kind of precondition for establishing a climate for accountable behaviors.

Accountability is not attained through use of fear, no matter how innocuous-sounding the fear-causing agent. For example, two words are often used interchangeably to elicit accountable behaviors: **expectations** and **standards**. Connotative interpretations of those words imply that an "expectation" is something a superior holds over a subordinate, while "standards" are criteria that have been prepared and issued by an undefined source. The word "expectation," though a mild term to administrators, can be a red flag for teachers. "Standards," on the other hand, can easily come from a collegially developed mission statement to which all professionals in the district have — without fear — pledged some allegiance.

Before work begins on the mission statement, you, as a curriculum leader, can begin building a climate in which accountability is made a professional reality. Here are specific actions you can take.

1. *List everything you think the district has accepted responsibility for accomplishing, either informally or formally.*

   In your list be certain to add any community based initiatives related to athletics, entrepreneurship, youth-at-risk, or integration. Although a more formal needs assessment process may be used later, this stage is simply a brainstorming activity you and your associates use to increase your own sensitivity to the wishes of the district's constituencies. For example, some rural states are giving serious thought to converting curricular priorities to such previously adjunctive studies as entrepreneurship, statistics, and technology.

2. *Prioritize the list from most to least important.*

   Though you may think it presumptuous to undertake such a task yourself, you need to practice an exercise you'll soon be asking others to perform. It isn't easy, and you may find yourself saying that all aspects of the curriculum are equally important — a perspective which can sabotage accountable behaviors. To avoid that condition, simply ask yourself what the logical and traditional role of school has been — and what has previously been or could be relegated to community agencies other than schools. Narrowing your focus to essentials helps accountability become possible.

3. *Using your prioritized list, pick the top few responsibilities that unquestionably belong in the school.*

   Those responsibilities that schools might totally or partially relinquish, if allowed, could include functions like certain sports programs, special interest courses, and time-consuming services. Be as exclusive as possible so that a focus can be sharpened on specific and very identifiable student learning needs.

4. *Now that the focus has become a bit sharper, write a paragraph which succinctly outlines the primary purpose of your school district.*

   This exercise gives you practice in word-smithing — saying something clear and meaningful in just a few chosen phrases. It is the kind of statement that parents, patrons, and older students should be able to understand and appreciate... primarily because it centers on student learning. It is also a statement that the district's educators could use in the most practical sense, thereby moving it out of the realm of mere product and into that kind of process which permeates the district's professional culture. Remember, your statement is just a product of informal practice; imposing it on others is not the idea. It should go no further than a few colleagues for their serious critique.

5. *Informally visit teachers, administrators and other district personnel, and casually ask them what they believe the primary purposes of the schools are, and keep a log of their responses.*

This activity works best if you are in a teachers' lounge or at a school lunch table, wherever you can find three or four educators willing to talk about their work in a somewhat casual atmosphere. Don't write while listening to them; copy recollections back in your office. If you wish, start the discussion by saying that an article you read suggests that most American educators aren't really sure what school is for, and, if they are, can't agree as to its primary purposes. That should elicit some pretty interesting responses!

6. *Organize a few informal meetings to "Focus on Essentials," inviting representative educators and board members to converse about the primary purposes of schooling, and keep a log of their general perceptions.*

Two or three meetings, with ten to fifteen educators and board members attending each meeting, should be even more instructive. This time have a few pre-set questions and take notes during the meeting. The participants should understand your motive — that educational accountability isn't possible if: (1) educators aren't clear as to their responsibilities, and (2) society has so many expectations that educators can't meet them all. Meetings shouldn't exceed 90 minutes, and participants should know that they'll get copies of your log. Ideally, those meetings will stimulate even more dialogue in the district. At this time do not invite community members to any meeting; though they'll be included in later activities, it is more important at this point for educators to sort out their ideas and viewpoints among themselves.

7. *Ask your superintendent (if you do not hold that position yourself) to schedule board meetings — or a portion of them — for the exclusive discussion of matters pertaining to curriculum and instruction, and use the first session to discuss your activities and findings pertaining to school purposes.*

Boards of education typically spend no more than five percent of their meeting time on matters directly related to the academic program. That situation frustrates many board members, even if they feel more comfortable discussing routine property, personnel and maintenance needs. The academic program is the logical heart of any school organization, and board members appreciate opportunities to talk about it in some structured and substantive way. Give them that chance yourself, and as time goes on give them other opportunities to have dialogue with the district's educators. Specific suggestions are offered in later sections of this book.

8. *If most conclude that the perception of school purpose among district educators and board members is too diverse or murky, suggest that it may be time to start developing a district mission statement that focuses on essentials.*

Preliminary remarks about a district mission statement should reveal its importance in establishing accountability, and your intent for it to become much more than a piece of paper. To work, it must have the impact of a constitution, wherein its principles permeate the culture of the district. A good analogy is our own American system of government, as everything we do is weighted against a set of standards found in our Constitution. Americans are a reflection of their Constitution, and similarly, a district's educators and students should be a working reflection of their stated mission.

Follow-up Strategies

Before organizing the district for the collegial development of a mission statement, there are some other things to attend to. If your district isn't already sponsoring a quality program to enhance the professional growth of its educators, you should prepare a proposal that suggests such an initiative. The proposal should recommend more than on-site inservice days and awareness-level lectures from experts; it should request enough funding for teacher-leaders, administrators, and others to attend seminars and conferences. Secondly, you should do more to upgrade your own skills as a curriculum leader by carefully analyzing the components of real organizational renewal. In addition to material produced by the Curriculum Leadership Institute, we suggest that you read general books on organizational management theory. Don't restrict your reading to books on educational institutions alone.

The Role of District-Level Administration in the Model You Choose

Administering an academic program is probably the most essential aspect of any school administrator's job. And, in this day of increased teacher decision making and involvement in managing curriculum, the responsibility for controlling and maintaining the quality of academic programs also belongs to every classroom instructor.

For many years academic governance suffered a kind of benign neglect, as school boards and administrators spent most of their time and energy on the "big four" of school management: finance, personnel, facility, and the law. District level administrators concentrated much of their time on the big four, leaving academic matters under the control of a curriculum director or supervisors, the whims of individual classroom teachers, and building principals — to the extent they had the time and interest. This circumstance resulted from no conspiracy to reduce school effectiveness; it happened because the components of the big four are nuts and bolts tangible, visible to the public, and sources of real concern among taxpayers who are accustomed to holding public servants accountable when it comes to money, employee selection, plant maintenance, and avoidance of litigation. Superintendents were once quick to say that they got more phone calls about the big four in one day than they received in a week about the academic program. And those "academic" concerns tended to focus on such mundane matters as grade disputes, appropriateness of class assignments, teacher unfairness, concerns about students covering assigned materials during an extended absence, and the district's standing in the race to attain the highest achievement test scores on some norm-referenced assessment instrument.

All of that began to change in 1983 with the issuance of the *Nation at Risk* report, because administrators and teachers were asked questions they had rarely heard before: "Why is that subject taught?" "How come my child is having so much difficulty in college math when she had two years of "A" in high school algebra and geometry?" "Why is there so little geography, economics, and advanced science taught in your high school?" "My high school junior has had American history from 1492 to 1870 *three times*; when is he going to get the rest of it?" "What's the point of covering that miserable textbook from cover to cover when the students will forget most of it anyway?"

Questions posed before, but having a greater impact after 1983, included some of these: "Why is school so boring?" "Why does my child want to drop out of school?" "What good is school anyway except for college preparation?" "What do you mean my child won't be promoted to the next grade?"

Fenwick English, a prolific educational writer, administrator, college professor, and curriculum consultant, began talking about the need for administrators to take greater interest in managing academic programs. He introduced the idea of "curriculum mapping," and talked about the importance of getting control of runaway and directionless scholastic activities. He attacked curricular gaps and redundancies, administrators who weren't sure of what was taught in their own buildings, and the educational theorists who thought that teaching to the test was an academic sin. English was among the first to tell district administrators that they needed to get a better handle on academic programs, because no longer were state departments of education interested in taking full responsibility for dictating and monitoring a school district's curriculum. He also said that common issues, such as those reflected in the above questions, needed definite answers from real scholastic leaders.

The problem with that kind of admonishment was that it was aimed at people who didn't really know how to get control of the curriculum. The main strategies most administrators used were to issue a few directives, appoint some ad hoc committees, hire a curriculum specialist, and find a consultant. Few superintendents had any interest in becoming involved personally, as problems associated with the big four were as pervasive and time-consuming as ever. So-called "solutions" to the curriculum problem rarely worked because nobody realized that minimal attention given to a major problem is not only ineffective, it can often backfire. There are untold American school districts in which the term "curriculum development project" elicits everything from amusement to open hostility.

Adjusting Priorities

The first step toward overcoming disdain or open resentment of academic planning is to replace the big four with the "big five," locating the curriculum and instruction program in a position at least as important as personnel, and more important than the other three. Creating the change isn't easy, as it requires much more of board members, administrators and teachers than taking a pledge to reform their thinking. It means the changing of agendas so that boards, administrative councils, teaching faculties, and parent advisory groups talk about curriculum and instruction more than any other topic. It means that money is budgeted for improvements in curriculum and instruction, an amount that extends beyond expenditures for teachers, textbooks, and facilities.... money budgeted to provide extra time, space, training, and informal dialogue necessary to build the school district into a cohesive academic unit. A certain discipline is necessary to make all that happen, because intensive examination and discussion of curriculum and instruction will <u>not</u> be innately satisfying activities. Unlike other topics in the big five, academic considerations are often slippery, vague, controversial, hard to draw conclusions about, and almost impossible in terms of developing locally recognized expertise. But conditions can be created to make the job easier, and those conditions flourish within a well-organized governance system.

Model Selection Basics:

- The model should define accountability as being allegiance to a cooperatively developed and implemented mission.

- A curriculum that is designed down from a clear mission, which contains specific standards for student learning, causes accountability to be better understood by those who teach and evaluate the quality of student learning.

- Accountability based on top-down expectations of administrators or external agencies, through use of traditional supervisory techniques or norm and criterion referenced examinations, creates a dysfunctional climate in the school or district.

- Systems accountability (focused on the cooperatively prepared and implemented mission) works because the district's key players are thoroughly involved in creating processes that lead to quality student learning.

- Curriculum leaders can create that climate by (1) thinking deeply about what educators must focus on (as essentials) to better serve their students and community, (2) opening a dialogue among local educators and lay leaders to help them consider learnings that should be essential, and (3) use that dialogue to initiate development of the district mission.

- Create a perspective among administrators and board members that makes curriculum and instruction at least as important as policies having to do with finance, personnel, building maintenance, and legal issues.

CHOOSING THE CURRICULUM COORDINATOR

Before any other action is contemplated, a superintendent and board should select — or reaffirm confidence in — a district curriculum coordinator. That job can be given to either a teacher or administrator, and — depending on the size of the district — may be a full or part-time assignment. The position should be allocated a respectable remuneration and stature within the organizational hierarchy. Since it is such a key role, a superintendent must give considerable attention to personal and professional qualifications, and avoid being swayed by such factors as seniority and credentials. Among those qualifications would logically be these characteristics, that the appointee: is obviously intelligent, has the ability to interact effectively with others, demonstrates creativity, gives attention to detail, writes and speaks well, understands and uses democratically dynamic leadership styles, and manifests a high degree of personal and professional accountability. The search for a curriculum coordinator, if one isn't already in place, should be limited to the organization's roster of employees since it is essential that the appointee already have a local track record that is known and respected by colleagues. Too many districts search for superstars outside the organization instead of identifying and nurturing local talent. The practice of hiring high powered outsiders virtually assures a year or two of interpersonal "waltzing around" before getting down to business. Moreover, superstars usually acquire that status via credentials and ego enhancement techniques — neither of which is useful in a leader who is expected to roll up sleeves and vigorously interact with others in a collegial decision-making format.

Coordinator Selection Basics:

- **The coordinator should be selected from the local faculty and staff.**

- **The coordinator should be intellectually capable and work effectively with others.**

- **The coordinator should be creative, and capable of giving attention to detail.**

- **The coordinator should write and speak well.**

- **The coordinator should understand dynamic leadership principles, to include the ability to conduct an effective meeting.**

- **The coordinator should demonstrate a high degree of personal and professional accountability.**

PREPARING THE ACTION PLAN

Once a coordinator is in place, the appointee's first task is to research and write an action plan. The plan is prepared after a careful review of the district's current status is completed. That review examines curriculum development and maintenance procedures over the past three to five years. Our experience reveals that districts vary from doing nothing more than maintaining textbook adoption policies to trying one or two intensive curriculum projects that more than likely fail. It is important, however, to use any previously-developed processes or materials that seem to be effective and can be interwoven with future efforts. While teachers become annoyed over failed projects in which they have put much time and effort, they become even more upset when something good that came out of the earlier enterprise is blithely ignored or discarded in the new one.

The coordinator should also investigate processes used by districts that have apparently been successful in their projects, and do some *very* selective reading. Most books on curriculum are written by and for theorists, while educational practitioners are crying for "how-to" manuals. Over-theorizing curriculum development within the first five years of work in a district that needs to give much attention to the basics is a sure way to sabotage an entire project. Theorizing *is* important, but only after an organizational culture has been established in which attention to crucial details and communication systems is accepted, and becomes a matter of habit.

The action plan should be primarily written for the superintendent and board of education, although a critical mass of teachers and other professional educators in the district must have a chance to review and critique it. It must be concise, clear, and augmented with graphics, timelines, and budgets. It must be designed as a reference to be used in conjunction with a formal presentation as well as follow-up reading. Literary style and careful attention to detail will make the document both more appealing and readable, so a table of contents is included as well as headings, subheadings, and the wide variety of formats now available with most desktop publishing equipment.

The plan's contents should incorporate a brief introduction, a few important concepts to understand, the actions to be accomplished during the first year, materials to be produced that first year, intended progress timelines, a proposed budget, and a recommendation as to how the project should be evaluated at the end of year one. If our Accountability Based Curriculum Model is used, the plan would specifically include: (1) a glossary which explains acronyms and professional jargon, (2) a proposed table of organization for academic program administration, (3) an overview of essential curriculum personnel, (4) the make-up of committees and their intended functions, (5) training procedures, (6) techniques used to develop a mission statement, (7) the action agenda for curriculum development, (8) first year timelines, (9) method for preparing a long-range plan, and (10) proposed first year budget. A complete sample of a plan of action is located in the appendix to this book.

Action Plan Basics:

- Preparation of the action plan is the initial responsibility of the curriculum coordinator.

- The purpose of the action plan is to outline what is to be done the first year. In the vernacular, it is the plan for "getting the show on the road."

- Although all of the district's teachers, professional support persons, and administrators have an interest in the action plan, the plan should be primarily written for the board of education and superintendent. Therefore it should be written clearly and without use of educational jargon.

- To the extent possible, the plan should interweave past efforts at curriculum development and school improvement.

- The plan should include (1) a brief introduction, (2) a few important concepts to understand [including a glossary and table of organization], (3) an overview of essential curriculum personnel and committees, (4) actions to be completed the first year — including mission statement development, preparation of the long range plan, and training procedures [focusing on the subject area committee's action agenda], (5) materials to be produced the first year, (6) intended progress timelines, (7) a proposed budget, and (8) a recommendation as to how the project should be evaluated at the end of year one.

STUDYING AND ADOPTING THE ACTION PLAN

The action plan is written by the coordinator, but even the best writers and leaders need to have their work critiqued. The orginal plan in this model provided for a critique by the administrative team and board of education, and that continues to be a recommendation. However, many districts also use the newly formed steering committee, described below, to review and critique the action plan. The advantage in asking a steering committee to check the action plan is that a critical mass of teachers becomes involved in the process.

The administrative team, board of education and steering committee should evaluate the plan in terms of its clarity, efficacy of processes recommended, appropriateness of timelines, and adequacy of the proposed budget. Administrative teams and boards of education will certainly have a special interest in these two areas: release time provisions for teachers and the budget. Justifications for recommendations in those two areas must be logical and well researched.

The steering committee should be asked to focus on processes and timelines, because teacher members of that committee and their building level associates are the people who must shoulder the burden of making everything work. Most teachers now have a good sense of how much real time and effort it requires to satisfactorily complete a major undertaking, especially if they are able to establish mental scenarios for accomplishing specific tasks.

An action plan must be adopted by the board of education and accepted as realistic by an administrative team and steering committee. Although modification of an action plan is certainly a possibility at some point in the first year, it is much easier to modify an existing plan than feel your way along without any guidelines at all.

Basics of Studying and Adopting the Action Plan:

- **The critique is conducted by the board of education, administrative team and newly appointed steering committee.**

- **Justifications for teacher release time for meetings, and amounts shown in the budget should be logical and well researched in preparation for talking with the administrative team and board of education.**

- **Justifications for processes and timelines should be logical and well researched in preparation for talking with the steering committee.**

IDENTIFYING THE STEERING COMMITTEE

The steering committee is an ad hoc group with one essential purpose: to write the bylaws that guide the academic program's decision making process. It can also be used to critique the action plan. Ideally, the steering committee should exist no more than two or three months.

A steering committee is appointed by the district superintendent, and should include a good representation of teachers, professional support persons, administrators, and a board member or two. If the district has a history of including parents, patrons, or students on such committees, those individuals should be officially designated leaders — such as a PTA or student body president. Using that criterion for selecting non-educators can set a precedent for future appointments of that kind; that parents, patrons and students should be represented by *position* — not personality.

The size of the steering committee should be limited to 15 members, as meetings of more than that number tend to reduce participant involvement. Smaller districts may sponsor a smaller committee, but larger districts should resist the temptation to make it substantially larger. In small districts it is generally a good idea to make all administrators members by virtue of their office, and to select other educators on the basis of their proven leadership abilities. As with the curriculum coordinating council, it is leadership ability that counts more than simple representation of buildings, grade levels, or subject areas. Moreover, the concern over voting power has no merit inasmuch as all decisions are to be made by use of informal consensus.

The work of the steering committee, although limited in scope and brief in duration, is very important to the on-going development of the restructuring program. Our experience is that many members of steering committees ultimately serve on the newly formed curriculum coordinating council, which is the permanent governing body for the academic program.

One might ask why an ad hoc steering committee is necessary. Why not simply appoint a curriculum coordinating council immediately? The answer we discovered over the years is that systemic change requires a "constitutional convention" before a government is formed. The constitutional convention principle overcomes many negative attitudes among those a future governance system will manage. Permanent councils appointed by superintendents or boards of education usually encounter stiff opposition at some point in the school improvement process.

<u>Steering Committee Basics</u>:

- **Superintendent or designee chooses up to 15 members.**

- **Superintendent chooses members on the basis of leadership ability of teachers, administrators, board members, and professional support personnel (representation is a secondary concern).**

- **Superintendent or designee chooses parents, patrons, and students according to position.**

- **Chair of steering committee is appointed by the superintendent or designee.**

- **Steering committee is ad hoc, so its agenda is limited to the preparation of bylaws for academic program decision making, and possible critique of the action plan for establishing a governance system for curriculum and instruction.**

- **Steering committee should be sunset within two months of it's appointment.**

PREPARING THE BYLAWS

Bylaws are the rules and procedures under which the curriculum coordinating council agrees to operate. They also indicate the relationship between the council and all other governing bodies in the district, including the board of education and administrative team. They establish procedures and standards that will govern the CCC and its individual members. They are adopted by the CCC, accepted by the superintendent and board of education, and made available to all certified personnel in the district. The bylaws constitute a working document that provides ongoing guidance, as well as a means of settling procedural misunderstandings.

Bylaws should be written and scheduled for periodic revision, and address the following: definitions, functions, meetings, decision making processes, quorum, channels of communication, agenda development and procedure, maintenance of meeting records, amendments, and personnel. The following example is a set of bylaws actually used by a school district. It is presented here not for the purpose of copying verbatim, but to provide a format that can be used in preparing bylaws that fit your local circumstances.

Curriculum Coordinating Council Bylaws

Definition

The Curriculum Coordinating Council (CCC) is a representative group of district personnel that advises the Board of Education, through the superintendent, in matters concerning curriculum development and instructional planning. The CCC will serve as a sounding board for certified personnel in curriculum matters.

Functions

The major functions of the CCC will be to:

1. *Communicate to the superintendent and the board of education long-range plans for curriculum development and review.*
2. *Establish and coordinate a systematic, ongoing process for evaluating curricula.*
3. *Establish and coordinate a systematic, ongoing process for resource selection.*
4. *Act as the communication link between the certified staff, the superintendent and the board of education.*
5. *Study curriculum concerns of certified personnel, the superintendent, and the board of education.*
6. *Coordinate subject area committees to develop and implement high achievement, results based curriculum.*
7. *Promote and encourage communication between buildings and levels within the district.*
8. *Recommend to the superintendent and board of education a yearly CCC budget.*

Meetings
GENERAL PROCEDURES: *The CCC will meet a minimum of once a month for the purpose of carrying out its functions. A primary meeting date should be established for each month and noted on the district calendar. A second meeting date each month should also be tentatively reserved for use if needed. At the beginning of each school year members will be informed of all regular meeting dates. Notification of all extra meetings shall be given at least five days prior to the meeting. Special meetings may be called as needed by the coordinator, superintendent, or at least five members of the CCC.*

DECISION MAKING PROCESS: *All decisions shall be by consensus of those members present.*

QUORUM: *A quorum constitutes a simple majority of the total membership. Meetings will not be conducted unless a quorum is present.*

CHANNELS OF COMMUNICATION: *All recommendations of the CCC will initially be made to the superintendent by the district curriculum coordinator, who serves as chairperson of the CCC. In the event that the superintendent does not support the recommendations of the CCC, the coordinator will have the opportunity to address the board of education.*

AGENDA DEVELOPMENT AND PROCEDURE: *Agenda items for consideration by the CCC may be proposed by the members, by certified personnel, the superintendent or by members of the board of education. The items should be submitted to the chairperson at least ten working days prior to the scheduled meeting of the council. The agenda and notification of the meeting shall be distributed to members of the CCC, one copy per building for posting, and to each member of the board. Distribution shall occur at least five working days prior to the scheduled meeting. The coordinator shall determine the amount of time to be spent on each agenda item.*

MAINTAINING MEETING RECORDS: *Records of meetings and materials submitted to the CCC shall be forwarded to the coordinator who will maintain a master file for reference purposes. A copy of these records will also be kept on file by the secretary. Minutes of all meetings shall be kept by the secretary. Minutes will be forwarded to the coordinator, CCC members, the superintendent, members of the board of education, and to each building for posting. Summaries of subject area committee meetings shall be forwarded to the coordinator.*

Amendments
The mission statement and the bylaws are subject to review at the beginning of each year. If changes, corrections, or updating is determined to be necessary after this analysis, then the CCC will make the amendments following the standard procedure for decision-making.

Personnel

CURRICULUM COORDINATOR: The position of curriculum coordinator shall be a permanent one. The coordinator shall serve at the discretion of the board and shall be recommended to the board of education by the superintendent. This recommendation may occur only after formal application and a personal interview with the superintendent. The applicant must meet the following educational and professional requirements, and must exhibit a willingness to commit a minimum of two years to the curriculum development process. The coordinator must have had at least five years of effective teaching experience. The coordinator must demonstrate leadership ability, an interest in the curriculum development process, an ability to be objective yet able to energize a group to positive action, and an ability to communicate. Finally, this individual must demonstrate a professional attitude and be inclined toward detail work. The salary will be a stipend payment representing a percentage of the teacher base pay as well as a negotiated amount arrived at by mutual consent of the applicant and superintendent, with ultimate approval given by the board of education. The salary will be reviewed yearly as will the number of hours worked. The duties of the curriculum coordinator are these:

1. *Works with the superintendent in monitoring needed changes in board policies relating to the district's instructional and curriculum programs.*
2. *Assists the curriculum coordinating council in the development and the effective organization of instruction and curriculum into a meaningful and coherent working relationship at the elementary, intermediate, middle level and senior high schools.*
3. *Emphasizes to each board member, administrator, and instructor the value of quality curriculum development and utilization of the curriculum documents in every classroom, K-12.*
4. *Monitors curriculum document usage in order to assure the curriculum plan K-12 is being implemented.*
5. *Monitors the latest research, trends, and developments in curriculum and instruction, and disseminates such information to appropriate personnel with the intent of providing philosophical direction to curriculum development.*
6. *Chairs the meetings of the CCC to assist in interpreting the curriculum and instructional programs of the district, and participates in discussions as needed.*
7. *Assists in coordinating activities of the subject area committees.*
8. *Assists in curriculum document development and in selection of textbooks and resource materials as necessary.*
9. *Encourages certified staff members to attend professional meetings and take advantage of other educational opportunities.*
10. *Participates in appropriate local, state, and national professional meetings related to curriculum and instruction.*
11. *Acts as a resource person for the CCC, all subject area committees, technology adviso-*

ry committees, and any curriculum study committees that may be added in the future.

12. Works with the CCC on the development and updating of policies and manuals relative to curriculum and instruction.

13. Works with the CCC to prepare an annual budget, to be submitted to the superintendent and board of education.

14. Serves as a liaison between the CCC, superintendent, and the board of education, assuring that all are well informed.

15. Serves as chairperson of the CCC, with the following specific duties:
    a. presides at all regular meetings
    b. prepares agendas for all regular meetings
    c. provides for notification of all meetings
    d. calls all special meetings
    e. assists in conducting inservice activities
    f. in cooperation with the superintendent, selects CCC members and provides their training, using current CCC members as resources
    g. with the approval of CCC members, appoints and trains members of subject area committees
    h. monitors attendance of CCC members
    i. receives all written resignations from CCC members
    j. prepares an annual report on the activities of the CCC to be submitted to the superintendent and board of education
    k. recommends yearly committee goals and objectives
    l. represents the CCC at all appropriate public functions, and board of education meetings, or appoints a CCC member to represent the committee
    m. assures that all district committees adhere to the goals of the mission statement and the long range plan.

VICE-CHAIRPERSON OF THE CCC: The vice-chairperson is an administrator who has a minimum of one year's experience as a CCC member. This individual will serve as an administrative liaison between the CCC and the administrators. The liaison will ensure that curriculum matters are dealt with in a manner consistent with the goals of and the decisions made by the CCC when administrators encounter these issues in their own administrative meetings. The administrative liaison will be appointed by the superintendent on a yearly basis by the March administrators' meeting. No additional salary will be allotted for this position. The duties of the vice-chairperson are these:

1. Fulfills all the duties of the chairperson in that person's absence.
2. Confers with the coordinator on curriculum matters or issues that arise.
3. Informs the chairperson on issues and concerns of administrators.

MEMBERS OF THE CCC: The members of the CCC shall be representative of the certified personnel employed by the district. Members of the CCC will be selected on the basis of interest and professional qualifications for the job. Interested parties will be asked to fill out an application and submit it to the coordinator. The coordinator, as the CCC chairperson, and the CCC vice chairperson, will work with the superintendent in making the final selections. However, principals will be asked for their input on teacher applicants and periodically will be asked to make recommendations. Member replacement will be made to maintain appropriate representation. The board of education must approve all new members as well as current members yearly before salaries can be paid. Additional provisions are these:

1. TERMS: Members will serve for an initial term of three years and may reapply for subsequent three year terms with no restriction.

2. RESIGNATION: A CCC member may resign at any time. A letter of resignation shall be written and submitted by the resigning member to the CCC chairperson at least one regular meeting prior to the effective date of the resignation. The resigning member's constituency shall then be notified immediately by the CCC chairperson. The vacancy shall be filled promptly from the constituency according to the selection procedures.

3. COMPOSITION AND REPRESENTATION: Member selection should provide for a variety of personal and professional traits, assuring that all grade level categories are represented: elementary, middle level, and high school. There shall be:

primary teachers (K-2)	2
intermediate teachers (3-5)	2
middle level teachers (6-8)	2
high school teachers (9-12)	2
administrators (by level)	3
support person	1
superintendent (ex officio)	1
board member (ex officio)	1
coordinator (ex officio)	1
Total	15

The planned working number for the CCC will be 14-16 individuals. The board of education will be invited to select one of its members to serve on the CCC. Ex officio means these persons are on the CCC by virtue of their positions and they do not apply for membership.

4. SALARIES: The CCC members will each be paid a stipend for their membership.

Each member will also serve as a chairperson or a committee member for a subject area committee, and will receive an additional stipend for that work. In accordance with board policy, administrative personnel may not receive stipends. Stipend amounts are itemized in the district salary schedule. Salary deductions will be made for CCC members who are absent from more than a total of three meetings, based on the following descriptions. A member will be excused from attending one CCC meeting, either regularly scheduled or called, without a salary reduction. In addition, a member may be absent from no more than two subject area committee meetings. A member must be in attendance a minimum of 75% of the meeting time to be eligible to receive the prescribed stipend. Salaries will be paid on a monthly basis, pro-rated equally each month.

5. *DUTIES: The duties of <u>individual</u> CCC members are:*
    a. *attends all regularly-scheduled meetings of the CCC and assigned subject area committee meetings*
    b. *maintains positive communication between CCC and building faculties, emphasizing teacher ownership of curriculum planning*
    c. *completes a training program in the curriculum development process model being used in the district*
    d. *assists in training other CCC members, SAC members, or participants in the district's curriculum development process*
    e. *chairs a SAC or will serve as a member of such committees in the event no leadership positions need filling (SAC chairpersons are appointed by the CCC chairperson)*

6. *DUTIES OF THE CCC AS A WORKING GROUP:*
    a. *establishes meeting dates and length of meeting*
    b. *reviews, on an annual basis, the council bylaws*
    c. *develops and then reviews, on a yearly basis, the district mission statement*
    d. *develops a long-range plan for curriculum development, resource selection, and curriculum document revision — with an annual review of progress and direction*
    e. *assists the CCC Chairperson in selection of subject area committee members who are not CCC members*
    f. *plans an annual calendar for committee work*
    g. *establishes guidelines for subject area committees and approves work completed by these groups*
    h. *establishes guidelines for a technology advisory committee and approves work it completes*
    i. *assists the curriculum coordinator with the preparation of the yearly budget for curriculum work*

    j.   *recommends what is produced from subject area committees to the superintendent and board of education for approval*

    k.   *conducts teacher inservice, emphasizing the importance of teacher commitment in implementing the curriculum at the classroom level*

    l.   *initiates formal evaluation procedures of curriculum every five years, by analyzing student test scores, class visitations, surveys, teacher interviews, and group information-gathering sessions to determine the effectiveness and value of the curriculum documents*

SECRETARY: The curriculum coordinator and superintendent will select an individual to serve as secretary who is not a member of the CCC. The salary for this position will be reviewed annually and adjusted based on proposed hours of work and the level and type of production required. The duties of the secretary are:

1. *Attends all meetings of the CCC.*

2. *Takes accurate and thorough notes of proceedings.*

3. *Types and duplicates notifications and minutes of all meetings, then distributes them to all CCC members, the superintendent, board of education, and two copies to the curriculum coordinator. Items will also be sent to all school buildings for posting and to other designated certified personnel.*

4. *Maintains all CCC minutes, correspondence, and other pertinent documents.*

5. *Performs necessary secretarial tasks for the timely completion of CCC and subject area committee projects.*

6. *Demonstrates a willingness to work closely and cooperatively with the curriculum coordinator and all CCC members for the success of the curriculum development process.*

Subject Area Committees

    Subject area committees are appointed by the CCC in accordance with that body's long range plan for curriculum development. A subject area committee (SAC) will be formed for each subject area to be analyzed. The primary responsibility of this group will be to formulate an outcome based curriculum by following an action agenda prescribed by the CCC.

    SELECTION: Prospective members of each SAC should show an interest in curriculum development and have one year of successful classroom teaching experience. Exceptions to this rule may occur when a middle level or secondary teacher must be appointed to the SAC because of district size and the importance of that teacher's involvement. Council members will choose SAC members using previously mentioned criteria as well as building and grade level representation to guide the selection process. The number of individuals appointed to a SAC may vary according to subject; however, no K-12 SAC should be larger than 20-25 or smaller than five or six.

TERMS: Members of subject area committees should understand that the committee will meet regularly — and at length — the first one or two years and regularly in shorter meetings for the next two years. Therefore, the minimum term of appointment is three to four years.

RESIGNATION: A SAC member may resign if the position represented is not filled by just one teacher. If a resignation is submitted by a member holding a key teaching role, a process must be established by that member to maintain the integrity of the curriculum building process. In all cases involving the work of the subject area committee, the council has the right and obligation to make whatever decisions necessary — to include removal and appointment of SAC members — in facilitating the successful completion of the SAC's work.

STIPENDS: SAC members will receive stipends in accordance with the policies of the board of education and the CCC.

LEADERSHIP: All subject area committees will be chaired by a member of the CCC. Chairs will preside at meetings, schedule meetings and plan agendas, monitor attendance, work closely with the council chair and curriculum coordinator, report progress to the council at each of its meetings, insure completion of curriculum documents according to a schedule established by the council, and personally present completed curriculum documents to the council.

DUTIES OF MEMBERS: Members are expected to attend all committee meetings, complete assigned tasks, maintain positive communication between the SAC and building faculties, and maintain positive communication between the SAC and the CCC.

— —

Please note that the bylaws statement, as modified to fit local needs, is the only document that may be a replication of another district's efforts.

Bylaws Basics:

- Preparation of the bylaws is the function of the ad hoc steering committee.

- The purpose of the bylaws has two components: a policy that guides council functions, and a policy that establishes the relationship between the council and all other governing bodies in the district.

- Bylaws are adopted by the council, accepted by the superintendent, and included into board of education policy.

- Bylaws are used to provide ongoing guidance, and as a means for settling procedural misunderstandings.

- Bylaws are written to meet local needs, but should include *definitions, functions, meetings, decision making processes, quorum, channels of communication, agenda development and procedure, maintenance of meeting records, amendments, and personnel.*

CHOOSING THE CURRICULUM COORDINATING COUNCIL

A district level curriculum coordinating council should be inclusive in terms of membership and have extensive authority over the academic program. Council membership must be representative of the district's primary components, and the selection process should be rigorous. To give the council real authority, it is recommended that members serve with pay for a period of three years or more.

Initial actions of the council are to initiate preparation of the mission statement; develop a long range plan; select, train and oversee the work of subject area committees; and conduct an on-going evaluation of the academic program's effectiveness. After the initial stages are complete, the CCC becomes the final conduit through which trends and new concepts are shared with district personnel, and the district's think tank or theorizing unit for keeping the academic program on the cutting edge of educational practice.

The curriculum coordinating council is essential to the success of any curriculum development and maintenance project because it offers long-term stability as *keeper of the vision.* It serves as a clearinghouse and locus for decision-making, thereby stimulating broader leadership and program ownership among teachers, administrators, and support personnel.

Organizing a Council

The most difficult aspect of any project is getting it started. It is the responsibility of the superintendent and curriculum director to begin the process by creating the steering committee of key teachers, administrators, and support personnel. As discussed before, that committee must be representative of the district's diverse components, but should be no larger than 15. The steering committee writes the bylaws that tell how the council is selected, and outline the nature of its action agenda. A simple schematic can show how the CCC fits within the district's organizational structure (see Table I below).

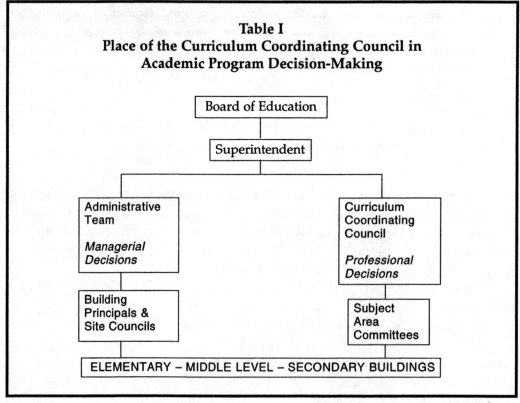

Table I
Place of the Curriculum Coordinating Council in
Academic Program Decision-Making

As can be seen in Table 1, the curriculum coordinating council reports only to the superintendent and board of education, and is in a decision making role which is parallel to that of the administrative team... but limited to matters having to do with curriculum, instruction and student learning. Note how the table of organization shown here follows the principles shown in the section, *Distinguishing Between Educational and Managerial Functions* on page 28. This kind of organization causes the curriculum coordinating council to be a very powerful body in terms of professional decision making. Although the council never deals directly with issues pertaining to personnel matters, financial planning, or building maintenance, it exercises considerable power over academic planning and implementation. Academic planning groups of the type described here are uncommon, so a council will have its authority challenged often. Consequently, it takes time for a district's stakeholders to accept and work with the new decision making culture.

Reciprocity works well in this model, in that administrators are represented on the council and the curriculum coordinator is represented on the administrative team. This depiction of the curriculum coordinator's status indicates that the primary decision making authority must reside at the district level, though many site based management strategies are appropriate in the Accountability Based Curriculum Model.

The curriculum coordinator is to be given *line* authority, and likely already has such authority if that person is an associate or assistant superintendent. If the curriculum coordinator does not possess regular line authority, it should be granted by the board in terms limited to *academic program management* — whether the appointee continues to be a building principal, part-time teacher, or member of the support staff. The line authority of a curriculum coordinator is focused on academics, and is thoroughly authorized via the bylaws of the council. The key point is that the coordinator should have **real** authority to get things done, but not have so much authority that there is an open ended opportunity to interpret policies and dictate arbitrary action.

The membership of the council is extremely important for it to achieve and maintain status within the district. The people who serve must do so for a lengthy period of time (at least three years) and should be recognized as being key leaders in the organization. Because they are leaders, council members should be able to deliberate in a professional manner, make decisions, have the courage of their convictions, communicate effectively with colleagues, and take action when necessary. Such characteristics are infinitely more important than mere representation according to grade levels, buildings, job responsibilities, and/or certification — though each of those classifications should be considered. Also of some importance are considerations having to do with years experience and academic credentials.

Table II gives an example of the possible membership of the CCC. For a district the size of our mythical "Pleasant Valley," this council is as large as it should get. Notice that representation is fairly uniform, a condition which may not exist in your situation. In addition, it is sometimes advisable to include a representative of those who serve as professional support personnel (e.g. counselors, librarians, or psychologists).

Table II
Possible Membership of the CCC

Curriculum Coordinator	(Chair)
Primary Teacher (K-2)	Hoover Elementary
Primary Teacher (K-2)	Eisenhower Elementary
Intermediate Teacher (3-5)	Hoover Elementary
Intermediate Teacher (3-5)	Eisenhower Elementary
Middle School Teacher (6-7)	Pleasant Valley Middle
Middle School Teacher (7-8)	Pleasant Valley Middle
High School Teacher (9-10)	Pleasant Valley High
High School Teacher (11-12)	Pleasant Valley High
Administrator	Elementary
Administrator	Middle Level
Administrator	High School
Superintendent	ex officio (by office)
Board of Education Member	ex officio (by office)

It is particularly important that Curriculum Coordinating Council membership be obtained via application. Other techniques have been tried and found unsatisfactory, including election, administrative appointment, and volunteering. Elections tend to be popularity contests that rarely result in a total council membership that is both competent and representative. Administrative appointments are often viewed with suspicion, and volunteering makes the process seem trivial and the council insignificant. An application process gives credibility to the future status of the Curriculum Coordinating Council, and allows full involvement and a sense of fairness. Refer to the "Sample Invitation to Apply for CCC Membership" and "Sample Application for CCC Membership," to get an idea of how application documents can be prepared.

Steering committee members can assist in helping associates understand the process, and should be willing to recruit as necessary. It is possible that members of that committee will want to apply for council membership, and they should be encouraged to do so. Please note in the example letter on page 63 details pertaining to application processes, remuneration, responsibilities, training, and bylaws. Probably the most important paragraph in the letter is next to last, especially the sentence that reads "Though selection criteria may include academic credentials and years experience, of greater importance is the ability of applicants to effectively study and discuss issues, make decisions, support those decisions with appropriate action, and communicate with others in the district." That sentence gives support to district leaders who might need to do a little recruiting among those who are new to the profession, but have much to offer in the way intelligence and decision making ability. That perspective aligns with the concept of promoting leadership as the primary selection criterion, and includes those young people who are ambitious in the need to fully assert their professionalism.

The sample application for CCC membership is found on page 64. Note its simplicity, that it is essentially a letter the applicant completes in six parts: (1) reason for applying, (2) previous experience with academic decision making in the district, (3) previous experience with academic decision making outside the district, (4) a statement that shows the existence of a philosophy, (5) a statement that shows the applicant's understanding of skills associated with good communication, and (6) any other points the applicant may wish to include. Also note that it is devoid of any references to credentials such as degrees earned, articles written, and presentations made. That kind of information can be included in the last section at the discretion of the applicant.

SAMPLE INVITATION TO APPLY FOR CCC MEMBERSHIP
SAMPLE APPLICATION FOR CCC MEMBERSHIP

TO: District Educators

FROM: Bill Smith, Curriculum Director

RE: Curriculum Coordinating Council

DATE: February 21, 1996

One of the first steps in implementing our new academic program management plan is to create a Curriculum Coordinating Council. The new Council will have 14 members consisting of educators who represent all major district functions and divisions. Included will be teachers, support personnel, administrators, and one member of the Board of Education.

The selection process starts with a formal application by those interested in serving. The application form is attached to this letter, and the process will be explained by your principal and/or another colleague with whom you work. Appointments to the Council will be made by the superintendent and me with the advice of others on the district's administrative team.

Those appointed to the council this March will serve rotating terms of one to three years. Council members appointed in subsequent years will serve three year terms.

The Curriculum Coordinating Council will be the most important academic program decision-making body in the district, as its actions are subject only to the review and approval of the Superintendent and Board of Education. Meetings will be held two to four times monthly for about 90 minutes each, and members will be paid $12.00 an hour. Council responsibilities this spring will focus on initial preparation of the District's mission statement and long-range plan. The Council will also oversee the selection of subject area committees and other matters pertaining to implementing the curriculum development model.

I will provide Council training and will work closely with members as they move through each step of this year's agenda. The first meeting will be conducted from 3:30 to 5 p.m. on March 14, 1996 in the library of Hoover Elementary School.

Anyone interested in providing leadership to the district is encouraged to apply. Though selection criteria may include academic credentials and years experience, of greater importance is the ability of applicants to effectively study and discuss issues, make decisions, support those decisions with appropriate action, and communicate with others in the district.

Applications should be submitted to my office no later than 5 p.m. on March 2, 1996. Please feel free to contact me if you have questions or wish to discuss any aspect of the application process.

SAMPLE APPLICATION FOR CCC MEMBERSHIP

PLEASANT VALLEY PUBLIC SCHOOLS

Application for Membership on the
Curriculum Coordinating Council

February, 1996

Please complete this application form and submit it to Bill Smith on or before 5 p.m., March 2, 1996. Applicants may be interviewed as necessary. All those who apply will be notified as to the status of their application by March 9, 1996.

Name _____

School _____

REASON FOR APPLYING FOR CCC MEMBERSHIP:

PREVIOUS EXPERIENCE IN ACADEMIC DECISION-MAKING WITHIN PVPS. (COMMITTEES, CURRICULUM PLANNING, OTHER SIMILAR ACTIVITIES)

PREVIOUS EXPERIENCE IN ACADEMIC DECISION-MAKING IN ANOTHER EDUCATIONAL ORGANIZATION (OTHER DISTRICTS OR ORGANIZATIONS THAT INCLUDE EDUCATION AS PART OF THEIR MISSION)

PLEASE STATE YOUR PHILOSOPHY OF ACADEMIC LEADERSHIP (FOCUS ON HOW <u>ANY</u> PROFESSIONAL LEADER — TEACHERS, SUPPORT PERSONS, ADMINISTRATORS — CAN IMPROVE A DISTRICT, BY MENTIONING APPROPRIATE CHARACTERISTICS AND ACTIONS)

PLEASE DEFINE GOOD DISTRICT-LEVEL COMMUNICATION (TECHNIQUES, ATTITUDES, RESPONSIBILITIES)

OTHER INFORMATION THAT SUPPORTS YOUR APPLICATION:

The Council's First Meeting

Although every CCC meeting is important, the first one establishes the pattern for what will happen later. Educators, like everyone else, enjoy the special feeling they get when given first class treatment. New CCC members who walk into a board of education meeting room to find tasty refreshments, notebooks with their names on them, writing materials, name plates, and a professional secretary ready to take notes, are certain to think that somebody means business. That perspective is made even more solid when the meeting starts on time, a carefully prepared agenda is followed, contributions are expected from each member, and concrete discussions are made. Members are no less impressed when the meeting ends on time with a firm commitment to taking action, and the announcement of the next meeting time and place. Three days later, when all district educators receive professional-looking and comprehensive meeting minutes, everyone will know that this council is likely to have more clout than most district committees.

The first meeting is also important from the standpoint of initiating process-es critical to the success of the model. The "big three" agenda items are **mission state-ment development, establishment of the long-range plan, and selection and train-ing of subject area committees.** Therefore, the next section pertains to mission state-ment development with emphasis on initiating *discussion* of the district mission.

Council Basics:

- **Leadership is the primary criterion for council membership,** as the council has extensive authority over the academic program.

- **Initial council actions are to initiate mission statement development, develop a long range plan, create and work with subject area committee(s), and con-duct evaluation of curricular effectiveness.**

- **The council serves as *keeper of the vision,* so its stability is important.**

- **Council selection is based on provisions in the bylaws. The only effective means of selection is via application.**

- **Applications should include a cover letter that explains the role of a council member and an application form.**

- **The council serves as the professional (academic program) decision making body in the district.**

- **The first meeting of the council should be especially well organized and focused.**

INITIATING DISCUSSION OF THE DISTRICT MISSION

For some school districts the era of the mission statement has come and gone. It has come to those districts that properly developed a mission and now use it thor-oughly and effectively. It is a bygone concept in those districts that prepared a mis-sion paragraph or slogan with no concrete meaning or purpose except to adorn school foyers, administrative offices and board of education meeting rooms.

Districts that developed and effectively use working mission statements are able to overcome many problems other districts cannot seem to solve. In those districts the magic of a good mission statement is not the ease in which it is memorized or how impressive it looks when framed and hung on the wall, but rather the extent to which it influences a sense of accountability and the design down process of curriculum development.

Mission: The Decision Making Point of Focus

Mission statements in the model we advocate are continuously consulted to identify the district vision in terms of board of education goals, budget allocations, curriculum content and design, staff development, student activity programs, and short and long term planning. Because of the mission statement, district educators have a point of focus that includes the principles, goals, beliefs, and even intended actions to which they can hold themselves accountable.

This more precise way of thinking about a mission came from concepts created by William Edwards Deming. Deming says that an organization which is committed to producing quality goods and services must *identify a purpose and be constant in the effort to achieve it.* When applied to educational institutions, this constancy is created through a shared allegiance to a commonly agreed upon mission. The unifying vision held by all educators in a district helps define direction and enables focused decision making on such matters as academic program development, professional growth projects, long-range planning, and budget allocations. Without such focus, decisions tend to be governed by whim, fancy or trend.

Deming also says that commitment to quality must result in a consensus regarding principles, goals and individual beliefs — not in the form of blind dedication, but rather in the sense that human participants in an organization must seek opportunities for merging ideas and practices. He says that quality outcomes are caused by a deep sense of accountability to what the organization stands for and the feeling of being an inherent part of it.

Expectations of teachers and administrators are better clarified when beliefs, goals, and principles are agreed upon. Defining expectations of teachers and students helps *eliminate fear,* which Deming believes is critical to building trust and collaborative effort among workers. Once trust is built, educators begin to *break down barriers of communication,* which Deming also advocates as a concept of improving performance. Not knowing which direction the district or its administrators are headed from year to year leaves teachers dealing with the unknown. Unknowns create fear and build walls between people. A mission which is specific in content and purpose and is adopted by the Board of Education, provides direction and enables people to talk about what needs to happen and what decisions should be made.

Once the goals of a district are defined and supported through the decision making process, professional training needs begin to surface. Mission statements that go beyond simple slogans, by clearly defining expected outcomes of the teaching/learning process, bring about an *emphasis on long-range planning* and *focused staff and organization development* — both Deming concepts for effective management. When the direction in which the district is headed is determined, educators know where they are going. Then and only then can they decide how they are going to get there and how they are going to grow as individuals.

Finally, Deming stresses a *reduction in the mobility of management*. When all mission statement components are in place, and it is adopted by the board of education and supported through board policy, changes in management do not result in roller coaster rides for school personnel. Stability is maintained because the "keepers of the vision" include all district personnel, the board, and especially the curriculum coordinating council. Building and central office administrators are hired in accordance with their ability to fulfill the district's mission.

Components of an Effective Mission

Educators are diverse in their philosophies and beliefs. Bringing about a foundation of shared beliefs is accomplished through the process of mission building. Research has found that what makes good teachers is not their knowledge or methods, but the beliefs teachers hold about students, themselves, their goals, purposes, and the teaching task. A really effective mission statement reflects this finding. Our four components of a quality mission are: purpose, student learning goals/exit outcomes, accomplishing the curriculum, and a statement of accountability.

The Purpose of the Mission

The purpose component explains why the district exists. In outcome based districts, that rationale rests on three essential beliefs: (1) all students can learn and achieve success, (2) success breeds success, and (3) schools control the conditions of success. Therefore, the purpose of school districts using our model is to continuously define what is to be learned and to provide instruction which enables students to achieve success. That purpose reflects the ultimate means and ends of education, so a strong curriculum governance must be connected to a mastery teaching and learning model that uses success-based lesson design and delivery.

Purpose statements which only pledge to deliver quality education or provide opportunities for students to reach their fullest potential are weak. Schools can't be satisfied to *deliver* or *provide* opportunities for students to learn. Schools must be aggressive in their purpose by pledging that students will learn and achieve defined curriculum outcomes at a success level.

Student Learning Goals/Exit Outcomes

The second component of the district mission is to identify goals or outcomes of learning which all students are expected to achieve. These goals are broad in that they reflect the K through 12 educational process and program. The Accountability Based Curriculum Model considers curriculum to include all student learning, both academic and affective in nature. This means that for every defined goal or exit outcome stated in the district mission, there must be a sequentially developed curriculum of goals/outcomes which begin at the kindergarten level and culminate at grade 12. Each grade or course level throughout the system must have a benchmark of progress toward achieving exit outcomes.

Not only must sequential outcomes be defined at these grade levels, they must be measurable. Without systematically assessing student learning throughout all K-12 grades, students can move through the system without being held accountable for achieving defined standards of performance. Social promotion or providing credit for attendance then occurs, allowing students to graduate into society illiterate and incompetent. Until outcome specific assessment is conducted, teachers never really know what is learned. All they know is that students have been exposed to learning, and that is not good enough because it is not accountable!

Accomplishing the Curriculum

Not including methods or techniques that will be implemented by all classroom teachers and support personnel within the district is inexcusable. The wealth of literature that validates teaching practices and techniques which result in successful student learning is so overwhelming that educators can no longer choose what they want to know. Truly professional men and women do not ignore research and validated practice in their fields, yet teachers often resist training in effective instructional practices by justifying their own techniques as being creative and motivational. Wouldn't it be interesting to watch how these teachers would respond to a doctor who wishes to be creative and ignore research and validated practice? Creative surgery or medication might be chosen, but only as a very last resort.

Longitudinal studies now support teaching techniques that give attention to learning styles, effective elements of instruction, cooperative learning, and outcome based instruction with a mastery learning component. It is also known that mastery learning requires extensive resources and a team effort, to include teachers, support personnel, and instructional assistance.

When educational research reveals that by the year 2000 over twenty million Americans will be uneducable and untrainable due to the failure of the public education system, it's time to draw the line. It is time to expect that the intended curriculum will be accomplished through quality teaching and quality learning.

Statement of Accountability

The fourth and final component of the district mission is the statement of accountability. Without defining who is responsible for achieving the other three mission components, the statement is not workable because no one is held accountable for its implementation. District administrators must pledge their allegiance to decision making which results in developing and maintaining curriculum, training and supporting teachers, and providing resources for success based teaching and learning. Teachers must pledge allegiance to performing quality leadership and effective instruction in order for students to achieve the clearly stated exit outcomes. Board of education members must also pledge their allegiance to decision making which furthers progress toward the attainment of the district mission and provides support for teachers, administrators, and other staff members dedicated to fulfilling their roles and responsibilities in achieving the mission.

Accountability statements should also reflect the role of students, parents, and the community in achieving the mission. Involving them in the accountability statement reflects a shared commitment that reasonably recognizes that schools do not operate in a vacuum. Without parents who value education at least enough to see that their children attend school regularly, and students who are willing to learn, attempts to accomplish the very best curriculum, instruction, assessment, and resources within the district are all in vain. Communities that ignore the need for providing adequate facilities and other resources for quality education impair the process of mission attainment. Good accountability statements recognize the collaborative effort of all stakeholders in the vision. School personnel might be keepers of the dream, but poor student attitudes and lack of parental and community support can turn dreams into nightmares.

Preliminary Activities Before the Writing Begins

Now that a design for the mission statement has been discussed, it is necessary to create conditions in which faculty, parents, students, patrons and other district stakeholders make initial contributions to the pending document. The process for doing that can vary among districts and communities, so our recommendations are limited to possible *meeting formats, areas of focus,* and *techniques for gathering information.*

The *meeting format* we recommend for faculty members and other distrcit educators center on the large group — small group — large group sequence of activities. In a small to moderate size district it may be possible to bring all educators together on one day, in a single location, for about two to three hours. Members of the curriculum coordinating council open the meeting by explaining its purpose and describing the process to be used in conducting discussion. Teachers are then organized in groups of six to ten so that there is a good mix of educators in terms of grades taught, leadership and support positions held, and departmentalized subjects taught. Council members and other district leaders then conduct each of the small group meetings, with a summarizing large group activity of 30 to 45 minutes held at the end of the day. The same process can be used in larger districts using a district within a

district process....breaking the district into high school regions and involving personnel from feeder middle level and elementary schools in those regions.

  Areas of focus for this meeting could, with some modification, be used in community meetings. In all cases, it is important to discuss the purpose of the schools,
what should be in a curriculum designed to meet that purpose, what students should
be able to know or do given the content of that curriculum, how teachers should
determine student mastery of the intended curriculum, and how accountability for
student learning should be defined.   Recorders in each group should take careful
notes of the discussion so recommendations can be accurately reported to the large
group at the end of the day, and later at a meeting of the curriculum coordinating
council.

  Techniques for gathering information in the small group meeting are closely
associated with the preparation of the leader, the skill of the leader in eliciting the
viewpoints of participants, and the openness of the leader to varied perspectives. All
perspectives should be noted and accepted as valid considerations, to be accurately
and sincerely reviewed by the curriculum coordinating council as it initiates the writing of a new mission statement. It is strongly recommended that everyone serving as
a small group leader thoroughly rehearse for the role, and be critiqued by other members of the curriculum coordinating council. Rehearsal and critique of this and many
other exercises of this type can mean the difference between a successful and unsuc-
cessful meeting.

  Community meetings can be organized and conducted the same way depending on the numbers of participants. Modifications can be made easily if the groups
are smaller, as might be the case with service clubs, church groups, or civic organizations.

WRITING AND INTERPRETING THE MISSION

  Our experience is that educational experts interpret the mission statement in
various ways. As discussed earlier, many educators see the statement as being nothing
more than a slogan or philosophical overview. They understand it to be a kind of free
standing preamble to a longer and separate list of goals and objectives, perhaps broken into categories relevant to subjects, buildings, or some other division in the district.

  We feel strongly that any organizational mission statement should be comprehensive enough to be structurally coherent and workable. Coherence means that
all components are carefully linked together, allowing a reader to get a relatively clear
and total perspective by reading just one document. Workable means that the lan-

guage and content of the statement can be translated into action with very little interpretation.

A coherent and workable mission statement, according to the model we have developed and implemented in many districts, ordinarily contains four distinct sections: *purpose, student learning goals/exit outcomes, accomplishing the curriculum* and *accountability.* Each section has already been described, but to review, the *purpose* statement is a concise paragraph that provides an overview of what the district is trying to accomplish, *student learning goals/exit outcomes* is an exposition of specific curriculum components, *accomplishing the curriculum* speaks to instructional organization and methods, and *accountability* establishes who is responsible for fulfilling the school district's purpose.

Mission statements that are written by those committed to an outcome based system are more concrete, specific and workable than are those prepared by educators who accept traditional school practices. A statement that recognizes the importance of exit outcomes and mastery learning will incorporate such words and phrases as *require, demonstrate, insure, essential learnings, accept responsibility, expectations* and *core curriculum.* The following example is a statement that has recently been completed by a district committed to exit outcomes. As you read this mission statement, critique it for specificity, alignment, and its potential for use by each subject area committee in designing and implementing a clear and focused curriculum. Also critique it in terms of how well it can be used by the curriculum coordinating council, administrative team, and board of education in making decisions about curricular priority and management. Do not critique it with the idea of replicating it in your own district, because the process is infinitely more important than the product itself. The only reason for its inclusion in this book is to show a model which may, as your district creates its own statement, be used for validation purposes.

USD 482 Dighton, KS
Mission Statement

Purpose of the School District

The mission of the Dighton School District is to ensure that through a challenging and diversified educational program students will develop and demonstrate essential problem solving, social, technical, and academic skills to be productive, responsible lifelong learners in a global society.

Student Learning Outcomes and Accomplishing the Curriculum

To accomplish this mission, the district will utilize curriculum, activities and services which promote the following student learning outcomes.

PROBLEM SOLVING SKILLS
The student will demonstrate these abilities:
• Identify issues and define problems.

- Gather, analyze and synthesize information.
- Consider various strategies and their consequences.
- Propose solutions.
- Apply the solution and evaluate the outcome.
- Recall and transfer information to new situations.

SOCIAL SKILLS
The student will demonstrate these characteristics and abilities:
- Be tolerant, kind, respectful, and understanding of others.
- Contribute to the maintenance of a positive work environment.
- Work both independently and cooperatively.
- Maintain a healthy lifestyle.
- Respond appropriately to diversity.
- Accept the rights and responsibilities of citizenship in a democratic society.
- Accept consequences for one's actions.

TECHNICAL SKILLS
The student will demonstrate the following:
- Knowledge of the personal implications of technology.
- Acquisition of technical skills.
- Analysis of the appropriate and inappropriate use of technology in society.

ACADEMIC SKILLS
The student will demonstrate mastery of curricular outcomes established for the following:
- Communications
- Natural sciences
- Social sciences
- Mathematics
- Health, physical education and recreation
- Vocational and technical arts

Achieving the mission of Dighton is an interactive process that requires communication and responsibility and is mutually shared by the following:

BOARD OF EDUCATION who will
- establish policies for quality education.
- allocate financial resources to pursue district goals.
- provide leadership and vision.
- support district personnel to encourage academic excellence.
- be politically and educationally informed.
- maintain confidentiality and professionalism.

DISTRICT ADMINISTRATORS who will
- provide instructional leadership and support at the district and building levels to encourage academic excellence.
- supervise the overall operation of the district as it relates to instruction, student activities, services and fiscal management.

- maintain confidentiality and professionalism.

INSTRUCTIONAL STAFF who will
- utilize the curriculum to teach and ensure learning.
- maintain a classroom environment conducive to learning.
- maintain confidentiality and professionalism.
- facilitate extra-curricular activities.
- actively support students and staff.

NON-INSTRUCTIONAL STAFF who will
- be cooperative and supportive of the system.
- interact positively with students and staff.
- maintain an environment that is safe, healthy and conducive to learning.
- maintain confidentiality and professionalism.

STUDENTS who will
- actively participate in the educational programs and experiences offered by the district.
- demonstrate commitment and effort to the learning process.
- cooperate with school personnel and other students.

PARENTS AND GUARDIANS who will
- provide a foundation for student learning and take an active and continuing role in the success of their child's education.

PATRONS OF DIGHTON who will
- provide resources, facilities, and support to ensure quality education.
- be receptive to new and innovative ideas in education.

In the Dighton statement there is a specific targeting of exit outcomes, defined as essential learnings prescribed for each subject and grade level. Clarity is achieved with regard to that district's four most important intentions: 1. problem solving skills, 2. social skills, 3. technical skills, and 4. academic skills. The district's educators want no confusion, so even more clarity is achieved in the accountability statement, which defines specific obligations for each category of key district leader.

The Dighton mission mentions instructional strategies and accountability in the *accomplishing the curriculum* section, instead of using a special section for that purpose. Other districts eliminate that element entirely, although we think it is a good idea to include it as a means of communicating to teachers the need to review the adequacy of the methods they now use. Below is what such a section looks like:

Recommended Instructional Techniques:

Recognizing that students have different learning styles, teachers are encouraged to use a variety of instructional techniques by choosing from strategies which:
- provide for both cooperative and independent learning.
- utilize lecture, inquiry based instruction and discussion.
- utilize manipulatives, technology, and community resources.

- utilize manipulatives, technology, and community resources.
- encourage parent involvement and communication.
- provide for in-class study time.
- allow for individualized and student centered instruction.
- support a discipline and classroom management plan that creates an environment conducive to learning.
- encourage teachers to share expertise.
- follow a well balanced sequential program.

Contrast the wording in Dighton's document to that shown in River Falls' mission statement below. The River Falls statement was written a number of years ago and reflects an educational mindset that was commonly applied in the 1960s and 1970s. Although it is a reasonably well crafted statement, it is overly comprehensive and vague. There are numerous hard to pin down words and phrases such as "help," "should," and "encourage." The educators in River Falls have declared their willingness to **provide** a solid academic program, but are not ready to **insure** student learning. Notice the references to helping students learn "to the best of their ability," and the primary emphasis on preparing young people to "become functioning citizens in a democratic society." Outcome oriented mission statements include such ideas as being quite important, but there is no preset notion about varying degrees of ability, nor is there a fuzzy set of altruistic assumptions about the nature of citizenship in a democracy. Instead, there is commitment to causing all students to learn the essentials, including details about how our system of government works.

River Falls School District
Mission Statement

Purpose of Schools

The public schools in River Falls exist to help young people by preparing them to become functioning citizens in a democratic society. To achieve that goal all students, to the best of their ability and by the completion of the twelfth grade, should be (1) academically functional, (2) aware of important cultural heritages, moral and spiritual values, traditions and lifestyles, (3) aware of vocational opportunities, (4) conscious of the importance of good health, (5) perceptive of the importance of one's image, and (6) appreciative of the fine arts.

Essential Goals for Student Learning

To achieve the purpose of the schools the following learning goals are established; that students should:

1. demonstrate at least a minimum competency level, as determined by district faculty members, in (1) reading, (2) mathematics, (3) social science, (4) health, physical education and recreation, (5) science, (6) the fine arts, (7) the vocational areas, and (8) all other language arts, including written and oral expression, spelling, penmanship, literature, and foreign language;

2. demonstrate a willingness to communicate in a positive manner with others by respecting their

rights, opinions, traditions, heritage, lifestyles, moral and spiritual values;

3. be able to identify and describe career possibilities toward which his/her education has provided initial preparation;

4. be able to identify and describe practices which develop and maintain a healthy lifestyle;

5. demonstrate a positive self-image; and

6. be able to identify and describe the importance of the fine arts to our society and lifestyle.

Recommended Instructional Techniques

In order to accomplish the above purpose and essential goals for student learning, teachers are encouraged to make use of the following techniques:

1. provide for student-centered instruction;

2. maintain a well-balanced and sequenced program of studies, leading to specific skills and/or understandings;

3. offer varied and interesting classroom activities;

4. utilize lecture, inquiry-based instruction, and drill;

5. utilize student involvement and decision-making through individualized forms of instruction;

6. utilize community resources; and,

7. encourage cooperative instructional efforts with other teachers.

To the extent that parents and patrons of River Falls actively support their schools, the Board of Education, the administration, the teaching staff and support personnel will accept responsibility for the growth of students in the areas mentioned under the Purpose and Goals sections of this statement. The students will be accountable for taking advantage of the various opportunities and experiences in education which are provided by the schools.

Again, it is very important that no one reading these examples assume that it is acceptable to simply replicate any currently written mission statement for use in a local district. To use an existing statement word for word destroys the mission's purpose. It is the process of building and dynamically using a mission statement that makes a real difference, and that activity is time consuming and sometimes difficult. The step-by-step *process* we recommended is discussed in the next section.

INSTITUTIONALIZING THE MISSION

An individual assigned the leadership role in mission statement development and implementation should understand that the endeavor is just as important for staff development as it is a means for generating a product. At the outset, the mission statement leaders must give much attention to the proposed process, and selection of district educators who will serve as the brainstorming body responsible for initiating and coordinating statement building activities. A district with a curriculum council already in place may use that group alone, or expand that group to enhance the representation of various district constituencies. If a curriculum council is already operating under a busy agenda, it is possible to select a special committee of district leaders. In any case, it is important that the group be very representative of district thinking, include the best and most respected educators available and be no larger than 15 to 20 members.

Here is an example of a proposal that can be used in making a presentation to a board of education and/or superintendent. This proposal assumes that the district curriculum council is not available to initiate and coordinate mission statement building activities.

Developing and Instituting the Public School District Mission Statement — A Proposal

Purpose

A mission statement is important to every organization as a means of keeping members continually cognizant of what their collective efforts are supposed to accomplish. When a succinct and well-written statement is absent, the organization's members can consciously or subconsciously develop and execute their own individual missions. That condition may or may not serve the best interests of the total organization; the usual assumption is that the lack of a commonly held mission causes confusion and inefficiency, and is likely to degrade the quality of the organization's "product."

The world's strongest governments are those with viable constitutions, and our most dynamic business organizations adhere to thoroughly prescribed policies and goals. The best educational organizations have mission statements that clearly set forth a *purpose, essential goals for student learning, recommended instructional techniques* and an *acceptance of accountability.*

Process and Personnel

A school district interested in developing a mission statement needs to use a process that is both efficient and inclusive. Though some may believe those conditions are not compatible, they *can* be if these principles are followed:

1. Identify and select the organization's strongest formal and informal leaders to initiate the process.

2. Choose a coordinator of that small group who:
   a. is both task-oriented and sensitive to individual perspectives;
   b. can write well;
   c. can conscientiously weave in the opinions of those who contribute generally acceptable ideas;
   d. can accept criticism of his or her writing or level of sensitivity; and,
   e. can bring closure to the developmental task through use of an appropriate timeline and friendly persistence.

3. Work at gaining consensus of the organization's members and approval by formal leaders and constituencies through:
   a. leaders developing a carefully constructed first draft of a proposed mission statement;
   b. leaders developing and instituting a process whereby that first draft is thoroughly reviewed and critiqued by all professional staff members;
   c. leaders instituting a process whereby all criticisms are collected, reviewed and incorporated into a second draft;
   d. leaders repeating steps "b" and "c" as many times as necessary;
   e. leaders accepting a lack of continued (serious) criticism as acceptance by consensus;
   f. leaders using the draft that is finally accepted by the professional staff for presentation to lay advisory committees and the board of education;
   g. leaders seeking approval of the final draft by the board of education;
   h. leaders submitting the approved draft to the curriculum council for use in the development and refinement of curriculum documents and evaluation techniques; and
   i. the curriculum council submitting the new mission statement for posting in district buildings, and publication in both district and community media.

Timeline
September 1 - 15
Selection of 10 - 15 formal and informal leaders who represent the district's primary professional constituencies.

September 16 - 30
Initial meetings of leaders to begin the writing process.

October 1- 31

Faculty, administrators, support personnel review and critique.

November 1 - 25

Final draft prepared as approved by the professional staff.

December 1 - 23

. Final draft, as prepared by the professional staff, is submitted to lay advisory groups and the board of education for study.

January 1 - 31

Input is received from lay advisory groups; approval is sought from the board of education.

February 1 - 29

Approved mission statement is submitted to the curriculum coordinating council for use in curriculum development, improvement, and evaluation; council begins disseminating the mission statement for posting and publication.

March 1 - Ongoing

Mission statement is institutionalized.

There are many points made in the proposal that can't be emphasized enough. Point one stipulates that the organization's strongest *formal and informal* leaders are *chosen* to serve on the committee. Volunteerism is not an acceptable approach; the district's senior leaders must identify those teachers, counselors, librarians, nurses and junior administrators who are most capable of effectively thinking through concepts and interacting with their colleagues. Those individuals should be given background on what is being proposed, then asked to serve on a schedule that is compatible with their day-to-day work. That means considerable attention should be given to timelines and the details of coordinating meeting activities.

Point two discusses the characteristics of a good group leader. Many districts use an administrator, while others use a teacher or professional support person. The individual's day-to-day job description is immaterial, as that leader *must* meet the criteria shown: task oriented, sensitive, good writer, open to ideas and criticisms, and capable of bringing closure to activities.

Point three covers the most critical aspects of the initial process. However, not mentioned in the items under that point is the importance of room size, furniture arrangement, refreshments, an agenda and a general business-like demeanor.

Meetings must be comfortable, interactive and begun promptly; they should provide opportunities for decision-making and the development of action plans; they are expected to end on time and with a clear indication of what has been decided. Follow-up on those decisions is absolutely essential.

Committee members should receive a clear rationale for mission statement development and use, and it is beneficial to allow them to write down their own perspectives of the school's purpose. A brief discussion after the sharing of those perspectives is revealing to everyone — primarily that there are so many diverse opinions. Nothing underlines the need for a mission statement better than that exercise.

The committee's leader is then responsible for preparing a complete draft of a simple mission statement. Depending on the size and composition of the committee, the leader may either present the entire draft or portions of it for deliberation. The leader should aggressively recommend revisions, even to the extent of criticizing his or her own original theories, phrasing, or textual structure. Rubber stamping the leader's product is not the purpose of a committee; committee members are expected to be viable and dynamic spokespersons for their schools and the profession in general. Active deliberation causes minds to work better and good ideas to appear on paper. Moreover, it causes a greater commitment among participants and added interest in becoming statement advocates when a draft is being considered by other members of the staff, the board of education and groups of lay persons. Therefore, though Point 3(a) on page 77 is brief, the task of creating an acceptable draft could take many meetings to accomplish.

Points 3(b) and (c) — review, critique, incorporating new ideas — are essential in assuring that all employees of the district have had a chance to influence the statement's text. The following document is a sample of guidelines used when the draft is disseminated to the district's personnel.

Guidelines to Committee Members for Discussion
Leading....From the Committee Chair

1. Be sure that the proposed Mission statement is in the hands of all faculty and staff members at least 48 hours prior to your meetings. If you have time and opportunity before the meeting, it is a good idea to ask your colleagues if they have had a chance to read the statement and, if they have, what their responses are. That kind of informal interaction will give you clues as to what might happen in a meeting, and could possibly avert extended discussions on relatively minor issues.

2. Develop a mental agenda before going into the meeting. The agenda might look something like this:
   a. "My" thoughts as to why a mission statement is now so important.
   b. Brief review of how our statement was developed.

    c. Some commentary on how the statement will be used.

    d. My personal level of commitment to the mission statement concept and document itself.

    e. Call for participant discussion on:

      (1) format;

      (2) perceptions of the document in general (organization, phrasing, structural appearance, etc.); and,

      (3) criticisms of content in each section.

3. If you feel quite positive about the document, you should let that attitude show. Be an advocate but *do not* become defensive; copy down negative criticisms and assure participants that their concerns will be *seriously considered* by the mission statement committee.

4. Indicate that a draft of the revised mission statement will be issued to all faculty and staff members after the next committee meeting, and that you should be contacted if there are additional concerns. Unless there are serious concerns, the committee will begin preparing its presentation to the Board of Education. **All faculty and staff members should know that the statement, when it is presented to the board, will be characterized as a product of all professional educators and support personnel. Please make that point very clear.** Try to avoid a situation in which a minority position becomes solidified.

5. Possible questions or comments you might encounter during the meeting are:

    a. *How is this statement different from the goals set by the board?*
The board's goals only partially pertain to the academic program per se, and that portion would certainly not be as comprehensive and precise as our statement. The board and committee will examine and resolve any discrepancies between Board goals and the Mission Statement.

    b. *How will we assure that the mission statement is more than mere window dressing?*
All committee members and the administrative team agree that a systematic process must be developed to assure that the statement has an appropriate and long-lasting impact on academic decision-making.

    c. *Is this particular mission statement to be used forever?*
No. A procedure will be devised which provides for continuing review of the statement's adequacy and procedures for amending it when necessary.

    d. *Do other districts have mission statements of this type?*
Yes. Many school districts use mission statements and many more are considering their development.

    e. *Is it possible that this mission statement could be used in faculty and staff evaluation?*
Yes. Though that may intimidate some, the statement is a clear expression of dis-

trict priorities as prepared by the professional staff. That is certainly better than being evaluated on the basis of assumption, whim, or fashion.

How a mission statement should be used by each governing body and employee in the district is another important consideration. Although we might be accused of spending too much time on the mission statement component of our model, we do so because its proper use is so essential to the actual implementation of long-lasting program change and real professional accountability. Maintenance of a mission statement requires considerable commitment and discipline, and the litmus test for its success is whether or not it is still considered an essential part of district governance five to ten years after completion.

Keeping mission concepts alive as day-to-day processes is infinitely more important than the mere existence of a document. Institutionalizing day-to-day processes means that a practice becomes so habitual that it is perceived as fundamental to the very existence of an organization.

Our American system of government is the best example of how a mission statement, when dynamically institutionalized, can guide a huge organization for many years... even centuries. The Constitution of the United States works because it is regularly reviewed, debated, interpreted and used as the basis for our entire body of laws and most cherished traditions. That system has been emulated by other nations, subordinate governmental units and many other organizations from religious clubs to youth groups. It is such a pervasive system that news articles each day discuss issues in the context of rights, responsibilities, due process and other matters that cause an examination of "constitutionality."

Although the American Constitution is an example of how a good concept can become institutionalized, there are far too many organizations in this nation that do not regularly reflect the country's governance system; two such organizations are industry and the public schools. In those organizations practitioners have rarely perceived a mission as being something created by and for the employees and the consumers of products and services. In the past, the most common mission of industry appears to have been the acquisition of profit. The mission of the public schools has been the sorting of students into very competent, marginally competent and incompetent categories; and (using such categories) credentialing those who complete academic units or programs.

Today, American industry is changing its mission to focus more on the quality of products and services; profit is still an important factor, but only in the context of the organization's survival and ability to assure quality over time. Schools are also moving in that direction by developing missions that promote quality learning for all students. In both instances, the accomplishment of that task must be characterized by dynamic, ongoing and broad based involvement of all who are part of the organization. In schools, such personnel include teachers, board members, parents, patrons, administrators, professional support staff, students and non certified employees.

The Board's Use of the Mission Statement

Boards of education in many districts with which we work spend 15% to 25% of their total annual meeting time on matters pertaining to curriculum and instruction. This is accomplished because of a board's willingness to (1) meet somewhat longer, (2) conduct special meetings, and/or (3) identify specific times in which nothing can be discussed *except* curriculum and instruction. During those sessions the superintendent insures that the mission statement is readily accessible; it may even be reviewed briefly before deliberations begin. Agendas usually include reports and discussions orchestrated by the curriculum coordinating council. Some boards, before making any decisions regarding new goals, programs or activities, conscientiously review the mission statement to determine whether or not such actions are in compliance. By keeping the mission statement available for continuous reference, the board (including its newest members) become involved with the concepts of organizational purpose, theoretical vision, academic outcomes and techniques for program development.

The Administrative Team's Use of the Mission Statement

District administrators are frequently involved in meetings, some to take care of managerial concerns and others to resolve issues that may arise. Occasionally, administrators hold one to three day retreats for the purpose of long range planning. The mission statement is a greater influence on administrators when it is made available in meetings, because administrators — when functioning individually — are too busy to reflect on its philosophical and procedural points.

Meetings that are managerial in nature should make use of the mission statement in terms of setting priorities. For example, a meeting might be scheduled to discuss bus schedules, custodial services, personnel policies, budget allocations and a new state mandate that would impact food service. An agenda review might identify the following mission related issues: bus schedules could be changed in such a way that a critical aspect of the middle school program is harmed; a possible reduction in staff could seriously interfere with the district's ability to teach critical skills; adjusted allocations of the budget might improve one aspect of the academic program while harming another; and a change in lunch schedules might adversely affect a special program designed to help the district meet its academic mission.

Meetings held to deal with issues are often related to the mission. Let's say that a group of parents is concerned that a new human sexuality or values education program is inappropriate. Although the board had certainly approved the program's implementation, it is up to the administrators to design a strategy to handle complaints. The presence of a mission statement, with a component that justifies sponsorship of such a program, can be helpful ...especially if parent/patron advice was sought in adopting the statement, and if board minutes reflect thorough consideration of the mission when the program was approved.

Retreats are usually meant to promote long range planning, and often focus on personnel, facilities, budgets and staff training. At least one administrator who attends such a retreat should serve as the mission statement monitor, one who weighs each area of discussion against authorizing or encouraging elements of the statement. That individual should be allowed to play "devil's advocate" as necessary, so that everyone, the superintendent included, stays on a path which is mission oriented.

The Curriculum Council

It is the district's curriculum coordinating council, under the leadership of the curriculum director, that should set the tone for mission statement use. A council works in two areas: (1) the nuts-and-bolts oversight of the academic program, and (2) the intense theorizing that causes council members to be the most forward-thinking leaders in the district. That dual role, management and "think-tank processes," requires disciplined vigilance in the use of a mission statement. On the one hand, managerial actions should always align with the mission; on the other hand, think-tank style brainstorming sessions should be no-holds-barred in style. That freewheeling intellectual exercise is necessary even when everyone assumes that a mission and the processes fostered by it "ain't broke." The American Constitution, as good as it is, has flaws and omissions that need correction from time to time, and concentrated thinking and discussion can lead to real improvement via amendment or upgraded interpretations. Even if intense discussion only modifies a program within mission statement parameters, or results in no overt action at all, the exercise itself clarifies thinking and promotes professional growth.

It is the curriculum director's job to assure that the district's mission statement is sitting on the table, and that it is referred to on frequent occasions. In fact, the curriculum director's diligence in keeping everyone on track in terms of mission concepts and decision-making processes is critical to the success of our model.

Subject Area Committees

A subject area committee should operate under appropriate constraints, one of which is the district's mission statement. Other constraints may include the presence of existing curriculum guides, norm or criterion referenced achievement tests used by the district, or state issued curriculum guides. However, the chair of a subject area committee must be certain that the committee is allowed, especially at the beginning of its existence, to explore new ideas in terms of how student learning can be improved in both scope and level of intensity. After that broad-based exploration has occurred, it is then possible to narrow the process by merging the new with what now exists. The district mission statement should be reviewed in the second or third SAC meeting and, using a process that will be described later, a subject area mission should be prepared which complies with the district's statement. It is that subject mission that should be the foundation for all future deliberation.

Faculty Meetings and Inservice Education

A major problem many districts have is the choosing of topics for staff meetings and inservice education. In districts that are focused on a mission statement there should be little debate, because all staff meetings and inservice education are based on the need to adjust practices to better meet the tenets expressed in the district's written mission. For example, if a mission statement mentions student self-esteem (as it probably should) a curriculum council, curriculum director or building principal may become concerned that insufficient attention is being given to that particular goal. If there is concurrence among key members of the faculty and staff, then faculty meetings and more general inservice education programs could be sponsored in order to overcome the assumed deficiency.

Organization Discipline

Quality outcomes are the result of an organizational culture that is characterized by disciplined behaviors; not the kind that are humorless and based on mechanical or bureaucratic drudgery, but are rather built into the organization's day-to-day culture. That kind of culture exists when key leaders (an ever-expanding group) have a vision of the future and courteously, respectfully and diligently guide others toward accepting that same vision. Drudgery and fear will kill organizational discipline faster than any other condition, so the trick is to maintain feelings of fun and excitement while moving forward in a systematic and assertive way.

All of us can think of organizations that have very serious purposes and disciplined activities to accomplish those purposes, yet certain leaders are able to keep the atmosphere light and refreshing. Some churches are examples of such organizations, as are businesses like Southwest Airlines and Disney World. In those organizations the participants, members, or employees know that they are involved in serious work, but that the organization's long range success depends not only on getting the work done but having a good time while doing it.

Curriculum leaders, like all who lead, must be able to have fun, laugh at themselves a little, and chuckle over silly ideas and stupid mistakes... yet make everyone feel affirmed and important. Good leaders also know when to push forward, back-off, apologize, chastise and mend fences... all in the effort to discipline those in the organization to keep their eyes on the mission, and to maintain the energy needed to accomplish it.

Mission Statement Basics:

- The mission statement is a focal point for everything the district does, as it defines the nature of accountability. (*Accountability is allegiance to a cooperatively prepared and implemented mission.*)

- William Edwards Deming's principles for good organizational management require a mission statement that is more *process* than product.

- A working mission statement requires coherence and alignment, starting with a <u>Purpose</u>, <u>Exit Outcomes</u> (that are aligned with the purpose statement), <u>Accomplishing the Curriculum</u> (teaching methods), and <u>Accountability</u>.

- Mission statements are effective to the extent there was a good process for their development, and there is a good process for their use.

- The curriculum coordinating council must spend plenty of time in organizing and conducting meetings with educators and community members, following clear information gathering models and procedures.

- The wording of a mission statement is very important, noting that the emphasis must always be on student learning as described in specific and clearly identifiable ways.

- After the mission statement has been initially drafted, a clear process should be used for its adoption and institutionalization.

- As much time should be given to the adoption and institutionalization processes as was given to the initial stages.

- Timelines for developing the statement can be useful projections, but must be applied flexibly.

- Processes for using the mission statement should be developed for the board of education, administrative team, curriculum coordinating council, subject area committees, and faculty meetings.

DEVELOPING THE LONG RANGE PLAN

Imagine:

- a school board approving expenditures for the next fiscal year without benefit of a district budget;
- a committee selecting plans for a new high school, with no student enrollment projections available;
- an administrator requesting permission to hire new teachers, with no plan for specific numbers, subject areas, or grade levels.

It would be difficult to find anyone involved in the educational process who would not consider these examples ludicrous. Long range planning is considered essential when it comes to facility expansion, faculty growth, student enrollment projections, or budgeting. Yet in more districts than not, academic decisions are made every year with absolutely no long range plans other than perhaps a schedule for textbook selection. Those who wish to establish true educational accountability and implement effective reform must recognize that long range planning is as important in the academics as it is in the "Three F's": Fiscal control, Facility maintenance, and Faculty management.

Textbook Selection

Too often academic planning is limited to textbook selection. To rely on this practice is to accept the concept that printed resources — rather than the district's educators — should drive curriculum development and maintenance. In the first place, we must remember that textbook content goes way beyond the essential and includes much that is superfluous. And because textbooks are designed with the something-for-everyone sales concept, teachers on selection committees never find a perfect book; instead they choose the one that comes the closest to what they're seeking. In turn, there is rarely a unanimous choice among all representatives of the selection committee. For example, primary grade teachers may like Company A's books the best, while intermediate teachers prefer the format or content of the books by Company B. If they consider switching companies half way through the grades, they run the risk of encountering too many overlaps or gaps. Consequently, the textbook selection process rarely results in the purchase of materials that are most appropriate and well articulated horizontally (classroom to classroom, building to building) or vertically (across the grade levels).

An emphasis on textbook selection takes away from teachers the responsibility to make serious decisions about curriculum content, scope, and sequence. In effect, it becomes a roadblock on the path to achieving the district's mission. Some teachers have, through the years, come to use the textbook as a crutch for the entire teaching process: what to teach, when, and how. If the outcomes necessary to accomplish the mission require deviating from the text, the teachers feel frustrated or overwhelmed. They're frustrated by a lack of resources for reteaching procedures or corrective activities, and they're overwhelmed by the belief that they must get through everything in the book.

Likewise, reliance on textbook selection hinders the creative teacher who desperately wants to conduct alternative forms of instruction, but has no framework other than the textbook for accountability. Both kinds of teachers — and all those in between the two extremes — need to be given the responsibility for curricular decisions. They are the trained professionals and they — not the textbook authors or publishers — are the ones who are expected to get results with students.

Think of it this way: Who would go to a physician who relied on a single publisher's medical journals for making a diagnosis or prescribing treatment? We expect our doctors to be knowledgeable about good health in general, as well as symptoms of problems, and either to know what treatment to prescribe or to have a wealth of resources (both written and human) to rely on. Is not the professional training of our teachers parallel to this example? Their years of education and experience qualify teachers for the decisions that need to be made regarding education of our youth. The decisions should not be limited to, or dictated by, what is included in a textbook.

One last point needs to be made about the inadequacies of academic planning based on textbook selection. Once upon a time, the textbook and an occasional supplemental filmstrip were the only media available to most classrooms. Today, we live in a media-intense world. A district that doesn't take advantage of the multitude of resources available not only limits the teachers in their professional capabilities, but also fails to prepare young people for the world in which they must live and work as adults. Resource and media specialists should definitely be included in the deliberations of curriculum councils and subject area committees. With all of these professionals working together, textbooks can be gradually withdrawn as the sole source of information, and textbook selection concerns can be put on the back burner by a district interested in true reform and restructure.

How Do We Begin?

The body most responsible for developing the long range plan is the curriculum coordinating council, and it should complete a tentative plan within the first year of the improvement program. As discussed earlier, the council's first charge is to coordinate the development of the district's mission statement. When the statement is completed — or nearly so — then the council begins work on the long-range plan, using the mission statement as a guide. Council members ask themselves: What are the most imperative purposes and goals of the district? The answer to this question is the necessary link between the mission statement and the long-range plan.

We need to know for developmental purposes that there are three basic parts to a good long range plan, and that we start the plan by considering the timing for each. Thus, after considering the *what* (most imperative purposes and goals), members of the curriculum coordinating council address the questions:

1. *When* will a curriculum document be developed initially;
2. *When* will the curriculum be implemented and validated; and
3. *When* will supplemental resources be identified and evaluation processes created?

Answering these questions requires a number of considerations. A primary one is: Which subject areas should be given attention first? Obviously, the answer to this question varies from one district to another; it depends not only on the imperative purposes and goals identified in the mission statement, but also on the district's current strengths and weaknesses among the subject areas.

In considering the order of attention to be given, we also have to consider which subjects should be given *longer* attention than others. This also depends on current strengths and weaknesses. If a subject area has many weaknesses, it is likely to take longer to identify and implement the steps necessary to eliminate those weaknesses. There are also some subject areas that, even if they currently have strong programs, will require a longer time period for the process just because of their scope and complexities. The subjects often referred to as the "big four" fit this category.

The "Big Four" — Never Tackle More Than One at a Time

The "big four" subject areas are those core curriculum areas that are required for all grade levels, K-12. They are: mathematics, science, social studies, and language arts (communication). When a district implements a curriculum improvement model, secondary teachers have an advantage because of departmentalization. A science teacher would not be asked to serve on a committee studying the language arts curriculum, nor would a social studies teacher be placed on a mathematics committee. Each secondary teacher would be considered for only one subject area committee, and if there are many teachers in a department, some teachers would be asked only to provide input; they might never actually serve on a committee.

On the other hand, in most districts, the elementary teacher teaches all of the core subjects. When trying to decide who will serve on the mathematics committee and who will serve on the science committee, etc., we are drawing from the *same pool* of teachers each time, and regardless of who is working to develop the curriculum, all elementary teachers are expected to implement and validate those curriculums. When elementary teachers must work with three of four new curriculums all at once, they can quickly become overtaxed and intellectually fragmented. The result is "curriculum improvement burnout." The improvement model will fail because no teacher can sustain the energy level to do a good job of teaching *and* continually devote the time and thought required for effectively teaching curriculums that are more focused and challenging than reliance on textbooks or traditional curriculum guides.

The way to avoid this problem is to sponsor just *one* of the big four subjects in any given year. Each year, as another one of the four is initiated, a different set of elementary teachers is selected for committee work, and all elementary teachers have a minimum of a full year before having to implement a new curriculum in another subject. Limiting the big four to only one a year does not mean that only one subject can be sponsored in a year. Other subjects can be studied simultaneously as long as they do not involve large numbers of elementary teachers. For example, along with one of the "Big Four," a district could also study the business subject area, and home economics, or perhaps a vocational curriculum.

Don't Forget Interdisciplinary

Another consideration required of the curriculum coordinating council as it develops a long range plan is: To what extent should traditional subjects be given interdisciplinary treatment? "Traditional" subjects include both core and noncore curricula. In the former, consider language arts. Much attention has been given lately to "writing across the curriculum." Where, when, and how will this be included in the long-range plan? An example of a noncore curriculum that often is interdisciplinary is health. In many districts this traditionally has been a separate subject; it now is often considered more interdisciplinary because it fits in physical education, science, and required human sexuality courses. It can also be worked into many other subjects because physical, mental, and emotional health affect our everyday lives. In developing a long range plan of when each curriculum is developed, implemented, validated, and evaluated, interdisciplinary topics must be carefully thought about and included.

How Long Will It Take?

Most long range plans are five to seven years in length, although they can be longer in larger or more complex districts. That's probably not the answer you wanted. Most districts begin an improvement plan because of both internal and external concerns and desires for actual improvement. Particularly because of external concerns, district educators would like to have immediate results — the quicker, the better. But quick fixes are exactly what the term implies — a quick-fix — not an effective or lasting accomplishment. The basic rule to follow is: Give the process enough time for thoroughness. To go back to the examples in our opening paragraph, would you build a new high school without taking the time to obtain and study enrollment projections, or budget demands, or tax bases? Or, as another example, if you assign your students a major research project, do you expect them to put in the time required to do the research thoroughly, or will you accept a "quick-fix, I-looked-up-a-few-things" product? If you really want to improve your present school plan, then you — the educators — and your school and community patrons must be willing to make the commitment to do the job right!

In addition to the rule for thoroughness, a second rule dictates the five-to-seven-year timetable, and it is one that was discussed above. The rule is: Do not burn out teachers by pushing too hard, too quickly. Remember that while the teachers are actively involved in implementing the improvement process, they also have a primary commitment to the right-now education of their students. When too much is pushed too fast, *something will suffer.* In this case it can be at least one of three things: the improvement program itself, the current quality of education of the students, or the general energy, enthusiasm, and degree of commitment of the teachers.

Outcome Based Requires Faculty and Staff Development

If the district is moving toward use of an outcome based model, then a long range plan must also incorporate plenty of faculty and staff development activities. **No assumptions should be made** with regard to faculty understanding of a model, or their readiness to use it. It is easy for those involved in the planning to be so wrapped up in the model and its processes that they begin to feel that's all they talk about, and that surely they've discussed it so much that their colleagues understand and make the same commitments they do. This, of course, is a fallacy. No one can have the same degree of understanding until directly involved in training, considerations, and discussions. Time spent preparing a new model will be wasted if the teachers — any of the teachers — are left behind in its execution.

The Content of Long Range Planning

So far we have discussed long range planning in the academic program. Specifically mentioned is the relative importance of academic program planning when compared to the "Three F's": Fiscal control, Facility maintenance, and Faculty management. Considerable time and effort are expended in those three managerial arenas, while academic planning is too often limited to textbook selection. It is doubtless an understatement to say that reliance on textbook selection procedures is inadequate, but what more can be done? We pointed out that *much* can be done, and that such initiatives must begin with the curriculum coordinating council and the district's mission statement.

It is critical that a long range plan be viewed in two ways: (1) identifying existing components of the academic program that are to be examined and developed, and (2) examining and developing those components systematically over time. For example, a district that selects the examination and development of the mathematics curriculum for school year 1997-98 will actually be spending three years in that activity: 1997-98, 1998-99, and 1999-2000. The most intense activity will occur in the first two of the three years, because it is in those years that curriculum documents are prepared, implemented and validated.

A Conservative Approach is Best

The long range planning process we advocate functions under a relatively conservative philosophy of curriculum management. The word "conservative" is used in the sense that curriculum is defined as consisting of discrete subject fields that have existed in public schools in this country for over a century. We use that conservative perspective *not* because we are ignorant of recent calls to make curriculum more interdisciplinary, or because outcomes in student learning should take precedence over completion of grades and courses. Those ideas are acknowledged and in many ways accepted. Our conservatism in long range curriculum planning is based on the concern that so many other aspects of the recognizable school structure are being dismantled and reassembled that dramatic changes in fundamental academic categories could cause a serious overload on the system.

At this point in our journey toward outcome based restructure, it is better to say that discrete subjects and courses can be arranged in a suitable scope and sequence, and that they can be organized around appropriate — even interdisciplinary — outcomes. Therefore, a good long range plan can and should recognize the future by being created with some interdisciplinary dimensions in mind. Such is the case with the example shown on the following page.

This example of a long range plan overview is actually being used by a K-12 school district. There is nothing sacrosanct about the codes that are shown; they are merely ways to communicate what will happen, and when. There are certain features of the plan that may need explanation, particularly: (1) what is entailed within each coded stage, (2) the logic behind the sequenced arrangement, and (3) the rationale underlying certain groupings.

There are five codes used in this plan. Each denotes major areas of effort, primarily by subject area committees, although other governing bodies and key district leaders are certainly affected in significant ways. The five codes, as shown in the plan, are: 1. (C) curriculum development; 2. (I) implementation of the plan in the buildings and classrooms; 3. (V) validation of the plan in terms of teacher use, student learning and external influences; 4. (R) resource selection, to include appropriate textbooks; and 5. (E) evaluation of the curriculum in terms of program use and student learning. Note that in this long range plan the district does not include a technology curriculum. It does have a technology resource advisory committee that gives advice to each subject area committee with regard to emerging technologies, especially those that might impact the subject being reviewed.

LONG RANGE PLAN
Pleasant Valley Public Schools

<u>Abbreviations</u>:

       C....Development of curriculum documents
       I.....Initial Implementation of the new curriculum
       V....Validation (internal and external)
       R....Resource selection
       E....Evaluation

Subjects	96/97	97/98	98/99	99/00	00/01	01/02	02/03
Social Studies	C	I/V	R/E				
Science		C	I/V	R/E			
Mathematics			C	I/V	R/E		
Communications				C	C	I/V	R/E
Foreign Language					C	I/V	R/E
Business	C	I/V	R/E				
Home Economics	C	I/V	R/E				
Industrial Education	C	I/V	R/E				
Speech/Theater					C	I/V	R/E
Art			C	I/V	R/E		
Music			C	I/V	R/E		
Health		C	I/V	R/E			
Physical Education			C	I/V	R/E		

Curriculum Document Development
(*C* - Year 1 of 3)

     Following the long-range plan, a curriculum coordinating council appoints a subject area committee (SAC) in the designated year. The initial charge given to that SAC is to create a scope and sequence/curriculum document. Unfortunately, curriculum documents have the reputation of being dismal products of a complex and unwieldy bureaucracy, so they often are ignored or disdained — especially in grades 9 through 12. Obviously, it is not our intent to perpetuate that tradition.

     One way to avoid that syndrome is a step by step process which includes these stages: (1) information gathering, (2) analysis of data and decision making, .(3) the design down process for curriculum development, and (4) implementation. Those stages will be discussed in greater detail later, but they call for something other than business as usual because *full recognition is given to the importance of the existing curriculum and the role of classroom teachers in making decisions about it.* Our information gathering strategy, while lengthy and laborious, gives total credence to the notion that the "school district is already doing a good job — we simply want to find out why and how, and what might be done to make its programs even better." Analyzation and decision-making focus on *what is,* while taking into account the external influences imposed by learned societies, state curriculum mandates, norm and criterion reference tests, and perceived/assessed societal needs. The design down process assures that all aspects of the curriculum are aligned, starting with the district mission and ending with the content and procedures for daily instruction.

Please note that the initial development of the curriculum in *communications (language arts)* can take two years. That field of study is comprehensive and complex, so it is important for it to be given special treatment. Such treatment is necessary even when foreign language is dealt with as a separate category. Reading is now treated as an inherent part of the communications curriculum and should never be considered separately.

Finally, as discussed in greater detail in the next section, implementation covers faculty development, internal validation, resource selection, and ongoing evaluation.... categories treated as distinct entities in the long range plan.

Implementation (*I* - Year 2 of 3)

Probably the most significant problem in most curriculum development projects is that nothing much is done after the paperwork is finished and documents are produced. Committee members often feel relief that the work is "now finished" and that appreciative teachers will make good use of the products of their efforts. As most of us know, that assumption is patently false. Curriculum documents placed in teachers' mailboxes with a brief memo as to their use are destined for an almost immediate demise. Time, paper, energy and professional expertise have been wasted.

The implementation of our model can easily constitute almost the entire faculty and staff development program of the district. In fact, there are those who can claim that *the best kind of staff/faculty development is curriculum development.* The point is that implementing a new curriculum, particularly one founded on principles of outcome based education, requires extensive training of teachers, administrators, and support persons. There are also numerous implications for site based management, because the internal dynamics within each building must be more interactive, collegial, and focused on total-school management of reteaching activities, corrective programs, and enrichment opportunities.

It is the responsibility of the subject area committee to assure that appropriate faculty/staff development activities are conducted within each building. That will likely require the assistance of principals, building leadership teams, and particular support personnel such as media specialists. It may also require the services of an outside consultant who can more vigorously and specifically guide the transfer of intended curricular outcomes to actual use in the classroom.

Validation (V - Year 2 of 3)

A subject area committee will have given some attention to validating the proposed curriculum during its actual preparation, particularly with regard to external influences and mandates (learned societies, tests, and state-imposed objectives). Just as important as those validating criteria are the opinions of teachers as they attempt to implement the new curriculum. Are students ready for the material? Is the difficulty level appropriate? Are the units sequenced logically?

Again, site based principles can be applied because gathering validating data must be ongoing and systematic. That requires leadership and well defined processes, because haphazard monitoring produces inconclusive results.

Resource Selection (R - Year 3 of 3)

We debated this point at length, and our conclusion is that resource selection must come *after* implementation and validation. The reasoning is that, to escape textbook-driven curriculum design, schools must select resources after they have identified curricular components. The issue, of course, focuses on how implementation of a new curriculum can occur without the resources that are aligned to it. Our answer is that a new curriculum will not likely be alien to older materials, and the experience of implementing a program without totally compatible textbooks will encourage teachers to make better use of other available materials.

Probably even more critical is the necessary inclusion of technology as part of the resource pool. Because of that need, we strongly recommend that school media specialists become involved with subject area committees, and that there be a permanent technology resource advisory committee to guide SACs as they prepare and implement curricula.

Evaluation (E - Year 3 of 3)

As any educational researcher will say, evaluation processes must begin at the onset of a project, and we certainly agree. In fact, the curriculum coordinating council should have a clear plan for: (1) determining how well the improvement program is working in terms of teacher use, and (2) gauging the extent to which student learning is continuously improved.

While broad guidelines are implemented by a CCC, a SAC must give focus to the second point: the extent to which outcome-based curriculum and instruction are having a positive impact on student learning. That process must have multiple parts, to include a comprehensive monitoring and testing program, follow-up studies of graduate and transfer students, and general observation of the academic climate. As one might expect, the processes just described can be complicated and time-consuming, necessitating careful planning and execution; hence the reason for waiting until the third year to give the effort serious and specific attention.

CHOOSING AND TRAINING

Long Range Plan Basics:

- Long range academic planning is as important as planning for budgets, facilities, and personnel.

- Good academic planning is much more than textbook selection.

- The long range plan is created by the curriculum council.

- The "big four" subject areas are dealt with one year at a time, not simultaneously.

- The plan should be seven years in duration... or long enough to do a good job.

- The plan should include more than preparation of curriculum documents; faculty development, validation, resource selection, and continuous evaluation must be shown.

- A long-range plan includes information about when a targeted subject is to be studied, and the configuration and extent of that study.

- The plan must avoid overloading a district's "change circuits."

- The plan is laid out in a table that uses various codes, all of which symbolize stages of extensive work that is coordinated by a subject area committee.

- The first stage is study and development using a step by step process, and the creation of a workable curriculum document.

- The second stage is implementation, emphasizing faculty development as its principal means.

- Third is a validation stage that monitors teacher opinions about a curriculum's "workability."

- Fourth is an activity commonly known as textbook adoption, but — in this model — is the more comprehensive *resource* selection.

- The final stage is a focused evaluation that determines the extent to which students are learning.

SUBJECT AREA COMMITTEES

Two of the most important tasks of the curriculum coordinating council are choosing members of subject area committees, and training them to effectively implement an action agenda. Selecting SAC members who are willing to work and make the process go smoothly is an essential aspect of quality curriculum building. This process is presented in great detail in Part III of this book, but an overview is provided here as it relates to the governance component of the model.

Choosing the Subject Area Committee

The long range plan triggers the appointment of subject area committees, so a curriculum coordinating council should have no difficulty making that decision year after year. However, there may be occasions when the council will change the long range plan and select a subject area committee for a year not previously designated. There is no reason why that shouldn't be done; the long range plan is not set in concrete, but is merely a way of guiding future decisions.

Members of the subject area committee are appointed by the council. In small districts, teachers working at the middle and high schools must serve on the committee. All who teach in self contained elementary classrooms will probably not be able to serve, but will send representatives from buildings and grade level categories. While leadership ability is an important consideration in the appointment of subject area committees, representation plays a larger role here than for membership on a curriculum coordinating council.

It is recommended that the curriculum coordinating council decide how it wishes to select SAC members, since the appointment should neither involve application processes nor voting. In the sample bylaws shown on page 51, the council provides for the appointment of any teacher with a year or more of successful classroom teaching. In many larger districts the buildings, grade levels, or departments are asked to send representatives, and the local teachers decide who that person is going to be.

The SAC should be chaired by a member of the curriculum coordinating council or someone who is in direct contact with it. This point is an important one, since committees only function at the pleasure of the council — and must report to it regularly. The chair must be a respected professional educator in the district, but not necessarily a teacher of the subject being considered by the committee. Nor does the chair have to be a secondary teacher. Some of the best committee leaders with whom we've worked have been elementary teachers, counselors, and building principals.

Training the Subject Area Committee

Training the subject area committee is an important task, because without training the committee will neither understand the action agenda nor execute effective curriculum building strategies. So that a subject area committee may hit the ground running in the fall semester, a good time for training is immediately following the last week of school.

We recommend that a subject area committee be given a two to three day training program, and that members of the curriculum coordinating council participate in the first year. Either the curriculum coordinator or an outside consultant can conduct the training using materials found in Part III of this book, or using publications specifically prepared for workshop use by the Curriculum Leadership Institute. Training must be conducted especially well the first year, and held each summer within the district's initial long range plan.

Basics of Choosing and Training Subject Area Committees:

- Subject area committees are chosen in accordance with the long range plan.

- Long range plans can be changed at any time, if a council believes new priorities require it.

- Members of subject area committees are chosen by the council using a technique of its choice, although application and voting processes are not recommended.

- Members can be identified by those in buildings, grade levels, or departments.

- Chairs of subject area committees must have a close working relationship with the curriculum coordinating council, and will preferably be a member of the council.

- Training of a committee should occur over a two to three day period at the close of the school year.

- Training should include participants from the council, and be conducted by the curriculum coordinator or an outside consultant, using materials found in Part III of this book.

ON-GOING COUNCIL FUNCTIONS

Insuring Internal Communication

Meetings

Productive meetings are the heart of curriculum development and leadership. With the current movement toward greater involvement of stakeholders in academic program decision making, curriculum leaders are faced with increasing numbers of meetings.

This may be a problem! One of the major complaints among curriculum workers is unproductive meetings. Unclear objectives, no written agenda, lack of leader control, and poor decision making seem to be commonplace in education at all levels.

This poor meeting syndrome often leaves curriculum workers discouraged and unmotivated. Fenwick English has written that poorly run meetings are primary killers of enthusiasm and energy among educators. The warning signs of poor meetings, according to English, are glazed eyes, nodding heads, and agitated movements. These signals are all too familiar to anyone who has been in education for any length of time.

It should be noted that unproductive meetings are not exclusive to education. A recent national survey of top executives, as reported in The Wall Street Journal, revealed that meetings account for the greatest amount of unproductive time in business. According to the survey, meetings came in first for lost time followed by telephone calls, paperwork, travel, and office gossip.

Why do bad meetings plague both education and business? We contend that the answer is simple — leaders in both fields have not been trained or taught how to conduct productive meetings. Rarely do professors of education and business include productive meeting skills in their course syllabus. The same is true with professionals in the field. One can search in vain for administrative staff development programs on how to run effective meetings.

In this section we focus on four major components of running a productive meeting: (1) preparing, (2) conducting, (3) closing, and (4) follow-up. We recommend that the curriculum leader address each of these components by posing a series of questions.

Preparing

The heart of a successful meeting lies in preparation by the leader. Questions that need to be addressed by the curriculum leader are:

1. What is the group's purpose and assignment? What, exactly, are the charge, and tasks or goals?

2. What are the short range and long range plans for achieving the assignment? How many times will the group meet and where?
3. What is the time frame for the group? What are meeting dates, and beginning and ending times?
4. Are the people in the group the most appropriate individuals to carry out the mission? Should the group include teachers, parents, administrators, students, or others who represent certain constituencies?
5. How will the physical environment and "creature comforts" impact the progress of the group? What is needed in terms of tables, temperature, space, seating arrangements, and food and drink?
6. How should the written agenda address the major issues facing the group?
7. How will the group's deliberations be recorded? Who will take notes or minutes, and how will that information be distributed?

All of these questions must be addressed by the curriculum leader prior to the meeting. Many of these questions can be addressed by **preparing a clearly written agenda.**

Conducting

Preparation is the first critical step of running a successful meeting. Conducting the meeting is the second major component. Questions the curriculum leader must address before, during and after the meeting are:

1 Have I communicated the purpose and significance of the meeting?
2. Have I communicated the necessary information concerning the short and long-range plans?
3. Am I fostering communication between group members and myself?
4. Am I following the planned agenda in a timely, logical, and efficient manner?
5. Does the group have the necessary information to discuss and take action on agenda items?
6. Am I aware of the group dynamics which elicit productive and nonproductive roles by group members?

One of the most important skills in the conducting of meetings is metacognition or thinking about what you are doing while you are doing it. Thinking about what you are doing and what the group is doing while following the prepared agenda is a difficult task that requires practice.

Closing

Closing is the third component of a successful meeting, and it is as important as beginning the meeting. Questions the curriculum leader must consider when closing a meeting are:

1. How can I best summarize the important ideas or decisions made by the group?
2. How should this committee act on conclusions or decisions? What recommendations or actions should be taken?
3. Does this group need to meet again?
4. If necessary and appropriate, what agenda items need to be considered for the next meeting?
5. What actions need to be undertaken to make the next meeting even more productive?

At the end of the meeting the curriculum leader must be able to synthesize the salient points of the meeting and report them back to the group. At the same time the leader must be able to identify the next steps for the group.

Follow-up

Those events which follow the meeting are also crucial to successful curriculum work. The group leader must become credible to those individuals who have contributed their time and efforts in the meeting. Questions the curriculum leader must consider are:

1. How will I acknowledge, deal with, or act on recommendations, suggestions, or decisions of the committee?
2. How can I recognize and reward group members for their contributions? Recognition might include both public and private expression of appreciation, including thank you notes and verbal expressions of gratitude.
3. To whom should I distribute accurate minutes of all committee actions?

Meetings do not have to be long and unproductive. Curriculum leaders can master the running of meetings by asking the above questions prior to scheduling a meeting. The following *Instructional Leadership Audit* can be used by the busy curriculum leader as a template for productive meetings.

Preparing

In relation to preparing for a meeting, (check)

_____ 1. Do I consider <u>timing</u> when scheduling the meeting (e.g. time of day, day of week, potential conflicts)?

_____ 2. Do I consider the <u>physical environment</u> of the meeting place (e.g.

tables, temperature, light, comfort)?

_____ 3. Do I prepare a <u>written and/or oral agenda</u> which is shared with participants (e.g. items of consideration, activities, issues)?

_____ 4. Do I create and use agenda items which are derived from or connected to the <u>Long Range Plan</u> (e.g. interactive plan, and action plan which identify where the school district is headed or going)?

_____ 5. Do I recognize the <u>different audiences</u> that will be present at the meeting and do I recognize their <u>respective needs</u> (e.g. _Teachers_ — how does this relate to my class and my students? _Administrators_ — how does this relate to our building and teachers)?

_____ 6. Do I consider the <u>degree or level of motivation and/or experience</u> of the group participants (e.g. volunteer vs. draftee, veteran teacher vs. new teacher)?

_____ 7. Do I consider the <u>necessity of the meeting</u> before planning and holding the meeting (e.g. canceling meetings which become unnecessary)?

_____ 8. Do I plan for "<u>creature comforts</u>" during the meeting (e.g. food, drink, rest breaks)?

_____ 9. Do I <u>prepare</u> myself for the scheduled meeting (e.g. know my roles and responsibilities, understand the agenda)?

Conducting

In relation to conducting a meeting, (check)

_____ 10. Do I communicate the <u>significance</u> of the meeting to all group members (e.g. value, benefit, relevance of meeting)?

_____ 11. Do I communicate the <u>purpose</u> of the meeting to group members (e.g. charge, tasks, goal)?

_____ 12. Do I establish effective <u>nonverbal communication</u> with group participants (e.g. nonverbal/verbal behavior consistency, eye contact, gestures, physical proximity)?

_____ 13.   Do I communicate <u>roles and responsibilities</u> which are expected of group participants (e.g. note taking, following, leading, listening)?

_____ 14.   Do I foster <u>communication</u> between and among committee members (e.g. allowing questions, permitting clarification statements)?

_____ 15.   Do I strive for <u>objectivity</u> with all committee members (e.g. exhibiting fairness, just treatment, equal consideration)?

_____ 16.   Do I strive for total <u>group involvement</u> (e.g. equal opportunity for input during group exchange)?

_____ 17.   Do I allow committee members to identify and discuss <u>unplanned agenda items</u> which were not on the planned agenda but are relevant and important to the success of the task (e.g. the issue of resources emerges during group discussion and committee leader facilitates discussion because of relevance and importance to success of task)?

_____ 18.   Do I recognize the <u>nonproductive roles</u> initiated by group participants and the significant impact of these roles on group effectiveness and efficiency (e.g. dominating, apathetic, impatient)?

_____ 19.   Do I make provisions for <u>accurate record keeping</u> of the committee proceedings (e.g. notes, minutes, summaries)?

_____ 20.   Do I make committee work <u>exciting</u> (e.g. use of humor, creating celebration atmosphere, having fun, risk taking)?

_____ 21.   Do I encourage <u>creative and divergent thinking</u> (e.g. permitting opposing points of view, reinforcing risk taking behavior and ideas)?

Closing and Follow-up

In relation to closing a meeting, (check)

_____ 22.   Do I establish <u>closure</u> in the meeting (e.g. summarizing, giving assignments, scheduling dates for future meetings)?

_____ 23.   Do I set the agenda for the next meeting?

_____ 24.   Do I provide opportunities (when appropriate) for group participants to <u>assess the effectiveness</u> of the meeting (e.g. assessing whether goals were achieved, suggestions for improving next meeting)?

_____ 25.   Do I express <u>appreciation, provide public recognition, or supply rewards</u> for effective committee participation (e.g. thank you notes, verbal expressions of appreciation, certificates of service)

_____ 26.   Do I <u>acknowledge, deal with, or act on</u> recommendations, suggestions, or actions of the committee (e.g. incorporating recommendations in procedures of the organization, using ideas to perform next task)?

_____ 27.   Do I distribute minutes or records to the appropriate persons?

Formal and Informal Messages

Business and industry spend much time with internal communication, claiming that poor communication within a company can be one of the most serious problems faced by executives. William Edwards Deming's admonitions deal with that issue in many ways, because a breakdown in communication can result in poor quality outcomes in terms of product or service.

As stated earlier, school districts have natural divisions that cause serious communication problems: between or among elementary, middle level and secondary grades; between teachers of different subjects; between teachers and administrators; between teachers and professional support staff; between the board of education and teachers; between students and teachers; and between parents and teachers. We're certain you can identify many more examples. The problem is no greater in a school district than that seen in a large and diverse business; the difference is the amount of time and effort the two organizations put into resolving the problem. Schools and school districts have not allocated the kind of time, money or effort that businesses give to the problem, mainly because the quality of the bottom line (student learning) means something different to educators than to those business people concerned about product perception in the marketplace.

A business cannot fault the product itself for being inferior, except in those instances where subcontractors or parts suppliers are accused of shoddy work. Schools, on the other hand, can easily point to a student's inferior mental ability, poor attitude, dysfunctional background, and a myriad of other inherent problems over which — it is claimed — the school has no control. The basic school reform tenets of the 1980s and 1990s dispute that position. Essentially, every movement from effective schools to outcome based education says that a school can control many of those circumstances if it simply gets its act together.

For an organization to get its act together it must have strong internal communication mechanisms. In the school restructuring model advocated in this book, the primary responsibility for developing, implementing and managing those internal communication mechanisms lies with the (1) administrative team and (2) curriculum coordinating council (see Table 1 on page 60). The *administrative team* must be clear in its communication about policy, budget, schedules, monitoring programs, personnel supervision, and personnel evaluation. The *curriculum coordinating council* must also be clear in its communication about academic philosophies, missions, curricular content, curriculum management, management of instruction, and evaluation of curriculum effectiveness in terms of student learning.

Entire books have been written about internal communication in organizations, so we are not able to adequately cover the topic here. However, there are a few basic principles we can offer:

- Use common sense, which tells us that good communication requires openness and honesty at all times. It also tells us that people will not accept new practices unless they feel that any ideas they hold have been solicited, discussed and appropriately applied.

- Avoid making assumptions about the adequacy of communication by maintaining a constant check that insures everyone is moving forward at similar levels of knowledge and practice. Members of curriculum coordinating councils will experience enormous professional growth in a relatively brief time, and their colleagues in the buildings will not keep up unless CCC members are diligent in systematically nurturing a similar kind of professional growth on the job.

- Be careful that an elitist environment is not created. It is easy for those working in the decision making mainstream to allow the development of organizational pecking orders, a condition which is detrimental to feelings of ownership. A new curriculum will suffer fatal attacks and sabotage if teachers feel as if they are on the outside looking in.

We recommend that you read any good literature on organizational communication and apply the principles advocated in that material. Most of those publications will offer tips on such matters as: how to decide to communicate through memo or personal contact, how to write memos that do not confuse or offend readers, how to conduct good staff conferences, and how to act on a myriad of other principles associated with quality human interaction.

Making Innovation Inclusive

The word *inclusive* in this book refers to two conditions: (1) inclusion of all stakeholders in a district when it comes to curriculum development, implementation, and management; and (2) inclusion of the growing body of knowledge being generated by all the various reform movements. Both definitions of inclusion are good descriptors of the organizational catchword of the 1990s: <u>systemic</u>. *Systemic change* means that new practices are so pervasive that they permeate every aspect of the institution, and the only way that can happen is to create conditions in which everyone becomes (and feels) involved, and all good ideas have a chance to be planted and grow in a nurturing environment.

The business of stakeholder involvement, as important as it is, must be carefully overseen and managed. We've already shown how district educators may be involved directly or indirectly in the work of the curriculum coordinating council and subject area committees. The extent to which students, parents and patrons are involved is determined by the steering committee as it creates the bylaws. The steering committee may decide that, in addition to the inclusion of board of education members, seats on the council should be open to representatives from the high school student government, parent-teacher organization, and community chamber of commerce. The bylaws may also provide one council seat to be filled at the discretion of the superintendent and curriculum coordinator, in case community representation should be expanded to accommodate a positively assertive special interest group.

Although leadership is the primary consideration, and decision making is done by consensus, care must be taken that there is a good representative balance of members serving on a curriculum coordinating council. A simple plurality of council members should be district teachers and professional support persons.

The growing body of knowledge now available about educational reform must be considered by a curriculum coordinating council. We strongly advocate the examination of all perspectives, including those presented by such diverse groups as the Coalition of Essential Schools, Association for Supervision and Curriculum Development, Effective Schools Network, and the Network for Outcome Based Education. A major problem for most districts in the past is that many professional personnel developed great ideas for improvement (through conference attendance or reading) but had no place to plug them into the system. They could use those ideas in their own classrooms, but the system did not accommodate expansion of those practices to other settings. The council and subject area committee structure opens new opportunities for such expansion to a system-wide program, because the practice of moving good theories into practice is a primary responsibility of academic program governance.

No educator should feel that the use of this district improvement model pre-
cludes use of other good ideas. True, some curriculum development ideas are alien to
the eight principles used as a foundation for the Accountability Based Curriculum
model, but most other innovations can be used in their current form or as modified.
We believe this strongly supports our position that the ABC model, once executed, is
a template for local decision making which can move in any direction that improves
the quality of student learning.

Monitoring Progress

Monitoring progress can take various forms, and is performed by the council
in both an informal and formal manner. Informal monitoring is simply a matter of
maintaining open communication between council members and district stakeholders. When it comes to formal monitoring, there are three techniques: (1) continuous review of the mission and how well it is being implemented, (2) the internal and
external validation of curriculum, and (3) continuous collection and evaluation of
data on student learning.

The board of education, administrative team, and curriculum coordinating
council should always have the academic mission statement in a place where it can be
regularly discussed and aligned with decisions made. That process alone stimulates
systematic monitoring of progress. Many districts discuss mission statement review
in their bylaws, including processes for how it should be used and amended.

In the previous section on the long range plan is a brief description of internal and external validation processes. Validation is also discussed in much greater
detail in Part III of this book. Internal validation is a formal way to intensively and
precisely monitor the implementation of new curricula. External validation compares
new curricula with external standards set by states, learned societies, and accrediting
agencies.

Continuous collection and evaluation of data on student learning is a function required by many state and regional accrediting agencies, and is therefore another way to monitor progress of the curriculum development program. There are limits to the value of most data about student learning for essentially three reasons. First,
there is an over-reliance on standardized norm referenced tests, state criterion referenced tests, and miscellaneous soft data coming from employers of graduates, post
secondary vocational schools, and traditional four year colleges and universities.
Second, most districts have traditionally collected neither soft nor hard data about
students, so local educator expertise and district willingness to budget research offices
are both inadequate. Third, accreditation processes that suggest that *school improvement is data driven* are appropriate only in circumstances in which control of the current academic program is firm enough for data driven changes to cause tangible

reforms in the real or taught curriculum.

While we certainly agree with the principle that school improvement is data driven, we do not accept that practice as a place to start restructuring. Monitoring a curriculum that is not yet coordinated and well managed, by focusing on the adequacy of student learning, is an exercise in frustration. However, after a curriculum component has been restructured using the accountability based model, it is definitely time to evaluate its impact on all students. See Part III, *Evaluating the New Curriculum According to Student Learning.*

Working With Building Administrative Teams and Site Councils

Using the leadership model described earlier, there are two decision making bodies that serve as agents of the board of education: the administrative leadership team (ALT) and the curriculum coordinating council (CCC). With the help of bylaws and good leadership, those two decision making groups, over time, should be able to work together reasonably well. A little more difficult to control is the relationship between and among those two groups and the building level site council (the principal and advisory groups to the principal).

Building level administrators and site councils must operate under policies that are explicit regarding the extent of their powers. The ALT should have policies that clearly prescribe the authority a building site council has over personnel, budgets, and other purely administrative matters. In the same way, the CCC should have policies that clearly prescribe the authority a building site council has over curriculum and instruction.

In brief, the curriculum coordinating council holds all power — subject to board of education review — over matters having to do with curriculum content and design. A building administrator or site council may advise the curriculum coordinating council on curriculum content and design, but neither one can make arbitrary decisions about those two areas of interest. However, it is highly appropriate that a building administrator or site council work with the CCC or subject area committee in implementing, maintaining, and monitoring the curriculum.

For example, once a curriculum has been prepared a subject area committee must make sure it is implemented through good faculty development activities. Those activities will include a combination of formal and informal training sessions that occur in the buildings. Those training sessions, ranging from formally organized workshops to informal peer coaching, cannot be conducted solely by a subject area committee. That committee must obtain assistance from persons in the building who are designated as leaders, namely, administrators and professional members of a site council.

Building leadership is as important as ever. But, in this model, building leaders must understand their opportunities and limits with regard to curriculum development and implementation. And it is the curriculum coordinating council's job to indicate what those opportunities and limits are.

Making External Mandates Work

The more state agencies get involved with school reform and restructuring, the more they produce new accreditation standards that focus on the quality of student learning. Some of those standards are quite specific, as in Michigan's Core Curriculum process; others such as that used in Kansas' Quality Performance Accreditation, are fairly broad. Usually associated with those accreditation standards are assessments of student learning, requirements for collection and use of data on student learning, and managerial processes such as site councils.

The major problem associated with those new accreditation processes is that they force a new managerial culture onto a district, one that invariably costs more money and makes more work for local educational leaders. Even worse is the need to form new administrative and communication media that may or may not align with a model such as the one discussed in this book. For example, mandates requiring building site councils are vague enough that a district may make assumptions that simply are not inherent to the mandate. When that is done, a site council may be given more power than is either expedient or appropriate.

Also, there is a natural tendency for district leaders to organize new committees that are task specific, at least in terms of the tasks which seem to be included in the mandate. For example, some states write mandates that include broad outcomes; districts then create new committees to deal with each of those outcomes. When new committees are added to the list of committees already in existence, then committee proliferation is more than an annoyance — it is downright dysfunctional to the smooth functioning of the organization.

Making those kinds of external mandates work for a district already involved in making internal improvements is a matter of focusing on what is right for student learning and for the district's smooth operations. Today's state mandates and policies usually involve matters more pertinent to curriculum and instruction, so it is important that a curriculum coordinating council have an extensive opportunity to evaluate the mandate in terms of what makes sense for the district, and develop recommendations that align with local priorities. Sometimes this means that council recommendations do not align with the mandate's language, in which case the superintendent should gain a good understanding of the council's rationale. If that rationale is solid, the superintendent and board of education should carry that recommendation to those in the state agency assigned responsibility for mandate compliance. It has been our experience that most state agency personnel — at some level — will gladly consider the variance recommended, and modify the mandate's application accordingly. There are two reasons for that: state mandates are in a state of flux right now, and most state personnel are interested in helping a district get into motion with regard to reform and restructure. Only petty bureaucrats will call for mandate compliance when common sense dictates otherwise.

An example of a modification that has worked well for us has to do with avoiding committee proliferation. Instead of developing committees to meet certain target goals established by accrediting agencies, we interweave the target goals into the work of the *curriculum coordinating council, administrative leadership team,* and/or *individual subject area committees.* That makes sense in that most new target goals for district improvement focus on school climate and the quality of curriculum, instruction and student learning. Creating another layer of bureaucracy is avoided by placing the responsibility for meeting target goals required by accrediting agencies in one of those three existing bodies, not in new target goal committees.

PART III:
LINKING ACADEMIC PROGRAM GOVERNANCE WITH THE IMPLEMENTATION OF NEW CURRICULA

As previous chapters have outlined, a district that commits to an improvement model must first set up a system of governance. The curriculum coordinating council (CCC) is the governing body for this model. The first task of the CCC is to coordinate efforts to develop and institutionalize the district mission. The second task is to devise a long range plan for curriculum development, implementation, and ongoing evaluation. The tool for *executing* the long range plan is the subject area committee (SAC).

THE SUBJECT AREA COMMITTEE

To understand the differences between a subject area committee and curriculum coordinating council, we should review the purposes of the council. Remember, a CCC is a **permanent** body of a district's best educational leaders. Its purposes are:

1. to establish and maintain the model for academic program governance;

2. to serve as "keepers of the vision," assuring compliance with the district mission statement, governing by-laws, and the long-range plan;

3. to theorize, discuss, and take action on issues pertaining to curriculum, instruction and student learning; and

4. to serve as an educational "transformer" in the integration of external influences and mandates, so that they positively influence rather than short-circuit existing change processes.

Most of the above purposes are self-explanatory, with the possible exception of the last one: the transformer concept. When mandates are imposed, or other external influences affect district decisions, much attention and energy are focused on responding to these demands. One of the first problems encountered is that so much attention and energy are used in this case that little is left for the original change processes the district had implemented.

The second problem is that a new mandate may cause a feeling of panic and in the rush to respond to it, action may be taken that is actually in conflict with the original long-range plan. In either case, the original plan is short-circuited. It is imperative that members of the CCC use their leadership skills to assess the situation and make decisions that assure that the new plans are implemented without interrupting the flow of existing ones.

The SAC is not a permanent body like the CCC, but is an ad hoc group that exists no more than three or four years at a time. It is led by a member of the CCC whose primary task is to maintain liaison between the two bodies. The SAC is subordinate to the CCC and is much more limited in its scope, since it deals with a single subject area. Its purposes are:

- to follow an action agenda for developing curriculum in this subject, with an accompanying comprehensive curriculum document (one or two years);
- to implement and validate the document through faculty development activities and evaluation strategies (one year); and
- to identify resources that support the validated curriculum and establish on-going evaluation procedures (one year).

When these tasks are completed, the SAC, while not really dissolved, is inactive for about two or three years, then it begins the process again. This means that the entire process is repeated every five to seven years. The repetition is necessary to keep the curriculum current and valid. Needless to say, the process is much easier the second and subsequent times it is implemented. Membership of the SAC may change somewhat for repeat processes, but much of it remains the same. (See Membership Selection below.)

The most intense developmental work of the SAC occurs in the first year (or two) of the process, when the curriculum document is being prepared. The next phase, which is devoted to extensive training and monitoring, requires a medium amount of time and energy. The last year of activity for the SAC — establishing the evaluation and resource process — is the most moderate.

MEMBERSHIP SELECTION

When the curriculum coordinating council has completed the long-range plan and thus knows which subjects will be addressed each year, the next step is to appoint the first subject area committee. Regardless of the size of the district, the general makeup of the SAC is the same. Obviously it is comprised of teachers who teach this particular subject, and they should represent as many grade levels as possible. However, other certified personnel are also assigned to SACs, including administrators, special education resource persons, counselors, or media specialists. In situations where there is only one teacher for a subject area (such as home economics), several subjects are combined into one SAC, such as vocational/technical: home economics, industrial arts, business, computer applications.

As mentioned above, each SAC should also include a representative from the CCC. It is not necessary for this person to teach the particular subject being addressed; his or her main purpose is to serve as a liaison between the two groups, and to help direct the action agenda <u>process</u>, which is consistent regardless of the subject at hand. The number of people to be assigned, and how to select them, varies according to the size of the district and is explained in detail in the following sections.

SMALL DISTRICTS
(Approximately 60 or Fewer Teachers)

The amount of leeway a CCC has in selecting members of the subject area committee depends on the size of the district. Ideally, a SAC would have one teacher for <u>each</u> elementary grade level, as well as two or three middle level and two or three high school teachers. However, small districts don't have that many teachers, and the numbers they do have must be distributed across the subject areas.

Keep in mind that curriculum development begins in only <u>one</u> of the "big four" subjects each year, to avoid overtaxing elementary teachers who must implement all four of these core subjects. In a small district every teacher will eventually serve on a SAC; the only "selection" that takes place is determining <u>which</u> SAC to assign each elementary teacher. The CCC must look at the total number of elementary teachers and keep in mind that they will need representatives from this group for at **least** four subject area committees. So, for example, if there are 12 elementary teachers, three could be assigned to each of the "big four" subject areas. If there are as many as 16 elementary teachers, four could be assigned to each committee, and so forth. *A district that is so small as to have only one or two elementary teachers on a committee would be putting a tremendous burden on these teachers and should consider joining another district to work as a consortium.*

If all elementary teachers are expected to serve on a SAC, the CCC should ask them to rank order the subjects according to interest, with the understanding that they may not get their preferences if too many teachers choose the same areas. In making the assignments, the first consideration is grade level representation. Each SAC should have no fewer than three or four elementary teachers, with the representation split as evenly as possible between primary and intermediate levels. As long as those criteria are met, teachers can be assigned according to their subject preferences. However, if a particular subject area is selected by only one group (all primary and no intermediate or vice-versa), or is selected unevenly (three intermediate and only one primary) then the CCC must revert to teachers' second, third, or even fourth choices to be sure both levels are fairly represented.

Districts of the size being discussed here usually have only a few secondary teachers of the targeted subject area (one or two middle level and one or two high school teachers). If the total is six or fewer, all of those teachers should serve on the SAC. In some small districts, the secondary level may have a problem similar to the elementary — one teacher may teach more than one of the "big four" subjects. This problem should be addressed just like the primary/intermediate situation: there should be at least one middle level teacher and at least one high school teacher on each SAC, and no one teacher should be asked to serve on two committees. Along these same lines, the CCC must consider the number of preparations — or separate courses — for which the middle and high school teachers are responsible. Although the teachers can work together to help each other, two to three preparations per person is a maximum. If there are more than six secondary courses, then more than two secondary teachers will be needed on the committee. Again, if the district has too few teachers to meet these criteria, they might want to consider working with another small district as a consortium.

In summary, the **minimum** make-up for a K-12 subject area committee of a small district would be six members: three elementary teachers (at least one of whom is primary and one is intermediate), one middle level teacher, one high school teacher, and one member from the CCC. Adding an administrator or member of the support personnel would greatly enhance such a small group. If the district has more teachers than the number needed to meet minimums for all SACs, additional appointments should be distributed fairly evenly among the various subjects.

MEDIUM SIZE DISTRICTS
(Approximately 60-100 Teachers)

Districts is this category can appoint subject area committees with good representation of grade levels. In most cases, all teachers in the district will serve on a SAC. The "big four" subject area committees should have one or two teachers for each elementary grade level, plus two or three middle and two or three high school teachers. Elementary teachers will also serve on other committees that span the K-12 grade levels, such as health or computer/technology. All secondary teachers serve on the committee for their major teaching assignments, such as fine arts or math.

Committee size for K-12 subjects ideally will be between 10 and 20 members. Groups larger than that are difficult to manage because discussions take longer and logistics, such as meeting rooms and release time, can be problematic. However, the CCC should use common sense; if keeping the memberships under 20 means that all but just a few teachers will serve on a SAC, then they should go ahead and increase the numbers so that all teachers will be involved.

LARGE DISTRICTS
(More than 100 Teachers)

Larger school districts can (and have to) be much more selective when considering who should serve on subject area committees. In these districts, not all teachers will be on a committee; therefore the CCC should consider two kinds of representation when selecting members. The first is *representation* in terms of buildings, grade levels, and teachers of the targeted subject. For K-12 subjects, all grade levels should be represented. Additionally, as many buildings as possible should be represented. Those districts that have more than a dozen elementary schools will **not** be able to have all buildings represented on each SAC. In such cases, the CCC should rotate representation among the schools; in other words, certain schools will have teachers serving on the social studies SAC, while another set of schools will have representation on the science SAC, and so forth. The following recommendations are provided for minimum and maximum representation in SACs of large districts.

Minimum	Maximum
1 teacher for every grade level, K-8........... 9	2 teachers for every grade level, K-8............................. 18
3 high school teachers of varied courses........ 3	4 high school teachers of varied courses......................... 4
1 administrator or support personnel........1	1 administrator or support personnel........................ 1
Total 13*	23

* These examples assume that one of the people selected for the SAC is also on the CCC. If this is not so, then a CCC member should be added, increasing the total by one.

The second kind of representation to be considered in selecting SAC members is a *representative mind-set*, which means those selected must have a positive attitude toward communication and its importance to the success of the project. The ideal member might be compared to an ideal representative in government. Not only does such an elected official represent a specific geographic population, but he or she (ideally) communicates frequently with constituents and takes their opinions into consideration when making decisions. The same should be true for members of the SAC.

In very large districts, the fact that there are so many teachers of a subject (particularly K-12 subjects) makes curriculum development even more challenging. A committee that must determine what all teachers of the subject think is important, and reach consensus on those ideas must be comprised of dynamic individuals who are recognized as leaders among the staff.

Leadership should be viewed much like the concept of representative mind-set. Those persons selected as SAC members should understand that advocacy, consensus-building, and compromise are all functions of leadership. Members must be willing to take a position on issues, and be able to advocate that position both within the committee setting and when communicating with other colleagues. In order to advocate a position, members must know how to dynamically lead positive deliberations. And as a part of making those deliberations positive, they must keep an open mind and have a clear sense of when compromise is in order. When positive and dynamic discussions take place, and the need for compromise is understood, then consensus is a natural outcome.

Effective decision making is a function that parallels those just described. Many businesses and agencies can attest to the fact that members of some committees can defend, debate, and reach a consensus of opinion, but then not know what to do — what kind of action to take regarding that opinion. SAC members must be able to make decisions based on the information available and opinions expressed (within and outside of committee membership), and then not only take action on them, but effectively communicate the decisions and action plans to others.

The bottom line is: When selecting SAC members, begin with the idea that all buildings and grade levels must be represented, as well as classifications of personnel — teachers, support staff, and someone from administration. Then look within these clusters for particular individuals who can demonstrate skills associated with leadership, decision making, communication, consensus building, and commitment. These attributes are just as important, if not more so, than subject knowledge.

THE CHAIR

In some districts, members of the subject area committee choose their own chairperson; however, in most districts, this selection is made by the CCC. In fact, the CCC member who will be on the committee for liaison purposes is most often named as the chairperson. If there is a CCC member who is a specialist in the targeted subject area, then he or she would be a logical choice. But keep in mind the point made earlier, which is that it is not necessary for the CCC delegate, or the SAC chairperson, to be a specialist in the subject area. This person's primary responsibilities are to serve as liaison between the two bodies, to help direct the curriculum development **process**, and generally to keep the committee functioning smoothly. The necessary qualifications for those purposes are not based on knowledge of a particular subject, but rather that the person is a good leader, facilitator, and consensus-builder.

COMMUNICATION

Regardless of the size of the district, it is imperative that each SAC have a system for thorough and ongoing communication, and this must be kept in mind when appointing membership. In small districts where all teachers will serve on a SAC, it is important to assess personalities and be sure that each SAC has sufficient numbers of people who can provide leadership and communicate effectively with peers.

The larger the district, the more difficult it is to keep channels of communication active among all stakeholders. Districts with many different sites will not be able to have every building represented on the SAC, yet faculty in all buildings need some connection to the work that's being accomplished. Minutes of each SAC meeting should be sent to all buildings. The SAC should also consider sending out single-page bulletins that highlight progress and issues; these do not take long to put together and are usually more often read than complete minutes. Grade level and departmental meetings across the district are also good opportunities to communicate about the new curriculum. E-mail and other technological means can be utilized as communication tools. The point here is that when selecting representatives for the subject area committee, the CCC must look at personnel classifications, buildings, representative mind set, leadership, and also *effective communication skills*.

THE SAC ACTION AGENDA

As explained in the previous section, the subject area committee is an ad hoc group which serves to create, implement and monitor the curriculum for a particular field of study. The SAC must be carefully organized and supervised, because it is central to the successful implementation of a district's long range plan. Its action agenda must also be clear and easy to execute because the specific tasks under that agenda can be time consuming and challenging.

The SAC uses an action agenda process developed by the Curriculum Leadership Institute which districts have found effective because it is logical and includes all key educators. As outlined in the schematic on pages 9-12, creating the action agenda itself is the first step to be taken; the remaining steps are (2) gathering information, (3) analyzing information and making decisions, (4) creating focus areas and indicators, (5) creating a subject mission statement, (6) converting focus areas to purposes, (7) converting indicators to outcomes, (8) creating task analysis guides, (9) preparing the curriculum document, (10) soliciting document approval from council and board, (11) training faculty, (12) validating the curriculum internally, (13) validating the curriculum externally, (14) making adjustments to the document, (15) identifying appropriate resources, and (16) preparing an evaluation process.

As mentioned in the previous section, the steps are completed over a period of three to four years; refer to the schematic on page 92 to review how a timeline is written. The sections that follow explain in detail each step of the SAC's action agenda.

INFORMATION GATHERING

Information gathering is a process the SAC uses for accumulating, synthesizing, and graphically displaying information about the curriculum as it is now delivered. By focusing on the district's existing curriculum, SAC members are telling their colleagues that good things are already happening in the academic program, and that the comprehensive review is being conducted because the content of instruction needs to be better understood and focused.

Today's emphasis on teacher involvement makes this step critical to the success of your program. If done correctly, the information gathering phase will help teachers begin to understand that their professional perspectives are just as important as those expressed by so-called experts. However, at the outset, teachers may neither understand the process nor trust a curriculum leader's motivation for conducting it. It is therefore necessary to initiate the activity only after careful thought and preparation.

Information about the real curriculum includes more than the superficial, yet must be limited enough to be digestible. The real curriculum is an expression of everything that is taught to students under the assumption their behavior will somehow be influenced. It focuses on that which is intended, not merely incidental or enriching, and covers hidden as well as overt elements of the instructional program.

In other words, curriculum leaders seek topics covered and pursue not only information found in lesson plans and textbooks, but also those goals hidden in each teacher's priority system. Obtaining that kind of information requires use of questionnaires and follow up interviews.

The Questionnaire
The first step to gathering the necessary information is development and use of a questionnaire, and careful thought must be given to the document itself as well as the process to be used. The following questions and recommendations should be considered by SAC members as they begin this first step. Sample cover letters and questionnaires are also provided below.

1. <u>What specific information are we seeking?</u>
   Primarily, topics that currently are being taught each year in each course/grade level of this subject. Additionally, it would be helpful if teachers would indicate

(perhaps with an asterisk) the ten or twelve topics they consider most important.

2. <u>Are we clear on exactly what we consider to be included in this subject area?</u>
Example: a social studies SAC first decided that the subject included the obvious categories of government, history, geography, sociology and civics/citizenship. Next it was discussed whether areas such as philosophy, culture, careers, and politics were additional categories or whether they were included in the topic areas already identified. Finally, they debated whether economics was a business or social studies topic — or both, and what the difference would be between a business and social studies perspective.

3. <u>What will the questionnaire actually look like?</u> <u>How can we get the information we need without burdening the teachers with undue amounts of paperwork?</u>
The questionnaire should be a simple form that outlines categories and provides space after each one where teachers list the topics they teach in that category. Extra space is provided for categories not listed that the teacher deems important.

4. <u>Should any additional information accompany the questionnaire?</u>
A cover letter of explanation should accompany the questionnaire. It might include the following:
   a.   who/what the SAC is
   b.   definition of the subject area (the categories included)
   c.   why we want this information
   d.   what we want them to do
   e.   information that a short interview will also be conducted
   f.   to whom and when they should return the questionnaire
   g.   an example of a filled-in questionnaire page

5. <u>Who will take the responsibility for seeing that the questionnaire is typed and duplicated?</u>
If arrangements for subject area committees include secretarial assistance or help through a curriculum coordinator's office——great! Otherwise, the committee must delegate chores among members.

6. <u>When and how will the questionnaires be given to the teachers?</u>
It is recommended that someone from the SAC distribute them in person, with a verbal explanation. This can be done individually, or in a group setting, such as a faculty meeting. The cover letter — a written explanation — is used for later reference when teachers begin to fill in the information.

7. <u>To whom should the questionnaires be returned?</u>
    Make it as easy as possible for the questionnaire to be returned; in other words,
    teachers should be able to return them to someone in their own building (or
    department/section if your site is large).

Displaying the Data

When the questionnaires have been returned, the information they provide
must be properly recorded and displayed. A systematic and organized method of
recording and displaying information probably means that some sort of matrix is used
to associate grade levels with sub-categories. Such a matrix for social studies might
look like this:

THE REAL SOCIAL STUDIES CURRICULUM, BY TOPIC

	K	1	2	3	4	5	6	7	8	9	10	11	12
TOPICS PERTAINING TO *HISTORY*													
TOPICS PERTAINING TO *GOVERNMENT*													
TOPICS PERTAINING TO *GEOGRAPHY*													
TOPICS PERTAINING TO *ECONOMICS*													
TOPICS PERTAINING TO *SOCIOLOGY*													
TOPICS PERTAINING TO *PSYCHOLOGY*													

A matrix such as this one can be simply prepared by using strips of butcher
paper that are hung on the wall. SAC members use felt pens to write the topics from
the questionnaires on colored pieces of paper (e.g. green for American history, blue
for world history, pink for geography, and so forth); these colored papers are then
taped onto the butcher strips in the appropriate boxes. The use of this matrix — and
of the color coded attachments — provides a tremendous visual representation of the

current curriculum. If the matrix has so many pieces of green paper that you can hardly get them in the right boxes, but has almost no pink sheets, the committee knows immediately where the current emphasis is, and what category may be slighted.

In the next steps of the action agenda, the SAC will do some in-depth analysis and decision making about the topics being taught. However, at this point they just do some preliminary analysis — primarily looking for items that need clarification from the teachers who filled out the questionnaires. For example, if teachers from several different grade levels listed the same topic, are they all teaching exactly the same thing, or is the topic treated differently from one grade level to another ... and, if so, how? Sometimes teachers are too vague about a topic; for example, one may simply say she teaches "U.S. government." In order to really analyze the curriculum and make informed decisions, the SAC will need to know more specifically what is included in this instruction. This preliminary analysis allows the SAC to identify specific questions they still need to have answered, and leads them to the second part of the information gathering process: the interview.

The Interview

The preliminary information provided to the faculty — both verbally and in writing — should have made it clear that in addition to the questionnaires, information will be gathered through personal interviews. The following questions and recommendations should be considered by members of the SAC as they make their plans.

1. <u>When does the interview process begin?</u>

    It is recommended that interviews not be conducted until after the initial analysis of data. When the questionnaires are returned, the data are displayed and analyzed. During this process, it becomes obvious where additional information or clarification are needed. The SAC will usually identify a few questions that need to be asked of all teachers. Additionally, they will find that there are particular spots where they need more information, such as a particular topic in one grade level, a whole category across numerous grade levels, or a clarification question that needs to be asked of a particular teacher.

2. <u>Who should interview whom?</u>

    The answer to this question varies from one district to another, depending on the size of the district and other local circumstances. One consideration is whether to cross levels——in other words, elementary teachers interview secondary teachers and vice versa. Many SACs are not comfortable with this because their elementary and secondary teachers don't know enough about the different levels of learning in the subject to ask the right questions. Other SACs find the switching of levels to be an advantage because it crosses barriers, and they learn from each other in the process.

If your district has many different sites, then another consideration is whether to have SAC members interview in their own buildings or in a different building. Switching buildings helps cross barriers and open communication. On the other hand, it is not as convenient and thus can be more time consuming.

The SAC should discuss all considerations and make decisions that will be most comfortable for the teachers being interviewed. **It is recommended, however, that teachers not interview other teachers of their own course or grade level.** In this circumstance it is too easy to make assumptions about what is being taught, or to impose one's own views.

3. Is it necessary to interview all teachers not on the SAC? What if the information on the questionnaire is perfectly clear, and we have no questions?

All teachers who teach this subject should be interviewed. First of all, if only some teachers are interviewed, they may get the impression they didn't do as good a job of responding as those teachers not interviewed. Secondly, those teachers not interviewed may feel their views are not considered important. Finally, it is always possible to gather some additional helpful information, even from those whose questionnaire responses were extensive.

SACs in large districts may at first be overwhelmed by the thought of interviewing all teachers of this subject. However, it can be done, and our experience has shown that it is definitely worth the effort. An example is a particular math SAC with whom we worked. The total number of elementary and secondary teachers of math in this district was over 800! To accomplish the interviewing task, the SAC enlisted the help of the CCC and a staff development committee. One joint meeting was held with all three groups, to provide general and specific questions to be asked, and to discuss and practice the interview process. Assignments were based on proximity to the interviewers, and a timeline was established to meet the needs of those with the greatest number of assignments. When the process was completed, all committee members agreed it was one of the most positive professional exercises they had experienced, and that it contributed probably more than anything else to the buy-in and feeling of commitment from the rest of the faculty.

4. Where, when and how are the interviews conducted?

The questionnaires are distributed to the persons who will be doing the interviews. (If Mike is to interview Sarah, then Sarah's questionnaire is given to Mike.) The interviewer evaluates them, making notes of specific additional information needed. In most cases, this person then calls to set up an appointment for each interview. (In very large districts, blanket arrangements may be made without individual calls. For examples, a roving substitute teacher may be hired for the day, and all teachers are notified that the interviews will take place that day.)

A private place and time should be selected for the interview, to minimize interruptions. During the call, the SAC members should mention some of the kinds of information that will be solicited, to give the teacher time to think about responses.

When making the appointments and during the interviews, strive for the comfort and convenience of the ones being interviewed. We are asking them to do something, so we want to show our appreciation for their cooperation. In addition to considering their needs regarding time and meeting place, we should be sure to use a friendly, yet professional demeanor — keep a good balance between the two. (Not too buddy-buddy, but not stiff and formal.)

5. <u>What are we actually looking for in the interview</u>?

A. The main purpose is to seek clarity of the information provided on the questionnaire. For example, if the teacher lists the topic, "climate," what, more precisely, is taught about climate? Is it primarily just defined, with examples given of what the climate is in various areas, or do the students examine how climate affects industry, the economy, and so forth? Which geographic areas are included — local, state, regional....?

B. The second purpose is to identify the hidden curriculum. Although the cover letter should explain that we want to know about all topics taught, teachers are sometimes reluctant to list those that are not in current curriculum guides or textbooks. The fact that a teacher spends valuable time on something not in the current guide or text tells us that the teacher places a lot of importance on this topic; therefore, this is valuable information to the subject area committee. It is important during the interview to determine whether any such topics have been left off the questionnaire. This information usually can best be elicited during a "friendly conversation" part of the interview; if the teacher was reluctant to list it on the questionnaire, he or she is not likely to volunteer it later, nor to respond well to a blunt question.

C. In a similar vein, we also want to know whether the teacher has any particular strengths or favorites among the topics. If so, the teacher is somewhat likely to continue to teach that topic, regardless of whether we include it in the curriculum document. The fact that a topic is a particular teacher's favorite should not cause us to include it. However, it may turn out to be helpful information, especially if we are debating the merits of the topic or if we think it should be included but we aren't sure where to put it.

D. And finally, we need to ask if there are things now being taught that the teacher thinks should not be in the curriculum at this grade level. Remember, the teachers started out by listing what they are actually teaching. They may be teaching something because it is in the current guide or text, but the truth is, they question its validity.

ANALYZING THE REAL CURRICULUM

When the subject area committee has gathered information about the currently taught curriculum, the members must display this information in some way in order to analyze it. In the previous section was a description and illustration of a matrix that is hung on a large space of wall. The vertical columns of the matrix are long sheets of butcher paper, with grade levels written at the top. The horizontal rows are categories that have been identified for the subject; for example, social studies categories might be history, government, economics, sociology, and geography. Each category is assigned a color so that information can be displayed in a color-coded fashion. Colored sheets of 8 1/2 X 11 paper are cut horizontally into thirds. The information that is gathered from questionnaires and interviews is written with a marking pen on the appropriate colors of paper; these colored sheets are then taped in the appropriate box on the wall matrix. For example, if "government" has been assigned the color blue, and a third grade teacher writes that she teaches about rules in the community, then *community rules* is written on a piece of blue paper and taped in the box that horizontally lines up with "government" and vertically lines up with "grade three."

This means of displaying the information has been found to be extremely effective for several reasons. First, it is literally a visual representation of the currently taught curriculum. Educators can look at this wall display and immediately determine what is happening at which grade levels in the targeted subject. Second, the color-coding is very helpful in recognizing the degree of attention that is being accorded each of the subject's categories. And third, as the committee begins to make decisions about the curriculum, the colored sheets of paper can easily be added to, removed and set aside, or moved from one grade level or course to another until a tentative scope and sequence has been determined.

DECISION-MAKING

The information displayed on the wall that the SAC analyzes is about the **currently taught** curriculum. As committee members analyze this data, they must begin to make decisions about the curriculum as **they want it to be.** To get from the former to the latter, there are particular problems and considerations members must take into account.

REDUNDANCY

The problem that presents itself most obviously is *redundancy.* As committee members peruse the information from grade level to grade level, they will notice particular topics showing up over and over again. What they must decide is whether and how these topics are presented differently and whether it is really necessary for them to be repeated so many times.

Certain topics do, of course, need to be taught at more than one grade level; elemental comprehension is the goal one year, with more complicated concepts being taught in subsequent years. The key here is to be very specific about *what* students at each level are supposed to know or do regarding this topic. In traditional curriculum guides we often find that a topic is to be *introduced* at one level, *mastered* at another, and *reinforced* at yet another. The problem here is one of vagueness. If teachers are to *introduce* a topic, does that mean they should spend some time on it but not really expect comprehension and lasting learning, or does it mean they should teach only simple elements of the topic... and if so, how many and which ones? If a topic is to be included in more than one grade level, the SAC needs to identify very specifically what is expected at each.

Although some topics do need to be repeated, as just described, it is a fact that this is not necessary nearly so often as most of us tend to think. Many educators will say that a topic (perhaps *even the very same concepts*) needs to be presented again and again because it takes that many repetitions for students to really learn it! In reality, what's happening in these instances is usually one of three things:

A) The topic is presented too early —at too young an age— and therefore students are not capable of really learning it yet.

B) Students have had the topic so many times they're bored with it. They stop paying attention, "turn off," and thus don't internalize the information for lasting learning.

C) Teachers have so many topics to teach they can't give the proper time and attention to all of them, thus some topics are "taught," but real learning does not occur.

SAC members must take these situations into consideration when planning the curriculum and take steps to *eliminate the problem*, rather than just continue to repeat curriculum topics year after year.

Redundancy also often occurs either because teachers just aren't aware that something is being taught at so many levels or because a particular topic is popular and everyone wants to include it. In these instances the SAC must decide which is the most appropriate grade level for the topic and eliminate it from all others.

GAPS

There are two types of gaps that SAC members may find as they analyze the collected information. The first type is easy to discern: a category is weak or missing at particular grade levels. For example, suppose "geography" has numerous colored sheets for all grade levels except third grade —which has only one entry— and sixth grade, which has no entries at all. Immediately the SAC knows that little or no geography is being taught in these two grades. What the SAC has to decide next is whether that's an accidental or purposeful gap, and whether it needs correcting. (Example of an "accidental" gap: geography should be taught at this grade level, but isn't, due to lack of time, teacher confidence or interest, materials, etc. Example of purposeful gap: psychology is considered a social studies course, but no geography is taught in the psychology class.)

The second type of gap takes more intense study of the current curriculum. In most cases (with the exception of specialty courses such as psychology) the SAC will find that all boxes of the matrix have numerous topics listed in them, which means that **something** is being taught in every category in every grade level. But just because all these "somethings" are being taught doesn't mean that all of the important topics are being taught. A topic the SAC considers critical may actually not show up anywhere at all. These gaps are sometimes discovered early, as the SAC begins to make decisions about focusing the curriculum for each grade level and course; however, they sometimes are not noticed until later steps of the SAC's action agenda, when the subject mission and course purposes are written.

APPROPRIATENESS OF CONTENT

The SAC must also decide if topics to be included in the curriculum are appropriate in terms of *content* — in other words, if what is being taught is important and relevant for students in this school district. Here are a couple of examples:

1. An eighth grade teacher taught an extended unit about a rather obscure island he had once visited. While his personal anecdotes made the unit interesting, the

SAC determined the unit was not really relevant to their mission.

2. An elementary school in a rural area had an extensive curricculum about major cities of the United States, but almost nothing about rural life or the relationship between rural and urban areas. The SAC decided that study of the particular cities themselves needed to be eliminated and replaced by urban concepts in general, as well as rural concepts and the interdependence of various size communities.

APPROPRIATENESS OF STUDENT READINESS

This category is basically self-explanatory. It was alluded to in the section above on redundancies when it was pointed out that some topics are presented too early, when students are not really ready for them. In a similar vein, many topics remain in the curriculum at particular grade levels just because "that's when they've always been taught," yet with today's more sophisticated students, they may be more appropriate at an earlier level. The SAC should use research, knowledge of the students in their community, and common sense in debating the appropriate readiness level.

CONVERTIBILITY TO OUTCOMES

All topics can be converted to outcomes as long as the expected result is clear; in other words, what is the student supposed to know or be able to do in regard to this topic. However, the SAC may find that much of what appears on the matrix really has more to do with methods, activities, or materials than end results. For example, some teachers may list titles of books that they have students read. In a results based curriculum, we would need to determine **why** students are being asked to read those particular selections. Are there facts we want them to know? Are they analyzing a particular style of writing? Are they making comparisons... of events, behaviors, writing styles, time periods? The SAC must be careful not to include these kinds of nebulous topics in the curriculum. They should either eliminate them, or get more information from the teachers about the outcome, or intended result, of studying such topics.

EXTERNAL VALIDITY

The **first** consideration in terms of validity should be internal: what do SAC members **themselves** consider to be important for the students of this school district? When that has been determined, external factors must also be considered. Are there state or local mandates related to this subject? If so, then in most cases such mandates must be honored when designing the curriculum. (In some cases mandates can be circumvented if the district can provide alternatives, compelling evidence, or logical reasoning for noncompliance.) The SAC should also look at recommendations of the learned societies, such as NCTM standards for math, Project 2061 for science, research and recommendations of NCSS, NCTE, ASCD, PDK, and so forth.

SELECTIVE ABANDONMENT

As the SAC seriously discusses all of the above considerations, one thing will become abundantly clear: **teachers cannot bring students to mastery levels of learning if they are expected to cover all of the topics that have traditionally been included in the curriculum.** We often refer to curriculum in the United States as being a "Three - Four" curriculum, meaning that it is 3 or 4 miles long, but only 3/4" deep! The key to lasting learning is to stop trying to "cover" everything and instead concentrate on those things that are really important —and relevant— and guide students through a meaningful and in depth study of those topics. If you have any doubts about the validity of that statement, try this little exercise:

Picture in your mind a college course that you took at least several years ago. Picture the classroom, the professor... perhaps you can even see the textbook. Now ask yourself: can you remember everything that was covered in that course?

Now think about some things that you **do** remember from a course you've taken. Why do you remember them? Occasionally the answer to that question will be that you found the subject fascinating — you were really interested in it. But that would not be the case for everyone in the class, since we all have different interests. In most instances, you'll find that the majority of students have retained learning either because much time and attention were given to the topic (in-depth study) or because of relevancy — students **use** in real life what they learned in the classroom.

One of the most difficult tasks of the subject area committee is to narrow the curriculum to those most important and relevant topics — a process we call *selective abandonment.* Educators find it difficult to take things *out* of the curriculum primarily for one or more of these reasons: a) those topics have always been there; b) because they are all *in the textbook;* or c) because everything seems to be important. But the SAC must keep in mind that "less is more," and that in this information age, it's more important for students to learn how to find information and how to think, reason, and problem solve than to memorize information or simply be exposed to multitudes of material. It's true that deciding what to remove from the curriculum and what to keep or add can be a real challenge. However, that process can be simplified somewhat if the SAC will determine for each course and grade level a **focus area** and **indicators.**

CREATING FOCUS AREAS AND INDICATORS

Selective abandonment — the process of eliminating all but the most essential topics in the curriculum — is not an easy task. In most cases, when SAC members examine the information gathered for a particular course or grade level, they find a wide range of topics. A few are easy to identify as non essential, but many are not so clear cut. Consider as an example the following information that was gathered by the social studies SAC in Pleasant Valley.

PLEASANT VALLEY PUBLIC SCHOOLS
1st Grade
Social Studies

1. Labor in home, school, community
2. Trade – money, transportation, communication, goods, resources
3. Families provide basic needs – food, shelter, clothing, love
4. Local environment (physical features) – and how it influences the way we live
5. Seasonal patterns
6. Utilization of and dependence on earth's resources
7. Directions – cardinal, left and right
8. Globe and maps as models of the world – oceans, land masses, state and city
9. Rules are necessary in home, school, community
10. Americans value loyalty, freedom, responsibility
11. Citizenship includes knowledge of and respect for one's country and flag
12. Observing safety rules
13. Current events
14. People learn from and are dependent on each other
15. Place of the individual in the family, school, community
16. Families are alike and different
17. Personal identification – child's and parents' full name, home address (number, street, city, state), phone number, child's date of birth
18. The family is the basic unit of the society
19. Individuals are alike and different
20. Language is the way people communicate
21. The importance of a positive self concept
22. We can learn from the past about our nation and state
23. The flag salute
24. Some famous Americans
25. Cultural customs for holidays

Notice that of the 25 topics reported, seven of them (# 1, 3, 9, 15, 16, 17 & 18) actually include the words *home* or *family*, and numerous others indirectly refer to home or family (such as #14: people learn from and are dependent on each other).

The SAC therefore could logically conclude that home and family are definitely central to this first grade's social studies curriculum, and could become the *focus area* for the new curriculum.

Once a focus area has been identified, the process of selective abandonment is much simpler. The SAC now looks at each topic listed for the particular grade level and determines if that topic "fits" the focus area. If so, (at least for now) it remains in the curriculum — it is an *indicator* of the focus area. If it does **not** fit, it is removed. Let's look at the first few of the topics in our first grade example above to see how they would be handled.

1. Labor in home, school, community... Labor in the home would be included in the curriculum; labor in school and community would be eliminated.

2. Trade — money, transportation, communication, goods, resources... Instead of covering such a broad range of information, trade would be taught only as it is necessary for families to exist. In fact, it would be eliminated as a separate topic, and combined with #3 below.

3. Families provide basic needs — food, shelter, clothing, love... Would remain in the curriculum.

4. Local environment (physical features) and how it influences the way we live... Basically remains the same — as to how it influences the way we (families) live.

5. Seasonal patterns... Either eliminated, or combined with #4 above — how physical features and seasonal patterns affect the way we (families) live.

6. Utilization of and dependence on earth's resources... Eliminated.

When the SAC has finished identifying a *focus area* and the *indicators* for that focus area for each course and grade level, they'll find that this process has resulted in a tentative **scope and sequence** for the targeted subject. As they worked with each course and grade level, they would of course have weighed each topic against the considerations described in the section above, "Analyzing the Curriculum." When the tentative scope and sequence is completed, they should look at these considerations one more time, particularly in regard to *gaps*. Sometimes a SAC will encounter a topic they deem important, but that could be taught at a number of different grade levels. Deciding that it doesn't fit the focus area of a particular grade level, they will "temporarily" abandon it, but then forget to reinsert it anywhere else. When they have carefully examined the scope and sequence one more time and discussed the considerations described previously, they are ready to begin the design down process of curriculum development.

THE DESIGN DOWN METHOD FOR CREATING A RESULTS BASED CURRICULUM

A topical scope and sequence is not sufficient information to put in a curriculum document. Teachers need to know much more than just the topic they are supposed to teach "about"; they need direction in terms of depth, breadth, and precisely what students are supposed to know or be able to do regarding this topic. In order for the SAC to replace the former, trivial pursuit curriculum with one that is focused on essentials and student performance outcomes they must *align* the curriculum. This means that they start with the basic premise — the district mission statement — and work their way, step by step, down to the specific outcomes for a specific subject for a specific grade level, making sure that each step has stayed in line with the previous one.

Perhaps an illustration or two will help you picture this. A good illustration is that old song that says, "the hip-bone's connected to the thigh-bone; the thigh-bone's connected to the knee-bone," and so forth. You can neither connect a bone out of place, such as joining the ankle-bone to the hip-bone, nor can you throw in one that doesn't belong at all, such as a wing-bone on a human skeleton.

A second example is the box-within-a-box concept. You know the kind: when someone gives you a huge, wrapped package for your birthday, which you eagerly tear into only to find a slightly smaller box inside, and a slightly smaller box inside that one, until you finally get to the last one, which is only about two inches square. Obviously the boxes have to be filled in a certain order; the second-largest box cannot fit into the second-smallest box. Likewise, you can't throw in one that won't fit at all, such as a long-stemmed rose box into the selection of all square boxes. The rose box might fit into one of the largest square boxes, but how will you get the next-largest square box into the rose box?

The concept behind both of these examples should guide you in curriculum alignment. The SAC will work from the broadest, most general statements down to the very specific. Included in the total alignment process will be: the district mission statement, subject mission statement, purpose for each course and grade level, outcomes for each course and grade level, and a task analysis of each outcome, which results in the identification of learning strands, teaching methods, student activities, assessments, mastery criteria, and extensions.

To put these in the perspective of the box within a box analogy, the district's mission is the largest box. The subject area mission is the next largest box; it tells us why this particular subject is being taught in this district — how student learning in this subject helps accomplish the district mission. Box #3 must come from box #2: course and grade level purposes must be demonstrably linked to the subject mission. Box #4 continues the linkage: what specific outcomes are required of students to fulfill the course and grade level purposes? And finally, the smallest box: now that we have a specific outcome, how do we go about actually accomplishing it?

Another analogy that is helpful in explaining the design-down process is to picture a graduated funnel, in which the mouth (the widest part) represents the district mission statement, and the point (narrowest part) is the task analysis. We work our way from level to level through this funnel with the end results of our intended student learning. A graphic of the funnel is provided below; a copy of this can be placed on an overhead or made into handouts so educators have a visual representation of the design-down concept.

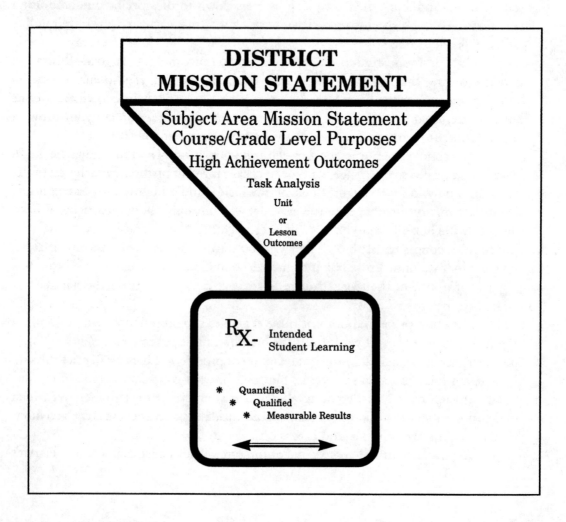

CREATING THE SUBJECT MISSION & COURSE PURPOSES

The subject area committee begins the design-down process by creating a subject mission statement. Two words that are useful in thinking about mission are **focus** and **coherence**. Focus is lacking in ordinary public school curricula because many teachers tend to think of their work as something they do, rather than as a medium through which students are given skills so that <u>they</u> can "do." In addition, subject matter is delivered in such a way that it rarely has a clear frame of reference with regard to the real world — the one that is now rapidly evolving. And much curriculum doesn't hang together very well, because no real thought has gone into grade to grade (vertical) and subject to subject (horizontal) coherence. That task has been left to textbook authors who do the best they can to piece together a program of studies, at least within the "series" with which they are involved.

Establishing vertical coherence is a function of the SAC's scope and sequence chart. The curriculum coordinating council maintains horizontal coherence as it compares one subject discipline to another. Establishing FOCUS is the responsibility of the SAC as it prepares the subject area mission statement. As mentioned in the section above, this statement is derived from the district mission statement. Members of the SAC carefully consider the district mission statement and then ask themselves how this particular subject directly relates to that mission, and what students will know, be able to do, or be like as a result of having studied this subject.

Some SACs prefer to write the subject area mission statement as a general statement, in paragraph form. Others prefer to have a short introduction, followed by subject exit outcomes — specific descriptions of student knowledge or behavior at the conclusion of their study of this subject. Following are numerous examples of both kinds of subject mission statements.

COMMUNICATION SUBJECT MISSION

SAMPLE I.

Students will read, write, speak and listen at a level that empowers them to contribute responsibly and successfully as members of a mobile society.

Reading Exit Outcomes — Students will:
1. analyze and evaluate various genres;
2. utilize and interpret technical information;
3. read literature for a variety of purposes, including enjoyment and appreciation;
4. respond to reading through writing, speaking, and listening;
5. recall, summarize, and integrate information they have read.

Writing Exit Outcomes — Students will:
1. recognize and demonstrate modes of writing appropriate to specific situations and audiences;
2. convey a clear message for a variety of purposes and audiences;
3. use the stages of the writing process;
4. evaluate their own writing using such instruments as the six-trait model;
5. demonstrate competency in the area of technical writing.

Listening Exit Outcomes — Students will:
1. respond actively to the speaker and message;
2. analyze and evaluate verbal and nonverbal messages;
3. use appropriate listening strategies for different learning purposes;
4. recognize and refrain from non-listening behaviors.

Speaking Exit Outcomes — Students will:
1. adapt to different communication situations and audiences;
2. demonstrate different speech genres;
3. deliver an organized verbal message and a purposeful nonverbal message;
4. acknowledge and respond to audience feedback.

SAMPLE II.

The purpose of the communication curriculum in _____ is to enable all students to think analytically and communicate effectively. This process is accomplished through the four essential components: listening, speaking, reading, and writing. Students will acquire, practice, and apply these skills in authentic experiences throughout the curriculum.

MATH SUBJECT MISSION
SAMPLE I.

Students in _____ will apply mathematical concepts and computational skills in reasoning, communicating and problem solving. Students will demonstrate the effective use of technological and informational resources.

SAMPLE II.

The mission of the mathematics curriculum in _____ is to promote students who share in the responsibility for their own learning. They will solve problems by thinking logically, communicating mathematically, and working both individually and cooperatively. The purpose of the mathematics curriculum is to require mastery level performance of core outcomes supplemented with learning extension so that students will be mathematically competent in the following K-12 mathematics outcomes. Students will:

I. demonstrate the appropriate use of number concepts, relationships, and operations;
2. utilize the properties, relationships, and processes of geometric shapes and values to interpret their relative positions;
3. demonstrate the ability to identify and compare unit values in judging the relationships of measurements;
4. translate a situation into a mathematical model and apply the solution to the real world;
5. utilize the correct terminology and symbolism of mathematics.

SCIENCE SUBJECT MISSION

SAMPLE I.

Students completing the _____ science curriculum will analyze, resolve, and apply science knowledge and technological solutions to real-world problems. Throughout the curriculum they will identify and evaluate the nature, limits, possibilities, issues, and history of science and will experiment with that which is already known to discover new and interesting interpretations and applications to everyday living.

SAMPLE II.

The mission of the science curriculum of _____ is student mastery of core outcomes as well as opportunities for extended learning. Upon graduation students will have achieved mastery of the exit outcomes, listed below, and the core outcomes in the classes in which they enroll, listed on the following pages.

SCIENCE EXIT OUTCOMES

Students will:

- justify decisions made relating to the environment and how it affects others;
- solve everyday life problems by using appropriate scientific tools, operations, methods and measurements;
- incorporate natural/artificial processes in explaining the existence of and changes in the universe;
- analyze the characteristic structures, functions, and interdependence of living things and/or non living things; and
- apply concepts, generalizations, and principles of matter and energy.

SOCIAL STUDIES SUBJECT MISSION

SAMPLE I.

Students successfully completing courses from the _____Pre K - 12 World Studies curriculum will analyze essential geographic, economic, historical, governmental, social and psychological facts and principles and apply them to contemporary and future human conditions. Students in World Studies curricula, including foreign language, will demonstrate an understanding of diverse cultures and apply the skills needed to participate in the changing global society.

SAMPLE II.

Students completing the _____ K- 12 social studies curriculum will demonstrate skills necessary to be productive and knowledgeable citizens, cooperative and independent learners, consumers and producers in a global market place, and social problem solvers. Success in achieving these skills will contribute to the student's positive self concept.

Converting Focus Areas to Purposes

When the SAC has finished writing the subject mission statement, which helps educators focus on why that particular discipline is in the curriculum and why students must master it, they are ready to determine the *purpose* for each course and grade level. In preparing the course/grade level purposes, the SAC continues to employ the two principles of alignment and focus. Just as the subject mission had to align with the district mission, so too must each course or grade level purpose align with the subject mission. The purpose statement tells us what we must accomplish, as related to this subject, in this particular course or grade level. If true alignment has taken place, then when all of the courses and grade levels accomplish their purposes, the subject mission will also have been accomplished.

To employ the principle of **focus**, we return to the focus areas that were prepared during the decision-making process. Remember that the focus area was determined in the first place by finding a common thread of topics for each course and grade level curriculum. That focus area now guides us in the development of course and grade level purposes. The focus area is expanded into a more descriptive statement of what students will know or do.

In the section on "Creating Focus Areas and Indicators," we used information gathered about the first grade curriculum as our example. The focus area that was identified for that first grade social studies curriculum was "home and family." Let's assume that the subject area committee of this particular school district wrote the subject area mission statement that is given as Sample I above. Members of the SAC would next ask themselves what it is they want students to know or do about home and family that aligns with the subject mission. The answers to those questions lead them to development of the course purpose as the following example shows.

Subject Mission:
Students successfully completing courses from the _____ Pre K - 12 World Studies curriculum will analyze essential geographic, economic, historical, governmental, social and psychological facts and principles and apply them to contemporary and future human conditions. Students in World Studies curricula, including foreign language, will demonstrate an understanding of diverse cultures and apply the skills needed to participate in the changing global society.

First Grade Purpose:
Students will analyze the relationships between self and family; compare and contrast family units by size, geography, history, and culture; and recognize the individuality of family units and rules. They will investigate needs that families provide, and social and environmental factors that affect the way we live.

Note how the purpose statement focuses on specific applications and is written in high achievement terms. The wording of these statements is critical to successful classroom implementation. The course purpose —as well as the essential outcomes that follow— must be stated in <u>measurable</u> <u>outcomes</u> language. This means that not only are ambiguous behavioral objectives not acceptable, but there can be no vague references about what might be <u>presented, introduced, taught, heard, learned,</u>

studied, or covered during the course of the school year. Instead, describe the student's **knowledge, performance,** or **behavior** in action terminology that can be measured, preferably stated in the higher cognitive levels of analysis, application, synthesis, and evaluation.

Although both Ralph Tyler and Benjamin Bloom offered us ways to think about outcomes, it was Bloom and his colleagues who actually gave us a linguistic structure for doing so through his "Taxonomy of Educational Objectives: Cognitive Domain," and it is in this taxonomy that we find the cognitive levels referred to in the previous paragraph. In the table shown on pages 141-142 are each of Bloom's descriptors, definitions, and a sampling of appropriate verbs and expected outcomes.

It must be said that Bloom and his associates refer to the six descriptors as a *taxonomy* and not a hierarchy. A taxonomy is simply a means of classification without regard to relative importance, a very significant distinction as one prepares course/grade level purposes and high achievement outcomes. It is probably true that the four descriptors listed first reflect higher kinds of thinking than the bottom two (knowledge and comprehension), but there is little reason to suggest that *evaluation* as a descriptor is any more important than *synthesis, analysis,* or *application.* All four of those descriptors indicate a relatively high level of cognitive operation, and that is all we need to worry about as the curriculum is developed.

Keep in mind that the SAC not only considers the cognitive levels during the writing process, they also avoid vague references. The following lists are frequently used terms to avoid when preparing purposes and outcomes, and some examples of acceptable alternatives.

AVOID THESE TERMS	USE TERMS LIKE THESE
present	apply
	illustrate
cover	analyze
	determine
study	interpret
	distinguish
learn about	evaluate
	produce
understand	compare/contrast
	debate
appreciate	verify
	defend
introduce	predict
	hypothesize
work with	improve
	show

Bloom's Taxonomy

Descriptors	Definition	Additional Verbs	Outcomes
Evaluation	*Judges information according to criteria and offers supporting opinions and evidence; critiques, compares, justifies concludes, discriminates, supports.*	Editorialize Decide Evaluate Dispute Rate Discuss Verify Grade Choose Assess Select Debate Appraise Defend	Judgment Panel Opinion Verdict Scale Value Recommendation Conclusion Evaluation Report Investigation Survey Editorial Decision
Synthesis	*Puts pieces of information together into a new plan, idea, or product; combines, creates, formulates, designs, composes, constructs, rearranges, revises.*	Hypothesize Imagine Modify Improve Invent Propose Infer Estimate Produce Forecast Design Predict Plan	Formula Invention Film Prediction New Game Story Poem Solution Art Product Project Media Products Machine Advertisement
Analysis	*Breaks down information into parts; differentiates, diagrams, estimates, separates, infers, orders, subdivides.*	Summarize Abstract Classify Dissect Compare Contrast Deduce Analyze Investigate Distinguish Categorize Examine	Questionnaire Survey Report Graph Chart Outline Diagram Conclusion List Plan Summary Category

Bloom's Taxonomy

Descriptors	Definition	Additional Verbs	Outcomes
Application	*Uses Information in different situations; demonstrates, computes, solves, modifies arranges, operates, relates.*	Show Apply Make Translate Illustrate Record Teach Construct Use Practice Determine	Demonstration Illustration Diagram Diorama Collection Map Puzzle Model Diary Report Lesson Solution
Comprehension	*Interprets communicated material without necessarily relating it to other material; explains, summarizes, converts.*	Restate Describe Locate Generalize Review Match Change Paraphrase Give main idea Reproduce	Diagram Description List Definition Fact Summary Reproduction Recitation Report Illustration
Knowledge	*Recalls specific information; identifies, names, defines, lists.*	Tell Recognize Locate Memorize Review Match State Read Relate Reproduce Choose	Labels Names List Definition Fact Test Reproduction Recitation Table

The following are additional samples of course purposes for a variety of subjects.

Kindergarten Mathematics Curriculum

(Focus Area: shapes and numbers)
Purpose: Students will analyze the definitions of and relationships among basic geometric shapes and they will use numbers to compare, analyze and solve problems, as well as to generate information.

High School Biology Curriculum

(Focus Area: Biology — plants and animals)
Purpose: Students will solve problems by using appropriate tools, operations, methods, and measurements, and they will analyze the characteristic structures, functions, and interdependence of living and nonliving things.

Fourth Grade Social Studies Curriculum

(Focus Area: geographic regions)
Purpose: Students will determine the relationships between state and region and compare and contrast regions in terms of geography, history, economics, culture and current events.

Sixth Grade Computer Curriculum

(Focus Area: keyboarding and word processing skills)
Purpose: Students will refine keyboarding techniques, apply word processing programs, and analyze software difficulties to select appropriate troubleshooting techniques from options presented.

Eighth Grade Physical Education Curriculum

(Focus Area: physical fitness and lifetime sports)
Purpose: Students will assess their individual performance levels of physical fitness and sports skills appropriate for lifetime wellness, set goals for and demonstrate improvement and maintenance of skill levels, and participate in a variety of rhythmic, coordination, and sports activities.

Ninth Grade Communications Curriculum

(Focus Area: plays)
Purpose: Students will read plays by authors representing a variety of cultures and time periods. They will evaluate and compare plays by purpose, style, use of language,

and societal conditions of the time period. Students will listen to and view audio and video presentations of selected play scenes. They will critique what they have read, heard, and viewed, both orally and in writing. Students will evaluate and improve their writing according to the Six-Trait Writing model.

First Grade Visual Arts

(Focus Area: primary colors, lines, shapes)
Purpose: Students will express emotions, use their imagination, and develop creative problem-solving skills by combining primary colors, lines, and shapes to create their own art. They will explore how and why people create art by viewing and discussing selected art work.

THE ANATOMY OF A HIGH ACHIEVEMENT OUTCOME

The subject area committee has now perused the district mission statement (which includes exit outcomes), written a subject mission statement, and prepared a purpose statement for each course and grade level of this subject. The next step in the design-down process is to prepare high achievement outcomes, but before that process is started, we need to have a good understanding of the definintion and concept of the high achievement outcome in general.

The concept and practice of *design down* requires careful academic program alignment, which means that no district should attempt the extensive preparation of high achievement outcomes until a solid foundation has been prepared. That is one reason why districts must be careful to avoid indiscriminate use of commercially pre-pared curriculum banks and criterion-referenced tests. Those instruments may or may not align with district missions and outcomes.

When we consider a design down model, we must think beyond just what will be prescribed in a written guide. For teachers to actually <u>accomplish</u> the missions, purposes, and outcomes that describe the district's reason for existence, there must be a substantive change in the teaching and learning processes. In fact, teachers must become so intellectually and scholastically engaged in subjects they teach that the con-cept of "essence" becomes increasingly clear to both them and their students. That cognitive shift from the idea of "covering material" to teaching and learning that which is fundamentally important to a student's well being and future growth is no small challenge. So, when we talk about the anatomy of a high achievement outcome, we are referring to much more than a string of words taken from an approved list ... although such a list is a good place to start.

That *list* is Bloom's taxonomy, which we referred to in the previous section. His taxonomy identifies and defines six descriptors, and provides commensurate verbs and outcomes which give structure to the process of designing high achievement outcomes.   (See Tables, pages 141-142.)

WHAT MAKES A HIGH ACHIEVMENT OUTCOME DIFFERENT?

A high achievement outcome is different from what is usually found in schools in that it starts with what students must do at a cognitive level that is truly challenging and interesting. It follows the premise that *learning is reflected in a change in behavior,* not simply a mental act with no behavioral consequence. A high achievement outcome is also different from the once touted "competency" concept, in which competency depicts a kind of minimum or baseline learning. A high achievement outcome has nothing to do with minimum competency; it demands that students stretch themselves in an academic discipline that requires deep thought and active scholasticism.

A high achievement outcome should have enough substance and relevance to be seen as important to both teachers and students. For an outcome to have that kind of substance and relevance it should entail in-depth examination and research. It is always easier to teach students who actually have questions about a subject under consideration. Yet most teachers constantly offer answers for which there are no questions. Student minds are passive and uninterested. There exists no mental imperative for the information being received, so students tune out. True, an instructional program has to have a beginning, and that beginning may not be especially exciting to students, but it needs ultimately to create a situation in which students become intellectually engaged in the subject matter.

So the difference between a high achievement outcome and other kinds of outcomes is a focus on: (1) behavior changes in students,   (2) concepts that interest, challenge and promote scholasticism of students, and   (3) research which serves as the basis for that scholastic growth. Investigative research and intellectual inquiry build on a natural human need. Inquiry also stimulates the habit of asking questions in an atmosphere characterized by dynamic forms of learning, which causes students to better understand the need for knowing the so-called "basics."

Dealing With Different Perspectives on Outcomes

Many professional educators and lay persons misunderstand what is, or should be, meant by the term outcome. In the comparative chart on page 146 are a few of those misunderstandings and how we respond to them.

Although misunderstandings are hard to overcome, we think the best goal of a high achievement outcome is this: *Students systematically investigate (research) substantive aspects of a topic, continuously create questions pertinent to that inquiry and use processes that build skills and knowledge of basic concepts sufficient to apply them.* The teacher's job is to organize the classroom in such a way that students can more easily

MISUNDERSTANDING	RESPONSE
The most important consideration in an outcome-based system is the ability of a student to satisfactorily complete some kind of summative assessment.	*William Edwards Deming says that we must stop our dependence on mass inspection to bring about quality. Deming points out that the only way to achieve true quality in anything is to give plenty of attention to the day-to-day processes of trying to attain it, and to check for quality at various points along the way... using many different techniques.*
The best curriculum is that which is very complete and comprehensive, so student outcomes should pertain to the amount of material they are able to cover in the time available.	*The best curriculum is focused on essentials that are taught to mastery, no matter how long it takes to achieve that mastery. "Trivial pursuit" curriculum is not a relevant concept. In fact, relevancy to student learning needs and social/vocational requirements is the most important consideration.*
Good "outcomes" have to come from some place besides the local district and community, preferably from educational experts who write textbooks or work in state departments of education.	*While every curriculum should be validated by checking outside points of reference such as the "learned societies" and other repositories of expertise, there should never be a total dependence on those sources. American education has always been controlled by local communities more than outside agencies, and that habit will not and should not be broken. All schools are only as good as the communities in which they are located, and the quality of the teachers who work in them.*

acquire basic knowledge, ask questions, reflect on responses, draw conclusions and apply knowledge and skills.

The Difference Between Objectives and Outcomes

Many educators, when they begin to consider outcome based education and thus examine sample outcomes, are understandably confused. They see little or no difference between outcomes and objectives, which they've been writing for years. Even when recognizing that there is a difference in wording in numerous examples, they wonder if the difference isn't simply a matter of semantics. Consequently, a question that we are asked time and again is, "What's the difference between an objective and an outcome, anyway?"

For some educators, the answer to this is simple: Nothing. The objectives they have been writing all these years are in fact outcomes. *However, these educators are rare exceptions.* Almost all of us have written some of our objectives as outcomes, but most of us have written just as many, if not more, objectives that do not include an *outcome* or *end result.*

An analogy that is used by many consultants and educators in trying to explain the difference is the sporting event. If we were to ask the football coach his objective for the big game tonight, the answer would probably be, My objective is to win the game. However, that may or may not be the actual *outcome.* In fact, the coach cannot control who actually wins the game because he has had no influence or control over the behavior of the opposing team. What the coach can control is the particular skills and conduct he wants his players to demonstrate, and the methods, activities, measurements, and expanded opportunities he guides them through to accomplish such. Consequently, while the coach's *objective* might be to win the game, the actual outcome depends on the player's demonstration of skills and conduct.

Another way to consider the difference between objectives and outcomes is to look at the history of "how we got from there to here." Originally we were taught to think of objectives as purposes. What is the purpose of the lesson you are about to teach? Therefore, the following objective was acceptable: "My objective is to teach the students about proper nutrition." This kind of objective will never be an outcome because it focuses on the teacher's performance, not the student's. So next we learned to state our objectives from the student perspective: "The students will learn about proper nutrition." That was certainly simple. But then came the question, "How do you know the students have *learned?*"

To remedy that problem, the next "new thing" to come along was the behavioral objective, an objective that states a behavior (or performance) that can be seen or heard. That kind of objective was certainly much closer to being an outcome: "The students will read chapter three, 'Nutrition,' and write answers for the questions at the end of the chapter." Now we have behaviors that are for the most part observable. We may actually hear the students reading or see them writing. Whether that is the case or not, we do have a product.... the written answers....that we can use to assess whether they know the information that is contained in chapter three. However, the objective above is an outcome *only* if our purpose is for students to read and write answers to questions!

The way that objective is stated, the end result we want is for students to be able to read and write answers to questions. The chapter on nutrition may possibly be only a vehicle for students to practice those skills; they might also read and write answers to questions in an English or mathematics text, or a *Weekly Reader* issue. The objective tells us nothing about what the student is supposed to know or be able to do regarding nutrition.

The following statement is an outcome that might replace the objective used in the previous example: **Students will list the basic food groups in the order they appear in the FDA nutrition triangle.** This statement is an outcome because it meets the following criteria:

*   *It contains a positive statement* — the students *will,* not should or may.
*   *It tells what the students will do,* not what the teacher will do or what the textbook outlines.
*   *It uses a verb that describes specific action* — students will list, not learn about or understand.
*   *It contains an end result* (the list) that relates directly to our intention (knowledge of nutrition); the learner is expected to be able to do something, and we know precisely what that something is.

Simple Outcomes and High Achievement Outcomes

The example used above is an outcome, and is certainly appropriate for the daily lesson level of instruction. However, it is what we consider a *simple* outcome rather than one that is classified as a <u>high achievement</u> outcome. Simple outcomes are a necessary part of instruction. They are used at the beginning level of instruction, when students must have background knowledge and prerequisite skills to accomplish the more challenging results that are ultimately sought. And those more challenging results are exactly what we identify, and then state, when striving for high achievement outcomes. They represent cumulative efforts, what we want students to know, be able to do, or be like by the end of a unit, or series of units, of instruction. High achievement outcomes are challenging and comprehensive. In most classes, five to fifteen such outcomes make up the entire year's curriculum.

The high achievement outcome should meet all the criteria described above for the simple outcome, plus four additional criteria:

*   *It must require a high cognitive level.*
    Students need to analyze or evaluate information and situations, synthesize prior

learning into new results and apply their knowledge or skills in realistic circumstances. They need to use creative and critical thinking processes, not just parrot back information that has been read or heard.

- *It must require dynamic student involvement.*
  Students need to be active, not passive learners. The word active tells us that the students must be doing something, that we must plan learning activities to accomplish the outcome. And if the outcome is high achievement, then the activities must go beyond listening, reading,and writing answers to questions. A good rule of thumb is to ask ourselves, "Can the students accomplish this outcome through lecture/discussion and reading of the text, but no other activities?" If the answer is yes, then we don't have a high achievement outcome. Lecture and use of the text can be very helpful in introducing and reinforcing various steps of the outcome, but they should play minor rather than major roles, and they should never stand alone.

- *It must be relevant to the students' lives.*
  This criterion is sometimes protested, primarily because it is misunderstood. It does not imply that everything that is taught must match students' current interests, nor that it must be put into practice today. But when students ask us, "Why should I learn this?" they are not asking an impertinent question. Why should they learn whatever it is we have planned? If we can't answer, then why are we teaching it? And when we can answer, let's be sure our reasons are not just platitudes.
  The subject of history provides us with a good example. Students frequently question why they need to learn about all those things that happened in the past, that are over and done with, and have no bearing on their lives today. The most typical response is that in order to understand our society as it is today, we have to know about major events that have already happened and how they shaped us. We must learn from our successes and failures. Furthermore, in order to know where we are headed, we have to know where we've been; we use past trends and events to predict the future.
  These are valid reasons, and students are usually willing to accept them at first. But typically what happens next? Students learn about all kinds of things that happened throughout history ... period. In more cases than not, they are not asked to explain their conclusions about how various events impacted society today. They are not asked to make predictions about where we are headed, and to justify their predictions according to past trends and events. Consequently, they don't see the connection that makes history relevant to their lives. The reasons provided for why they learn these things become empty platitudes.

- *It can be authentically assessed.*
  All outcomes, even simple ones, need to be assessable. This is nothing new to us; even when we were writing objectives, we were accustomed to making sure that we could assess what we were trying to accomplish. However, when writing high-achievement outcomes we need to think beyond the traditional paper and pencil test. We need to ask ourselves, "How can the students actually apply this learning?" How is it relevant to real life, and is there a way to determine whether students can make this transfer from classroom instruction to use in the real world? A high-achievement outcome is one that can be assessed by having students demonstrate specific skills and competencies that reflect real life situations or issues.

Applying What We've Learned

Let's return to the study of nutrition that we were using in our examples earlier, and analyze another outcome to see if it meets all of the criteria to be a high-achievement outcome: *Students will analyze a given menu to determine and list its nutritional contents. They will evaluate the menu according to FDA recommendations for a healthy diet, correct any deficiencies they may find, and justify their conclusions.*

A list of criteria for determining whether or not this statement is really a high achievement outcome is shown below, with explanations appropriate to each criterion.

Criterion #1: *Does it use a positive statement?*
Yes. It says the students will do these things (not "may" or "should").

Criterion #2: *Does it describe what the students will do?*
Yes. The entire outcome is stated from the student perspective; there is no mention of the textbook or what the teacher will do.

Criterion #3: *Does it use verbs that describe specific action?*
Yes. It says students will analyze, list, evaluate, correct, and justify.

Criterion #4: *Does it contain an end result, and does that result relate
                  directly to our intention (knowledge of nutrition)?*
Yes. Our intention is for students to be knowledgeable about the nutrition content of foods and what constitutes a healthy diet. We want more than mere awareness of these things; we want them to apply their knowledge. The end result of this outcome is that they will know how to determine nutrition content, because they will actually do so with a given menu. They will know what constitutes a healthy diet — at least according to FDA standards — because they will not only evaluate the menu accordingly, but will correct portions that they believe to be unhealthy, and justify their choices. We will have their lists, their recommended corrections, and their justifications as evidence of their learning.

Criterion #5:   *Does it require a high cognitive level?*
Yes. Students are analyzing, evaluating, and justifying, and the assignment also requires them to apply knowledge. All of these thought processes are considered to be in the higher cognitive domain.

Criterion #6:   *Does it require dynamic student involvement?*
Yes. Students are not just reading about good nutrition; they are actually analyzing and evaluating a menu, and justifying their conclusions and decisions.

Criterion #7:   *Is it relevant to students' lives?*
Yes. Not only is the topic of good nutrition relevant to their lives, relevancy is also present in what students are required to do with that topic. They learn the make-up of foods in terms of nutrition, and how to make nutritious food choices. These skills and knowledge are relevant to their lives today, and also contribute to our goals of long-term application and life-long learning.

Criterion #8:   *Can it be authentically assessed?*
Yes. Students are demonstrating skills and competencies that reflect a real life situation — they are analyzing a menu for its nutrition contents and health value.

Examples of High-Achievement Outcomes

A selection of high achievement outcomes for various grade levels and subject areas is provided below. These are intended as *examples* only, not as outcomes to put into your own curricula. As we have stated repeatedly, good high-achievement outcomes must be designed down from your district's mission statement by those who teach the subjects and courses. Outcomes appropriate for another district may not be the best choice for you.

These sample outcomes might be used as a guide for subject-area committees as they begin to write their own outcomes. They could also be used for a staff development activity: Teachers could evaluate these outcomes against the eight criteria to determine if they are indeed high achievement outcomes and specifically how each outcome meets each criterion.

SCIENCE

First Grade: *Students will research and develop hypotheses on the causes of shadows and the causes of changes in shadows.*

Third Grade: *Students will observe examples of various kinds of mold; classify them according to characteristics; and differentiate them according to growth conditions.*

Fifth Grade: *Students will identify the components of proper nutrition and analyze the effects of imbalanced diets on laboratory mice.*

Seventh Grade: *Students will arrange a given set of organisms into a standard scientific classification system and will design their own classification system for nonliving things.*

Ninth Grade: *Students will evaluate personal, community, state, and national energy conservation efforts, and justify conclusions.*

Chemistry: *Students will design an experiment to demonstrate energy changes associated with chemical changes and will describe real-world contexts for this phenomenon.*

SOCIAL STUDIES

Kindergarten: *Students will design and share with classmates profiles of themselves that include physical characteristics, family membership, and personal interests.*

Second Grade: *Students will illustrate the expanding relationships of self to family, neighborhood, and community.*

Fourth Grade: *Students will analyze and report the significance of landforms, climate, and natural resources to the economy of each of the geographic regions of the United States.*

Sixth Grade *Students will compare and contrast the history, culture, economics, and political divisions of selected countries from each continent.*

Eighth Grade: *Students will evaluate and justify conclusions about the Revolutionary War's impact on the American culture of the time, and determine how other countries of the world were affected by that event.*

American History: *Students will analyze the causes of the Civil War and interpret the moral and economic arguments that prevailed during its conduct.*

American
Government: *Students will determine and report or illustrate ways in which the U.S. Constitution has affected and reflected changing values*

in our society.

MATHEMATICS

First Grade: *Students will identify, order, and compare numbers to 100.*

Third Grade: *Students, using play money, will determine the total value and identify the exact money needed for simulated purchases up to $9.99.*

Fifth Grade: *Students will create a floor plan of a one-story building and determine the perimeter and area of each room.*

Seventh Grade: *Students will conduct a survey, calculate the data according to percentages, and prepare a line graph to depict the results.*

Algebra I: *Students will brainstorm real-life scenarios that require working with unknown quantities. Given hypothetical values for the known quantities of the scenarios, students will write and solve appropriate equations.*

Geometry: *Students will create a conditional statement and its converse and determine the truth or falsity of each.*

Alg. II - Trig.:   *Students will form quadratic equations from applicable physical data and find the solution to these equations or determine that no solution exists.*

LANGUAGE ARTS

Kindergarten: *Students will analyze given sets of print materials, pictures, and objects to determine the common beginning sounds. They will create booklets, illustrations, models, pantomimes, or role-plays to demonstrate the appropriate sounds.*

Second Grade: *Students will edit given sentences to correct mistakes and/or improve writing style; they will categorize the edited portions to eventually deduce the appropriate rules.*

Fourth Grade: *Students will distinguish among simple, compound, and complex sentences, provide examples of each, and develop paragraphs as extended sentences.*

Sixth Grade: *Students will develop and implement a strategy for researching an approved topic, and will prepare a written report of the research, complete with bibliography.*

Eighth Grade: *Students will differentiate and write examples of each of the following kinds of paragraphs: descriptive, expository, cause and effect, problem and solution, and comparison and contrast.*

Tenth Grade: *Students will select and develop theses to: (1) prove a point, using inference, analysis, deduction, and conclusion; and (2) persuade, using eloquent diction, devices of suspense, analogy, and personal anecdotes.*

Twelfth Grade: *Students will read a given set of short stories to identify and compare elements of fiction, including theme, plot, symbol and irony, character, point of view, emotion and humor, and fantasy. Additionally, students will evaluate each story according to how well it achieved its purpose and the significance of its purpose.*

CONVERTING INDICATORS TO OUTCOMES

Now that we understand what a high achievement outcome is and how to write one, we're ready to convert the topical curriculum to one that is outcome based. At this point we return to the focus areas and indicators that were prepared earlier. Remember that the SAC spent a good deal of time and energy in the decision-making process, selectively abandoning non-essential topics until they had created a focus area and indicators for each course and grade level. Their next step was to prepare a subject area mission statement, and then to convert each focus area to an outcome-based course or grade-level purpose. Likewise, the indicators will now be converted to the high-achievement outcomes.

In previous sections, we have been using as an example the first grade curriculum from Pleasant Valley. Let's look again at the subject mission, course purpose, and then the first indicator to see how we would convert that indicator to a high achievement outcome.

Subject Mission:

Students successfully completing courses from the Pleasant Valley Pre K - 12 World Studies curriculum will analyze essential geographic, economic, historical, governmental, social and psychological facts and principles and apply them to contemporary and future human conditions. Students will demonstrate an understanding of diverse cultures and apply the skills needed to participate in the changing global society.

First Grade Purpose:

Students will analyze the relationships between self and family; compare and contrast family units by size, geography, history, and culture; and recognize the individuality of family units and rules. They will investigate needs that families provide, and social and environmental factors that affect the way we live.

Indicator #1: labor in the home

This indicator is appropriate to several parts of the grade level purpose, particularly: the relationship between self and family, the individuality of family units and rules, and the needs that families provide. Therefore, the purpose has guided us in terms of what we want students to know or do regarding the topic of labor. The next step is to phrase that information in the form of an outcome. Our first attempt could result in the following:

Students will describe jobs or chores that are performed by the various members of their families and recognize that jobs and chores vary among individuals and family units. They will determine and list benefits of accomplishing jobs and chores, including the provision of basic needs. Students will prepare responsibility charts to record ways that they personally help with labor in the home.

Having written this outcome, the SAC members now compare it to the eight criteria to be sure that it is a high achievement outcome. Let's check the criteria now.

Criterion #1:   Does it use a positive statement?
Yes. It says the students will do these things (not "may" or "should").

Criterion #2:   Does it describe what the students will do?
Yes. The entire outcome is stated from the student perspective; there is no mention of the textbook or what the teacher will do.

Criterion #3:   Does it use verbs that describe specific action?
Yes. It says students will describe, recognize, determine, list, and prepare.

Criterion #4:   Does it contain an end result, and does that result relate
                      directly to our intention (labor as it applies to home and family)?
*Yes. Our intention is for students to know what labor is and its importance to each
family even though the particulars vary from one family to another. We want more than
mere awareness of these things; we want students to show responsibility and pride in their
own contributions. The end result of this outcome is that they will recognize that even
though each family is unique, work is necessary to provide for a family's needs,. Students
will demonstrate that they can contribute by keeping a record of their own chores.*

Criterion #5:   Does it require a high cognitive level?
*Yes. Describing jobs and chores does not in itself require a high cognitive level,. However,
students may have to do some investigation to come up with the information; additionally, they are making comparisons, and they have to determine the benefits of the labor, both
of which require a higher level of thinking. They also must apply learning by providing
data appropriate to their own families, and by accepting and documenting their own
responsibilities.*

Criterion #6:   Does it require dynamic student involvement?
*Yes. Students are not just listening to general discussions. They are providing personal
information, applying thinking skills, participating in the performance of chores, and
making and sharing charts.*

Criterion #7:   Is it relevant to students' lives?
*Yes. Recognizing the importance of work for all family members, and sharing in the
responsibility and performance of work is relevant to a student's life now and in the future.*

Criterion #8:   Can it be authentically assessed?
Yes. The descriptions, lists, and charts are all derived from real situations and applications.

APPROACHES TO MAKING THE CURRICULUM INTERDISCIPLINARY OR INTEGRATED

As educators study the model and receive training in the SAC's Action Agenda
— particularly the steps of decision-making and writing outcomes — we are often
asked about interdisciplinary and integrated curriculums. Educators sometimes confuse the two, thinking they are one and the same thing, but they are actually quite different. In an **interdisciplinary** curriculum, we work with a *particular item of essential*

learning that is not unique to any one discipline. Educators say, This is important and we want to be sure we're teaching it… but which subject, or subjects, should include it? An **integrated** curriculum deals with *connecting the disciplines.* It has nothing to do with a particular "something" that needs to be taught, but rather with the fact that subjects should not be isolated; students need to see the interconnectedness of all the disciplines. These curricular approaches are discussed in great detail in a later section of this book, in conjunction with thematic instruction. However, a general understanding is needed at this point, to see their role in the curriculum development process.

Interdisciplinary Curriculum

The interdisciplinary curriculum consists of those items *essential for student learning* that are not not unique to a particular subject discipline. Such an item may even be developed into a subject or course offering in itself, but even then its implementation is not necessarily limited to that particular slot. An example of such an interdisciplinary curriculum is technology education. No school district can ignore the importance of technology education because some aspect of it is always essential for student learning. Districts have recognized this fact by offering everything from a wide range of technological courses to at least one basic computer class, which is usually required for all students in the regular education program. But knowledge and use of technology are not limited to special classes nor to any single or specific discipline. For example, the computer can be an instructional aid in almost all subject areas. Students apply learning experienced in the special class, such as how to actually operate the computer. But use of the computer in other classes also requires that the outcomes of those classes include more specific application, such as how the computer can enhance learning of subject matter, aid in the accomplishment of tasks, or how particular programs work.

Technology Plus Others

Other examples of interdisciplinary curriculum topics are: career education, writing across the curriculum, self-esteem, citizenship, and consumer education. Educators should also consider anything that is essential learning for their own student populations. If your community or state relies heavily on a particular industry, that topic might be considered for the interdisciplinary curriculum. For example, in a farming community or state, agriculture could be emphasized in terms of careers, economics, or its role in local, state, national, and global concerns. All of the topics above are relevant to the entire district.

Additional topics may be identified for individual schools — topics that are unique to a particular school because of its own student population, but are not unique to a single discipline or single group of students. An example of such a topic is the study of a particular culture that is relevant to the majority of students who attend the school, or even E.S.L. (English as a Second Language)... if the *majority* of students come from non-English speaking families. Specialized schools, such as magnet schools, also must plan for their own unique interdisciplinary curriculum.

Who's In Charge?

Both the Curriculum Coordinating Council and the Subject Area Committees are responsible for ensuring that interdisciplinary outcomes have been included in the district curriculum. However, the focus for each is quite different. The CCC looks at general topics and considers them in terms of their necessary depth and complexity. They must then decide *where* to include these topics, and whether they need to be taught as separate courses or if they can be interwoven with existing disciplines. Because of the broad nature of the topics, they "fit" in many places. Most of them are also applicable to real life for the students; consequently, it's important that application is demonstrated in many areas, yet needless duplication and repetition must be avoided. Although this all sounds terribly complicated, the process is not quite as complex as it may seem when considering general descriptions. A look at the process itself and a specific description should prove illuminating.

Writing Interdisciplinary Outcomes

First of all, keep in mind that the interdisciplinary outcomes you identify should be written in the same way as any high achievement outcome: they must meet the eight criteria we have described previously. Second, recognize that some interdisciplinary topics, such as self-esteem and writing across the curriculum, must be woven into existing curricula, while others, such as technology or career education, can either be woven in, taught as separate units, or both.

The specific example that we've chosen for illuminating that strategy is *citizenship*. This topic is a part of the interdisciplinary curriculum that can be taught both as a woven-in element and as a separate unit. In fact, to assure mastery by all students, many districts offer it both ways at certain grade levels.

Citizenship fits all of the complications referred to earlier. Demonstration of citizenship skills is expected of students in all subjects of all grade levels, therefore it "fits" everywhere, and deciding exactly what to put where becomes challenging. This broad applicability also makes it tempting to list vague objectives rather than specific outcomes. For example, in a list of expected citizenship skills, one often finds "getting along well with others." Granted, this is a behavior that we would like all students to demonstrate, but the wording is much too vague, is not stated in high achievement terms, and does not require intellectually engaged students. We must also ask ourselves: Are we actually going to teach this — with specific lessons — and if so, how and when?

There *are* lessons for all grade levels and subject areas that can teach this type of behavior. Primary grade children can discuss rules at home and school, make comparisons, help establish classroom rules, and analyze and evaluate what is or isn't fair in specific situations. Students of all ages can participate in activities based on moral dilemmas, decision-making, and conflict resolution; the complexity of the activities determines the appropriate grade levels. Activities can be incorporated into the various subject disciplines: examining the behaviors of characters in literature, analyzing historical events and decisions in social studies, discussing fair play at recess and physical education, and evaluating moral dilemmas in science and technology.

Teaching to Interdisciplinary Outcomes

When the interdisciplinary outcomes have been identified and *properly written,* the selection of teaching behaviors and student activities is no longer complicated. In the example given above, instead of saying that the students will "get along well with others," we can make a distinct and measurable statement such as, "The students will identify and evaluate the issues in a given set of conflicts and support one or both sides of each issue."

The wording of the latter statement includes high achievement terms and requires intellectually engaged students. The outcome can be taught to mastery and assessed accordingly. Application can be measured by presenting a variety of additional situations — with different circumstances — and having students identify and defend issues. Application is furthered in the students' own processes of "getting along well with others." When conflicts arise, students can be directed to apply the learning: "What is the issue here? Support your point of view." Peer evaluation can be applied in stand-off situations; young people are more inclined to adhere to the opinions and decisions of their peers than to those of adults, and having participated in practice situations makes them more confident about the fairness of a real-life application.

Woven-in or Stand Alone?

Depending on the core outcomes identified for citizenship education, separate units or course offerings may be necessary for the upper grade levels. Nine-week, semester, or year-long courses might be offered in such areas as: The Court System, Criminal Justice, The Constitution, Civics, The Mock Trial, Conflict Resolution, Criminal/Civil/Juvenile Law, Corrections, Law Enforcement, Voting or Politics, The Citizen as Consumer, The Law in General, Rights and Responsibilities, and so forth. All of these course offerings have the potential to allow us to meet our designated outcomes. But obviously, they are not all necessary. Having identified the outcomes, we must choose only those courses necessary to achieve them.

Using Extensions

Just as disciplinary outcomes must be supplemented by extensions, so must interdisciplinary outcomes. Not all students will learn at the same rate. We need a few separate courses, or a number of lessons within a course or subject, to provide correctives or enrichment. Some of the separate courses described above can be offered as enrichment courses for the accelerated students. Others — even semester or year-long classes — can be offered as correctives. For example, a semester class on conflict resolution might be required of students who cannot identify or evaluate acceptable solutions to conflict situations. The Citizens as Consumers Class could be made available to students who have not demonstrated the ability to recognize both their rights and responsibilities as consumers in the real world of their own communities.

These extensions need not be offered only as separate courses; they can also be woven into other subject disciplines, and presented through a variety of teaching methods. A cooperative learning activity can be an excellent vehicle for studying about representative government, how the election process works, or solutions to real or imaginary community problems. Dilemmas can be role-played. Corrective activities can be implemented through children's stories (or more advanced literature selections), simple case studies, or projects that require citizenship research and skills. Art and music courses can include lessons related to license, copyright, and freedom of expression. Math classes that include study of fractions, percentages, estimates, or graphing might use taxes and government budgets as real-life examples for application. The world of sports is now a big business and includes not only high finance, but rules, laws, contracts, ethics, gender issues, drug problems, and a host of other law and citizen-related issues.

The SAC's Role

Remember that the CCC looks at interdisciplinary outcomes to decide if they can be woven into existing courses or if a separate course needs to be organized. Additionally, as overseers of all subject curriculums, they will evaluate each curriculum as it is completed to see that interdisciplinary outcomes were included. While the CCC makes these more general decisions, the Subject Area Committee makes very specific ones.

Keep in mind that the SAC does not just "dream up" outcomes for their subject; the outcomes that are to be taught come from the design-down process. In that process, the very first thing the SAC looks at is the *district mission statement.* Members of the SAC must read that statement critically; as they examine the purpose section and the exit outcomes, they will find not only items inherent to their particular subject, but also the kinds of interdisciplinary outcomes described above, and they must ask themselves how their subject can help accomplish each of these. Then, as they continue the design-down process, they do the "weaving-in" described previously.

The subject mission will reflect those interdisciplinary themes they've identified, as will the course and grade level purposes of the appropriate levels that they've identified for instruction. And then, of course, it is the SAC who actually writes the specific outcomes.

If the CCC has determined that a separate course is needed for an interdisciplinary topic, even though the topic is not unique to any particular subject, they still have to assign it to a Subject Area Committee for curriculum development and writing. In some instances, a *separate* SAC is appointed; this is particularly the case with a topic as pervasive as technology. In other situations, the new course is assigned to the existing SAC with which the topic seems most compatible. For example, one of the citizenship courses described previously would be assigned to the social studies SAC. On the other hand, a cultural diversity course might be assigned to social studies, or perhaps to fine arts... depending on the approach the CCC had in mind for its implementation. But whether the topic is assigned to a new or existing Subject Area Committee, is up to that SAC to actually develop the curriculum.

Remember....

The important thing to remember in working with interdisciplinary outcomes is that the same principles must be applied to them as we apply to subject outcomes:
   (1) interdisciplinary outcomes must be essential to student learning;
   (2) they must be taught to an identified mastery level;
   (3) student learning of the outcomes to mastery level must be assessed, with extensions provided when necessary; and
   (4) all instructional steps must be aligned with district and subject missions, and grade level and course purposes.

The Integrated Curriculum

The integrated curriculum is one in which the *disciplines are connected* through their curriculums. While this is an extremely desirable kind of curriculum, it is also an extremely complicated one; therefore, **we do not recommend that districts try to do a complete integration of the curriculum when they are first switching to a design-down, outcome-based system.** It is difficult enough for educators to switch from the old "cover everything" curriculum to one that has been selectively abandoned and stated in terms of high achievement outcomes without also trying to figure out how to tie together the outcomes for all of the disciplines.

Consider this analogy. Suppose someone invented a brand new number system. While it is superior to our present one in terms of what it can accomplish, it is nevertheless completely different from what we're used to; in fact, it no longer uses any of the familiar numerals 0-9. Now of course we must teach this new system to our students. But suppose we said to our intermediate level and high school students,

"You must learn to multiply, divide, and determine fractions... and you must learn the concepts of trigonometry and calculus... but you must do so while using this brand-new number system instead of the one you've been using all these years!" How overwhelming that would be! Would it not make more sense to teach the students how to use the new number system and **then** —when they're comfortable using the new system— teach them the mathematical concepts and computations?

The same theory should be applied to the curriculum development process. As the long-range plan is executed for the first time, educators should concentrate on use of the design down process and preparation of high achievement outcomes within individual disciplines. When teachers have become accustomed not only to writing, but to teaching high achievement outcomes, then integrating the curriculum will be a much easier process.

However, there <u>are</u> some steps that can be taken in the early stages to begin integrating the curriculum areas. Primarily this involves having each Subject Area Committee (after the first one) examine the curriclum documents from all previous committees to familiarize themselves with focus areas and general content. Then as new committees begin their work, they can consider common focus topics. It is not necessary for all subjects to be linked to the same focus area, but if a single focus can be carried over to even one or two other subjects, some integration has taken place. Consider the following examples for River Falls's first, fifth, and tenth grades.

River Falls's long-range plan listed the big four subjects in the following order: social studies, science, math, and communications. In developing the social studies curriculum, the following focus areas were identified for grades one, five, and ten respectively: home and families; westward expansion; and world history.

When the Science SAC analyzed the first grade curriculum, they discovered that most of the topics dealt with different kinds of animals — pets, farm animals, and zoo or other wild animals. So obviously "amimals" would be the focus area for first grade science. However, the SAC took this idea a little further, and made the focus area "animal *families*" in order to tie it into the social studies curriculum. The outcomes then approached the various categories of animals (tame/wild) through a particular family, such as the cat family: domestic cats, jungle cats, and so forth.

When the Math SAC met, they did not tie into "families" as a focus area; however, they did use the idea in suggested activities. When students were expected to count, compare, and communicate numbers, it was suggested that the vehicles used be related to human or animal families, such as: Which of these is larger... the cat family or the bird family? Meanwhile, the Communications SAC used "families and animals" as a two-part focus; students listened to and read stories about families as well as all kinds of animal stories. They wrote and talked about their own families as well as their pets, and their experiences with other animals at parks, farms, or zoos.

In grade five, the focus area of westward expansion was carried over from social studies to communications. Students read fiction and non-fiction selections about the pioneers, the gold rush, and life on the plains, as well as numerous westerns. They kept journals and wrote letters during a social studies simulation in which they were pioneers traveling the Oregon Trail. They wrote reports, poetry and creative stories about westward expansion and life. They learned songs and listened to stories related to the focus; they gave oral reports and participated in role-plays and discussion groups. Although this first time through the Science and Math SACs did not choose to use the same focus area, members of those committees are already beginning to brainstorm ways they can integrate their subjects with that common focus when their committees begin the process again in a few years.

We offer River Falls's tenth grade as yet one more example of using the "common focus" approach because of a dramatic change that resulted. Originally, in communications, the focus for tenth grade was American literature, eleventh grade was British literature, and twelfth grade was world literature. However, the social studies sequence was world history for tenth, American history for eleventh, and American Government for twelfth. To better integrate the curriclum, the sequence was changed so that tenth grade has world literature (historical), and eleventh grade has American literature. Twelfth grade was changed to current world literature; British literature was eliminated as a separate course, but is included in both the tenth and twelfth grade curriculums.

These examples show ways that Subject Area Committees can begin the process of integrating the curriculums during implementation of the first Long-Range Plan. As we've pointed out before, revising the curriculum the second time through is so much easier because through our continuing evaluation processes, we know teachers are using the planned curriculum; we also know that by that time, teachers better understand how to write and teach to high achievement outcomes. Therefore, during the second round of curriculum revision, SACs can give their time and attention to more fully integrating the separate disciplines.

CREATING TASK ANALYSIS GUIDES

Thus far, we have examined these aspects associated with the preparation of high achievement outcomes: the working definition of a high achievement outcome, clarification of some common misunderstandings, the difference between an objective and an outcome, converting indicators to outcomes, and criteria for verifying the authenticity of high achievement outcomes. Most educators find the process difficult at first, but with practice and — more important — the opportunity to work with colleagues, they soon get the hang of it.

Keep in mind that we don't just dream up high achievement outcomes that sound good; to the contrary, our efforts are directed through the design down process. Likewise, now that we've prepared our outcomes, we must each ask ourselves, How will I go about teaching these? It is important to think this question through, otherwise we may have an outcome that sounds good but is not practical when it comes to putting it into action. Also, it is a fact that many teachers are accustomed to simply covering material rather than teaching to specific outcomes. Identifying — and including in our curriculum document — the components of teaching to an outcome will be a tremendous benefit in helping these teachers make the transition. Additionally, once a task analysis has been completed, it's a big time-saver for all of us. Time is something that is always too limited for teachers. And if any of the curriculum is new, or slightly different than what we've taught before, we may become frustrated in trying to teach it. Just because we don't have the time to think through all the components and how we will accomplish them, we may do a less-than-satisfactory job, or even revert to the old "covering material" methods.

The approach to use in determining what it takes to accomplish a high-achievement outcome is the **task analysis** process. A task analysis is just what the name indicates: we **analyze** an outcome to determine the **tasks** that must be completed. You may be accustomed to thinking of these tasks as learning **strands** or **units** of instruction. The terminology is not important; call them whatever you like, but do determine just which knowledge and skill components must be taught in order for students to accomplish the outcome.

Tasks — The Nucleus of the Outcome

A *nucleus* is a central point of focus around which matter is gathered. The tasks form the nucleus of the outcome because they are the central focus around which all other instructional decisions are made. Keep in mind that an outcome is an **end result** — it is what the students now know or can do after participating in the learning process. A **high-achievement outcome** is cumulative. Students have acquired knowledge and skills that they now put together into one end result. The tasks are those separate "pieces" of knowledge and skill that students put together. Let's look at an example. The following is a high achievement outcome for second grade science:

Students will survey the number and kinds of pets owned by class members, and prepare and interpret bar graphs of results. They will also determine and demonstrate the proper care and treatment of pets.

To identify the tasks, we simply analyze the outcome; what are the separate parts of knowledge and skill that lead up to the desired result? In this example, the following tasks are necessary: (1) definition of and processes for conducting a survey;

(2) conducting the survey; (3) components and interpretation of bar graphs; (4) making bar graphs of survey results; (5) interpreting the prepared graph; (6) determining proper care and treatment of pets; (7) demonstrating proper care and treatment of pets.

Notice that in the first step of the analysis we simply identify the tasks; at this point we are not concerned with wording. However, once the tasks have been identified we then think of them in terms of unit or lesson outcomes. It is not at all uncommon for teachers who are just beginning this process to identify the desired outcome, but then use the same vague teaching processes to try to get there.

For example, a 7th grade social studies teacher was planning instruction for an outcome that required students to locate specific geographic descriptions on maps and globes. When asked how he would teach this skill, the teacher replied that the first task involved knowledge of specific vocabulary words, so he would **introduce** the words, have students **study** them, and then **test** the students on their knowledge of the words.

In the discussion that followed, his colleagues quickly pointed out that they had no idea what he actually expected from his students. "Introducing" words is something the teacher does, and it doesn't require a response from the students; did he expect a response? If so, what? For what purpose were students supposed to "study" the words? Were they to memorize the definition of each? Should they be able to spell them correctly? Were they to do any sort of application with them, such as use them in a sentence or find them on a map? Likewise, how, and on what, would they be "tested?" Would they simply have to match words and definitions; would they be given a word and asked to supply the definition; would they have to give an example of how or where the word is used?

In more instances than not, our methodology doesn't really change. What changes is that we think through, and identify, the end results of the methods and activities we choose. Ask yourself what you plan to do in your class tomorrow, and then ask, Why? What is the expected result of those efforts? For example, if tomorrow you want students to read a newspaper article about the selected topic, ask yourself: For what purpose? What result do I expect? Do I want them to know everything in the article? Do I want them simply to become aware of the issue? Do I want them to identify the issue and give the opposing points of view? Identifying the expected outcome of each lesson will help provide the teacher as well as the students with focus; instruction and actual learning are both greatly enhanced.

So, once the high-achievement outcome has been analyzed to identify the tasks, then each task is stated in outcome terms. In the science example above, the first task is "definition of and processes for conducting a survey." The first part of that is simple: students will <u>define</u> <u>survey</u>. The second part takes just a little more thought. Obviously we're going to teach the processes, but to what result? Do we want students to list the steps of a process, explain a process in their own words, give examples of different kinds of processes, or demonstrate a process? If they can do any of these things for one process, is that acceptable, or must the result be for two (or even more) different processes? Identifying the end result in this way not only makes it easier to plan how we'll proceed with instruction, it also simplifies the assessment process. It's much easier to determine whether a student can or cannot "list the steps of the survey process" than to determine whether a student "knows what the survey process is."

Returning to our science example above, the tasks could be stated as the following outcomes. Students will:

1) define survey
2) list and explain the steps for conducting a written survey
3) conduct a written survey on the numbers and kinds of pets owned by class members
4) examine and identify components of given sample bar graphs
5) interpret the given bar graphs
6) create and interpret bar graphs depicting the data collected in the pet surveys
7) participate in class discussion and inquiry to determine the proper care and treatment of pets
8) demonstrate the proper care and treatment of pets in simulations
9) demonstrate the proper care and treatment of classroom pets

And Now... The Rest of the Story

Identifying the tasks (strands, units) is the first step of the analysis process. It is followed by determining **teaching methods, student activities, means of assessment, criteria and evidence for mastery, and extension activities.** The first two of these, teaching methods and student activities, are directly related. The thing to keep in mind is that teaching methods identify only what the *teacher* will do, and student activities explain what the *students* will do. As mentioned above, the teaching methods, in most instances, will not vary that much from what the teacher is accustomed to doing. Identifying the methods to be used simply helps the teacher think through the best way to achieve expected results. If background information is required, then lecture and class discussion may be your best choices. When students are ready to actually work with the skill or concept, you need to determine how you will direct them. Is a cooperative learning activity appropriate? A simulation? Guided practice of written assignments?

In answering these questions, the relationship between teaching methods and student activities becomes obvious. If the *method* chosen is cooperative learning, then obviously the *student activity* is going to be a cooperative learning activity. However, in describing the student activity, we describe the <u>particular</u> cooperative activity.

Returning to our example of the science outcome, task #2 says that students will list the steps for conducting a written survey. Our sample teacher chooses cooperative learning as the *method* for teaching this skill. For the student activity, she chooses the following jigsaw activity: The class is divided into groups of four. One person from each group gathers together for instruction on step one of the survey process; the second person from each group learns step two, and so forth. Then group members teach each other what they have learned. Students continue teaching and coaching until each person in their group can list and explain all four steps of the survey process. On her task analysis form, the teacher lists "cooperative learning" under the heading of Methods. Under the Student Activity heading, she writes, "Jigsaw activity: four steps of conducting a written survey."

This process is continued for all of the tasks that comprise an outcome. For each task that has been identified, we simply ask ourselves: what method will the teacher use, and — correspondingly — what exactly will the students do? A task may require only one method and/or activity, or it could require several; it all depends on the complexity of the task and how much discovery, practice, or transfer of learning are required.

The following tables list examples of teaching methods, and activities that require dynamic student involvement (a criterion of a high achievement outcome). These lists are helpful references when preparing a task analysis in that they: 1) help clarify the distinction between methods and activities; and 2) provide alternatives for teachers who have difficulty thinking of new approaches.

TABLE ONE: METHODS

PLANNED FROM THE TEACHER'S PERSPECTIVE...
THE TYPE OF ACTIVITY OR THE VEHICLE THAT WILL
BE USED TO ACCOMPLISH A TASK

lecture
guided discussion
field trip
problem-solving techniques
directed research
directed reading or writing
peer task (two students work together on the assignment)
peer tutoring (one student helps the other)
small group assignments or cooperative learning
whole-class collaboration on assignment
guest speaker or interaction with a resource person
demonstration

guided practice
use of media (audio, visual, print)
software programs
brainstorming
role-play
simulation
modeling
mentoring
conferences
contracts
independent study
events (field day, fair, contest, program, service project)
Directed activities (panel discussion, debate, game,
      tournament, experiments, projects, surveys, interviews)

TABLE TWO: SAMPLE ACTIVITIES
THAT REQUIRE DYNAMIC STUDENT INVOLVEMENT

conduct a survey
graph results of a survey or research
collect samples or examples
sketch a picture or plan
inspect (a place, product, project)
search for specific items or clues
identify problems
propose solutions
create (a song, story, play, product, model)
combine elements of drama, music, dance, art
reorganize (a process, product, book, paper, group)
suggest improvements
evaluate (a product, idea, plan, occurrence, event, process, ad, speech)
determine criteria for evaluation
establish a set of rules
plan/participate in an event (cultural fair, field day, environmental
      program or project, community service, play, field trip, fund raiser)
role-play
participate in a simulation
make up own worksheets for practice/drill
write/produce a song, jingle, commercial, rap, skit, play
interact with a resource person
conduct experiments

conduct research
make up a game
demonstrate a process
write (a poem, story, essay, explanation, constitution, skit, play)
make posters, murals, collages
make maps
analyze (a document, process, problem, situation, event)
teach someone how to do something
collect data
create a dictionary, glossary, journal
draw conclusions
make decisions/justify choices
classify (terms, objects, places, ideas, events, behaviors, data)
evaluate own work, progress/set goals
work cooperatively in a group
prepare a bulletin board
make an audio or video tape
make inferences, predictions
form and support opinions
make up problems for others to solve
determine relationships (between items, groups, processes, ideas, events, issues)
invent a new product or service
compare/contrast (stories, items, events, ideas, styles, issues, results, processes)
determine/evaluate consequences
debate
participate in panel discussion
conduct an interview
produce a newspaper, television program
solve problems (real-life applications)
prepare budgets
create (art, cooking, sewing, woodworking, machine, writing)
change (a story, event, process, idea, product, bill or law)
write letters, editorials
distinguish between fact and opinion
evaluate rules/laws
brainstorm
make/solve puzzles
determine/evaluate qualifications (for a position, office, honor)
identify points of view/persuade/select different viewpoints
make charts, flow charts, diagrams, graphs, timelines
participate in a community or governmental meeting/process/project
conduct a campaign

make or interpret cartoons

conduct a mock trial

establish and apply a rating scale or ranking system

devise a system (for record-keeping, time management, note taking, sharing of
   responsibilities, handling conflicts)

create and demonstrate a new way to do an assigned task

test an idea

use software programs

respond to imaginary situations (what if…, suppose you…, imagine that…)

prepare a contract (or other "legal" document)

conduct/write case studies

find an alternative (procedure, technique, solution, use)

plan a trip or tour, including all relevant background information

find or create an analogy

develop a handbook

keep a critic's log of television programs, books, or movies

identify the steps used to learn something/complete a task (metacognition)

Assessment — The Real Test of Instruction

There are lots of incidental things that we teach that we may not even assess. These are the little everyday kinds of things, or the additional little tidbits that we know some students will find fascinating; they're an added bonus for anyone who chooses to remember or use them. But we all know that those things we've identified as **necessary** knowledge or skills require not only careful instruction, but some form of assessment to determine if students have indeed learned that which was intended. When preparing <u>outcomes</u> we must ask ourselves, Can this be assessed, and if so — how? (If it cannot be assessed, we have a problem with the outcome.)

In completing the task analysis, there are additional points to consider for the assessment portion of our planning. The first thing to consider is that each <u>task</u> should be assessed. Waiting until all tasks have been completed and then assessing the total outcome causes instruction to be less effective and more time-consuming. If some students have not achieved the outcome it may be difficult to decide just exactly which part they didn't understand. Or, it may turn out that a first step was learned incorrectly — one that is necessary for all other steps to be successful — thus requiring the student to start over and repeat the entire process. On the other hand, frequent, formative assessments allow us to correct errors and misunderstandings before they are compounded.

A second rule to follow in our planning is to look at the verb used in the outcome. Whatever the verb indicates students will do, the assessment must verify that they can in fact do it. For example, if the outcome says that students will *compare* things (places, issues, items), then our assessment needs to have students making a comparison. If the outcome says they will *list*, then the assessment requires them to make a list. This seems so obvious, yet after careful examination you will be amazed at the number of times the planned assessment does not match exactly the stated outcome.

The third thing to consider is authenticity. We often use as an example the young child who received a perfect score on a written test about simple fractions, but could not help his mother prepare half of a simple recipe. **Educators, in general, seem to be convinced that a paper-and-pencil test tells us whether a student knows or can do the intended outcome.** While a written test can be a good indicator of student achievement, it should not be considered sole proof of student learning. It is only *one* indicator. What else will convince you that the student really knows or can do that which you expect? How will the student use this in real life, and is there a way to have the student do that in class? Answering these questions will lead to appropriate choices of assessment when preparing the task analysis.

Sometimes the student activity that has been planned can also serve as the assessment instrument. For example, in the science outcome that we've been looking at, one of the tasks is for students to demonstrate proper care and treatment of pets. Our sample teacher has chosen simulation for one teaching method; for the student activity students will be given situations involving pets, and they must demonstrate how they would handle each situation. This activity is also an assessment tool. Simulations might include such things as how to pick up a kitten or puppy, how to approach someone else's dog, what or how much to feed certain kinds of pets, or ways to protect an outdoor pet from inclement weather. In each case, the teacher documents whether the student does or does not demonstrate proper care, and then decides whether additional instruction is necessary.

The teacher is also planning to use an on-going exercise that will serve as both a student activity and an assessment. She has several classroom pets, and students will be assigned the responsibility for care of the pets throughout the school year. Again she can evaluate how well the students accept the responsibility and whether they demonstrate proper care. This fulfills another criterion of good assessment, which is that students are reassessed periodically even after instruction and the original assessment for the outcome have been completed.

The topic of assessment, and the next two components of the task analysis — mastery and extensions— are dealt with in greater detail in later sections of this book. For now it is important to know that during the task analysis process, educators must decide and describe each of these instructional elements to assure that they are accomplishing the outcome.

What's Good Enough?

In traditional approaches to education, after an assessment was given, the teacher evaluated the assessment, recorded the score in a gradebook, and then went on to the next lesson, regardless of how well students had performed. In a results based approach, teachers do all that they can to bring students to mastery. This means that if students don't do well the first time through, extended learning opportunities are necessary. The questions that immediately come to mind are, How well must they do? What's good enough? And what are we looking for to convince us that the student has indeed "mastered" this task?

The answers to these questions form the *criteria* and *evidence* for mastery of a task. Criteria and evidence are, for the most part, the same thing... with one subtle difference. When we ask ourselves what we're looking for — what our expectations are — we answer the questions by determining a set of **criteria**. For example, we may say that a student must solve a written set of math problems with 80% accuracy. The written set of math problems is the means of assessment; 80% accuracy is our criteria for mastery. Or, for students performing a science experiment, we may say they must do the experiment <u>independently</u>, use all materials provided, and reach the same result at least twice. Performing the experiment is the means of assessment; doing so independently, using all materials, and reaching the same result at least twice are our criteria for mastery.

The **evidence** that we're looking for is something more tangible — it's the proof that the student accomplished that which was expected. You might think of evidence as <u>something that you could put in the student's portfolio</u> if you so desired. So, in our examples above, the math test itself — the actual pieces of paper showing the student's work — would be the evidence. In the case of the science experiment, there are a number of ways to provide evidence; we might use: a videotape of the student performing the experiment; a rating sheet filled out by the teacher; anecdotal records of the student's performance; or perhaps a lab record completed by the student or another observer.

As mentioned before, the topic of mastery is discussed in much detail in a later section of this book. But as educators work through the task analysis process for an outcome, it is important that they determine the criteria and evidence for each assessment in order to know whether students are ready to move on or whether they need extended learning opportunities.

One More Thing

There remains one more part to the task analysis process, and that is the determination of extensions. When a task is assessed and we find that some students are not able to do that which we expect, what do we do next? As mentioned before, the traditional answer to that question has often been "nothing." We record the poor score in the grade book and move on to the next step. However, outcome-based instruction and mastery learning require a different approach. If we <u>know</u> that a student has not learned what we expected, then obviously we have not yet taught it to that student. We may have presented material and provided learning opportunities, but we have not taught students to do something until they can actually do it.

Occasionally the problem exists simply because the student has not had enough practice to become proficient at the desired skill. In these cases, "more of the same thing" is acceptable. However, just as often the problem is caused not by a lack of practice, but by a lack of understanding. Repeating the exact instruction, especially if it's done more slowly the second time, may be all that's needed for some students. But it's also a fact that many students don't understand something the first time because of particular methods or activities that were used; therefore, repeating the exact instruction isn't going to help them a bit. What we have to ask ourselves at this time is, How else could this be approached? How could we provide for a different learning style? Or perhaps, Could this be broken down into even smaller pieces; or could another student explain how he or she approached the process? Our past teaching experiences allow us to anticipate problem areas, so in the task analysis process we plan ahead for alternative methods and activities that could be used with students who need further assistance. These methods and activities are referred to as *correctives.*

Just as important as planning ways to reteach specific tasks is the need to plan *enrichment* activities. There are always those few students who catch on to something so quickly that they're ready to move on when most of the class is just getting a good start; holding them back is boring and does not provide the challenge they need. We also often find ourselves in situations where part of the class can successfully complete the task, but other students need correctives. Teachers in this situation often ask, If I take time to do correctives with some students, what do I do with the rest of them? The answer to that question is also enrichment activities. The important thing to consider in both of these instances where enrichments are needed is once again not just to do more of the same thing, or just to provide busywork. Enrichment activities need to be interesting and challenging ways to expand the knowledge or skill associated with the task at hand.

Let's look one last time at our science example to consider both a corrective and enrichment activity. One of the tasks is for students to create bar graphs depicting the data collected in the pet surveys. Our sample teacher didn't have students start out by graphing the actual survey information. Instead, she provided very simple data that students could graph with only one bar, then increased the amount of data for them to graph with two or more bars. As expected, some students struggled with the one-bar sample, while others could accurately design multi-bar graphs right from the beginning.

For those students who were struggling, the teacher planned a corrective activity in which students used building blocks to represent numbers in the data. She had them count and stack the numbers of blocks that corresponded with the numbers in the given data. Next, she gave them crayons and large-square graph paper and had them color a square on the paper each time they selected a building block, until they could see the relationship between the building blocks and the bar they had created on paper.

Meanwhile, the students who were proficient at bar graphs were working on a cooperative group activity. The teacher had asked them to come up with a list of ways that bar graphs could be useful to them in their lives. The students came up with an impressive list that included such things as graphing their spelling (or other subject) scores to determine progress, how their allowance money was used, how their class was doing in the physical fitness activities currently underway in physical education, and which school lunch items were most often eaten or wasted (hoping they could influence future menu selections). The teacher then gave them the option of selecting one of their suggestions to work on together, or of making individual selections to complete by themselves. If they chose a group project, she would have them collect the data and prepare a bulletin-board bar graph; if they preferred the individual projects, she would ask them to collect and graph the appropriate data and then share the results with the other class members.

Correctives and enrichments both need to be related to the task at hand. While this is generally understood about correctives, it is not always applied to enrichments; teachers often plan an "enrichment" activity that has nothing to do with the particular outcome on which the class is working. (See p. 358 for additional detailed information about extensions.)

How to Use the Task Analysis

A simple form can be used for teachers to complete the task analysis process. The form is printed on standard 8-1/2 x 11 papers that are turned horizontally. A blank line is printed at the top of the first page; the teacher will write the outcome to be taught on this line. The rest of the page is divided into columns with the following headings: TASKS, METHODS, STUDENT ACTIVITIES, ASSESSMENTS, MASTERY CRITERIA/EVIDENCE, and EXTENSIONS. (These may be prepared on one or two sheets of paper, according to preference.) Then the teacher fills in the columns with the information appropriate for the outcome listed. Examples of completed task analysis sheets for one outcome in each of the "big four" subject areas are provided on the following pages.

Completed task analysis sheets should be included in the curriculum document. Information should be provided to make it clear that while the outcome and tasks are required teaching for all teachers of this particular course or grade level, the methods, activities, assessments, criteria/evidence, and extensions are only suggestions. Teachers should of course use whatever means they choose to teach the outcome. An outcome-based education adage says that it isn't so important <u>when</u> a student learns something, as that she learns it. Likewise, it isn't so important how a teacher teaches something, as that he teaches it. However, most teachers find the task analysis sheets in their curriculum documents to be extremely helpful and time-saving. Some teachers use the suggestions exclusively. Others begin with ideas of their own, but turn to the suggestions when they need alternatives for students with different learning styles or those who need additional instruction.

Teachers should consider the task analysis to be a lesson plan. Here is an outcome; specifically, how am I going to teach and assess it? When they have outlined all the categories, they may even choose to go back and indicate which task and activity they plan to do on day one, which they will do on day two, and so forth. There is no need to write a second set of daily plans.

When the curriculum document is first distributed, it is not really considered a finished product. It must be validated by the teachers who use it, and changes or slight modifications are often needed. Likewise, through validation and staff development processes, additional suggestions can be presented — to add to the task analysis sheets. Teachers who were not on the Subject Area Committee may have terrific ideas that have not yet been shared. And all teachers — whether or not they served on the committee — often come up with new ideas when they actually get into the instructional process. If all of these ideas are added to the task analysis sheets during the implementation year, the revised document will be a tremendous resource for any teacher, new or experienced, who teaches this subject.

There is an additional use to consider for task analysis forms and the task analysis process: they make a terrific staff development activity for districts just beginning outcome-based education. The activity should be led by the curriculum coordinator or another educator who thoroughly understands the process of teaching to outcomes. Staff members are provided with blank task analysis forms. The coordinator selects a topic that is common to all, and leads the group to state the topic as an outcome, and then analyze the outcome to fill in the rest of the form. The coordinator carefully guides discussion so that all of the questions suggested in this section are addressed. After working together on one or two samples, teachers can work in small groups to prepare a task analysis sheet for something each of them actually teaches.

The following pages are sample task analyses for one outcome in each of the big four subject areas.

Grade Level or Course: Grade 1 Science

Outcome: Students will research and develop hypotheses on the causes of shadows and the causes of changes in shadows.

Tasks to Accomplish	Teaching Methods	Student Activities	Means of Assessment	Mastery Criteria and Evidence	Extensions
Research the causes of shadows.	Class discussion.	Discuss experiences: where have we seen shadows? what kinds of shadows have we seen?			Have students work in pairs or small groups with assigned roles.
	Trip to playground.	Observation: find shadows on playground. What makes them?			Visit the library; find and read stories about shadows.
	Classroom experiements.	Use lamps, flashlights, projector (any other light sources) — experiment to see how shadows are made.	Teacher observation: Evaluate student participation in research activities.	Each student must actually manipulate the materials, not just observe. Active particpation is the only criterion.	
Develop hypothesis for causes of shadows.	Class chart and discussions. Cooperative group experiements.	Make class chart together: examples of paired items (light source and object) that make shadows — draw conclusions to reach hypothesis: light shining on object makes shadow of the object.	Students explain in their own words that light shining on an object casts a shadow of that object.	yes or no (can or cannot) criterion. Student must be able to make the statement.	Students perform tests with the specific items of the assessment to verify or refute their conclusions.
			Given a set of pictures of objects that includes but is not limited to pictures of various light sources, students circle the pictures that could cause shadows.	80% proficiency.	
			Students choose appropriate tools and demonstrate causing a shadow.	Each student must successfully create at least one shadow.	

Grade 1 Science (continued)

Tasks to Accomplish	Teaching Methods	Student Activities	Means of Assessment	Mastery Criteria and Evidence	Extensions
Research causes of changes in shadows.	Cooperative group experiments.	Work cooperatively in groups; use light sources, people, objects, and diffusers — place people and objects in front of light in different positions, distances, through diffusers (containers of water, prisms, etc.). Record experiment — illustration or writing.	Observation of student participation. Evaluate records of experiments.	Active participation by each student. Words and/or pictures must show position of objects relative to light source.	Give oral explanation of experiments. Visit museum or view prints to see how shadow is used in art work. Create pictures using shadow.
Develop hypothesis for causes of shadows.	Share results of experiments; class discussion.	Groups share illustrations or written records with rest of class, draw conclusions to reach hypothesis: size and shape of shadow affected by variables — distance of object from light source; position of object; additional object between a light source and object.	Students name one (or more) variable that affects size/shape of shadow and explain — orally or through illustration or demonstration — how shadow is affected. Given a list of variables, students indicate those that affect changes in shadows.	Student's explanation must be accurate. 90% proficiency.	Students place an object in front of a light source and trace the shadow; repeat the process several times, moving object closer or further from light. Compare tracings to conclude that distance affects size of shadow. Students use hand puppets to produce a "shadow play." Puppets used in front of light source to act out story; audience watches shadows on the wall. Students vary distance and position of puppets relative to light to create "giants," miniatures, or strange-shaped characters.

Grade Level or Course: Grade 3 Mathematics

Outcome: Students, using play money, will determine total value and identify exact money needed for simulated purchases up to $9.99.

Tasks to Accomplish	Teaching Methods	Student Activities	Means of Assessment	Mastery Criteria and Evidence	Extensions
Define money and identify value of coins and bills from penny to $5 bill.	Use models to guide discussion. Small group activities.	Class discussion. Matching games. Distribute money randomly; students come forward when their amount is called.	Given play money, students respond to "show me." Shown a coin or bill, student names amount.	Student will be asked to show each coin and bill at least twice. Must have 100% accuracy. 100% accuracy.	Flash card recognition. Examine and identify coins from other countries.
Determine different combinations to equal same amount.	Demonstration followed by guided practice.	Use manipulatives to discover combinations. Practice worksheets.	Written test. Play "Let's trade" (If I give you my coins for yours, is it a good deal?)	90% At conclusion of trading period, all students must have same or greater amount of money that they started with.	Second set of manipulatives. Wrap coins for exchange at bank.
Find the sum of 2 or 3 money amounts.	Lecture/demonstration: adding with decimal point and dollar sign, estimating.	Practice worksheets. Oral responses requiring estimation and mental math.	Written test. Challenge: estimate amount needed for...	80% Student estimates must be correct to nearest dollar for two of each three attempts.	Use play money to count amounts needed. Make up samples for classmates to estimate.
Determine value of a purchase; identify combinations of money needed.	Cooperative learning.	Each group given a variety of items to purchase; determine appropriate combinations of money.	Evaluate group decisions.	Group may use any coin/bill combinations, but must have correct total — 100% for items assigned.	Peer tutoring. Activities to do during family shopping trips.
Determine total value of multiple items and identify exact money needed.	Simulation.	Play store – use play money to purchase multiple items in store.	Evaluate store participation and accuracy. Present each child with item to purchase; require exact amount.	Shopper and clerk check each other's accuracy (as well as teacher). Students erring on 2 or more purchases will need correctives. 100% accuracy.	Use catalogues to choose items and determine money needed. Guest speaker from retail business to discuss applications.

Grade Level or Course: Grade 7 English

Outcome: Students will read a selection of their choice from the required 7th grade reading list; plan and participate in group presentations about the stories; compare problems or dilemmas of main characters or actions taken; and write short evaluative essays about the character behaviors using correct grammar, spelling and punctuation.

Tasks to Accomplish	Teaching Methods	Student Activities	Means of Assessment	Mastery Criteria and Evidence	Extensions
Review basic punctuation and grammar.	Brief lecture and use of questioning.	Small group work: prepare practice sheets; trade, work, and correct.	Written quiz.	90% proficiency.	•Write sentences requiring particular grammar/punctuation determined to be problem. •Peer tutoring. •Read short stories; find examples of appropriate grammar/punctuation. •Computer self-help program.
Select and read stories.	Assist students with appropriate selections. Individual conferences as they progress.	Read. Conference with teacher. Outline highlights to share later with group.	Individual conferences to check: acceptable reading rate; comprehension; outlines.	Reading rate should allow conclusion by 5th day. Student must accurately summarize selected portions to demonstrate comprehension. Outline must be in proper form and must correlate with amount read each day.	•Paired students read a selection together. •Students prepare an audio recording of selected book for others to listen to.
Make vocabulary lists; create dictionaries.	Conferences. Supervise computer project. Emcee game.	Make vocabulary list as story is read. Use software to create dictionaries. Play Jeopardy-type game to practice use of vocabulary and spelling.	Vocabulary list is evaluated. Participation and success in game. Spot quizzes as conferences continue.	Vocabulary list must include at least 5 words per day, correctly spelled and defined. Students must correctly answer at least one question for game participation. Spot quizzes: 75% proficiency on spelling; 90% on definition.	•Cooperative learning for small groups needing additional practice. •Expand dictionary by adding words from other classes, interests.
Groups of same story plan and make presentation.	Cooperative learning strategies.	Discussion, decision-making and action for skit, panel discussion, puppet show, collage presentation, rap, etc.	Products and performances: by total group participation, clarity, detail.	Everyone in group must have a role in product and presentation. Clarity and detail must include accurate and chronological descriptions of major characters, dilemma, solution, and conclusion.	•Make presentations to other classes.

Grade 7 English (continued)

Tasks to Accomplish	Teaching Methods	Student Activities	Means of Assessment	Mastery Criteria and Evidence	Extensions
Make comparisons.	Whole class discussion. Group project.	Group work to prepare bulletin board that lists and compares characters and actions.	Compare main characters of earlier-read stories to bulletin board information (application).	Student must accurately describe at least three similarities or differences between previous story and selected one from bulletin board.	•Start with simple, well-known short story, e.g., fairy tale; identify main characters and actions; repeat with progressively more sophisticated stories; compare each set. •Compare own behaviors/choices to book character's. •Identify current events/issues that parallel book problems/dilemmas.
Write essays; peer critique; make corrections.	Instructions. Guidance to individuals as needed.	Write essays to evaluate actions of main characters. Use personal dictionaries for vocabulary/spelling. Partner critique rough draft; make corrections.	Summative*.	Student may have no more than three errors each in spelling, grammar and punctuation. Comparison must be accurate and supported by at least three examples.	•Students select any characters from stories of their choice to practice identifying, evaluating, and comparing characters/behaviors. •Oral evaluations. •Write simple summaries. •Peer tutoring. •Select main character and write story with alternative solution. •Attend movie and evaluate/compare character behaviors to book's.

*Summative evaluation: Provide short story to read. Students write short essay on character behavior...analysis and comparison to unit's characters. No peer critique. Teacher checks content (analysis, evaluative thinking) and writing skills (grammar, spelling, punctuation). Students provided rubics (File E-7).

Grade Level or Course: High School American Government

Outcome: Students will analyze the impact of American political behaviors and political participation on functions of government and creation of public policy.

Tasks to Accomplish	Teaching Methods	Student Activities	Means of Assessment	Mastery Criteria and Evidence	Extensions
Analyze political behavior and participation.	Lecture & discussion: general; political cartoons.	Take notes. Analyze selected readings. Whole class discuss and interpret cartoons.	Questioning; written test.	Each student must either respond to oral question or refute/support someone else's response. Written test: 80% proficiency.	Foreign exchange students explain systems and participations in their countries. Conduct interviews of family members or friends to determine why they vote and what influences their vote.
	Cooperative learning.	Make political cartoons; present to class for interpretation/discussion. Make campaign posters.	Evaluate cartoon presentations and campaign posters.	Cartoon must reflect a real situation, which must be identifiable in depiction by majority of class. Poster must be legible and include t least three major points about candidate/issue.	
	Moderate debate.	Debate voter rights.	Evaluate debate participation and content.	Students must: stick to the issue; give supporting evidence; justify conclusion.	Interview county clerk regarding voting rights.
Evaluate the way government reacts to public opinion in forming public policy (Party politics)	Lecture & discussion.	Note taking; discussion; present own opinions.	Evaluate participation and discussion content.	All students must participate; content must be relevant.	Organize support within the school for political candidates.
	Cooperative learning.	Design party platform. Organize a political campaign.	Evaluate platforms and campaigns plans.	Must match rubric distributed to students (teacher's file C-4).	Chart campaign issues; determine influences of priorities.
	Moderate debate.	Debate: Face the Nation; political issues.	Evaluate debate participation and content.	Must match rubric distributed to students (teacher's file C-4).	Participate in a real political campaign.
	Editorial assignment.	Write or give oral editorial regarding political candidate or platform.	Evaluate editorial.	Opinion must be logical and supported by detail. Written reports evaluated for content only (not spelling/punctuation).	
	Guest speaker.	Interview political candidate.	Written summative test.	Evaluated according to rubric distributed to students (teacher's file C-6).	

Task Analysis Basics:

- A task analysis is the process of analyzing an outcome to determine specifically how it is to be accomplished.

- The first component to be identified is the set of learning tasks (units or strands) that are required to achieve the outcome, and these tasks should be prepared in outcome terms as well.

- The remaining components include teaching methods, student activities, assessments, criteria and evidence for mastery, and extensions.

- The task analysis can be recorded on a simple set of forms; completed forms should be included in the curriculum document

- Although the tasks are basically the same for all teachers, the remaining components may vary from one teacher to another; teachers may plan these components to fit their own teaching styles and ideas.

- A task analysis takes the place of traditional lesson plans.

- A task analysis can be a great benefit in helping teachers make the transition from "covering" the curriculum to teaching to outcomes.

- A task analysis helps provide focus, which greatly enhances both instruction and learning.

- A curriculum document that includes task analyses for all the outcomes is a tremendous resource for all teachers teaching the subject.

- A task analysis can also be a useful staff development tool as educators begin the outcome-based processes.

THE CURRICULUM DOCUMENT IN A RESULTS BASED SYSTEM

Most of us in education remember the curriculum guide as being a large document suitable for placing in a drawer and ignoring. Reasons why guides stay unused may vary, but so much time is spent on their preparation that disuse ought to be a major concern in every district. Teachers have a right to feel angry over devoting so much energy into the writing of a guide, only to see it wasted or even lost.

Our research into the matter has resulted in the conclusion that guides are rarely used because they are: (1) not respected enough for teachers to feel true ownership; (2) overly complicated and hard to use, especially for those teaching multiple subjects; (3) insufficient for meeting the needs of highly creative teachers; and (4) disseminated to teachers with very little attention given to on-going faculty development (to include newly-hired teachers).

In this section, attention will be given to overcoming those four problems. But first, we need to examine the curriculum guide in this era of outcome-based education and mastery learning, and how it is different from what we've come to expect.

Curriculum Guides: The Old Versus the New

Older curriculum guides are based on scope and sequence charts, units of instruction, and topics to be covered. Often topics are written in terms of student competencies so that the teacher may identify what should be learned before students move to the next level of learning. And just as often those topics or student competencies are broken into incredibly infinitesimal categories, creating long lists that can intimidate even the most precise teacher.

Traditional curriculum guides are created with so much detail included because the committee that creates them wants to be certain each aspect of the learning program is covered, and that student competency is the result. Teachers feel intimidated because the committee, through the curriculum guide, tries to micro-manage the teaching act....a logistically and psychologically inappropriate function. Textbooks are easier to use because in general they focus more on *units to cover* than on student competency. Teachers tend to fall back on what makes them feel more comfortable, so curriculum guides based on "trivial pursuit" *student competencies* are shelved in favor of textbooks based on "trivial pursuit" *topics to cover.* Both result in a minimally effective instructional program.

As we think about the new kind of curriculum document, it is important to understand that the goals of traditional educational programs and the newer outcome-based/mastery learning systems are fundamentally different. As indicated previously, the academic program is to be *designed down*, with high achievement outcomes in mind. And in most cases, such a high achievement outcome will focus on an application that can be understood and respected by students. In other words, the teacher is to focus on the use of a skill or new area of knowledge, not on the little pieces of learning that may or may not be necessary to master the application.

Most teachers find such a holistic notion of teaching and learning to be disconcerting in that there is a fear that students will be given insufficient guidance in mastering the "basics." It makes more sense to them to help students understand basic principles of a subject before they begin applying them on a larger stage. They say, "students must learn the fundamentals associated with reading before they can use their reading to solve problems and reach higher levels of thought." Advocates of outcome-based education have no quarrel with that idea so long as the teacher never forgets that the ultimate high achievement outcome is more important than the learning essentials that go into it. As things stand now, some teachers have a tendency to think of reading as a science unto itself when, in fact, it is simply a cognitive tool which allows human beings to do something else more effectively and efficiently.

One reason why students who initially loved school learn to dislike it may lie in the fact that what was once seen in kindergarten and first grade as meaningful and challenging has become trite and of little consequence in their lives. Reading, writing, and calculating are intellectual tools for accomplishing something more, and that "something more" should be found in high achievement outcomes that, by their very definition, are *not* "trite and of little consequence." That idea under girds the structure of an outcome-based curriculum document; its focus is not on incidental topics or highly specific competencies, but rather on outcomes that have real applications for students in their current lives, and in both their short-term and long-term future.

Overcoming Typical Curriculum Guide Problems

As mentioned earlier, there are four reasons why curriculum guides are all but useless in most districts: *no teacher ownership, complex formats, a sterile and bureaucratic appearance that discourages creativity,* and *inadequate use of faculty development for guide implementation.* There are numerous reasons for those inadequacies.

Ownership Problems: Districts commonly appoint curriculum committees of teachers who represent their colleagues, and the same process is true of the model used by the Curriculum Leadership Institute. The difference is that the Institute's model follows an Action Agenda (see p. 119), which begins with a fairly precise information-gathering technique that focuses on what teachers are currently doing within the "real" (actually taught) curriculum. Moreover, the model's Subject Area Committee is designed to confer dynamically with all teachers and support personnel in the district as they go through the process of analysis and decision-making. The next steps of the Action Agenda are also inclusive, in that a subject mission statement must be collaboratively built, and the development and implementation of the curriculum are considered to be long-term procedures that are inherent to faculty development. Contrast that way of doing things with the more commonly applied methods used by *ad hoc* committees, which sometimes devise a curriculum guide exclusively out of external mandates and use decision-making processes that rely solely on the intuitive powers of committee members.

Complex Formats and Bureaucratic Appearance: The second and third problems are related and center on a penchant for developing a complex format for curriculum guides. While scope and sequence charts are useful, it is much less helpful for teachers to gaze upon page after page of precise competencies and charts that depict graduated levels of instruction and student learning. While the general concept of "I" (for Introductory) is easy enough to understand, it is actually too vague to be of any use in directing instruction. If something is to be "introduced," does that mean that a full concept is taught, but no real learning is expected, or does it mean that only "some" material is taught, and if so... how much? Likewise, what does it really mean when "R" (for Reinforcement) or "E" (for Extension) are used? And, unless it is carefully defined and commonly accepted, "M" (for Mastery) is more akin to "M" for Mystery.

Our claim that curriculum documents should not follow such a format may be viewed by some as conflicting with the entire previous section — the task analysis process, which is a very detailed prescription for teaching to an outcome and includes identification of mastery levels and extensions to be used. However, there are two vast differences between the "introduce, master, reinforce" curriculum guides and one that lists high achievement outcomes supported by task analyses. In the former, what is specific is the **topic** — not what is meant by "introduce" or "master." Additionally, as pointed out before, those topics (all required) are so narrow that teachers feel micro-managed and that they are allowed no creativity.

In contrast, what is required in the second type of document is the **outcome** — what each student must be able to do as a *result* of participating in the learning process. Specifically what that learning process is varies from one teacher to another. The task analyses included in the guide are samples only. Their use in faculty development activities helps each teacher learn how to get rid of vague claims that something has been "taught" or "mastered by students." Instead, **teachers assert their own professionalism and creativity** in determining <u>how</u> to teach, assess, and evaluate learning and they use the task analysis process to specifically document the process. Teachers who are less creative or just prefer more direct prescription often choose to use the sample task analyses as written. Likewise, teachers who have balked at curriculum guides before, particularly experienced teachers who have a creative bent, are not opposed to following a curriculum document if it isn't confusing, immersed in trivia, and characteristic of rigid and bureaucratic thinking.

Inadequate Faculty Development: Finally, the most serious problem with curriculum guides is that few districts take them seriously enough that they are systematically implemented through intensive and on-going forms of faculty development. Too often the guides are placed in teachers' mailboxes with a note attached that indicates the principal's desire that they be used... mainly because fellow teachers put so much time into their development. That's it! There is rarely a systematic method for helping teachers understand the rationale behind a new document or to show them how their teaching is to be influenced by it. There is no monitoring of the document to check for intended improvements in the program or the quality of student learning, and there is no mechanism for making modifications that respond to changes in the academic program. Moreover, in this era of outcome-based education, any document using high achievement outcomes will simply confuse teachers who have not been prepared to accept the new paradigm.

Proposed New Format for Curriculum Documents

Curriculum documents need to be kept simple and easy to use. That is the most important principle when a Subject Area Committee begins to put their decisions in writing. It must be remembered that there is no such thing as a fool-proof curriculum document, and that each will be used by highly intelligent professional educators who are expected to transfer the intended academic program to effective classroom instruction and quality student learning. True, even the most capable teachers will need to be taught how to use new documents, but that use must be translated into "interacting with," as well as "being directed by." In short, teachers are not pawns in a system; they *are* the system, and materials used to help them do their jobs should recognize that fact.

Ordinarily, our style of curriculum document contains eight essential components: (1) *Introduction*, (2) *Acknowledgments*, (3) *Effective Dates of Document*, (4) *District Mission Statement*, (5) *Subject Area Mission*, (6) *Grade Level/Course Purposes*, (7) *High Achievement Outcomes*, and (8) *Sample Task Analyses*.

Introduction: The introduction is merely a statement that describes the document and offers directions as to how it ought to be used. This section is also a good place to indicate the importance of on-going faculty development, and how that program will be conducted. Above all, faculty members should know that the document does not stand alone, that it is merely a volume of pages developed so that more substantive communication can occur among all the district's educators. Although it describes essential learning outcomes, it is not the end-all in terms of curriculum development and maintenance.

Acknowledgments: It is always important to recognize those who spent so much time preparing a document. Acknowledgments are expressions of appreciation that mean much to those who spent many hours working on what sometimes can be a tedious task.

Effective Dates: Amazingly, there are curriculum documents that provide no indication whatever of when they were written. It is critical that documents have publication dates in a prominent location, and that subsequent changes be dated as well.

District Mission Statement: The district mission statement, which is the working "vision" for everything done in the academic program, should be in all curriculum documents. All pages after the district mission statement should meet the test of "design down" alignment, a test that should be administered frequently by the Curriculum Coordinating Council and Board of Education.

Subject Area Mission: The specific mission of the subject area should be included next; this is especially important in those cases where the subject area is the product of interdisciplinary curricular fusion. For example, whole language processes require units of instruction that are thematic in nature. In that situation it is easy to forget the primary mission of a subject area if curricular themes and units of instruction are both nontraditional and based on high achievement outcomes. There is no such thing as too much clarity in the focus of an intended curriculum, and it is here that clarity of focus becomes imperative.

Grade Level/Courses Purposes: As indicated in previous sections, topics are narrowed according to a focus area, which is then extended into a specific purpose for each grade level and course. Those purposes should be listed on a page or two near the beginning of the document, and also shown above the lists of high achievement outcomes designated for each grade level and course.

High Achievement Outcomes: Under each grade level or course purpose are listed five to fifteen high achievement outcomes. These outcomes not only identify **essential** student learning topics, but state precisely what it is the students should know or be able to do at the conclusion of instructional processes for those topics.

Sample Task Analyses: As explained earlier, the task analysis is a process that helps teachers change from "covering material" to actually achieving a desired specific result. When a teacher has a finished set of task analyses for all of the outcomes in his or her course or grade level, they are terrific time savers in terms of lesson planning, assessment, and documentation or grade reporting. However, completing those task analyses is *at first* time consuming and fairly complicated. **It is imperative that staff development be planned to provide training for all teachers in the task analysis process.** It is equally important that at least some task analyses for each grade level and course be included in the document so that teachers can use them — just as they are — or as samples to follow when they do the task analysis process themselves during implementation of the new curriculum.

Curriculum Document Basics:

- The Subject Area Committee develops the curriculum document by following an Action Agenda that requires interaction and collaboration with other district educators.

- The format of the document should be simple and direct rather than lengthy, complex and overly detailed.

- Curriculum documents should be systematically implemented through intensive and on-going forms of faculty development.

- The curriculum document includes eight essential components: Introduction, Acknowledgments, Effective Dates, District Mission Statement, Subject Area Mission, Grade Level/Course Purposes, High Achievement Outcomes, and Sample Task Analyses.

APPROVING THE CURRICULUM DOCUMENT

When the Subject Area Committee has completed all components of the curriculum document and is satisfied with the finished product, the document is ready to be presented to others for approval. The first group to critique the document is the Curriculum Coordinating Council. For the most part, this critique is just a formality. Remember that every SAC has at least one member (ordinarily the chairperson) who is also a member of the CCC; this person has been providing reports at every CCC meeting about the SAC's progress, including important discussions held, decisions made, and any dilemmas or decisions needing CCC input or approval. Therefore, the completed document should hold no surprises. However, CCC members will be anxious to see the end result of the year's work, and they also need the opportunity to examine the new curriculum in detail, pose and receive answers to questions that come up upon examination of the document, and offer any suggestions they may have as to format. CCC members should also check to be sure the new curriculum adheres to any policy that has been set and — if it is not the first subject's document to be presented — that it is consistent with previous documents and any interdisciplinary outcomes that have been determined.

When all questions and suggestions have been satisfied and the CCC has approved the completed document, it is ready to be presented to the Board of Education. Just as there should have been no surprises about the document for the CCC, the same is true for board members. In most districts, at least one board member serves on the CCC. So, just as the SAC chairperson has been keeping the CCC informed of decisions and progress, the board's CCC member has been keeping the rest of the board equally informed. However, at this time the document is <u>formally</u> presented to the board for approval. The presentation is made by the curriculum coordinator, the SAC chairperson, and any other SAC members who are available. Two or three of these representatives should address the board, pointing out specific components that make this document different from previous ones. Remaining members of the SAC are introduced, but they are there mainly to show their support for the new document. Questions from board members are fielded by any member of the group.

It needs to be made clear to both the CCC and the Board of Education, that **while this document is to be viewed as the new curriculum, it has not yet been implemented or internally validated**; therefore, it is not a final version, and some changes will undoubtedly be made during the coming school year. Some boards approve the new document during the same meeting at which it is presented; others accept the document but delay approval until the next meeting so they can peruse it in greater detail. If board members have minor suggestions about the document, these can be addressed during the implementation/validation process. However, any major concerns may require another meeting of the SAC for correction. The board votes to approve the document, and is bound by the same guidelines as for any other decision requiring a vote — usually a simple majority is required for passage.

VALIDATION OF THE NEW CURRICULUM

As you know, a major part of the theory underlying the governance structure of our improvement model is based on the work of William Edwards Deming. Deming is essentially a management theorist <u>and</u> industrial statistician. That point needs to be made because Deming mixes careful analysis with intelligent ways of working with human beings. He emphasizes the idea that the production of quality goods and services is not possible without precise analysis and humane management practices, and that those two conditions must be mutually reinforcing. While most Americans find that idea to be good common sense, they quickly learn there is much more to it when implementation is attempted.

American managers tend to believe that the only good method for checking quality is to assign supervisors to constantly look over a worker's shoulder. The supervisor, who theoretically has a clear set of criteria as to what quality should be, makes certain that the worker meets those criteria to the letter. The worker, on the other hand, learns to resent the supervisor and even the company's criteria for quality, and that conscious or subconscious resentment leads to a subtle sabotage against the organization.

While teachers rarely have supervisors standing over them watching every move, there is a penchant in this era of "accountability" for administrators to find different (supposedly better) ways to "check quality." The most common method we hear about is the criterion-referenced test that is supposed to prove whether the teacher is doing a good job by assessing student knowledge of a prescribed and taught curriculum. Most teachers dislike that idea if it is a <u>primary</u> means for checking instructional quality, as much as Deming would dislike product testing as a primary means for checking worker commitment to excellence.

The Accountability Based Curriculum Model is focused on a mission and <u>everyone's</u> commitment to it—and that commitment most especially involves the teacher. A teacher who is treated respectfully as a professional partner will commit to quality as it is presented and interpreted by the organization's mission statement.

Deming's Methods and the Practice of Curriculum Validation

In the Subject Area Committee's Action Agenda, some validation takes place during the curriculum development process, but most of it falls in the second year as teachers implement the new curriculum. Validation is simply a pilot test to make sure the curriculum document works the way it should. And, like anything new, that document is not likely to be problem-free. Problems must be identified and corrected as much as humanly possible before material resources are selected and a long-term evaluation program is implemented.

In Deming's world of industrial management he would insist on attention to detail in validating the use of a procedure or tool. Every process and piece of equipment would undergo intense scrutiny to be certain that tolerances are as close as possible, and that all procedures lead to consistent quality. In an automobile, a doorlatch that doesn't cause the door to shut with perfect flushness and alignment with the body will be redesigned or completely replaced. There is no such thing as "that's good enough," but rather there is an attitude that upholds standards no matter how much extra time and work are involved. For a process to be valid in Deming's world of industry, standards cannot be set without attention to detail ... ..how does the doorlatch perform after it has been opened and shut 10,000 times, or does it keep the door aligned after the car's body has been twisted in both directions .5 of a centimeter? And if the door hasn't remained aligned, does it exceed the baseline tolerance of only a .15 cm. variance?

Is that definition of validation alien to us who are educators? It may not translate into how we work with human beings, so let's use an example that is a little closer to our professional home. A few years ago a community college district asked for our help in designing and implementing a curriculum that was to be market-focused. The college district had already analyzed the needs of businesses in the region and had drawn conclusions as to what vocational programs were necessary to make its students good prospective employees in local industries. Next, they had analyzed their current course offerings, and found them to be everywhere from archaic to totally irrelevant in terms of vocational training.

The administrators worked with the instructors in developing a series of courses that were better aligned with market needs, and began systematically validating them according to how well students could perform the functions needed by local businesses. They found that some courses were out of proper sequence, that a few left out essential areas of learning, and that others tended to cover too much material. They also found that traditional students weren't ready for certain sophisticated concepts, while the nontraditional students who had been in the workplace before coming to college had little difficulty.

All of this information was systematically assembled, recorded, and used in the redesign of the curriculum. Deming would have approved, because the program's quality was assessed in terms of whether the student could perform in a quality manner at the end of the training program. The college didn't use industrial statistics to make the appropriate changes, but it did follow an analytic and systematic procedure. It also thoroughly involved the instructors, because a validation process has no long-term meaning without the committed ownership of those who must make revised programming work.

True, a K-12 public school district is neither an auto plant nor a community college with a vocational mission, but both of those examples can be instructive. A public school district that commits to outcome-based curriculum and instruction must promote both quality and instructional focus in highly tangible ways. Curriculum validation is the first process through which those goals are accomplished. To be valid, an outcome-based curriculum document must focus on essential areas of learning and promote high quality teaching. That document must take into account student readiness and self esteem, the needs of society and the marketplace, qualifications for admission to some sort of post-secondary education (vocational or college), accreditation, and the perspectives of learned societies, as well as those associated with norm- and criterion-referenced tests that are currently in vogue.

Methods for Validating a K-12 Curriculum

Let us assume that the Pleasant Valley School District has developed an outcome-based curriculum document in science. The document contains all the elements we've discussed in our model, including the district mission statement, subject area mission statement, course and grade level purposes, ten to fifteen high achievement outcomes per course or grade level, and student learning tasks for each outcome. An extensive faculty development program was started just before school was out for the summer to show teachers how to use the document. That faculty development program was continued at the beginning of the new school year and it helped teachers develop their own task analyses for accomplishing the intended outcomes. Throughout the year, teachers were taught how to use cooperative learning strategies and methods for incorporating a knowledge of student learning styles into the instructional program. Methods to assess student learning were also covered in some detail, with particular attention given to helping teachers develop portfolio assessments appropriate to expected levels of learning.

This faculty development program was interwoven with a feedback system so that teachers affected by the new curriculum were encouraged to share successful strategies with one another, and to discuss their frustrations and concerns. This new curriculum document, unlike past ones they had received, was not presented to them as being perfect. They knew it probably had problems, and that some of those problems could be serious.

Teachers were told that it was more than just appropriate to report problems—that it was absolutely essential if the curriculum was to last more than a few months. They were also told that their concerns and recommendations would not be ignored or lost; that every statement about the new curriculum would be heard, seriously studied, and applied to a modification program if other educators involved in the project agreed. Teachers were initially skeptical that their suggestions would be accepted, and even more skeptical that a system could be employed that would actually move their ideas into some sort of definitive action. Teachers accustomed to past forms of lip service had to be shown that this was really a different way of doing things.

What were teachers shown? They were shown processes and forms that indicated a district commitment to the outcomes approach to learning, and those processes and forms were divided into two validation components: internal and external. Internal validation was a function of the teachers themselves, while external validation focused on the influences from **constituencies** (parents, businesses, colleges, and community groups) and **agencies that oversee the schools** (state departments of education, accrediting associations, and organizations that create and administer tests).

Although internal and external validation should be considered separately, they must at some point merge to have an influence on the academic program. Let us first consider them separately.

Internal Validation

Internal validation usually applies to five considerations: (1) appropriateness of content, (2) appropriateness of sequence, (3) student readiness, (4) suitability to teaching methods, and (5) availability of resources. Here are the questions that should be asked in each of the above categories:

1. **Is the course content appropriate?**

Is each of the ten to fifteen high achievement outcomes for students at this grade level pertinent to essential learning goals shown in district and subject area mission statements?

Is it possible to create assessments for each of the high achievement outcomes that focus on performance and real-life applications?

2. Is the sequence of instruction appropriate?

Some outcomes stand alone and can be taught at any time of year, but others must be taught in order. Is the listed sequence of outcomes used in this class or course appropriate, or should the outcomes be reorganized in order to facilitate student learning? ("A" should be learned before "B," and "B" must come before "C"?)

Is the sequence logical and appropriate not only within a class or course, but from one class/course to the next?

Is sufficient reinforcement of learning built into the curriculum of this course or class to assure retention of learning?

3. Are students ready for this curriculum?

Are learning expectations at levels either too abstract or too elementary for students in this course or class?

Have students been given sufficient prior learning experiences to meet the challenges associated with the high achievement outcomes used in this course or class?

Can all students achieve success — and be challenged — at the newer level of expectation?

4. Is this new program suited to my teaching methods?

Does the new curriculum fit with my current teaching methods?

If new teaching methods are recommended, do they seem to improve the quality of student learning?

5. Are resources available to support the teaching of these outcomes?

Can we identify and locate any of the following resources to support the teaching of these outcomes: textbooks, miscellaneous publications, other print materials, software, manipulatives, audio or video aids, community resources, human resources, or models?

If inadequate resources are available, what specific kinds of resources are needed to assure quality teaching and student learning?

A simple form can be developed and duplicated for teachers to fill out througout the year as they teach the new curriculum. On the top of the page is a place for the teacher to indicate which outcome is now in progress. Next appears a set of questions such as those listed above. In many cases, a one-word response — "Yes" — is all the teacher needs to reply. However, space is provided after each question for comments. If the answer is "no," then the teacher writes a brief explanation of the problem, or the space can be used simply for more detail or for suggestions.

It is important that these forms be returned to the SAC on a regular basis. If revisions are necessary, they can be thoughtfully considered and made throughout the year rather than left to the hectic last few weeks of school. Some districts have teachers fill out the form whenever they complete an outcome. Others have teachers submit a form each week, even though they haven't completed the outcome. Teachers often find that *some parts* (tasks) of the outcome are good, while others are more troublesome, and responding to the separate tasks provides a clearer picture of the strengths and weaknesses of the particular outcome. **In fact, in many districts, teachers use a task analysis form in place of the regular lesson plan book for this particular subject.** Questions such as those above are printed on the back of the task analysis forms, and copies of the forms are submitted to the SAC. In this way, the SAC members have not only the responses to the questions they've asked, they also have numerous task analysis sheets to include in the final, revised document. This makes the curriculum document a tremendous resource as it not only lists the outcomes to be taught, but provides suggestions from all the teachers for teaching methods, activities, means of assessment, and extensions.

External Validation

As mentioned earlier, external validation is a matter of aligning the curriculum with the expectations of constituencies and agencies that oversee the schools. Most often such external validation must be managed at the district curriculum coordinator level. That individual, or someone assigned to that office, should be responsible for building a data-base which can be shared regularly with both the curriculum coordinating council and subject area committees. Some accrediting agencies already ask districts to sponsor individuals who are responsible for creating a data-base; they are occasionally referred to as "resource specialists" or "directors of institutional research." They accept responsibility for creating and disseminating surveys, and performing various other kinds of functions that would generate information as to the perspectives of external groups. They must also take responsibility for conducting follow-up studies of students, to determine whether or not the school district's program is adequately preparing graduates and transfer students for their subsequent educational or vocational experiences.

Although the curriculum coordinator collects much of the research and data related to external validation, the SAC is also actively involved in the process. Many SAC members belong to subject-specific professional organizations and through publications and conferences keep up with the research and recommendations from these learned societies. And all SAC members must evaluate external considerations during both the developmental and implementation stages of the new curriculum.

The SAC first begins its external validation early in the first year during the decision-making process. As they work toward selective abandonment of current curriculum topics, they consider the recommendations of the learned societies, such as NCTM standards, AAAS Project 2061, and so forth; additionally, they check state mandates to see if their curriculum choices are compatible. Other external factors are also evaluated throughout the writing process, such as content and processes emphasized in standardized tests, college admission requirements, and state assessments. These factors have less impact and should not drive the curriculum, but still should be considered as another means of validating the new curriculum.

The SAC's external validation continues during the second and third years of their Action Agenda. As the curriculum is implemented and as plans are made for long-term evaluation procedures, criteria such as test scores and success in post-secondary schools and employment are developed.

When extensive data must be collected, treated, and evaluated — for external validation or accreditation purposes— we believe it is particularly important that a district not assign that task to the SAC or some other committee. In all but the smallest districts the job should be given to an administrative specialist who has enough clerical help and funding to do the job well. That person would logically be supervised by the curriculum coordinator. In very small districts (30 teachers or less), the curriculum coordinator might be able to perform that function with sufficient release-time from roles other than those associated with curriculum and instruction.

Validation Basics:

- The practice of validating an outcome-based curriculum involves both systematic processes and the thorough involvement of the teachers who are asked to use it.

- The curriculum is validated *internally*, which means it is evaluated by the teachers who teach it, and *externally*, which means it aligns with the recommendations of learned societies and expectations of constituencies and agencies that oversee the schools.

- Internal validation is conducted in the same year as *implementation* through intensive staff development, and each process depends on the other.

- The primary questions in an internal validation program are: appropriateness of content, appropriateness of sequence, student readiness, suitability to teaching methods, and availability of resources.

- Submission of task analysis forms, through which teachers document how they taught and assessed each aspect of the outcome, is an even more effective means of internal validation.

- External validation begins during the SAC's decision-making process and continues through the implementation process and through long-term evaluation procedures.

- External validation focuses on recommended standards, content and processes associated with standardized tests, post-secondary education and employment requirements, mandates, and learned society research.

- All school districts need a good data-base on which to make decisions; the task of collecting, treating, and evaluating extensive data should be assigned to an administrative specialist.

CURRICULUM IMPLEMENTATION THROUGH A SOUND FACULTY DEVELOPMENT PROGRAM

Let's say it right up front: most of us received inadequate preparation as teachers. The reason for that can be traced to a university/college culture that unduly influences undergraduate "professional" schools of education. Unlike law and medical schools, which enjoy a degree of independence from the internal politics of higher education, schools of education find themselves enmeshed in traditional university thinking regarding scholarship, academic rigor, promotion, and tenure. Because of pressures imposed by university traditions, teacher educators are hampered in trying to change programs to be more responsive to the needs of our nation's young people and the schools they attend. .

All of us can point to unfortunate conditions in our own preparation programs: inadequate field experiences, poorly articulated curriculum, instructors who didn't practice what they teach, professors who hadn't been in a P-12 school in decades, and classes that featured "mickey mouse" subject matter. Moreover, many of the courses in general education and liberal arts and sciences were taught in lecture sections by professors who were less than interested in actually involving students in the subjects they taught. Philosophy of education reigned supreme, but there was precious little study of such critical areas as classroom management and discipline, day-to-day methods that accurately assess student learning, and curriculum decision-making. Either by design or by default we were taught to depend on prepared instructional materials instead of learning how we could develop and conduct a challenging and interesting classroom program ourselves. Finally, it is fair to say that many of us were more greatly influenced by our supervising teacher in the student teaching program than by any of the classes taken on campus.

Because of the leadership of educators such as John Goodlad and accrediting bodies such as the National Council for the Accreditation of Teacher Education (NCATE), changes are slowly taking place in our professional preparation programs. In the meantime, public school educators must make up the deficiencies by causing faculty and staff development programs to do two jobs: (1) extend into practice the good aspects of preservice teacher education, and (2) help beginning and more seasoned teachers learn important concepts and practices that were either ignored or given inadequate coverage in their college preparation. Those two on-going faculty development needs would be necessary even if there were few faults in the preservice preparation of teachers, largely because no college can develop an optimally effective teacher in just four or five years.

The Purpose of Faculty Development

Faculty development programs are just like any other kind of educational program: *They should cause a change in behavior that actually improves student learning.* If that criterion were to be applied rigorously, many faculty development programs in which teachers now participate would be deficient. August or September inservice days before school begins are usually a disaster; they are scheduled at a time when teachers can think only about what they must do to initiate the school year. Consequently, administrators try to schedule speakers who are both effective and highly entertaining. Their impact on the teachers, no matter how stimulating the speech, is likely to be minimal. And there is no doubt that the "change in behavior" criterion is met rarely, if at all.

Many administrators and inservice education directors recognize the problem with August or September inservice days, so they now schedule workshops at other times of the year. A number of districts have joined regional service centers or district consortia, which do a better job of focusing on the specific needs of specific educators. Regional service centers offer a menu of workshops for various types of teachers and educational support staff, and often those workshops are many hours or days long. Because educators who participate in those workshops are interested in the content, probably because it pertains to their specific work assignment, there is a much better chance that their behaviors in the classroom or workplace will be positively affected. That is good, but unfortunately the overall impact on student learning is likely to be minimal. The reason is that individual educators working in isolated circumstances do not constitute a total high-quality program; it is akin to an automobile assembly line in which those who make and install dashboards become deeply involved in quality control, while all other technicians continue to operate as they have in the past. Cars rolling off the end of the line have great dashboards, but everything else is inferior.

If it is fair to say that current faculty development programs do not meet the "change in behavior/improved student learning" criterion, then what is better? We advocate that *the best form of faculty development is curriculum development!*

Curriculum Development as Good Faculty Development

William Edwards Deming says that organizations committed to real improvement must view their workers much differently today than in the past. Workers are not merely pawns in a system, with the only reward for their efforts to be a salary and benefit package. He says that salary, benefits, and pats on the back for meeting the expectations of executives are not enough to improve quality. Workers must feel that they are an inherent part of the enterprise, valued members of a team that can take pride in what it accomplishes.

Faculty members and those educators who support their efforts are much more than workers. They are professionals who should be making important decisions about how their work is to be conducted and how those decisions can be implemented assertively and effectively. Teachers who are in a position to assert their professionalism are much more likely to be a positive force in the drive to improve instructional programs and the overall quality of student learning. It isn't possible to assert one's professionalism sitting in an auditorium listening to the most recent educational guru, or participating in a faculty meeting in which the principal gives announcements, directions and admonishments. It isn't possible to assert one's professionalism when a teacher who has participated in an effective workshop finds that no one back home pays any attention as to how newly discovered ideas can influence the total program of the school. Asserting professionalism is possible only when an organizational dynamic is created that systematically allows open communication and vigorous faculty interaction. The key term in the previous sentence is "systematical-ly," because the necessary kind of organizational dynamic is not merely the product of a leader's personality or drive; it is a pervasive way of doing things, a setting that accepts and even encourages creativity and diverse thinking in the collective effort to produce high-quality.

Curriculum development is the best form of faculty development because it involves teacher teams making important decisions about what should be taught and when it should be offered. Teams talk about the fundamental mission of the school, and how to align the school's activities with that mission. They discuss definitions for mastery and the methods for assessing student learning that are in accordance with such definitions. They study the recommendations of the learned societies and con-duct various forms of action research in order to improve the quality of academic pro-grams and student learning. They conduct meetings of community members, par-ents, students and other constituents, which produce additional recommendations for improvement. And, probably most important, they conduct meetings in which teachers, administrators, and support persons are able to discuss issues and make deci-sions as professional colleagues.

What would happen if no more August and September inservice meetings were scheduled (except for new teachers)? Time usually scheduled for inservice edu-cation would be used to get school under way smoothly and efficiently.

What would happen if no more "speakers" were scheduled for faculty inser-vice days? Teachers could meet in groups to engage in dynamic discussions about the curriculums they are teaching and the results in terms of student learning. They could raise questions, propose solutions to problems, and share successful methodologies. A menu of workshop opportunities might also be available, but with the caveat that workshop participation is for the purpose of improving the total academic program as much as for helping an individual teacher. And there would be ways to make certain that new-found ideas are actually connected to systematically applied improvement projects.

What would happen if teachers and other educators in the district were encouraged to attend professional meetings at state and national levels, and become active in the learned societies (such as the National Council of Teachers of Mathematics)? If educators returning from such meetings were automatically includ-ed in substantive discussions that keep colleagues up-to-date on changes regarding essential learning for students, the district would be in a better position to produc-tively theorize its way toward creative improvements.

And what would happen if teachers (individually and in teams) were encouraged to conduct various forms of action research, not for some college course, but because the results of that research would be useful in improving the quality of curriculum, instruction, and student learning? Action research that leads to an improvement of conditions in a school or classroom, which in turn causes better quality student learning, is always worth the extra time, money and effort.

The obvious follow-up question to the questions shown above is: "What structure is necessary to make certain curriculum development does, in fact, become the best kind of faculty development?"

Curriculum Development, Faculty Development and Structure

Many districts have governing entities for both inservice education and curriculum development. Some states offer teachers the opportunity to obtain recertification points through carefully planned and executed district-sponsored programs. Usually the process involves the submission of a district inservice plan, under which faculty members set their own professional growth goals and activities. Faculty members who meet those goals accumulate sufficient inservice points for recertification. A committee oversees that process, taking care of necessary paperwork, conducting needs-assessment surveys to determine the interests of the teachers, and organizing workshops.

It is our recommendation that professional development committees that oversee district inservice education programs limit their activities to the filing and reporting functions that are important for recertification. Needs-assessment surveys and the organization of key developmental workshops should be eliminated, although there may be opportunities to sponsor certain generic programs of general interest to the district's educators.

The district's curriculum council and its subordinate committees should be responsible for the most important aspects of faculty growth. The curriculum council's members should frequently work with other district teachers and administrators to communicate goals, receive recommendations, and conduct deliberations on various issues pertinent to the district's programs. In districts that use our model, council members will have frequent meetings with groups of teachers to: (1) discuss mission statements, bylaws, long-range plans, and other procedural matters, (2) develop definitions for mastery learning and outcome-based education, (3) prepare baseline procedures for implementing and validating curriculum, (4) develop guidelines for the selection of instructional resources, (5) review processes for the use of portfolio assessment, and (6) create workable techniques for the creation of student assistance components.

Subject Area Committees will dig into those matters even further, using procedures and guidelines established by council actions. In particular, the SAC must plan and conduct faculty development activities for the implementation and validation of the new curriculum.   Too many times, in traditional settings, curriculum guides were prepared in isolation by a committee and then placed in teachers' mailboxes when they were completed.   Period.   No staff development was planned for introducing the new guide or for any follow-up to see if it was being used or if it was valid.   Ask any group of teachers who have received their new guides in this manner what happened to those guides, and you will find an overwhelming response that the guide ended up on a shelf or in a drawer... or lost.

In our model, the curriculum documents are distributed at a well-planned faculty development meeting.   Various members of the SAC take the rest of the faculty through the document almost page-by-page, explaining what is new or different and highlighting examples.   Validation forms are pointed out, and instructions are given for how and when the forms are to be completed and returned.   General questions and concerns are answered and discussed.   Teachers are then given a period of time before another meeting is planned, so that they can peruse the documents on their own, contemplating how they will teach and assess the intended curriculum.   In fact, in many districts, this first meeting takes place right at the end of the school year, so teachers have the entire summer to become familiar with the new curriculum.

The introductory meeting just described is highly recommended as a first step, but *that meeting cannot stand alone!*   Subsequent faculty development sessions must also be planned.   An excellent agenda for the second session is based on the task analysis process, particularly if that process itself is new to the faculty.   SAC members show and discuss a completed task analysis for one of the outcomes.   They then select an outcome that does not already have a completed task analysis and coordinate efforts for the entire group to accomplish one together.   Finally, they break into small groups, each of which collaborates to do a task analysis for an actual outcome of each member of the group.   In districts where the task analysis process is not new, the first step (showing a completed example) could be skipped; however, step two — completing one together — is a good refresher, and step three — the small group work — is a tremendous help to all because of the collaboration and sharing of ideas.

Additional faculty development sessions planned throughout the year can focus on continued sharing of ideas, training in pertinent areas such as cooperative learning and portfolio development, and discussions of strengths and weaknesses of the new curriculum, mastery and expectations, and ways to provide extended opportunities for learning.   Unlike traditional inservice days, these sessions are viewed by faculty members as productive, relevant, and highly professional.   And the feedback they provide to the SAC members for validating or revising the curriculum is invaluable.

It is easy to see that the combined actions of the council and its subordinate committees will more than serve a faculty development function.   In addition, we strongly advocate the concept of teacher leadership in many settings: conducting community meetings, speaking to local service clubs, preparing articles for the news media, making presentations to professional meetings, and writing for professional journals. Sometimes that leadership can be in the form of teams consisting of teachers only, administrators and teachers, support persons and teachers, teachers and parents, and other appropriate configurations. The practice of teachers serving as leaders in adult settings is an important aspect of professional growth, because it is the respect given by other adults that makes us feel truly competent.

Curriculum Implementation/Faculty Development Basics:

- Faculty development is guided by the district's curriculum council under the premise that individual and program growth must be thoroughly linked.

- Faculty development is focused on the idea that educators should be encouraged to assert their professionalism, that they are totally involved in discussions and deliberations, and that they are frequently given leadership opportunities.

- Awareness-level workshops and meetings are scheduled only when necessary, and followed with substantive opportunities to discuss what was learned, and to integrate that learning with the district's total mission.

- The effectiveness of the faculty development program is constantly checked in terms of program improvement and the quality of student learning.

- State plans for recertification through local inservice education programs are carefully integrated with strategies that improve curriculum design and encourage outcome based instruction and mastery learning.

- Administrators encourage teacher attendance and participation in state and national professional meetings. At the time that they approve such trips, the administrators identify a block of time ... such as a faculty meeting, breakfast or luncheon, early dismissal day, or whatever is necessary ... to provide the opportunity for these teachers to lead follow up, substantive discussions with colleagues.

- New curriculum documents are introduced to teachers through well planned faculty development meetings; they are *not* just placed in teacher mailboxes.

- The implementation and validation of the new curriculum are supported through systematic faculty development strategies. These include instruction and guidance for the task analysis process, sharing of ideas, training in pertinent areas such as cooperative learning and portfolio development, and discussions of strengths and weaknesses of the new curriculum, mastery and expectations, and ways to provide extended opportunities for learning.

MAKING REVISIONS TO THE NEW DOCUMENT

During the implementation/validation year the Subject Area Committee should continue to meet on a regular basis in order to validate the curriculum and make any necessary revisions. The SAC will receive *internal* validation information from two sources: (1) the validation forms that teachers fill out and return each week (or when they've completed teaching an outcome), and (2) the discussions that are held during faculty development sessions related to this subject. Based on this information, the SAC first determines whether changes do indeed need to be made. When a curriculum is new, and especially if it is one that requires modification of teaching behaviors, teachers may say that "it isn't working." Through the written comments and discussions, the SAC must analyze the situation to determine if the problem is really with the curriculum itself or with a teacher's frustration with change. If the problem is with the curriculum, then the SAC rewrites whatever portion is necessary to make the correction. If the problem lies in *teaching to* the new curriculum, then plans should be made to provide assistance through such means as continued faculty development, administrative support, mentoring, or peer coaching. (See also EVALUATING CURRICULUM: TEACHER USE.)

Some of the necessary curriculum changes are minor. The SAC may need simply to change a word or phrase to clarify an outcome. For example, part of a seventh grade science outcome said "students will demonstrate an ecosystem." Teachers were immediately confused about what that meant, so the outcome was reworded to say, "students will create a project to illustrate an ecosystem." Sometimes the vague wording of an outcome takes a little more thought to correct. For example, a third grade social studies outcome stated that students would "compare the geographic regions of Kansas." During implementation, it was discovered that some teachers were guiding students to compare industries and economics only, others were comparing topographies and landmarks, and yet another teacher was comparing physical size, population, and history. The SAC had to look at the course purposes and outcomes for third grade and several other grade levels to determine just what it was they wanted students to compare, and then state the outcome accordingly.

Sometimes major changes need to be made in the curriculum. It may be determined that an outcome is not grade-level appropriate, which means it needs to be moved to a different grade level, which in turn can cause problems if the new grade level already has too many outcomes or if the outcome in question does not relate in any way to the focus area of the new grade level. In this case, the SAC must determine just how essential the problem outcome is. Can it be selectively abandoned? If not, then a major "shake-up" may have to take place among two or more grade levels or courses, possibly even effecting the overall purpose of those grade levels/courses.

Other outcomes —particularly those requiring lots of hands-on materials—

may be difficult to implement or validate if those materials are not available. This situation becomes a real "catch-22"; the SAC is reluctant to recommend large expenditures of money without knowing that the outcome will be appropriate and yet it's almost impossible to determine if it's appropriate without the necessary materials. In this situation, one of two things usually happens. In the first instance, the district purchases a **minimal** amount of materials —fairly generic ones that can be used in a variety of circumstances— so that the teachers can implement the outcome at least at an exploratory level, and then predict its appropriateness based on this preliminary instruction. In the second case, the SAC relies on teacher experience and knowledge of student abilities to predict the appropriateness of the outcome even if it cannot be thoroughly implemented the first year. If all other outcomes for the grade level or course are appropriate and the outcome in question "fits" well within the set, the outcome stays in place and materials are purchased for the following year.

All problems reported by teachers, whether minor wording questions or major dilemmas, need to be given appropriate attention by the SAC. And once decisions are made, teachers need to receive feedback so that they know their concerns are taken seriously and trust can be established.

During this same school year, members of the SAC are also working on external validation. Although they've already considered the curriculum according to mandates and standards or other recommendations of the learned societies, they continue to examine the research and keep themselves apprised of new information that may impact the curriculum they are implementing. In addition, they review the content or results of any norm-referenced tests that are given during the school year to see if the tests align with what's being taught, and how well students are doing. Although externally developed tests do not drive the curriculum, they do help stimulate dialogue about the content of and criteria for good curriculum. In most instances the SAC will find that the external factors they've analyzed do indeed validate the curriculum — in other words, they provide **evidence** that the new curriculum is what they want it to be. Occasionally, however, the SAC will find that they've overlooked something important or that minor changes will improve the curriculum; in these cases, they make the adjustments just as they do for problems encountered through internal validation.

When all curricular changes have been made, the curriculum document is once again presented to the curriculum council and then to the board of education for final approval. When that approval has been received, the effective dates of the document are changed and then the revised document is printed and distributed to teachers.

EVALUATING CURRICULUM: TEACHER USE

Experts who evaluate curriculum and instruction ask essentially two questions when checking academic program effectiveness:

1. *Are teachers using materials and processes that support the intended curriculum?*
    —and—
2. *Are students learning the intended curriculum?*

This section of *The Curriculum Leader* discusses the first of those two methods for assessing academic program adequacy, because students will never learn an intended curriculum if it isn't thoroughly taught.

The kind of curriculum management that assures adequate classroom instruction is a serious problem in most districts. Common causes for such management problems include the tendency for teachers to rely on text and workbooks that may or may not match the district's priorities, or teacher insistence on the kind of academic freedom that openly disdains external control of curriculum. Those conditions are ordinarily grade-level specific: elementary teachers use vast quantities of published material while some high school teachers emulate the free-wheeling style of a favorite college professor. Whether it is one of those or some other reason, converting a loosely-managed system into one that is carefully sequenced and outcome-based can be traumatic to many teachers.

Teachers Are "Somebodies"

Evaluating the extent to which teachers plan and conduct instruction based on the intended curriculum requires acceptance of a certain philosophy, and considerable thought as to appropriate procedures. The philosophy that we have been advocating is that teachers must be treated as professional persons, and that their opinions should be respected both collectively and individually. The quality of student learning will not improve when teachers are forced to comply with mandates through oppressive administrative monitoring. Teachers who are manipulated as if they are pawns in a system will react negatively, and either consciously or subconsciously subvert new practices.

Before we are accused of extreme naivete when it comes to personnel management, it is important to acknowledge the existence of recalcitrant teachers. We know of teachers who will rebel no matter how enlightened our approach to human resources development, and we know that dismissal, transfer, or disciplinary action is sometimes the only solution to change-induced personnel problems. But there is a fine line between professional dissidence and outright rebellion, and dialogue and time are the best ways to identify which is which. Curriculum leaders and those administrators who support change processes must exercise the kind of patience that accepts skepticism from all types of teachers, from those who can articulate an intelligent rebuttal based on sound pedagogical principles to those who simply fear change because it isn't comfortable. Both are valid concerns that only sincere dialogue and time can remedy. Time and intense dialogue with dissident teachers can serve to modify the change initiative in very positive ways, by bringing those who doubt into the circle and by inserting elements of their ideas into the original innovation.

We leaders in educational innovation must accept the premise that teachers are important "somebodies" who are not to be treated as mere subordinates. If William Edwards Deming could make a statement like that for workers with limited schooling, surely we can say that for well-educated teachers. That must be our overriding philosophy, a philosophy so strong that it transcends the American penchant for making changes *now!* Educators won't knuckle-under to those superiors who expect immediate action in all matters pertaining to change, because human beings simply will not respond to that kind of unnecessary pressure. The principles of time and dialogue, practiced under a philosophy of patience and a clear long-term model for restructure, will create real changes in teacher functions and the quality of student learning.

Procedures to Evaluate Teacher Use of the Intended Curriculum

Now for the tough part. If we were discussing industry, this is where we might talk about Deming's Total Quality Management (TQM). TQM is an idea that is remarkably simple, one that is so uncluttered with sophisticated processes that it could even be called "common sense." To assure quality products and services in industry, workers need to define and create processes for achieving near perfection. Logic says that the way for workers to do that is to talk to each other about such processes, and to be trained in techniques that can make them better at what they do. They use teamwork and statistical measurements, and create checks for quality all along the assembly line. They learn to evaluate themselves in non-threatening ways by working closely with each other and their supervisors. Supervisory functions are less difficult because the team has a tendency to supervise itself, by recognizing good work and by chastising those who lag behind.

In schools, teachers are physically and professionally isolated from each other. Teamwork, while partially successful when there are serious attempts to make it work, is not inherent to the ways schools are organized. TQM becomes difficult because the teaching function is segmented by cubicles, walls, and hectic schedules. Moreover, different school buildings host different kinds of students, and such cultural diversity influences how a curriculum will be taught. Under those circumstances, one standard for curriculum content and quality of student learning is difficult to communicate and impossible to implement evenly.

If time, opportunity, and wide ranges in student needs restrict teacher inter-action, and if teacher interaction is the key to stabilizing and monitoring the effec-tiveness of curriculum and instruction, then perhaps something should be done to change conditions which impede that interaction. Yet in virtually every school dis-trict we are told that meeting times are impossible to find: morning meetings are out because teachers use the time to get ready for class, noon meetings won't work because the lunch hour is too brief, planning periods are scratched due to classroom supervi-sory needs or negoiated rights, after school meetings are a problem because coaches can't attend, and evening or Saturday meetings are not feasible because of contract stipulations. We know that many of those reasons are a smoke screen for a much deeper concern, that teachers are tired of going to meetings that decide little and pro-mote no meaningful action. Moreover, they are annoyed with the underlying purpose associated with many meetings, that teachers who attend them are really being "inser-viced." Being "inserviced" is a passive condition, something like a car getting a lube job. Feeling "worked on" instead of "worked with," teachers often walk away from the "inservice" professionally numb, personally demeaned, and thoroughly irritated.

It is our belief, based on considerable experience, that teachers will attend and enjoy meetings when they are truly involved, and when those meetings result in meaningful decisions and solid action. So the first consideration when evaluating teacher use of a curriculum is the process for preparing and conducting truly out-standing TQM-type meetings. The second consideration is to interpret acquired information to determine how it can offer clues as to the quality of curriculum and instruction. Finally, a curriculum leader should have some idea as to what to do if problems are detected that the meeting process itself is unable to resolve.

Preparing and Conducting TQM-Style Meetings

A TQM-style meeting is really a combination of faculty development and an assessment of quality teacher actions. A curriculum leader's responsibility is to make certain the meeting is structured so that a special kind of atmosphere is created, one in which participants can become dynamically involved in real and exciting decision-making. Perhaps the best way to picture such a meeting is to think of another group of professionals who have come together to tackle a really difficult challenge: engi-neers trying to determine the best design for a critical airplane part, doctors debating the pros and cons of certain treatments for a chronically ill patient, or lawyers delib-erating the best strategy for an up-coming case.

We have all seen movies or read books in which certain professional persons have created a "think tank" atmosphere for their meetings, thereby making the meet-ing climate stimulating for both participants and outside observers. It is marvelous to watch film documentaries of great human accomplishments, because a featured part of the process is almost always some kind of vigorous team deliberation. We know that people who participate in such meetings may walk away elated, satisfied, frustrated or even a little angry, but any negative feelings they might harbor do not include a perception that the meeting was a waste of time. They know that a vigorous exchange of views is the way both individuals and an organization get better, and they also know that their membership in the group is important to the on-going quality of the endeavor. Their opinions may not hold sway right now, but they know that tomorrow an idea they offer may save the day.

The curriculum leader who is able to create a "think tank" atmosphere is both a full participant in the action and the person who must qualitatively evaluate the effectiveness of decisions, actions, and on-going programs. That kind of qualitative evaluation will work only when teachers function like the professionals they're supposed to be: they vigorously express points of view, give examples of how they do things in their classrooms, listen carefully to their associates when they express points of view, synthesize numerous ideas into workable plans, and make clear and workable recommendations for action. A meeting in which those elements are present is no place for complacent educators or those who feel that the proper role of teachers is to passively accept administrative dictates and prescribed printed resources. Such individuals are extremely uncomfortable with active deliberation, so it is the curriculum leader's task to meet that challenge by helping them become part of the process.

It is likely that teachers who become part of the process are making a commitment to establishing and maintaining the new outcome-based curriculum. Even if that isn't the case, they are at least engaging their minds on the issues at hand. Passive or openly hostile attitudes are easy to detect in a highly dynamic meeting, so conclusions drawn by a curriculum leader about who is using new curricula and associated instructional processes should be fairly accurate.

Preparing for a TQM-style meeting is a matter of working with the participants and leader, assisting in the creation of an appropriate agenda, and making certain predictions about likely outcomes of the meeting. In very small districts it might be possible for the curriculum coordinator to attend all grade level and department meetings, but in most school districts it is important that members of the curriculum council and the designated subject area committee share that responsibility. The curriculum coordinator and curriculum council or subject area committee members should be trained in how to help the designated leader (department or grade level chair) prepare and conduct a meeting, and how to work with participants and assess their level of commitment to using the curriculum. Therefore, the coordinator and council should identify opportunities to work with those subgroups of teachers, conduct the training necessary for those who will join the meetings, organize the process, and establish methods for acquiring essential information. Here is an example of how the process might work:

Jan, as the district curriculum coordinator, understands the importance of combining curriculum implementation, faculty development, and processes that assess curricular discipline. She also realizes that the most critical time for that process to begin is when a subject area committee is ready to issue a new curriculum document that is based on high achievement outcomes. She has spoken with the chair of the subject area committee, and knows that its new curriculum document will be ready after the summer workshop...about July 1. The SAC chair tells Jan that the committee has worked out a building-level implementation plan which calls for multiple grade level and department meetings. Those meetings will be led by SAC members, and the agenda will focus on explanations and discussion of course and grade level purposes and attendant high achievement outcomes. It is assumed that the meetings will clarify the meaning of those outcomes, and will cover the kinds of teaching methods, resources, and assessments of student learning required by the new system. SAC members will have sufficient knowledge of new processes to help the teachers, because they have received the necessary training in the summer workshop.

Jan asks the SAC chair for a two to three hour period of time during the summer workshop so that she can provide instruction on how to assess the quality of faculty participation. The SAC chair expresses a concern that many SAC members will not want to be in a position that requires them to evaluate their peers. Jan says that she is sensitive to that issue, and that this kind of evaluation is designed to be helpful and not punitive. She goes on to say that the kind of assessment conducted by SAC members is centered on the willingness and ability of faculty members to actually implement the new instructional system. A serious concern about one or two faculty members who are openly hostile to the project will likely be shared by other teachers in the meeting. That hostility, if based on rational skepticism, could be healthy and a way to stimulate positive on-going deliberation. On the other hand, there might be reason for alarm if hostility creates a distancing from the group or argumentative positions that serve to inflame, not enlighten.

Jan also tells the SAC chair that teacher recalcitrance is characteristic of certain individuals within varied settings, but that its presence in a school committed to outcome-based education is particularly serious. Teachers who are not comfortable in the new system need counseling and perhaps a different kind of educational assignment. SAC members should understand that point, and know how to express concerns in ways that are helpful to chronically dissident teachers. Their concerns could be given to the SAC chair, who in turn might talk with Jan. Jan will then work with building principals in arranging actions that are helpful to both teachers and the quality of student learning in their classrooms.

What will happen as a consequence of Jan's efforts? Our experience is that there will be a certain amount of suspicion and awkwardness at first, primarily because teachers are not accustomed to being open or trusting about their concerns. If they are dissatisfied, the usual approach is to mention something to the colleagues they trust, because any general discussion might be perceived by those in authority as belligerent griping. After Jan talks with the SAC members who will work with the teachers, she can expect continuing sensitivity on the part of some or all of them. Keeping dialogue open is the only way that sensitivity can be reduced, because trust-building is essential for progress to be made. Deming says that fear is the number one problem in most organizations, and fear is built on distrust and the perception that sincerity is not possible in hierarchical human relationships. Therefore, Jan, the SAC chair, and all building principals need to discuss that phenomenon very often. Reducing fear and distrust must be a number one priority on the part of all who are leading the development and maintenance of the academic program.

Interpreting Clues as to the Quality of Curriculum and Instruction

In the previous example Jan and the other curriculum leaders with whom she works are setting the stage for a different kind of evaluation, one that is merged with the faculty development process. Although that process is not a managerially neat way to obtain information about possible control problems, it is much more professional and qualitative in its approach. It also creates a need to define "red flags" in terms of teacher attitudes and behaviors. What are "red flags" that may be reason for a curriculum leader to be concerned? Here are a few of them:

- A group of teachers are hostile toward the new approach to curriculum and instruction because it may take away prerogatives they have come to appreciate. Perhaps they have had total discretion with regard to curricular content, or had access to a particularly large portion of the materials budget. Whatever their concern, they resent having to participate in the larger project because it will certainly take away rights, funding, or special forms of recognition. They maintain a contrary position by using their group for support.

- Teachers of certain electives dislike the program because it reduces the emphasis on tracking, and may even promote a greater emphasis on interdisciplinary processes. Changing the program will cause them considerable inconvenience, even to the point of making a wholesale conversion. They will make the effort to change only if they are properly reimbursed in terms of time and money.

- Teachers have heard so much about the accountability aspect of outcome-based education that they are certain the ultimate goal of the district is to create and implement processes to check on teacher effectiveness. They are so disturbed over that possibility that they find reasons why the new system won't work. Those reasons are usually focused on a lack of support from parents or the board of education, and on concerns that student psychological and physical problems are so great that it is silly to talk about mastery learning and high achievement outcomes. Those teachers worry so much about the situation that they are absolutely paralyzed, therefore limiting their efforts to "going through the motions" or simply "opting out" until they change jobs or retire.

We have dealt with the problems mentioned above, and others that are similar. Those kinds of problems are serious, and easy to detect when teachers meet to plan new programs. Interpreting the clues these teachers give is not really a problem. In the first example, anyone who has been allowed to lead a privileged professional life will not be happy with a program in which certain sacrifices will need to be made for the greater good of the organization. In the second example, teachers who have become accustomed to certain processes will not take kindly to hours of extra work to develop a program that has dubious merit in their eyes. And in the final example, it is clear that psychological paralysis will not only interfere with a new program's implementation, it will likely interfere with an adequate maintenance of the existing curriculum. Using those three examples, it is important to consider how the problems can be resolved ... .at least for the time being.

Resolving Problems That Interfere with the Delivery of Quality Curriculum and Instruction

We've suggested that the most significant "red flags" we've encountered in districts are: (1) teacher hostility because personal and professional prerogatives have been reduced, (2) teacher concern about having to design and deliver totally new instructional programs, and (3) teacher paralysis due to fears about accountability. It's also been indicated that these are real problems felt by some of the very best professional teachers in the district, and they will certainly manifest themselves as inadequacies in the "taught" curriculum. So how are those problems resolved?

The only immediate response is that there are no easy answers, but when teachers are *hostile over losing personal and professional prerogatives* we create conditions in which they can assume some leadership in designing and implementing the new process throughout the district. That is important, because those teachers are probably among the most innovative and "entrepreneurial" types in the school. While they may be a little hard to live with, they cannot be faulted for their energy and imagination. Instead, they should be encouraged to extend their entrepreneurial spirit to the total faculty via the leadership of councils and special developmental projects. In short, we have found that teachers who have gained special recognition and "perks" in the past have done so because they have innovative ideas and are real go-getters; the trick is to move that spirit from an individual or departmental setting into one that positively influences the total restructuring program.

Teachers who *must redesign their entire instructional program because of new approaches* do not complain because of laziness, but because they feel they've been "jerked around" before and resent having to develop new processes that they think will likely fail or be no better than what they are currently doing. It is important to acknowledge the validity of their arguments, because all of us have had such negative experiences ourselves. A curriculum leader is most uncomfortable when teachers inquire about where the model is currently successful, or what evidence is available which supports the idea that student learning improves because of the model's implementation. They want testimonials, concrete evidence, and the chance to see for themselves those programs that really work. Visits to showcase or prototype districts help overcome skepticism, as does the enthusiasm engendered when teachers attend high-powered workshops. Most important, skeptics need to talk one-on-one with teacher practitioners whom they trust, and who will give them feelings that the effort is actually worth it. One-on-one conversations are much more helpful than statistics that show improved standardized test scores, visits to districts, and powerful workshops.

Teachers who *fear the hidden accountability agenda are much more difficult to help*, because their feelings are both rational and irrational. They are rational in that there are educational reformers who advocate measurement of accountability via tests that are not prepared by teachers themselves, and who would use quantified outcomes of those tests to evaluate teaching effectiveness. It is irrational in that such processes, where they have been tried, had little real impact on the evaluation of teaching effectiveness. Moreover, there has been no wholesale dismissal of teachers because of poor standardized test scores, and very little in the way of disciplinary action. The approach we take to this issue is that individual districts must design workable programs under clear definitions of expected student mastery, and identify the assessment processes that make sense to them. There is considerable evidence that no governmental regulatory group will discipline or even chastise a district for creating and implementing an improvement model that they can logically explain in terms of quality student learning outcomes. That is especially true if community members also support the school's efforts. In brief, we indicate that no state-level accountability process will have an adverse impact on a district if the school has its act together, and is working closely with the community it is serving. It requires solid leadership to advocate that position when a state requires the taking of certain standardized tests, and threatens to link funding to student success levels, or to publish the results of those tests in the media. But doing what is right will help fearful teachers, and develop better quality student learning outcomes.

Evaluating Teacher Use of Curriculum — Basics:

- Adequate use of a new curriculum depends on how much allegiance teachers can give it, and allegiance depends on how they feel about the sponsoring organization and their role in it.

- TQM (Deming) calls for helping all members of the organization feel like "somebodies," and to break down barriers that impede that feeling. In schools, teachers will improve their feelings toward the organization if they can meet with each other and build a sense of teamwork.

- Meetings need to be carefully structured and conducted to be effective. A good meeting is a process of helping teachers build and evaluate their own programs, and the role of a curriculum leader is to intervene when feelings or conditions require it.

- Interventions require the identification of problems, interpretations as to what those problems really are, and methods for resolving those problems.

EVALUATING CURRICULUM: STUDENT LEARNING

In the previous section we talked about evaluating the curriculum in terms of teacher use — how to determine if teachers are actually presenting the intended curriculum. Let's assume that we have followed the guidelines offered and we know that our teachers are indeed presenting the curriculum that is outlined in the curriculum documents prepared by the Subject Area Committees. The key word that we need to focus on here is *presenting*. Presenting is not the same as teaching; in fact, there is an outcome-based education adage that says, YOU HAVEN'T TAUGHT ANYTHING UNTIL STUDENTS HAVE LEARNED IT. We can give entertaining lectures, use up-to-date media, and plan all kinds of activities, but none of this assures us that learning actually has taken place. So how do we know if students have "learned it"?

The first answer to this question is obvious, and one that is not new to experienced teachers: we must administer some type of assessment to determine if student learning has occurred, as well as the <u>amount</u>, or <u>degree</u> of learning, and the specifics of <u>what</u> has been learned. However, administering "some type of assessment" is not enough. In planning for assessment, we must ask ourselves a series of questions.

1. What about **alignment?** Does this particular assessment link directly to the intended outcome? Does it measure precisely what we're trying to teach, or does it include extraneous subject matter, or even content that is in no way related?

2. How am I measuring success (mastery)? If the student performs better now than before, is that satisfactory? Am I measuring this student's performance according to that of the other students? Or am I measuring the student's achievement against a specific, predetermined set of **criteria?**

3. Is **one** assessment enough to convince me of mastery? Is **one kind** of assessment enough to convince me of mastery?

4. **When** should I be checking for learning?

5. How should I **document,** or keep track of, student learning?

Alignment

The idea of alignment is so much one of common sense that most of us just assume we have indeed been testing for the intended outcome. However, close examination of our assessments often proves otherwise. Consider this example: the outcome says that students will recognize and name the shapes of circle, square, rectangle, and triangle. So the teacher asks the students to draw the four shapes.

First of all, the teacher is asking for more than is expected in the outcome. The outcome says recognize and name; it doesn't say create, draw, or even copy or reproduce. The former is much simpler than the latter. How many times have you personally tried to think of the answer to a question, but it won't come to mind? Yet if you see a selection of answers, you can identify immediately the one that is correct. Which is more important: that you recognize the right answer when you see it, or that you can come up with the answer on your own, with no clues provided? That depends on what we were trying to accomplish in the first place. And what we try to accomplish is affected by a number of factors, such as the developmental level of the learners, the relevance of the information to the learner's life, and so forth — all of which should have been taken into consideration when designing the expected outcome.

The second problem with the assessment that was used in the example is less obvious. Suppose Susan accurately draws all four shapes. The teacher might say, "See, she knows them all." But perhaps Susan thinks the rectangle is the square, and vice-versa. She still would have drawn both of them correctly, and the teacher might never realize that Susan has the two confused. In order to align the assessment accurately with the outcome, we have to ask ourselves, What precisely is the outcome, and what kind of behavior/performance demonstrates it? In our example the precise outcome is two-fold: **recognize**, and **name**. In order for the learner to **recognize** the shape, the learner must be **shown** the shape; in order for the learner to **name** the shape, the learner must **say** or **write** the name and in some way indicate which shape the name belongs to.

Criterion-Referenced Tests

Everyone who has been reading about education reform recognizes the term **criterion-referenced tests**, and for the most part, acknowledges the necessity and validity of this type of assessment.   What we want to know is whether a student has learned that which we intended to be learned. Measuring his or her performance against that of other students simply tells us whether the student has done better or worse than others; it still doesn't tell us whether the outcome has been accomplished. A student could get the highest score in the class but still have a very poor score, and obviously not really know the material or be able to demonstrate the skills. Or, a student could receive a very high score, but if we are grading only according to how something "strikes us" at the time, the score may not be valid. The only sure way to assess the student's learning is to decide, **in advance**, what criteria we're looking for, and evaluate student performance against these criteria.

Although the idea of criterion-referenced tests has been widely accepted, implementation of this type of assessment has been greatly hampered by the existence of a major fallacy in understanding its definition. Many educators are operating under the assumption that a criterion-referenced test must be a <u>written</u> test. This is simply not so! Criterion-referenced tests can be written or oral examinations, performances, projects, or even behaviors. The only "criterion" for a criterion-referenced "test" is that the students be evaluated according to a specific set of predetermined criteria!

If you're giving a short-answer written test, are there specific words the student must use to demonstrate learning, or are synonyms acceptable? If you're watching a performance or experiment, which specific skills or steps are you looking for to convince you the student can do what you expected? How <u>well</u> must they be performed? To perfection? With few errors? Well enough for others to recognize the result? If students are building models of geometric shapes, will you judge the finished projects by any criterion other than accuracy of shape? Does it make a difference what medium is used? Is size important, or neatness? If you're looking for mastery of expected behaviors, such as working cooperatively in a group, what constitutes success? Must the student be able to work cooperatively with anyone and everyone in the class, or is it acceptable for the student to recognize a personality clash with another student and ask not to work with that person?

Objective tests such as true-false, matching, fill in the blank, or find the solution usually have single, right-or-wrong answers and thus usually have only one crite-rion: correct answers, and mastery is set as a predetermined **percentage** of **correct answers.** On the other hand, essay tests, research papers, experiments, projects, or performances usually require several criteria. When trying to determine what the cri-teria will be, it is helpful at least to visualize the expected results, or if possible, look at a real example. If you still have papers or projects from previous classes, examine them and analyze the evaluation procedures you used, making a list of evident crite-ria.   If the students will be expected to perform, evaluate a similar type of perfor-mance outside of class, and make notes about your judgments. Conduct an experi-ment yourself, or ask a family member to do so, and make a list of what you're look-ing for as the experiment proceeds. If assigning an essay, think about writing the essay yourself, then prepare an outline of what must be included, or the way it must be writ-ten.

Most criterion-referenced tests that have multiple criteria can best be evaluat-ed by use of either a **checklist** or a **rating scale.** Checklists provide a systematic way of checking whether important characteristics are present in someone's performance or product.   Once the list has been developed, it's easy to use —you simply note whether the characteristic is or is not present. Keep the list fairly short, make sure each item is clear, and arrange the items in an order that makes the total list easy to use. Consider the following checklist for evaluating the first draft of a narrative para-graph. Because it is a first draft, the teacher is not yet judging the quality of what is written, but simply whether the components are present.

- _____ topic sentence
- _____ descriptive details
- _____ sequential order
- _____ all sentences are relevant
- _____ consistent viewpoint
- _____ summary or conclusion

A rating scale differs from a checklist in that instead of determining the pres-ence or absence of a behavior or characteristic, it helps us determine the <u>quality</u> of the behavior or characteristic. A rating scale is usually used to evaluate performance, and is based on a continuum rather than a list. You are probably familiar with the three- or five-point rating scale that uses general labels: poor, fair, average, good, excellent. Sometimes the words are listed below the continuum line; at other times they are assigned a numerical value, such as 1 = poor and 5 = excellent. You've probably been asked to use this type of evaluation procedure for presenters at conferences you've attended. While that type of rating scale is satisfactory for such a general purpose, it is not recommended for evaluation of student learning. Instead, develop a **rubric** to explain the basis for each rating. A rubric lists the categories that will be evaluated and — for each category — descriptive terms that are stated concretely. Consider the following example for evaluating a student's science experiment.

Category: Logical progression
Rating of "1" = haphazard or disjointed progression
- leaves out steps
- performs steps out of order
- inserts irrelevant steps

Rating of "2" = Acceptable progression
- completes all necessary steps
- steps are progressive, logical
- errors may occur, but are corrected in subsequent attempts

Rating of "3" = Effective progression
- completes all necessary steps
- steps are progressive, logical
- steps are performed correctly — no repeats needed
- steps are clearly defined & described by student as performed

Category: Conclusion
Rating of "1" = improper conclusion
- no conclusion formed
- conclusion is faulty — not supported by findings
- conclusion not stated clearly

Rating of "2" = acceptable conclusion
- conclusion aligns with hypothesis
- conclusion supported by 2 or more findings in any order
- conclusion recognized and clearly stated

Rating of "3" = clear & logical conclusion
- conclusion aligns with hypothesis
- conclusion supported by 3 or more findings
- findings are sequential
- conclusion recognized and clearly stated

The important thing to remember when designing the criterion-referenced test is that not only should the criteria be determined in advance, but they should be *communicated to students* before the test is assigned. We've all been students ourselves, but now that we're on "the other side of the fence," we often forget what it was like. Don't make that mistake. Think back about classes you have taken and the frustration you often felt when you knew a major assessment (written in class, or outside of class paper or project) was coming up, but you didn't know for sure what the instructor was expecting. Or perhaps expectations for the paper or project were clear, but grading procedures weren't. Wouldn't it have made a difference in the way you approached the creative writing assignment for English class if you'd known whether the instructor was more interested in your creative ideas or your proper use of mechanics? Would you have been more successful on that history test if you'd only realized that the teacher didn't care anything about all those dates you memorized, but wanted you to be able to describe cause and effect in detail? Would you have spent less time researching your project and more time constructing it if you'd known the project's appearance determined the major portion of your grade? Bottom line: pretend you're a student in your class. How can expectations be conveyed to **help you really learn** that which is intended?

One is a Lonely Number

There have been some very popular movies and T.V. shows made about law school students and the stress they endure because an entire semester's work — and success or failure — is measured only once: a written final examination at the end of the semester. Most law school classes, as well as some other college courses, are still conducted this way today. Of course, one of the reasons for this procedure is that the professors actually **want** some of their students to fail. Basically, their attitude is: We have too many students, and besides, we only want the elite — the very brightest — to succeed, so we must "weed out" the others. It works. Many students fail, but often times they fail because the stress and pressure are overwhelming and get in the way, not because the students haven't learned that which was intended.

An argument used by law school professors is that handling stress and pressure is an integral part of practicing law, so such examination procedures are valid and desirable because they also assess the student's ability to perform under pressure. The question of alignment is really debatable here. What's really being measured is the students' ability to take a *written examination under pressure* — not their ability to "think on their feet" when opposing counsel introduces unexpected evidence, or when a witness gives surprising testimony, or a judge overrules a crucial objection. This type of "performance under pressure" would be more accurately measured when students are put on the spot to analyze complicated cases during class, or when they participate in mock trials. And what about the content of the examination? Does it really measure what the student knows about legal cases and procedures? What about the student who really knows the material, but simply misinterpreted the question? Or what about the one who can accurately explain absolutely everything that was "covered" in class **except** the one thing that was asked on the test?

At this point you may be saying, But that's law school; we don't do that with K-12 students. However, many of us do — particularly in high schools. Perhaps we don't wait until the end of a course or even a semester, but we do plan only one assessment for a whole unit of instruction. When we do so we cheat ourselves, and our students. We cheat ourselves because we narrow the chances that we are accurately assessing student learning. And how can we be accountable for our teaching if our measurement of student learning is not valid? We cheat our students not only because the one assessment may not be accurate, but —more importantly — because if students have problems at the beginning of the unit, we only compound the situation by waiting until the end to discover that fact.

We need to administer both **formative** and **summative** assessments for the benefit of our students and for our own benefits — so that we know we're teaching effectively. Formative assessments are used throughout the unit of instruction; one should be administered for each <u>step</u> of the learning process.

Consider this example: A fourth grade core outcome states that students will compare the topography, climate, and natural resources of each of the six geographic regions of the United States. Suppose Mr. Brown has students investigate all of these components for one region, then they repeat the process for the second region, and so forth. When they finish with the sixth region, he administers a test in which he randomly assigns each student two of the regions and asks the student to explain the similarities and differences of each component. About a third of the class does not do well. They either leave out components completely, or they assign to a region characteristics that don't belong. How does Mr. Brown know where correction is needed? If students left out the part about topography, did they forget what the topography was for that particular region, or did they never understand what topography was in the first place? When they assigned incorrect characteristics to a region, were they confusing two regions, or were they simply listing familiar words they remember without really comprehending their significance to a particular area?

Mr. Brown's unit would be much more successful if he would administer frequent, short checks for comprehension. The day after they talk about topography — even if they had started their investigation of a particular region — he should assess whether students can explain, **today**, what topography is before continuing that investigation. The same thing should be done with "climate," and "natural resources." If the approach is to work with one region at a time, he should check to see that students can accurately describe one region before proceeding to the next. When the second region is completed, he should see if students can accurately compare the two before beginning a third. Not only does this process help Mr. Brown see where learning problems are occurring, and correct them before they are compounded, it helps the student focus on what's important and to see the relationships of prior learning to new information.

There is another problem that is caused by the "one-test syndrome." An example of this problem actually happened to one of this book's authors. Allow us to slip into a first-person narrative to share it with you.

Particularly during the years they are in school, many people report having a reoccurring dream in which they're headed for class to take a big exam and realize on the way that they've done none of the necessary preparation. Well, one year in college I found myself right on the verge of that situation, and it wasn't a dream. I won't bore you with how I got myself into such a predicament, but the fact is, I was facing a major exam for a literature course and had done <u>none</u> of the required reading. Since I prided myself on my good grades, the prospect of sure failure had me in tears. However, it happened that a relative of mine was taking the same class, and he came to my rescue. He had read all of the assignments, more than once, and had also practically memorized all of the lecture notes from class, and had analyzed the readings to see where the main lecture points applied.

My relative and I spent the entire day before the test "studying" together. Actually what happened is that he told me, in his own words, all of the stories in the assigned readings, and explained their significance according to the lecture notes. After each narrative, he would quiz me about the facts, issues, and relevant concepts. My only source of preparation for the test was what *he* had told me. Imagine my shock when I received an A on that test and he received a D!

What happened? Three things: first of all, the **criteria** for grading had not been shared with us. Although it was a literature class, the instructor graded more on proper writing mechanics than on content. I happened to be able to write well, and so was able to put my small amount of knowledge into proper form. My relative had a wealth of knowledge about the components of the literature selections and their importance to society, but spelling wasn't his strong suit, and he frequently used comma splices.

The second thing is, the instructor was **testing for things that had not been taught.** The class was a survey course in which only the literature was discussed. Not only was there no instruction on writing mechanics or techniques, there also were *no prerequisites* for taking this course. And yet the instructor graded more on the writing process than on knowledge of the literature. While I agree that students in a college course ought to be able to write well, one of several things should have happened here: students should have been required to satisfactorily complete a writing course before being allowed to take this class; the instructor should have taught writing as well as literature; or the instructor should have graded only on literature but required my relative to attend the writing lab for students needing help in this area.

The third thing that happened in this story is that because I had crammed for the test, my knowledge was very short-term. I was able to remember the things my relative had told me well enough to get them on paper the next day. But had we been tested on that same material a week or so later, I would have remembered little, if anything. On the other hand, the young man who coached me had done so without even referring to his notes. He could so thoroughly explain and compare each story's characters, issues, conflicts, and impacts, that I've no doubt he still could intelligently discuss them today, even though that was many years ago. So which of us really learned? According to the test results, I did. He practically failed. I hope the main point of this story is obvious: a single test does not measure true learning.

There's one more point that needs to be made here, and that is: one **kind** of test is also not sufficient. There is an abundance of research that supports the validity of different learning styles. And common sense tells us that if we all have differences in the way we learn, then we also have differences in the way we can best **demonstrate** that learning! Some people abhor the idea of an oral exam, yet there are others who would gladly <u>tell</u> you anything you want to know, but they just can't seem to organize their thoughts when they have to put them on paper. Some people can <u>show</u> you how to do something, but they couldn't explain it — orally or in writing.

Once again we have to ask ourselves, What is it we really want to assess? This is not to say that we should forget about interdisciplinary learning. If we want students to be able to write, then writing across the curriculum is an important tool for reinforcing these skills. And if students are not able to write well, then we all (all disciplines) need to keep working with them on the particular writing problems they experience. In the meantime, if what we want to know right now is whether a student comprehends the importance of climate to a region's economy, we must consider how to determine that information. An essay exam may be one means, but if the student writes so poorly that we can't make sense of what's written, then what we know is that the student needs lots of help with writing skills. But do we know if she comprehends the importance of climate to a region's economy? Perhaps she can explain it to us orally. Perhaps she can make a chart to illustrate the concept. We still need some means of assessing this particular outcome.

Another reason for using more than one kind of assessment is that, just as only <u>one</u> test may not be enough to assure that actual learning has occurred, using only one <u>kind</u> of test poses the same problem. This is especially true in terms of application. Consider the simple example of the elementary student who passes with flying colors the written test on simple fractions: that two fourths equal one half, and two halves make one whole, and so forth. Meanwhile, on the morning after he makes a perfect score on his test, his mother asks him to help make the pancakes for breakfast. She tells him to double the recipe, which consists of simple one-fourth and one-half amounts. And he doesn't have a clue. He is not able to transfer math class, paper-and-pencil learning to real-world application. If we want to know if our students have learned, we need more than one kind of example to be convinced.

Remember When

Let us stress again that not only are the number and kinds of assessments important, but the timing is equally so. Formative assessments are short, frequently administered assessments that help you determine whether everyday learning is occurring and progressing as you intended. These assessments do not have to be —should not be— long or complicated.

We are acquainted with a high school math teacher who presents a new concept and then lists on the board an extensive selection of pages and problem numbers in the math book that students can work for practice of the new concept. All of the problems are ones for which the answers are shown in the back of the book. She asks the students to check the answer for each problem before going on to the next; she doesn't want them to practice working them incorrectly. She tells them it's up to them how many problems they work for practice. She will not check all of their homework. However, if they have difficulty, they need to ask for help first thing when class starts the next day. When assistance is needed, she continues with instruction before assessing. And of course, students who claim they "don't understand" have to show the homework they attempted so teacher and student can analyze the work to see where correction is needed. (This eliminates the problem of kids not trying and simply stalling progress the next day.) Students then know that before anything else happens, they will have to work TODAY'S THREE PROBLEMS. It takes only about ten minutes of class time for everyone to work the three problems and the teacher to circulate, checking their answers. Yet with this short assessment, she gets a really good reading of whether students are indeed ready to move on, or whether more instruction or practice is needed for this concept.

The summative assessment, as its name implies, is a summary of all the formative assessments. This is the one that comes at the end of the unit, at the end of the next unit, the end of the semester, the end of the course. But each time we expand — from the end of one unit to the end of the next — we need to include a little something from the previous test. Remember the example of the author's literature test; real learning is lasting. We need to check that students haven't just "memorized for the moment"; that their so-called "learning" isn't just here today, never to surface again. Each summative assessment should include the spiraling effect: the first coil includes one or two items from the last test, the second coil includes an item or two from the test before that, and so forth. As the year progresses, probably only one question or technique needs to be included for those skills and concepts that have been checked repeatedly. Or perhaps you'll want to administer more than one summative test —a longer version for the last couple of units, a shorter version of only one or two items for everything tested previously.

And Then Comes the Question of Grading…

A question that is frequently asked is, Should we grade homework? If, by "grade," you mean check to see if work is done accurately, yes. (And you needn't check it all yourself. Students can check their own work in class.) If you mean assign a value that is averaged into the final score, the answer is no. This goes against the old paradigm, the way we've always done things. But once again, consider the *purpose* for assigning homework in the first place. Homework should be a way to **practice** new skills or concepts. It helps the students themselves determine whether they really have learned something (or already knew it) or whether they need more instruction. If we're already proficient at something, we don't need to practice. If students are already proficient at whatever we're teaching, then we don't need to teach it. And yet when a student brings in a homework assignment and only half of it is right, and we average that score into his grade, what we're doing is penalizing him for not already knowing what we are trying to teach!

Once again we're going to ask you to visualize yourself in a similar situation. Research tells us that most of the jobs our students will perform throughout their lives don't even exist now. Pretend that one such new job has just been created. It's related to education, and it's a wonderful opportunity, so you accepted the position when it was offered. But since it is all brand new, the only way you can learn what to do is through on-the-job-training, which a supervisor will provide.

So Monday morning arrives — your first day — and the supervisor sits down with you to explain the procedures. You have to work with education clients, and there are forms to fill out and research to be completed. It's fairly complicated, but the supervisor assures you she'll be available to answer your questions. She explains that you'll work with practice "clients" all week, and that she will check your work each day and provide needed help. On Friday, you must work through a practice client all by yourself to demonstrate that you're ready to handle your own real clients the following week.

The first day, you do have to ask lots of questions, and you make quite a few errors with your practice client. But each day, you become more proficient, and by Friday you're ready to "show your stuff." Sure enough, you complete the whole process perfectly — not one error! So the supervisor agrees that you're ready to have your own clients next Monday, and explains that two other trainees will also start that day. All three of you demonstrated your proficiency today, and all three of you received the same score.

Oh … by the way, the other two will be placed at the top salary level, but you will be working at two levels lower. Why is that? Well, because you had to ask more questions and you made more errors during the training process. What? Yes, you all performed at the same proficiency today, and you're all going to be doing the same work next week, but apparently you aren't listening. You didn't learn the process as quickly as they did, so you can't be placed on the same salary level. And yes, this is a permanent situation — you can't undo what's already been done.

Get the picture?

Keeping Track

One of the biggest roadblocks that keeps teachers from teaching to outcomes is fear of all the record-keeping. We have all these little formative tests to keep track of, as well as who's doing correctives, and who's doing enrichments, and when the whole class is ready to start something new. Record-keeping <u>will</u> take some time, but it needn't be as big a hurdle as you may have feared. As with any new thing we attempt, the biggest time consumption is at the beginning — getting organized. Once we have a system established, using the system isn't that complicated.

Many teachers who teach to outcomes still use the traditional gradebook system. Down the side of the page is each student's name. Across the top are designations for each assignment, for each step of the learning process. In many instances, a checkmark is all that's needed: yes, this step's outcome has been met; no, the student is still working on it. Scores, or letter grades are entered when the full outcome has been met.

While the gradebook is effective for "keeping track of," that's really all that it does. It provides a list of what the student has accomplished, and the final evaluation score of those accomplishments. But it doesn't really show us the work itself, or precisely how a student has improved, or why an outcome still has not been met. This kind of information can be valuable not only to the teacher, but it can be of great benefit to students by helping them become more actively involved in their own learning processes. And it can be accomplished by use of the portfolio. Although the portfolio is explained in great detail in a later section of this book, we offer a simplified description here.

A typical student portfolio is contained in an expandable, or accordian-style, file folder. Yes, there's one for each student. Yes, they will take up a bit of space, but a file cabinet or set of bins or crates on shelves can do the job. No, it will not take an inordinate amount of time for you to do all this filing; all but perhaps preschool children can do their own filing.

So what goes in the portfolio? Samples of the student's work collected over a period of time. Students should be given explanations at the beginning of the year about portfolios and that they will be used. They should provide input into what goes into their own folders. Portfolios may include "finished" items, such as written summative tests, photographs of projects, written reports, lists of books read, or even audio or visual tapes of debates or performances. But portfolios should not be limited to these final products. Students might also include such things as writing samples, "before" and "during" photos of a project as well as one of the finished version, notes the student made for a report or research paper, an explanation of how a problem was solved, data used for an experiment, or journal entries. When students include preliminary work samples in their portfolios, they become more aware of the importance of each step of the learning process and how one step relates to another, as well as to the completed project or learning experience.

The teacher should plan periodic times during the year to conference with each student about his or her work; the portfolio is used as the vehicle for the conference. Not only can teacher and student discuss current work, but they can evaluate progress by comparing earlier pieces to present ones. Evaluations are more thorough because comparisons are made over extended periods of time. Remember, too, the advice to use more than one kind of assessment — portfolios can facilitate this process greatly. You can't put a photograph or a videotape in a gradebook. Additionally, work samples can include not only a representation of a particular concept or skill that was learned, but an example of how that learning was applied.

Other benefits of the portfolio approach to assessment include:

- provides authenticity — actual classroom work is shown, not just resulting scores or grades

- integrates instruction with assessment

- permits assessment of a broader range of cognitive skills — beyond factual knowledge

- involves students in setting goals, evaluating progress, and planning

- assists the teacher with planning for effective instruction

- provides the student additional opportunities to demonstrate learning and show skill development

- promotes student interest, motivation

- involves students in metacognition, which facilitates future learning

- can be used by high school students to support applications for employment or college admission

- can provide tremendous assistance to tutors or teachers working with students who need extra help, such as students taking outcome-specific summer classes

There is one more point about portfolios that needs to be made. Some teachers are under the impression that everything in a student's portfolio is passed on to the next teacher. And indeed, some school districts do maintain a cumulative portfolio through the use of software programs. But teachers who are using file folders as portfolios can't visualize, nor can we, how to handle or store the mountains of material that a student would collect from kindergarten to graduation. The answer to this dilemma is that not everything is passed on. A portfolio should be thought of as an assessment of the student's work in this class only; it's possible that nothing will be passed on. On the other hand, particularly if a student is moving on without mastering _every_ outcome, it may be helpful for the next teacher to have some examples of where the student "left off," and what kinds of problems he or she was having. You and the student should decide together what, if anything, is kept from one year to the next.

Evaluating Student Learning of Curriculum — Basics:

- **The assessment must align directly with the expected outcome. Ask: What precisely is the outcome, and what kind of behavior/performance demonstrates it?**

- **The only sure way to assess the student's learning is to decide, in advance, what criteria we're looking for, and evaluate student performance against these criteria. The student should also be told in advance how learning will be assessed.**

- **Checklists and rating scales are helpful tools for assessments that have multiple criteria.**

- **Administer more than one assessment, and more than one kind of assessment, for each outcome.**

- **Use formative as well as summative assessments. Be sure summative assessments include the spiraling technique.**

- **Students should be _encouraged_ to practice new skills and concepts, and to learn from their mistakes — not be penalized for doing so.**

- **Portfolio assessments benefit teachers and students alike, as well as provide valuable information to parents and possibly to colleges or future employers. The benefits of portfolio assessment greatly outweigh the inconvenience they cause in terms of time and space.**

RESOURCE SELECTION UNDER A NEW CURRICULUM DESIGN

In previous sections of this book we've made the point that no curriculum should be textbook-driven, and that the process for selecting textbooks and other resources ought to occur after a curriculum has been written, implemented, and validated. That means, in most cases, that resource selection occurs in the third year of a three-year developmental process. By consciously causing that activity to follow a sequence characterized by development, implementation, and validation, curriculum leaders insure that local educators, parents, and patrons are in full control of the curriculum's content and student learning outcomes.

Although we strongly advocate the process just mentioned, rest assured that it is no easy task shifting from a textbook-driven curriculum to one in which resources are looked upon as merely supporting locally-determined academic programs and student learning outcomes. Textbooks and other published materials have dominated the educational scene for so long that it seems almost unthinkable to some teachers, administrators, parents, and students to remove them from their hallowed position of pedagogical prominence. Perhaps it is the notion that someone who writes textbooks is more credible as a curriculum decision-maker than someone who teaches school. Perhaps it is the idea that a major national publisher would never make the mistake of commissioning and printing a text that doesn't have solid value for young people. Whatever it is, the concept of "textbook as curriculum" is pervasive.

In fact, the "textbook as curriculum" perspective is so pervasive that two of the nation's largest states spend a great deal of time evaluating textbook worth, and screening out those considered unacceptable. In both states, coverage and accuracy are important criteria, with varying degrees of attention given to "appropriateness"... depending on the political, philosophical, and religious points-of-view of those responsible for selecting texts. The criteria applied in those states become significant to all other states because of the impact they have on the publishers' market. If only five social studies textbooks are acceptable in Texas and California, then a cost-effective strategy for publishers is to concentrate on the production and sale of those five books in *all* states.

Textbook publishing is more than a big business; using textbooks as the focal point of the curriculumt has really become the American way. In the late 19th century and early 20th century many states produced their own texts for use in the thousands of small individual schools and school districts that dotted our land. The reason for that approach then made sense, inasmuch as there was a need to standardize curriculum in an era of educational beginnings. Small schools, poorly prepared teachers, and a state's inability to monitor so many programs through accreditation made it seem logical to identify student learning needs, and to write textbooks that helped teachers accomplish those intended outcomes. And many of the old textbooks *did* have clearly identifiable student learning outcomes: arithmetic, mathematics, and science focused on both agricultural and mechanical positions; social studies was aimed squarely at the requirements and nurturance of good citizenship in a democracy; and language arts concentrated on good communication and the components of our evolving culture and the cultures that influenced it.

When states began to consolidate their thousands of separate schools and school districts into a few hundred, and were better able to manage their administrative, curricular and financial needs, producing state textbooks became inefficient and burdensome. States created curriculum guides and standards for accreditation, so it seemed logical to let private business provide printed materials to support instruction, so long as those materials were in line with the curricular goals of the state. Most states then sponsored textbook adoption processes that narrowed choices that individual districts had with regard to "approved" instructional materials.

In the mid to late 1960s, it became the vogue for states to allow individual districts considerable latitude in making decisions about curriculum and the materials used to support instruction. "Approved" lists of textbooks became longer and longer, and were finally abolished in many states. Accreditation became a *pro forma* function, with little attention given to curriculum and instruction. In fact, the main emphasis was on innovation that would: (1) make school more interesting, (2) give more attention to the self-esteem needs of students and (3) reduce the high school drop-out rate. In the meantime, elementary textbooks became dominated by certain pet processes for teaching basic skills, while secondary texts looked more and more like college books in which the content reflected the scholarly fascination of academicians. Elementary and secondary teachers became even more firmly entrenched into their separate camps, this time because one group thought that hammering away on basic skills was especially critical while the other group explored great ideas and pursued theoretical challenges of the day.

To make this scenario even more confusing, the state's relinquishing of curriculum management responsibilities to the districts created a tremendous leadership vacuum. Members of boards of education had no idea how to manage a curriculum, and administrators rarely, if ever, had a graduate course on curriculum design and management that was practical enough for day-to-day application. The only recourse for local districts was for teachers and principals to fall back on the wisdom of textbook publishers and choose individual textbooks and textbook series that *seemed* appropriate.

Is it any wonder that the subject of curriculum is perplexing to educators of the 1990s, and that both curriculum and the choosing of textbooks seem to be an unresolvable mess? We in the Curriculum Leadership Institute believe that the situation can be resolved with time and a commitment to systematic improvement, and this section will show how resource selection can be an inherent aspect of the overall improvement model.

Process for Selecting Resources

In our model, the body primarily responsible for selecting instructional resources is the subject area committee (SAC). Those who serve on a SAC are the most conversant with the content of a new curriculum document, and have spent much time working with faculty members and administrators in its classroom implementation. Because of the validation procedures that have been in place, SAC members already have a pretty good idea as to how adequate the current resources are, and what is needed to supplement or replace them. However, with the wealth of materials available today —print, manipulative, and technological— simply discovering "what's out there" requires a tremendous commitment of time and energy. Thus, a special Resource Advisory Committee (RAC) can make the job much easier for each group that is ready to select subject-specific resources.

The Resource Advisory Committee is a permanent, on-going committee comprised of faculty members, one or more administrators, certain special educators, media specialists, and (in some cases) community members. The role of this group is to research products and services in general, and to serve as the communication link between the district and companies and agencies that supply the products and services. To accomplish this, it is imperative that members of the RAC receive training in a number of areas. Among those areas are: (1) the different kinds of resources now available, (2) kinds of business organizations that create those resources, and (3) methods for working with companies interested in selling instructional resources. The RAC then works with an individual SAC in (1) procedures to collect specific data as to methods used to teach high achievement outcomes in each course or grade level, (2) techniques for treating those data so that clear selection criteria are developed, (3) processes for evaluating resources according to outcomes, (4) processes for selecting resources and distributing them to teachers, and (5) methods for training teachers in how to use selected resources. Establishing and training the RAC is important because it gives local educators an advantage in controlling the process of reviewing and selecting instructional resources. Without such training, all advantages are with company representatives interested in selling products to the districts.

Good Training Results in Smart Decisions

Any reader of *Consumer Reports* understands that it pays to know what product to buy in terms of: (1) its quality, (2) what it can do, and (3) how much it costs. The writers associated with *Consumer Reports* test products and examine their repair record. A *CR* test car will be driven and used like an ordinary motorist might use it, and that information is made available through narrative reports and various kinds of charts. A reader can look at those data, compare them to the data shown for other vehicles, and draw conclusions. A conclusion might be influenced by more than quality if the car has features that allow it to do something no other car can do. For example, a car with a poorly organized instrument panel and a bad repair record for its shock absorbers might be acceptable if it has a four wheel drive feature the reader needs. A poorly organized instrument panel is simply an inconvenience, and shock absorbers can be easily replaced with better quality products. On the other hand, if the cost of that car is so great that the reader isn't able to buy a new one, it might be concluded that what the reader needs is a two-year-old version of that car that has been driven with great care.

We know that only a certain fraction of the buying public reads *Consumer Reports* or some other publication which serves to inform and train prospective customers. Many people depend on sales persons to convince them one way or the other, because they make their purchases on the basis of brand loyalty or personal trust in the person selling the product. The American public, though, is not committed to brands as it once was … whether those "brands" are political parties or General Motors' automobiles. And, while trust is still a factor, it might be safe to say that it is no longer "blind trust."

Some school districts are "brand loyal" to certain textbook companies, or have a pleasant relationship with the sales representatives associated with those companies. While there are advantages to that method of operation, it is probably fair to say that a district's students are not being as well served as they could or should be in this era of intense change. Members of a RAC — and subsequently a SAC— if properly trained, will have a *Consumer Reports* mindset: they will make choices according to a product's **quality, performance,** and **cost.** That means that they will need background knowledge and a workable set of criteria.

Eight Step Training: Background Knowledge and Criteria

The ultimate goal of training members of a RAC is to help them develop and effectively use criteria for assessing the quality, performance, and cost of instructional resources. It is also meant to help them work with SACs to effectively coordinate internal procedures for data collection and curricular implementation. A good training program covers:
— resources available,
— organizations that produce resources,
— methods for working with organizations that produce resources,
— methods for collecting and organizing essential curricular information,
— methods for converting curricular information into selection criteria,
— evaluating a resource according to outcomes,

— processes for selecting resources and distributing them to teachers, and
— methods for training teachers to use selected resources.

Resources Available

Resources now include an amazing array of media, from standard textbooks to compact discs that hold huge amounts of information for display on relatively inexpensive table or laptop computers. Modems allow unlimited networking with distant sources of information, and other forms of electronic/mechanical wizardry are appearing every day. If companies that develop and produce that material had their way, every classroom would be filled with their publications and high-tech hardware. And the companies would then have a direct market not only for upgrading baseline purchases, but for the software necessary to keep everything functioning and up-to-date.

The trick is for a school district to acquire hardware and software to support its mission without investing in superfluous equipment. A RAC's job is to examine the products of publishing houses, computer companies, and other suppliers, to draw conclusions about the advantages and disadvantages of their products in a pedagogically generic sense. In other words, RAC members independently and objectively evaluate products so that they can help SACs compare available products to specific curricular needs.

The existence of a RAC allows each SAC to work with knowledgeable experts without all of them having to become experts themselves, or — as non-experts — coming into direct contact with sales persons, with the risk of being convinced to purchase something on the basis of charisma or misplaced trust.

Another RAC function is to remain slightly skeptical with regard to technology, because there are many aspects of a school's curriculum that do not need technological support. In fact, it is essential that a RAC recognize the value of certain free, inexpensive or locally available printed, or low-tech materials as possibly the best resources to support the development of specific student learning outcomes.

By avoiding the "gee whiz, isn't-that-neat" factor, a district can make smart decisions about available resources. Its decisions are more likely to be cost effective, curriculum focused, and outcome based.

Organizations that Produce Resources

It is probably correct to say that confusion reigns with regard to available instructional resources, and part of that confusion is caused by businesses trying to respond to a shifting market. Major publishers continue to produce textbooks as they have before, while modifying them to avoid past criticisms about inequities in race, culture, and gender. They are also working to correct problems of "dumbing down" and "fuzzy focus," by reworking trivial pursuit content that is not perceived by students as being pertinent to the real world. And, along with those efforts, companies must also find common ground between conservative state selection boards and districts (or states) that have shifted to the use of prescribed student learning outcomes.

Computer hardware and software companies are also confused by school markets that are both running short of money and changing their educational goals. Teaching technology as a discipline unto itself is still important, although it is changing due to the increase in user-friendly equipment and children who are technologically proficient. And the use of technology as a teaching tool seems to be entering a common sense era ... one in which educators choose the resource that best promotes learning no matter how sophisticated it appears.

The best business organizations in this era of change and confusion are those that listen and take time to understand the market. Too often we as educators wander up and down aisles of convention exhibit halls, besieged by sales people who peddle gimmickry. They tell us that the only way to break down the status quo is to introduce their products and systems.

The purpose of a district-sponsored RAC is to strip away the hype, and to open doors to those commercial organizations that are willing to become partners with client districts. And those organizations begin that process by listening and understanding our needs.

Working With Organizations that Produce Resources

Those who advise districts about resource selection have strict rules pertaining to the relationship between a district and business organization. The most prominent of those rules is based on a "we'll call you, don't you call us" principle. A RAC works with companies first on a generic basis, then later advises the SAC when it is ready to make subject-specific selections. Thus, the RAC and SAC learn about available products, obtain samples (sans sales pitch), independently review and compare samples, use the services of sales representatives only by invitation, limit sales pitches to responses to specific questions, restrict access of sales people to other district decision makers, and operate within a predetermined budget.

Being in charge of the selection and purchase of resources is no easy task. It requires careful planning and plenty of organizational discipline with regard to strategies and communication. Although business organizations should not be perceived as the enemy, they should be approached with the knowledge that some are more self-serving than others. As said before, the best businesses will become accountable partners who share your interest in improving the quality of student learning.

Collecting and Organizing Essential Curricular Information

In a district committed to outcome-based education, obtaining information necessary to choose appropriate resources is not a major problem. Educators understand the need for "design down, deliver up" thinking, in which high achievement outcomes are linked to course/grade level purposes which are, in turn, linked to subject area purposes and the district's mission. Therefore, only one question is necessary: What resources will best help students achieve the intended learning outcome?

It is at this point that the RAC and SAC begin working together. The RAC shares general information with the SAC about kinds of products available, which companies are willing to work with the district to meet local needs, and general quality and cost-effectiveness of particular products or kinds of products. The RAC then provides instruction to the SAC in steps they need to take for the decision making process. While the SAC will have a relatively good general idea about the kind of resources needed, it is important that specific selection criteria be applied — that certain prevailing principles be adopted to guide deliberation and decision-making.

Converting Curricular Information Into Selection Criteria

Selection criteria are specific guidelines based on both the district's goals and intended student learning outcomes. Here are examples:

____   *The learning resource connects generic knowledge to specific personal/vocational applications understood by students in the ____ grade.*

____   *The learning resource uses language that is challenging, but does not over-shoot the vocabulary of students in ____ grade.*

____   *The learning resource is logical and sequential in its approach to subject matter for students in ___ grade.*

____   *The learning resource stimulates creative and critical thinking in students in ___ grade.*

____   *The learning resource gives attention to the interdisciplinary nature of public school subject matter.*

There may be extensive additional criteria that pertain to the media themselves, such as quality of book bindings, print, pictures, graphics, and page layout. Electronic media will need to be evaluated for ease of use, cost-effectiveness, reliability, and servicing.

Evaluating a Resource According to Outcomes

Criteria applied to outcomes may require the use of "incorporation checks" based on specific learning elements and learning tasks. An "incorporation check" may need an established level of acceptance for any resource. One way to do such a check is to use a simple form while examining the resources under consideration. In traditional resource selection processes, teachers would examine a textbook by looking at such things as illustrations, general topics covered, instructional suggestions, and any special features such as charts, glossaries, or suggested experiments and activities. After finishing with one book, they would move on to the next, looking at the same kinds of features; after examining all books available they would select the one that appealed to them the most.

In an outcome based system, most teachers understand that they're looking for resources to support the outcomes, but they make the mistake of using basically the same traditional approach. They may have the outcomes "in mind," but they look at textbooks or other resources to get general impressions and often choose something because of its appearance, a particular feature, or because it *seems* to fit several outcomes rather than because it indeed supports the new curriculum.

Instead, teachers should start the selection process with the outcomes in front of them. As they begin to examine a resource, they should ask themselves how well that resource helps them teach outcome #1 and give a rating to the resource (on a scale of 1 to 5) for the first outcome. Then they rate the resource for how well it helps them accomplish the second outcome, and so forth. When they have worked through all of the outcomes, they average the ratings to obtain a final score. This process is repeated for all resources under consideration. The resource with the highest average score is the best choice in terms of supporting **all** outcomes. (See sample form below.)

Select a resource to evaluate. Look at each outcome you are required to teach. How good a resource is this for outcome #1? Give a score 1-5 (5=Best). Repeat for outcome #2, and so forth. If the resource does not address an outcome at all, record a 0. Figure the average rating for each resource.

RESOURCE NAME   *OUTCOME #*

	1	2	3	4	5	6	7	8	9	10	11	12	AVG
Example Holt	5	0	3	3	1	4	4	0	3	5	2	5	2.9

In an outcome based system developed by local teachers, there is a good likelihood that no one book or electronic medium will meet all resource needs. In fact, textbooks and other "regular" forms of resources may be less than 50% useful in their present form ... meaning that an individual book offers only half of the information necessary for students to meet intended learning outcomes. Is that sufficient incorporation to justify the purchase cost?

After criteria have been written and studied, a SAC must make solid decisions that might go so far as possibly eliminating the use of standard textbooks in favor of general reference materials, periodicals, and selected compact discs. Money usually encumbered for textbooks might be reassigned to cover the cost of field trips, special resource persons, or interactive video.

Whatever the case, it is imperative that no decision about resources be made without prior thought, the development of precise guidelines, and a systematic evaluation process. It is essential that district leaders be in charge of making final decisions, not those who represent business organizations that provide products and services.

Selecting Resources and Distributing Them to Teachers

As with the implementation of curriculum documents, initiating resources into the instructional program involves much more than sending a package with an attached note. Teachers want to be involved in the resource selection process, and must be given guidance on how to use new materials.

Decisions made by a SAC are always subject to approval and possible modification by the teachers asked to use adopted resources. In fact, it is expected that even an initial decision will broadly reflect the wishes of individual teachers and groups of teachers. That dictates use of an on-going communication which is both formal and informal.

Teachers, while their original opinions are important, must also be educated as to alternative options. Some very good teachers will want to continue use of traditional textbooks, so it may require time and effort to show them the advantages of alternative systems. And after teachers have received materials, they will need guidance on how to use them appropriately.

As in many other aspects of curriculum work, it must be recognized that gaining effective teacher involvement can be a frustrating challenge. Some teachers will take issue with the entire process, based on both philosophical and practical principles. And, as usual, their arguments are not groundless. But once a decision has been made about the use of outcome-focused instruction, flexibility must be achieved with regard to supportive resources.

Training Teachers to Use Selected Resources

By the time teachers receive new resources they are already acquainted with methods for outcome-focused instruction, and have probably been frustrated with their inability to locate adequate reference and supplemental teaching materials during the validation year. Most will likely be grateful for the new publications, hands-on materials, and electronic references they receive, but will nonetheless need guidance.

The key to a training program is that teachers must shift from the exclusive use of textbooks and their supplementary materials to the use of materials as references. In an outcome-focused system, teachers establish the direction and strategies for learning; resources merely provide background content and in-depth meaning. A resource should be a means for enriching instructional content by giving it more relevance and texture.

Teachers accustomed to using worksheets, workbooks, chapter quizzes, and other forms of "canned" teaching tools as *primary* media for instruction, may not have a good attitude about the new approach. While predetermined and drill-oriented instructional media are useful in spots, they have limited value overall. Training will certainly help those teachers build their own instructional tools, and show them how media can be used in accordance with interactive teaching techniques and methods that recognize differences in learning styles.

Resource Selection Basics:

- **An attitude of "textbook as curriculum" can be changed with the introduction of an outcome focused system and processes that encourage step-by-step change.**

- **A Resource Advisory Committee (RAC) helps district educators carefully analyze needs and creates smart consumers, those who make judgments on the basis of product quality, use, and cost.**

- **A RAC prepares a SAC to make smart decisions through an eight-step training program that improves an understanding of:**
  available resources,
  organizations that provide resources,
  how to work with organizations that provide resources,
  how to collect and organize curricular information,
  how to convert curricular information into selection criteria,
  how to evaluate resources according to outcomes,
  how to select and distribute resources to teachers, and
  how to train teachers to use selected resources.

PART IV:
LINKING THE RESULTS BASED CURRICULUM TO INSTRUCTION

THE MATHEMATICS CURRICULUM

The special resource person for this section is Connie S. Schrock, Emporia State University, Emporia, Kansas.

Introduction of the National Council of Teachers of Mathematics publication, *Curriculum and Evaluation Standards for School and Mathematics* (1989), placed new and critical attention on the mathematics curriculums in the nation's public and private schools. Those standards provide criteria to judge the quality of a mathematics program, with special attention given to: (1) concepts and skills that should be emphasized, (2) particular goals that are most appropriate, and (3) instructional methods teachers should use. Much importance is given to helping districts establish a foundation for what is valued in their mathematics program, and to show how a curriculum can be converted from a traditional format into one that is focused and applicable to real life needs.

Those who wrote the standards indicate that implementation of new concepts and practices should be evolutionary, not revolutionary, and that plenty of attention be given to logical scope and sequence plans that meet local needs. In other words, schools should not throw out existing mathematics curricula and implement something new in the space of just a year or two. Some teachers can remember when such a "quick fix" was implemented during the New Math Project of the 1960s, and how teachers, parents, and students were left confused and frustrated. Realizing that change is possible without such dramatic action, those who wrote today's standards say it is important to *review existing curriculum and integrate appropriate changes.* They make those recommendations because many topics currently taught are appropriate and well placed, and because the new standards are meant to be interpreted and integrated — not worshiped and imposed. There is a recognition that teachers need careful training and time to embrace the changes, inasmuch as only full teacher understanding and acceptance will cause a smooth and logical transition from the present curriculum to a new one. Teachers, and the students and parents they serve, must see for themselves how students can master a mathematics curriculum that also achieves local and societal goals.

Societal Goals

The standards are presented under a preamble containing four basic goals, that schools must produce: (1) mathematically literate workers, (2) lifelong learning skills, (3) opportunity for all, and (4) an informed electorate. Each goal seeks to prepare students for a very different kind of century, one in which there are many new jobs that require both technical and critical thinking skills. Students will need to be ready to analyze new situations and draw logical conclusions, so a mathematics curriculum must go beyond basic arithmetic and algebraic facts. It should also provide rich experiences within a variety of mathematical fields, and should convey mathematics as an approach to solving problems and interpreting information.

For example, even young elementary school students should be able to interpret and transfer this kind of knowledge: that if there is a 30% chance of rain on Friday and a 70% chance on Saturday, it does not mean that there is a 100% chance of rain for the weekend. Young students should develop that kind of perspective as a tool to be internalized for daily and long-term use, rather than view numbers and their relationships as abstract symbols and processes to be memorized for no discernible "real life" reason.

Student Goals

If the above four societal goals are to be met, teachers must help students achieve these five learning goals: (1) to value mathematics, (2) to become confident in the ability to use mathematics, (3) to become mathematical problem solvers, (4) to communicate mathematically, and (5) to reason mathematically. Those goals were created because the experts who wrote the standards are concerned that too many students never really achieve any high order learning outcomes because teachers have classified them as "low achievers" who need continuous and repetitive drill on the basics. To break out of that vicious cycle, the standards suggest that mathematics be thought of as a *science* rather than as simply a *skill.* For example, students who feel weak in computational skills may realize their strength in other areas such as problem solving and application, or if they shy away from computation, they may find value and confidence in estimation.

Currently, many middle level and high school courses are organized as separate classes for each topic. If the standards are to be followed, an ideal course would *integrate* the different topics as they are needed and as natural relationships develop. This integration method would allow mathematics to be taught contextually, thereby giving students an opportunity to build on their own understandings. While the classes might move ahead more slowly than is the case now, students would have opportunities to interact with mathematics from a position of intellectual and academic strength.

Curricular integration is not altogether new in mathematics, since it now is found in some algebra and geometry courses in which topics like probability and statistics are included. As a future consideration, given the current needs of industry to check product quality through statistical analysis, integrating that area of study throughout the mathematics curriculum might be a good idea.

Let's examine how the integration of probability and statistics with algebra might benefit student learning according to the five student learning goals mentioned above. If the teacher used concrete industrial examples in a kind of "Junior Achievement" setting, in which specific quality control problems were to be solved through mathematical analysis, then students might value the "real life" efficacy of quantitative evaluation. If taught well, perhaps through a combination of direct instruction and cooperative learning processes, the exercise could also increase student confidence, improve mathematical problem solving ability, and promote the use of mathematical reasoning in other similar situations.

The idea of integrating mathematical topics has clear implications for subject area committees in the development of a subject mission, course and grade level purposes, and high achievement outcomes. Although these examples should not be used word for word, the following design-down format might work for a district or school that is serious about integrating the mathematics curriculum grades K through 12.

Mathematics Mission Statement in a K-12 District

Students in this school district will demonstrate confidence in the use of mathematics through their ability to solve mathematical problems, communicate mathematically, integrate mathematics with appropriate technology, and apply mathematics to real world situations.

Mathematics Program Purpose for Grade 3

Students will apply number operations and principles of geometry to the solving of real life problems.

High Achievement Outcome for Grade 3

Students will identify, interpret and apply sequences or patterns to the solving of problems associated with simple construction projects.

Mathematics Program Purpose for Grade 9

Students will use algebra and basic mathematical reasoning skills to solve problems associated with the maintenance and improvement of quality in industrial products.

High Achievement Outcome for Grade 9

Students will develop a heuristic strategy for identifying real life but non-routine industrial problems, with particular attention given to using mathematical analysis to locate deficiencies in three products.

In preparing the above "design-down" format examples, questions were applied that should be asked in the development of a mathematics curriculum document: *Do the various mission and purpose statements focus on the most essential aspects of mathematics as an integrated and applied discipline?* and *Are the statements reflective of mathematics as a science rather than an eclectic series of random skills?*

When teachers write a task analysis based on a new high achievement curriculum, they must consider what should be done to make integrated learning really work for each student. The most obvious requirement is that teachers conscientiously help students learn why certain processes are used. When a student asks, "Why do we do that?" teachers must be prepared to answer in complete terms. For example, when teaching long division a teacher should fully explain why we "bring down" the next term or why we add zeros behind the decimal. Or when teaching division of fractions, the reasons for inverting and multiplying must be made clear. Rules given to students without insuring an understanding of their meaning are quickly forgotten, so a teacher must constantly ask, "Does what I say make sense?"

No less important for teachers is the belief that mathematics principles are not inherently difficult, and that all students can learn and apply them satisfactorily. Although the issues of mastery and summative assessment for mastery will be discussed later in this section, it is most important that formative "checks for understanding" be applied on a daily basis. A popular technique for such assessment is through student writing. Writing in mathematics is a good way to find out what students understand and why they work a problem as they do. By including writing in the mathematics curriculum, students better communicate their abilities and questions. Situations posed elicit student ability to solve problems and to think their way into certain "real life" applications, a method that underlines the importance of mathematics as a *science* which needs to be communicated in more than one dimension. While numbers alone can communicate, words and sentences provide a means for students to express their meaning in ways that are significant to both them and those with whom they wish to interact. Tangible reality is more important to children and young people than nebulous and abstract symbols, and writing about mathematical applications can make the subject almost as real as playgrounds, paper clips, erasers, pizza, and cake. And as students mature, the sophistication of their mathematical writing and real life applications should grow with them.

Local Needs and Reality

Real world applications may be different depending on whether students live in rural or urban areas, yet the need for mathematics remains constant. Local needs must be considered when a curriculum is revised, and those most acquainted with such needs are parents, patrons and the teachers themselves. The ABC model of school improvement suggests that information be gathered from teachers about the existing curriculum, and that members of a subject area committee (SAC) make basic decisions about appropriate course content, scope, and sequence. That process is important so that teachers may be given opportunities to assert themselves professionally, and can build the organizational dynamics in such a way that teachers will conscientiously implement the new program. The National Standards should be referred to *after* basic decisions are made about essential content, scope and sequence — but *before* the outcome-based curriculum document is prepared. This will cause an intellectual interaction between the local educational decision-makers and those who wrote the standards — a process we call validation.

Local needs must also be considered when mathematics resources are selected, because published materials and technological software must reflect the changed curriculum. While publishing companies state that they support and incorporate the NCTM standards, some are more diligent in doing so than others. Moreover, resources need to reflect local needs as well as the admonitions found in the standards. The ABC model indicates that the subject area committee is fundamentally responsible for selecting materials, and that under no circumstance should a textbook drive curriculum development and maintenance.

Technology

A visionary mathematics curriculum should incorporate technology to the extent a school or district can afford it. Instruction supported by calculators and computers allows students to model real-world uses of mathematics. This recommendation does not imply that the traditional instruction of basic skills be eliminated, but does encourage a balance between traditional techniques and those in which technological tools are used. Performance at higher cognitive levels is not tied solely to the quality of a student's computational skills. On the contrary, a significant aspect of problem-solving is the student's ability to choose the appropriate tool for the problem — given the availability of hardware and software, and the adequacy of budgets.

Calculators and computers, if properly used, must be considered viable tools for any public school student. The use of technology can reduce tedious calculations, thus providing time within a classroom presentation for analysis and creative thinking. Rather than dampening students' interest with an endless worksheet of long division, the skill can be introduced through hand computation and expanded through the use of calculators. With calculators, students can quickly convince themselves that any even number, regardless of its magnitude, is divisible by two.

Applications

The National Council's *Standards* are divided into four parts that pertain to grades K-4, 5-8, 9-12, and evaluation. Each grade level includes four standards which form the basis of the entire curriculum. They are *problem solving, communication, reasoning,* and *connections.* These four strands unify the program, illustrating mathematics beyond rules and procedures by emphasizing underlying concepts. When students are given opportunities to see applications of mathematics, they should be better able to recognize problem situations and patterns. Applications show them a tangible path to finding a solution, how to communicate the methods used in reaching that solution, and proof as to why the solution ought to be seen as valid. Rarely in real world applications will the crux of a problem be to regurgitate the sum $232 + 561$ or cos $\sim$/3. Most often, these numerical challenges are merely a small component of a much more complex set of circumstances. That is why a high achievement outcome used by a teacher must reflect that kind of essential "real life" application.

Manipulatives

Another step toward a strong conceptual understanding of mathematics is the use of manipulatives in the classroom. Manipulatives are anything students touch that will help them understand, and their extensive use can be beneficial from primary grades through high school. Models of conic sections and fraction bars give students reference points that give meaning to their pencil and paper calculations, but often that kind of manipulative-based conceptual development is lost in a barrage of rules and procedures. Curriculum leaders and teachers should remember that lifelong learners and users of mathematics became proficient with real life applications because a conceptual base was formed on which their mechanical prowess could grow.

Implementation Via Staff Development and Resource Selection

Staff development and resource selection are important responsibilities of a subject area committee. Only through good staff development will a curriculum based on tangible applications, manipulatives, and conceptual understandings be properly implemented in the classroom. And only through an insightful approach to selecting classroom instructional aids will teachers have the proper tools for supporting the instructional process.

Any change in curriculum must be made in a way that causes teachers to believe it is right and necessary. Teachers change methods only when they genuinely feel the adjustment improves their teaching or the performance of their students. Training to develop skills necessary to modify a curriculum will vary among individual instructors, as well as among schools and districts. Meaningful inservice activities provide an exchange of ideas between teachers who are implementing new ideas successfully, and those only now considering their implementation. Practices to follow for those coordinating an implementation strategy include concise presentations of concepts, clear demonstrations, group and individual practice, considerable grade level and departmental discussion, and on-site follow-up with individual teachers. The coordination and conduct of this kind of inservice should be the responsibility of a mathematics subject area committee, in cooperation with building principals and other key administrators.

In addition to changing teacher beliefs about the new curriculum and ways to teach it, the subject area committee must insure that sufficient materials and support are provided. Textbooks and other print and technical resources are an integral part of any curriculum, so their selection by the subject area committee must be made in accordance with curricular goals. The impact new resources will have on a teacher's perception of a concept and the ability to explain that concept must be considered. (See the previous section on resource selection for additional guidance.)

Evaluation

As the content and focus of our curriculum changes, so must the techniques to evaluate the success of that curriculum. This includes changing specific aspects of existing evaluation tools such as the written test, as well as introducing new techniques for assessment. Because learning is more important than testing, examinations must measure what is of value and not simply what is easy to test. To be certain that we test for valuable learning, it is essential that teachers diagnose what students know and understand in addition to what they do not understand. Open ended problems with multiple answers and approaches can help in this diagnosis. For example, instead of a memory test item such as "What is 150 divided by 3?", it is better to ask this question: "If you divide 150 by a number and the answer is between 2 and 3, what can you tell me about that number?." The latter question better elicits the student's understanding of division. By rephrasing the problem, "A rectangle has a side of length 3 and a side of length 4, what is the area?" to "Draw a rectangle which has an area of 12 square centimeters," the student is required to do more than simple multiplication skills to find a solution.

Other tools may also be used to assess student learning. Small group, cooperative learning projects teach students group dynamics skills and show them how to create meaningful products. Portfolio assessment systems encourage students to demonstrate what they perceive to be their achievements and progress in the course, causing them to be challenged to set their own goals for the short or long term, and to take greater responsibility for evaluating their own growth. The use of mathematics journals and notebooks encourages students to write clear explanations and design informative graphs, both of which verify that a student understands a concept. Student ability to take notes is also important because it has real-life applications, not simply because it is necessary for college preparation.

Some evaluation techniques involve more teacher time, but yield rich results.

These include personal interviews and observations of student problem solving. The use of those kinds of assessment tools is encouraged, but should be carefully considered inasmuch as change must be cost-effective with respect to a teacher's limited time.

Mathematics Basics:

- Improvements in the mathematics curriculum should be based on the recommendations found in *Curriculum and Evaluation Standards for School and Mathematics*, produced by the National Council of Teachers of Mathematics in 1989.

- The new *Standards* call for evolutionary change in the curriculum, indicating that much that is currently being done should be considered acceptable — with appropriate modifications.

- The *Standards* view student learning outcomes as pertaining to real-life applications, not simply as preparation for the next grade, course, or academic level.

- Students should value mathematical principles and become confident in their use. They should also be able to solve mathematical problems, and communicate and reason mathematically.

- The concept of integrating mathematical principles is recommended in the *Standards* as being particularly important, under an umbrella notion that mathematics is a science, not just a skill.

- Design-down concepts are important in a mathematics curriculum so that all district educators can remain focused on the fundamental reasons the subject is taught. No existing curriculum should be discarded in favor of something new that is theoretically based on the Standards; the curriculum-building format of this model is an important means through which the new *Standards* can gradually be implemented.

- The use of technology is important in a good mathematics curriculum, as are specific application exercises and manipulatives.

- A mathematics subject area committee should give careful attention to implementation through quality staff development and enlightened resource selection, and evaluation techniques must align with the values indicated in the subject area mission.

THE COMMUNICATIONS
(LANGUAGE ARTS) CURRICULUM

The special resource person for this section is Gerrit W. Bleeker, Emporia State University, Emporia, Kansas.

The following scenario actually took place recently in a first grade classroom. The teacher, Mrs. Green, asked her six-year-olds if they had ever heard a story about a gingerbread man. Most had not. She asked them if they had ever tasted a gingerbread man. Most had not. She asked them if they had ever helped their parents or older brothers or sisters bake cookies. Most nodded "yes." After several students shared cookie-making stories, Mrs. Green read to the class her favorite cumulative tale, "The Gingerbread Man." The children listened expectantly. When Mrs. Green finished reading, the class decided to make their own gingerbread man. Mrs. Green helped them read through the recipe and locate the necessary cooking utensils and ingredients. During the preparing process, the class reviewed and practiced math skills as they measured and mixed; talked about telling time as they set the oven timer; jointly decided how to "dress-up" their gingerbread man with raisins, red hots, and other candies; and speculated on how the gingerbread man would look and taste when he was baked.

After popping the class's creation into the hot oven, Mrs. Green ushered her class outside for recess. Upon returning to their classroom, the eager students discovered that their gingerbread man had escaped, leaving only a brief note on the oven door. Mrs. Green helped her first-graders read the note: "RUN, RUN, AS FAST AS YOU CAN, BUT YOU CAN'T CATCH ME, I'M A GINGERBREAD MAN. I'VE GONE TO VISIT THE PRINCIPAL!" The class scurried off to the principal's office to find their runaway friend. The principal informed his guests that the gingerbread man had visited his office, was no longer here, but had left a note for him to share with the first-graders. The principal helped the children decipher the second note: "RUN, RUN, AS FAST AS YOU CAN TO THE NURSE'S OFFICE!" And so they continued their search, going from nurse to counselor to media specialist, talking to new people, decoding new messages, making inferences and drawing conclusions. At last they found themselves in the custodian's broom-closet where they spied a note attached to a broomstick: "RUN, RUN, BACK TO YOUR CLASSROOM!" The excited first graders located their runaway friend waiting for them in their classroom, but no one wanted to eat him. The gingerbread man had come alive for them. "Besides," quipped one boy, "his feet are probably dirty!" Rather than consuming the ginger-bread man, the class decided to write him a note, sharing their feelings about making, losing, and finding him.

This sceond scenario is from a student teacher's lesson plan for a thematic unit on "Survival." The student teacher, Mr. Gray, introduced the unit by having his students bring to class newspaper and magazine articles which detailed how teenagers either survived or succumbed to major problems facing them. After sharing and talking about these real life situations, Mr. Gray asked his class of seniors to read Richard Peck's young adult novel, *Remembering the Good Times.* While reading the novel, each student kept a dialectical journal, describing in one column how characters in the book coped with major problems confronting them, and in another column speculating on how the student would have handled the same problem. The students' dialectical journals were used as a springboard for class discussion. After discussing a number of problems raised by the novel — divorce, suicide, affluence, social/economic cliques, crime/violence, adjusting to change — the students formed small interest groups and collectively researched one of the problems in terms of how other adolescents were dealing with it. Students were encouraged to request information, either by interviewing or writing letters. They could also use print and non-print resources in the school and public libraries. After completing their research, students wrote up their findings in the format of a television news investigator and took turns sharing the results with their classmates and other students from psychology and consumer education classes.

Even though Mrs. Green and Mr. Gray teach at different grade levels, use different materials, and employ different teaching strategies, the overall learning outcomes for each class are similar. Both instructors use a curriculum and methods of instruction which enable students to learn and master communications skills — reading, thinking, writing, speaking, listening — through the process of using language for real, worthwhile purposes. The students are at the center of the curriculum and are immersed in whole language activities. They are taught how to use language to find, process, evaluate, and respond to information. They learn to use language to discover what they know, think, and feel and then learn how to shape and manipulate language in order to communicate their knowledge, experiences, and feelings to others. In both instances, communications skills are taught in an integrated, meaningful context, not through piecemeal or isolated exercises.

Because the communications components are so closely interrelated, a strong communications curriculum strives to integrate all forms of language learning, although balance among each of the several communications areas will vary depending on grade level and purpose of the course. Studies show that instruction which carefully and systematically integrates these language processes is more effective than instruction which artificially fragments them. In addition to integrating English language learning experiences, the above two classroom examples show that the communications curriculum is interdisciplinary. On the elementary level, students learn to connect language arts (reading, listening, speaking, and writing) and mathematics, science, and art; on the secondary level, students learn to connect language arts skills and sociology, history, psychology, and economics. Moreover, the communications curriculum is, by design, spiral in nature. Significant language arts competencies begin at the earliest and most appropriate grade level and then are reinforced, built upon, and elaborated on as students progress through the K-12 program. Ideally then, the communications curriculum will aid students in steadily increasing the range, sophistication, and complexity of all their language arts skills.

Although the primary goal of our elementary and secondary schools is to produce students who can read, think, write, speak, listen, and use communication technology, not only capably, but joyfully, the bulk of the responsibility for teaching these skills is placed on the elementary classroom teacher and on the 7-12 communications teacher. And although efforts continue to implement "languaging across the curriculum" at the secondary level, these programs serve primarily to reinforce and practice the communications skills learned and mastered in the English classroom. Consequently, the communications curriculum must pinpoint in a unified and sequential manner at each grade level student learning outcomes in the areas of reading, literature, writing, speaking, listening, and using communication technology. These student learning outcomes are informed and shaped by six basic whole language or integrated language learning principles.

BASIC PRINCIPLES

1. Students are Empowered as Language Users

The communications curriculum enables students to become proficient and comfortable users of the language by immersing them in using language for real purposes and audiences. They learn to value language as a powerful tool for thinking, imagining, creating, analyzing, evaluating, and problem-solving. Discrete language arts skills are taught and practiced within the context of reading, writing, speaking, and listening; only when the rules of grammar, usage, spelling, and mechanics become an integral part of the language generating process does real language learning occur.

2. Reading is a Transaction Between Reader and Text

The communications curriculum recognizes that reading is a cumulative process of decoding, interpreting, and understanding the printed word. It provides for both guided and independent reading and encourages students to become independent, lifelong readers who appreciate and understand literature, both classical and contemporary trade books. It ensures that students learn reading strategies which help them engage and interact with whole texts. Since students want and need to think and talk about what they read, the curriculum also includes opportunities for them to respond to literature through writing, speaking, drama, and visual arts. Through reading and responding to a variety of literature, students gain insight into self and others, grapple with fundamental human questions, and learn about other times, places, and cultures. As students progress through the literature curriculum and increase their knowledge and understanding of literary forms and conventions, they also learn to interpret and analyze literature from different critical perspectives in order to help them understand the rich complexity of literature and to enrich their appreciation of good art.

3. Writing is Taught as a Process

The communications curriculum establishes a framework in which written composition is taught as a complex, developmental process consisting of at least three stages: planning, drafting, and revising. Since proficiency in writing is a developmental process, continuing all through school and beyond, most writing skills are never fully mastered, but are improved, strengthened, and refined. Additionally, the curriculum reflects the compositional theory that good writing grows gradually and naturally from within writers as they practice using their verbal resources in a variety of ways — modifying, shaping, and reshaping their material for a purpose and for an audience. Writing is not merely a collection of grammar rules, mechanical conventions, and proper spelling; it is a complex, intellectual and intuitive process by which students discover, create, and shape their experiences, feelings, and knowledge so that they may learn from these and communicate them clearly and coherently to others. Students learn by writing and they learn to write by writing — across the curriculum.

4. Speaking and Listening Skills are Taught Within a Communication Context

The communications curriculum recognizes that speaking is both a rhetorical and multisensory activity, involving not only voice and diction, but also nonverbal factors such as space, body language, and physical setting. By learning to speak for varying situations and audiences, students will become fluent, purposeful, and articulate oral users of the language. Moreover, listening, both an aural and visual activity, is taught intentionally in a communication context rather than through isolated drills and exercises. The curriculum provides for activities which enable students to learn how to be attentive, discriminate among sounds, perceive and discriminate among verbal and nonverbal cues, assign meaning, evaluate, remember, and respond intelligently and tolerantly. Speaking and listening skills are a sequential and integral part of the total language program.

5. Communication Technology is Considered a Primary Language Art

The communications curriculum reflects the impact of technology on communication — film, television, video and audio cassettes and compact disks, radio, the word processor, and computer programs. Media is taught both as an object of study and as a tool for communication. Students learn about the power and limitations of various communication media; they also acquire skills in receiving and presenting both experience and information through electronic modes. Students realize that new modes of communication require a new kind of literacy.

6. The Communications Curriculum is Integrated

The communications curriculum acknowledges that language processes are learned most naturally and meaningfully in whole contexts rather than as isolated skills. An integrated program enables students to make connections among the subject areas and to practice daily communication skills in a context of a unifying topic or theme. For example, elementary students studying an ecology unit may observe a natural habitat, take notes, draw sketches and label them, write reflections in their journals, make wildflower prints, read poems and articles about nature, sing songs about ecology, research the history of Earth Day, interview a conservationist, and design a nature collage. On the secondary level, students studying a unit on survival may read both fiction and non-fiction, discuss their reading in small groups, design their own survival kit, construct a language experience chart, research the topic, and create a video presentation. In both instances, students learn to use language arts skills in an integrated way to explore, to understand, and to share what they have learned about an issue.

Given these six underlying principles for effective language learning, an integrated communications curriculum contains learning outcomes similar to those set forth in the following three samples:

Sample One

Subject Mission Outcome (one component): Students will demonstrate the knowledge and skill to read and respond to a variety of literature.

Fifth Grade Outcome: Students will read with open-mindedness, curiosity, and a readiness to ask questions.

Learning Task: After reading a piece of literature, the student will generate questions concerning the motivation for the central character's actions.

Teaching Method/Student Activity: After reading the text silently, the students will write five questions on paper and take turns sharing them with the whole class. Student-generated questions will be used to discuss and understand the central character's behavior.

Means of Assessment: Informal writing assignment (list of questions) and teacher anecdotal record of class participation.

Sample Two

Subject Mission Outcome (one component): Students will demonstrate the knowledge and skill to write effectively and fluently.

Eighth Grade Outcome: Students will develop their own "voice" in writing and adapt it for a specific audience.

Learning Task: The student will write two letters describing the same incident, one addressed to a close friend and the other addressed to an authority figure.

Teaching Method/Student Activity: After practicing individual "voice" tuning exercises and participating in a whole class "audience" profiling activity, each student will write two letters. The teacher will confer with individual students during the writing process.

Means of Assessment: Peer evaluation of features of "voice" and "audience" in the two writing samples which will be placed in the student's writing portfolio.

Sample Three

Subject Mission Outcome (one component): Students will demonstrate an understanding of the impact of technology on communication.

Eleventh Grade Outcome: Students will analyze the effect of media on the communication product.

Learning Task: The student will write a paper comparing and contrasting a newspaper account and a television newscast of the same incident, noting specifically how each media shapes the message.

Teaching Method/Student Activity: Students will read a newspaper article and watch a taped television newscast of the same incident, brainstorm similarities and differences, and then each write a comparison and contrast paper.

Means of Assessment: Teacher evaluation of formal writing sample.

Communications Basics:

- The primary goal of a communications curriculum is enabling students to learn and master reading, thinking, writing, speaking, and listening skills through the process of using language for real, worthwhile purposes.

- Communications skills are best taught in an integrated, meaningful context, not through piecemeal or isolated exercises.

- It is important for students to understand the interdisciplinary nature of learning, and that the communications curriculum can and should be merged with other areas of learning.

- Six basic principles should be followed in implementing an effective communications curriculum:

  (1) students are empowered as language users,
  (2) reading is a transaction between reader and text,
  (3) writing is taught as a process,
  (4) speaking and listening skills are taught within a communication context,
  (5) communication technology is considered a primary language art, and
  (6) the communications curriculum is integrated.

THE SCIENCE CURRICULUM

The special resource person for this section is R. Scott Irwin, Emporia State University, Emporia, Kansas.

In spite of over three decades of massive (most estimates exceed $1 billion) funding for development and implementation of "exemplary" K-12 science curricula, it is well documented that two-thirds of America's kids are NOT participants in effective science instruction.

The professional literature in science education, curriculum development and implementation is replete with lamentations and depressing accounts of an all-too-familiar condition: In the face of all the reports of higher cognitive and affective gains made by K-12 students attending schools that have implemented an activity-based science program, a majority of our school districts continue to engage students in passive, science-flavored reading, memorization and regurgitation. And, in an alarming percentage of our elementary classrooms, science simply is not part of the "real" curriculum (what actually gets taught and learned).

For as long as most of us can remember, educators have struggled to be recognized and respected as professionals. We have always held this deep conviction that teaching was as noble and professional a calling as practicing law, medicine, dentistry, etc., despite its more limited material rewards. Yet, how "professional" are we when, 30 years after the development and validation of science curricula that has proven superior, two-thirds of all those responsible for teaching K-12 science have failed to engage their students in **doing** science?

Would you take your child to a pediatrician who, 30 years after the development of polio vaccine, failed to immunize his or her patients against this crippling killer? Would you consider that physician a "professional"? Then why should we regard as professionals those educators who practice negligence in the treatment for the intellectual health and growth of our children?

In this section, we will address most of the reasons our science instruction isn't as effective as it should be. And, we'll show how an outcome based curriculum development and maintenance model can help you and your teachers build a strong, viable science curriculum for your schools ... one in which students enjoy the achievement of meaningful, high level outcomes.

Professionals Must Have Ownership In What They Do

The philosophy advocated in this book is that teachers who are treated as professionals act like professionals. Their opinions earn our respect. Professionals also tend to learn from experience. So, let's examine a "worst-case" and "bad-case" scenario from the past three decades of science curriculum work, see what we've learned, and explore where we might go from here with a "best-case" scenario.

Worst-Case Example

A teacher from Centerville, USA returns home from an enrichment workshop (or graduate course from a nearby university), all fired up with enthusiasm over new approaches and materials for teaching science in the elementary school. She's armed with everything: sample teachers' guides, scope and sequence charts, videos, computer courseware, even a sample materials kit with all the goodies a second grade teacher and her students might need to do every experiment in a new curriculum. Upon sharing news of her wealth with her building principal and superintendent, she is immediately appointed as chairperson of the district's science textbook adoption committee, a position for which she has little or no training (but, what the heck, neither does anybody else, and besides, at least she **likes** to teach science!).

The other teachers on the science committee are quietly polite as they watch the videos of kids and teachers in action with a "hot" new hands-on science program. But they quickly conclude, "Who needs all the noise, mess, hassle and extensive daily preparation time, to say nothing of the hours of staff development needed to get ready to teach this stuff!" So, six committee meetings later, they vote to adopt the newest edition of some smooth-talking salesman's textbook, complete with annotated teacher's guide, blackline worksheet masters, colorful overhead transparencies, and a complete battery of short quizzes and longer tests for each chapter and unit. At its next meeting, the local school board accepts the science committee's recommendations but vote to NOT ORDER THE MATERIALS KITS that go with the science adoption. "That'd cost us more than the last reading and math adoption combined!" harrumphed the board president.

The new science program quickly settles into the same old pattern of science flavored reading... and nothing really changes.

Meanwhile, what happens to that enthusiastic and dedicated teacher who chaired the committee? At best, she's feeling a little disappointed and disillusioned about how science can or should fit into her students' lives. Perhaps she still directs an occasional student activity in her own classroom, one that seems to somehow highlight the concepts or theme of a chapter or unit in that new textbook.

At worst, she may be bitter and resentful toward the administrator(s) that set her up to fail; toward her peers who do not share her new found enthusiasm for science; and toward the directors and/or sponsors of that workshop that got her all excited about activity based science in the first place. After all, what do those university profs know about daily life in the elementary school trenches, anyway?

Bad-Case Example

Dr. Marie Sharpe, Associate Superintendent for Curriculum in Affluent

Suburbia, USA and Dr. Rupert Hipp, Curriculum Coordinator for The Inner-City Magnet Schools near Affluent Suburbia, attend a school administrators' convention during which they see a high-tech, multi-media presentation on a new middle school science program. To their credit, both administrators have long sensed the need for improved instruction in science for the early adolescent. They've read abstracts and articles from those studies showing it's the middle school years when kids get "turned off" to school (in general) and science (in particular). Both administrators return to their home districts with sincere motivation, confidence in their leadership styles, and very much aware of the degree of influence they have in matters of curriculum. Each administrator quickly assembles a Science Curriculum Committee. At their first meeting, each shows a "slick" video of highlights from the development and school based validation of this Science/Technology/Society based middle school curriculum. Some of the teachers on the committee have already heard about this new program. And all members were quick to note that it was funded by no less than the National Science Foundation and featured a talented, scientist-teacher writing and field testing team that worked closely for five years with the ultimate publisher of the program.

So, with nothing better to suggest, assurance that the money was available to purchase ALL necessary materials to implement the new program (lush budget in the suburban district; special grant funds for the "traditionally underserved" in the inner city district) and the forceful charisma of their respective curriculum leaders, the science committees from both districts cast a unanimous vote to adopt this dynamic new socially conscious science program for their middle schoolers.

What happens next in both school districts has a hauntingly familiar ring: In the affluent suburban district, a two-week-with-full-pay staff development workshop gets canceled when Dr. Sharpe resigns her position to accept the superintendency of another affluent school system. Instead of two weeks of training and practice using materials from their new science program, the teachers are left with the last half day before classes begin in August to unpack their new program on their own and get ready to teach it!

In the inner city magnet schools, even with supplemental government funding earmarked for improvement of science and mathematics teaching, the funding formula only provided for one science teacher from each middle school to attend a one week staff development workshop. Each of those teachers was then expected to return to his or her respective building, plan and direct pre-school inservice, and function as the science resource person for colleagues. All remaining middle school science teachers and their principals were minimally involved or informed of the selection of the new curriculum or the preparation and ongoing support that is so crucial to successful implementation.

Already slim chances for success were further damaged in both school districts when the commercial supplier of the program's laboratory materials failed to anticipate the nationwide response to the new curriculum and half the teachers still had not received complete science kits at Halloween. But the final 'kiss of death' for what might have been effective middle school science teaching crept over both districts during the second and third year of implementation when it became painfully obvious no long range provisions had been made to (a) provide ongoing staff development to science teachers new to either district, or (b) provide budgetary support for the routine, periodic replenishing of the consumable items that teachers and students need each school year.

What Have We Learned From Our Mistakes?

The 1960s, '70s, and '80s represent the greatest period of research and development in the history of science education. While none of the curricula developed during the period were ideal for all learners in all environments, a good portion of them met or exceeded the expectations of their developers and at least some of the school districts that tried them. Nevertheless, to the surprise of no one, there are easily as many studies revealing WHY so few students have experienced success in science as there are new programs purporting to define and achieve that success.

An analysis of schools whose students enjoy success in the sciences and those in which success is limited reveals some conspicuous differences. School districts with effective K-12 science curricula tend to have most or all of the following characteristics:

1. The teachers who are responsible for actually teaching science have the greatest influence on:
   a.   determining how their instruction serves the overall mission of the school district;
   b.   establishing a few, high level outcomes for students at each level of science instruction;
   c.   designing, selecting and validating the most appropriate science teaching materials and strategies to help students achieve those outcomes; and,
   d.   sharing in the planning and direction of continuous, ongoing staff development.

2. Teachers are well prepared in that:
   a.   they have strong backgrounds in both subject matter content and effective science teaching strategies and materials; and,
   b.   new teachers are recruited with emphasis on these attributes.

3. There is a well-funded, well-defined, well-managed system for providing teachers and students with an adequate, continuous supply of living and nonliving sci-

ence teaching materials.

4.   At all stages in the planning, implementation and evaluation of the science curriculum, building principals play an active, visible, supportive role.

Better/Best-Case Example

Greg is a biology and general science teacher in a medium-sized, consolidated rural high school in the Midwest. When he started teaching six years ago, and before his district began implementing a comprehensive, outcome based curriculum model, Greg admits to spending days of valuable classroom time drilling students on the classic Latin names for phylum, class, order, family, and species... especially for those Great Plains plants and animals that are part of his students' native grassland ecosystem.

Nowadays, this active, professionally motivated young teacher no longer spends so much time drilling for the memorization of long lists of "factoids." To be sure, Greg still describes and illustrates representative examples of how scientists classify living organisms. But, he spends much more time engaging students in both real and simulated field studies of the **interrelationships** among populations of organisms (producers-consumers-decomposers; predators and prey; etc.) in grassland, desert, marine, arctic and other ecosystems in all parts of planet earth.

"The problem solving processes my students practice in those ecosystem studies and the knowledge they acquire about   patterns and relationships among living things and their environment — these are **meaningful, transferable** skills, 'habits-of-mind,' and concepts," says Greg. "Our school district's solid commitment to an outcome based model for curriculum reform helped me break out of the cycle of teaching 'factoids'," he admits.

Not surprisingly, Greg is an active member of the Subject Area Committee (SAC) for science in his district. To make sure their efforts aligned with the overall mission of the school district, the science SAC focused on "What **all** high school graduates should know and be able to do in science, including interrelated achievements in mathematics and technology." Their one critical underlying principle was *LESS is MORE*, that the **understanding** and **applicability** of *fewer*, high achievement outcomes is much more important than the *quantity* of material covered.

The trickle-down effect of all this is like a breath of fresh air through such school districts. As Greg might describe it, "We spent **three years** with a dozen colleagues (a) sharing what we were already doing in science; (b) reorganizing toward a few, significant outcomes we'd like our kids to achieve at each grade level; and then (c) surveying and selecting the best *combination* of resources to achieve those outcomes; (d) training ourselves and our peers to use them; and (e) becoming our own toughest critics as we validate what does and doesn't work so we can continuously improve what and how we teach."

"You can't do all that without getting to know each other pretty well," insists Greg. "We may not agree on every little detail in this revised, streamlined science curriculum, but we definitely respect and support each other! And, most important, we, our students, their parents, our administrators and school board members all know and endorse WHAT we expect from all our students and WHY those expectations are worth achieving."

Does Every School District Have To Start From Scratch?

It's a poor use of time and talent to expect every science committee in every school district in the land to start from scratch in redefining how their science curriculum will help the total school district fulfill its mission. Fortunately, maybe for the first time ever, real help is on the way via "Project 2061" and **Science For All Americans.**

While reflecting on education, James B. Conant once recalled an exchange between Alice and the Cheshire Cat in **Alice in Wonderland,** to wit: "If you don't know where you want to go, any map will do." **Science For All Americans** is about scientific literacy. It represents a set of recommendations by the National Council on Science and Technology Education, a distinguished group of scientists and educators appointed by the American Association for the Advancement of Science (AAAS), on what understandings and "habits-of-mind" are essential for ALL citizens in a scientifically literate society. As part of the AAAS initiative called "Project 2061," **Science For All Americans** was written as the culmination of the first of three phases of a massive project to establish a conceptual base for reform by spelling out the knowledge, skills and attitudes all students should acquire in their total K-12 school experience. **Science For All Americans** is a strong endorsement of the "Less Is More" approach. In redefining only the basic core of learning in science, mathematics and technology that should be expected of all students, **Science For All Americans** includes only that subject matter content that can be defended as *essential, enduring and learnable.*

Phase II of "Project 2061" is now well underway. It involves teams of educators and scientists transforming **Science For All Americans** into several alternative curriculum models for use by school districts and states. During this phase, the project is also drawing up "Blueprints for Action" for reforming teacher education, organization of schooling, educational policies and educational research.

Phase III will be a widespread collaborative effort, lasting a decade or longer, in which many groups active in educational reform and improvement will use the resources of Phases I and II to move the nation toward scientific literacy.

When one considers the widespread movement toward a more outcome based curriculum in many schools, state departments of education and accrediting agencies throughout America, the timing of efforts like "Project 2061" couldn't be better.

Maybe every teacher in America really doesn't have to "reinvent the wheel."

You can obtain copies of **Science For All Americans** and/or the "Project 2061" newsletter, **2061 Today** by writing: Project 2061, American Association for the Advancement of Science, 1333 H Street NW, Washington, DC 20005.

Science Basics:

- **Research overwhelmingly supports an activity-based science program as being most effective.**

- **A science curriculum is also more effective when those who teach science are involved in planning and implementing the curriculum and the ongoing staff development needed to support it.**

- **There must be a well funded, defined, and managed system for providing an adequate, continuous supply of living and nonliving science teaching materials.**

- **Building principals must play an active, visible and supportive role for teachers to implement an activity-based program.**

- **SCIENCE FOR ALL AMERICANS represents recommendations for necessary learning for a scientifically literate society.**

THE SOCIAL STUDIES CURRICULUM

The special resource person for this section is James A. Hannon, Emporia Public Schools, Emporia, Kansas.

In 1989, the National Commission on the Social Studies in the Schools made public its report, "Charting a Course: Social Studies for the 21st Century."   The report embodies recommendations that clearly go beyond a simple reorganization of the scope and sequence of the cognitive curriculum. Indeed, careful examination of the Commission's findings suggests a thorough re-examination of our very vision of what ought to be the outcomes of social studies education and how these outcomes might best be achieved. Recognizing that not all social studies educators embrace the Commission's report in its totality, some of its more significant components will, none-the-less, be briefly recalled to provide some common ground for discussion and future application.

A New Vision

Perhaps the very heart of the Commission's recommendations is the recognition that, among the social studies, there is a certain body of knowledge and skills that must be *applied* effectively within the social, political and economic contexts of societies. Thus, when district mission statements typically suggest that students will become responsible, productive citizens, the logical implication for the social studies is that persons must be able to do more than obey the laws and make a living. It is imperative that people act and interact positively within and among societies and their institutions. To simply possess a particular body of knowledge and set of skills does not necessarily warrant the assumption that one can apply them to the real world. The Commission, therefore, emphasizes the application of social studies knowledge and skills to real life situations as the focal outcome for social studies education for the 21st century.

Content Recommendations

Recognizing dramatic changes in world events, it is no surprise that the Commission perceives society as being very global in nature. Specifically, it is recommended that social studies programs devote at least as much attention to significant world civilizations as is devoted to America. History and geography are regarded as the cornerstones of the social studies curriculum. Within that framework, other components of the social studies should be consistently integrated so that students possess a firm understanding of each upon graduation.

A Cumulative Curriculum

Recognizing that the elimination of redundancy and superficiality have been goals that have frequently eluded social studies curriculum designers, the Commission emphasizes the need to develop programs of social studies that are truly cumulative in nature. Social studies should be a constant in each school curriculum from kindergarten through grade twelve, with each subsequent grade level building on, not simply repeating, knowledge and skills learned earlier. Considerable efforts should be made to replace the memorization of superficial facts and concepts with in-depth studies that will increase the students' insight, understanding and abilities to apply what they have learned to real situations.

An Integrated Curriculum

A concern of many educators for some time has been the apparent inability of many students to apply knowledge and skills, particularly outside the context of the given course or subject in which they were acquired. The Commission recognizes that the social studies naturally affords some of the best opportunities to combine the diverse content of the school's curriculum. Given that application to real life situations is imperative, the integration of the various components of the social studies, both among themselves and with other content areas, is critical. The Commission particularly encourages the integration of the humanities and the natural and physical sciences within the social studies.

Methods and Materials

Most educators accept that all students can learn, but not necessarily in the same ways nor at the same pace. Further, it is generally accepted that acquisition of knowledge and skills from a variety of sources tends to reinforce learning, and that students can become more proficient in applying what they have learned to a variety of situations. To these ends, the Commission recommends that a variety of materials and methods of instruction be employed in the social studies classroom.

A Case for Outcome Development

The Commission's report intentionally encourages social studies educators to reflect upon the role of the social studies in preparing students for the future. Through serious examination, one recognizes that little has changed in the social studies curriculum for several decades. If one accepts the Commission's new vision of the social studies, then it is logically concluded that students must become both individual and cooperative learners who are capable of recognizing and solving current and future problems in appropriate ways. The social studies curriculum, therefore, must lead the student beyond the redundant memorization of facts and concepts. The outcomes of social studies education must be the development of persons who can effectively deal with the real challenges of a world that is becoming increasingly complex and global in nature.

The first, and perhaps most significant, prerequisite to relating the social studies to real life situations is to begin thinking in terms of learning outcomes that reflect what students can do, not just what they know! Consider the following examples of social studies outcomes.

Sample One

District Mission Outcome (one component): Students will be responsible consumers in a global society.

Subject Mission Outcome (one component): Students will evaluate policies for consuming natural resources.

Tenth Grade Outcome (one of five to fifteen outcomes): Students will design a policy for conserving important world resources.

Seventh Grade Outcome (one of five to fifteen outcomes): Students will demonstrate ways to conserve natural resources.

Fifth Grade Outcome (one of five to fifteen outcomes): Students will investigate the uses of natural resources and explain the importance of conserving them.

Second Grade Outcome (one of five to fifteen outcomes): Students will identify several products and relate them to the natural resources used in their production.

Sample Two

District Mission Outcome (one component): Students will demonstrate skills in problem solving and decision making.

Subject Mission Outcome (one component): Students will critique the impact of governmental policies on societies.

Twelfth Grade Outcome (one of five to fifteen outcomes): Students will critique the impact of the current economic policies of selected countries on the world community.

Tenth Grade Outcome (one of five to fifteen outcomes): Students will design a policy to fulfill an important economic need in the United States.

Eighth Grade Outcome (one of five to fifteen outcomes): Students will compare ways societies solve economic problems.

Fifth Grade Outcome (one of five to fifteen outcomes): Given limited economic resources, students will demonstrate ways economic choices are made.

Third Grade Outcome (one of five to fifteen outcomes): Students will distinguish between wants and needs and use shopping and budget simulations to demonstrate appropriate choices.

First Grade Outcome (one of five to fifteen outcomes): Students will recognize that people need money to buy the things they need.

The previous samples illustrate several important elements of the relationships between the new social studies curriculum and the design down model of curriculum development. First, they exemplify how the social studies curriculum emphasizes outcomes — what students will do based on real life or life-like situations. Second, notice the role of the social studies curriculum in achieving two components of a district mission. Although the district mission outcomes are rather generic, as most mission statements naturally are, the particular role of the social studies in achieving the district mission is exemplified. Application of higher order thinking skills is evident in all of the examples.

The examples also show that the curriculum is cumulative in nature. Successful achievement of the outcomes identified for each particular grade level depends to a considerable degree on the knowledge and skills previously required. There should be little time or need for redundancy here. Also recall that the integration of at least one component of the social studies within the context of the broader curriculum is represented here. In sample two, the ultimate objective is problem solving and the curriculum designers have used economics as one vehicle through which that particular objective will be achieved. Finally, the samples clearly reflect the "design down, deliver up" nature of an outcome based curriculum.

Perhaps the social studies lend themselves as well as, or even better than most disciplines to real life situations. This is one reason why it is so disappointing that we have continued to implement social studies programs in which students see so little relevancy. An outcome based program, however, inherently defies irrelevancy. When one begins to match properly articulated outcomes with appropriate learning tasks and assessments, this fact becomes even more apparent.

Consider how an outcome based program begins to take form in an actual classroom setting. As you read the following examples, keep in mind that it is the outcome that is essential. Learning tasks, teaching methods, student activities and even assessment will vary somewhat as the individual teacher applies his/her instructional approach. Also, keep in mind that there will probably be more than one learning task and more than just one form of assessment necessary for each outcome. The following examples are necessarily limited in those respects.

Sample One

Subject Mission Outcome (one component): Students will evaluate the impact of economic decisions on societies.

Eighth Grade Outcome (one of five to fifteen outcomes): Students will compare ways people solve economic problems.

Learning Task: Students will work cooperatively to solve an economic problem involving the relationship between productivity and the acquisition/distribution of wealth.

Teaching Method/Student Activity: Students will engage in a group simulated activity. Each student group will be given $1,500 in play money with the instructions to purchase items necessary to begin farming on the Great Plains in 1900. After research, each group must determine how the dollars will be most efficiently spent based upon need priorities and cost/productivity analysis of hand tools versus the modern machines of the day. Groups will present and defend their decisions to the class.

Means of Assessment: After class critique and discussion, each student will write a brief paper explaining ways people can work together to effectively solve economic problems.

Sample Two

Subject Mission Outcome (one component): Students will evaluate policies for conserving natural resources.

Tenth Grade Outcome (one of five to fifteen): Students will design a policy for conserving the world's natural resources.

Teaching Method/Student Activity: Students will simulate a world congress and produce an international policy for conserving natural resources. Students will be divided into teams with each team researching and representing the interests of a particular nation.

Means of Assessment: Teacher's anecdotal records of student participation in class discussion/debates and analysis of student research notes will be used to assess achievement of the desired outcome.

These examples give some insight as to how an outcome based social studies program may be applied in the classroom. Notice that outcomes, teaching methods/student activities, and assessments share one common element — application of knowledge and skills! In each of these examples the student is an active participant in his/her own education. Do not be misled, however, by the fact that these examples are taken out of context. Remember that in these social studies classes there are several grade level or course outcomes to be achieved. Also recall that the curriculum is cumulative. The assumption is that students have already learned the necessary skills and knowledge to perform the expected tasks. This has been achieved through the successful accomplishment of previous learning tasks in this and earlier grade levels. If students are not capable of successfully achieving the desired outcomes, the teacher will intervene with additional learning tasks to correct the assessed deficiencies.

Social Studies Basics:

- The NCSS report, "Charting a Course: Social Studies for the 21st Century," suggests outcomes for the social studies and how they might be achieved.

- The report not only provides content recommendations, it emphasizes a cumulative and integrated curriculum.

- The social studies curriculum must lead the student beyond the redundant memorization of facts and concepts. Learning must be related to real life situations and must reflect what students can do in those situations, not just what they know.

- The outcomes of social studies education must be the development of persons who can effectively deal with the real challenges of a world that is becoming increasingly complex and global in nature.

THE ARTS CURRICULUM

The special resource person for this section is Linda Willis Fisher, Illinois State University, Normal, Illinois.

The arts includes two major categories: VISUAL ARTS, referring to objects and experiences which include drawing, painting, printmaking, photography, film, ceramics, fiber arts, and sculpture and PERFORMING ARTS involving dance, drama, and music. Some programs include a third category, LITERARY ARTS, which encompasses composition of poetry, fiction, and plays.

The arts provide universal communication and expression that reaches beyond the differences in the verbal/written languages. Through the arts, one can gain a better understanding of the history and culture of past and present societies. The sounds of music, the movement of dance, the character roles of drama, and the images of the visual arts provide insight to an individual, a culture, or to a specific time.

Through arts education, students attain appreciation for their own artistic potential while acquiring the knowledge and skills useful for understanding the fundamental cultural values of our society. Arts experiences involve *passive* (appreciating) as well as *active* (expressing using materials and processes) learning.

Reform in Arts Education

Arts experiences in the schools have a history of emphasizing process over content with a concentration on the skills of art making and performing, and favoring the talented student. The reform of arts education programs calls for a comprehensive approach for <u>all</u> students which includes art making and performing, yet involves much more.

In 1988 the National Endowment for the Arts (NEA) released the study on arts education, *Toward Civilization: A Report on Arts Education,* in which a balanced education was defined as consisting of basic knowledge in three branches of learning — the arts, humanities, and sciences. The *Report* lists four purposes of arts education: to give our young people a sense of civilization, to foster creativity, to teach effective communication, and to provide tools for the critical assessment of what one reads, sees, and hears.

A comprehensive approach, referred to as discipline-based art education, originated in the visual arts. It integrates content from production, history, criticism, and aesthetics. Programs using this approach, appropriate for all arts areas, have the potential to develop intellectual skills and provide opportunities for creative self-expression. Students who consider the arts from the viewpoint of artist, historian, critic, and aesthetician become more perceptive about visual images, dance movements, musical compositions, and dramatic performances. As students learn about other artists and assess works of art, the quality of the student's own work improves measurably.

The art making/performing component of a comprehensive arts curriculum allows students, as *artists*, to present their ideas and feelings by creating expressive images, movements, and sounds. Productive members of future societies will need to be flexible, imaginative thinkers who can investigate and find multiple solutions to the same problem.

The study of the history of individual art areas acquaints students, as *arts historians*, to other times and cultures. In the next century, today's students will need to work cooperatively with others from different cultures; therefore, they will need to respect and appreciate cultural differences, yet recognize commonalities. The arts help to reach this goal.

Learning to critique and judge works of art increases students' ability, as *arts critics*, to think independently, creatively, and to make reasoned interpretations and judgments. Exposure to aesthetic issues helps students, as *aestheticians*, clarify the meaning of art in their own lives. The ability to think critically and creatively and to make informed judgments is essential for people of the 21st century.

Therefore, one can examine the benefits of arts education that extend beyond the appreciating and expressing mode. A comprehensive arts education program can facilitate development of the skills and characteristics important to students' success now and as members of the 21st century. A quality arts program helps to develop critical thinkers, problem-solvers, and decision-makers; cooperative workers; sensitive learners who appreciate and understand different cultures and cultural values; and confident individuals who recognize uniqueness in themselves and others.

Interrelating the Arts

As well as instruction in the individual areas, the arts can be presented together. Interrelated arts instruction is designed to enable students to recognize the same aesthetic concept in more than one art form as well as the natural relationship among the arts areas. For example, students can create a variety of lines using art materials and their bodies in space and time. Lines can be drawn on paper, improvised by sound, illustrated by a locomotor pattern, and characterized by walking, talking and gesturing.

Integrating the Arts

In addition to instruction of content knowledge and experiences within the individual art areas, each of the arts can contribute to learning in other disciplines of the curriculum. Learning-styles research has shown that the arts help students learn beyond lecture-type, language-only instruction. Integrated into the general education curriculum, the arts can help to achieve many of the aims of education reform. The study of the arts carries over into other subject areas.

A school with strong arts curricula produces non-artistic benefits. In a high performance environment where students are excited about learning, teachers attribute higher test scores on other traditional subjects to the integration of the arts for learning mathematics, reading, science, and social studies. The arts also provide a common language that enhances cultural understanding and appreciation in the increasingly diverse cultural settings in our schools.

A Broader View of Art Education

Students should be able to transfer their success in school to life in a complex and challenging future. Arts educators need to constantly convey to the community that their students are learning a variety of useful lifelong skills. One way to do this is for performances and exhibits to project a broader view of the arts curriculum. For example, printed programs can include a summary of course content, including the school's mission statement and the relationship of the outcomes and activities of individual courses. One student can write program notes describing concert selections, and another could introduce the work on the concert program or at the exhibit, explaining its important technical elements. At an arts festival students might demonstrate rhythmic patterns; dramatic interpretations; and drawing, painting, and sculpture techniques. During intermission of a dramatic production, creative drama students could present a scene from the drama being presented as it might have been conceived if written by others. Art exhibits could include a written explanation or photographs of studio experiences, portraying sequential development of the displayed art work, as well as describing objectives of the assignment and how multiple solutions were developed. Exposure to the knowledge content and critical thinking, problem-solving, and decision-making processes required in the arts will help the public understand the breadth of the arts curriculum.

It is important that the public be aware that the substance of the arts curriculum occurs within the curricular day rather than at public performances, school musicals, and art exhibits. Often these are the only results of arts programs the public sees; therefore many citizens conclude that the sole purpose of public school arts programs is to train artists and performers.

A Comprehensive Arts Curriculum

A comprehensive arts curriculum is part of the basic K-12 curricular program and consists of more than making and performing. It goes beyond holiday arts and crafts, marching band for athletic events, dance recitals, and class plays. Arts curricula must meet the needs of all the students, not just a talented few. The arts curriculum is an independent strand, yet dovetails with other core academic subjects across the curriculum. Just as all other subjects, arts education should be held accountable by an evaluation/assessment procedure.

The phrase, discipline-based art education, was coined by H. Dwaine Greer, Professor of Art Education at the University of Arizona, Tuscon, to describe a multi-faceted, comprehensive approach to visual arts education. The following definitions have been adapted to include the arts areas of dance, drama, music, and the visual arts. Such a comprehensive arts curriculum integrates ideas, skills, knowledge, values, and creative abilities from four arts disciplines:

1) **arts history,** which allows students to investigate and compare the arts made and performed from different cultures, places, and times;
2) **arts criticism,** which allows students to analyze and evaluate the structure, meaning and significance of works of art and to make reasoned interpretations and judgments about them;
3) **aesthetics,** the inquiry into understanding the nature, beauty, and experience of the arts, which allows students to formulate opinions about art and to articulate them using appropriate vocabulary;
4) **arts production,** which allows students to express their ideas and feelings by creating or performing in one or more of the arts forms.

When preparing an arts education program, curriculum developers can use the following list to review the program elements. The program is:
- a component of the school system's core curriculum.
- taught district-wide.
- taught at all levels of the K-12 curriculum.
- based on a written, sequential curriculum where content builds on earlier learning.
- integrated with other segments of the curriculum.
- taught to all children, not just those who are identified as talented or who express interest.
- emphasizing multicultural, gender, and global perspectives.
- promoting higher-level critical and creative thinking skills.
- emphasizing student's self concept.
- providing experiences with authentic works of art from various cultures through museum visits and attendance at concerts, dance performances, and dramatic productions; artists and performers in school programs; and other community resources.
- going beyond holiday arts and crafts, marching band for athletic events, dance recitals, and class plays; drawing its content from the four arts disciplines.
- assessable, because both teachers and students should be held accountable for what

is learned in the arts classes.

If such features are in place, the students will be provided with a high-quality arts education program.

Who Should Plan the Arts Curriculum?

The curriculum committee, comprised of arts teachers and classroom teachers who have received arts training, should develop a written curriculum that is comprehensive in content and sequentially organized. Committee members may obtain guidelines for essentials in arts education from a number of agencies and organizations including the Alliance for Arts Education (national and state levels), National Endowment for the Arts, American Council for the Arts, Council of Chief State School Officers, National PTA, National School Boards Association, Getty Center for Education in the Arts, and the John F. Kennedy Center for the Performing Arts.

Many state departments of education have developed frameworks from which comprehensive arts programs can be developed, such as the *Visual and Performing Arts Framework for California Public Schools*, and *Illinois State Goals for Learning in the Fine Arts*. Numerous state departments of education have also prepared documents in dance, drama, music, and the visual arts that provide curricular guidelines. Additionally, information can be obtained from individual arts area national organizations including DANCE/USA, National Dance Association, Music Educators National Conference, Educational Theater Association, and National Arts Education Association.

Implementation: Staff Development and Resources

Implementation of a new approach is a complex and ongoing process, but the time and effort of administrators, teachers, parents and students working together will result in an effective arts curriculum and an enhanced education for all students.

Staff development and resource selection are important to the successful implementation of a comprehensive arts curriculum. Implementing changes in curriculum from a studio/performance-based focus to a comprehensive approach can be accomplished through inservice such as intensive summer training institutes and building/district level workshops. Training for classroom teachers and arts specialists not familiar with a comprehensive approach should be a hands-on, collaborative process presented by their peers, local and regional arts specialists, and/or key people in the arts whom they respect.

If a comprehensive arts program which integrates history, criticism, and aesthetics with making and performing is to be effective, it is important that building principals be involved in the training so they will understand what may be, to them, a new approach.

Effective implementation and continued success of comprehensive programs in the arts depend greatly on knowledgeable district-wide supervisors of the individual arts and/or schemal arts supervisors. These supervisors must serve on, or at least work closely with, the arts subject area committee. Supervisors, as agents of the arts SAC, also work with the district curriculum coordinating council in overseeing the K-12 programs, not just in coordinating arts teacher efforts. At the elementary and middle school level, building or district leadership teams of classroom teachers and arts specialists can be formed to work with the arts supervisors. Secondary arts teachers should periodically meet with their respective arts supervisor for continual "checks and balances."

Once the comprehensive arts program is in place, continual progress should be shared with administrators, the school board, and parents. Arts specialists, classroom teachers, and supervisors will need to communicate closely; periodic review and evaluation should occur.

Resources for the support of the instructional program should include budget-line funds for building a library of artwork reproductions, audio and video tapes of dance, drama, literary, and music productions; equipment and materials for art making and performing; and provisions for field trips and for guest-artist visits to classrooms to share their experiences in their respective art forms.

Adequate instructional time for each of the arts disciplines is essential for a successful arts program. Time needs to be allotted for individual area content as well as for integrated experiences at the elementary and middle school levels. The secondary student should have a variety of arts courses from which to choose in meeting arts requirements for graduation.

An effective comprehensive arts curriculum can be developed and implemented in a number of ways using teaching approaches that meet local needs. The keys to success are: a supportive environment; adequate resources and policies; and a mix of imagination, patience, and determination to succeed.

Teachers of the Arts

Ideally, all students would be taught by certified specialists in each of the arts disciplines, which is the case in some regions of the country. This is not always realistic in many schools. It is possible, however, for elementary students to be taught by teachers who have received staff development training in the arts disciplines (dance, drama, music and visual art) geared to specific student age levels and who use a comprehensive, sequential curriculum to guide them. Hall Wildung, coordinator of comprehensive visual arts in the Robbinsdale, Minnesota schools, where team teaching (classroom teachers working in conjunction with an arts specialist) is used at the elementary school level, states,

There are people who say it would be nice to have the art teacher teach everything, but I can tell you that we have a lot of elementary art teachers who feel there is good advantage to team teaching, and I do too. The elementary teachers see kids bringing concepts and vocabulary that they've learned in the art class into their work in other disciplines. This is really one of the strong points of our program, because so many (classroom) teachers are now seeing opportunities for interdisciplinary work — with language arts, with science, with other subjects.

At the intermediate, middle, and high school levels, the arts programs should be conducted by certified arts teachers; in very large districts, these certified teachers are supervised by a specialist in all of the arts or by separate supervisors of the individual areas of the arts.

Students of the Arts

Students must know they need to prepare themselves to be responsible members of the 21st century. They need to know that arts experiences will increase their problem-solving and decision-making skills, and heighten their sensitivity to and respect for all people. And such experiences will also provide opportunities to express themselves as unique individuals.

Computer-based technology will require workers who can understand complex and fast-paced systems. To cope and compete in the ever-changing world, today's students must be versed in the language of the arts. Students need to know that the future society will need creative, imaginative people who can find multiple solutions to a problem.

Students need to assume a share of the responsibility in the evaluation process. Portfolio assessment procedures encourage them to describe what they perceive to be their achievements and progress, causing them to be challenged to set their own goals, and to take greater responsibility for evaluating their own growth.

Assessment

Even though the arts are considered to be of a subjective nature, educators must be aware of program outcomes that can be identified and measured. Student achievement can and should be assessed through homework, classroom assignments, studio work and performance, portfolios, and tests. An effective in-place evaluation systems allows for investigation and feedback.

Participants in **Arts PROPEL**, a cooperative five-year arts assessment project funded by the Rockefeller Foundation, are developing appropriate assessment devices for all the arts. In the visual arts, the traditional portfolio is often limited to students' own artwork. The current approach of a program like **Arts PROPEL** also includes essays, diaries, and research projects in the development of more comprehensive student process portfolios. These contain not only products made by the student but also written material that addresses ideas and information from the historical, critical, and aesthetic disciplines.

The student and the teacher should both be involved in the evaluation of a comprehensive overview of the student's learning. Following are strategies that can be used for evaluation and guidelines for who is responsible for each.

Student Responsibility
- Comprehensive Portfolio
  - Works of Art (visual images and objects, slides, photos, audio/video cassettes)
  - Journals
  - Research Papers
  - Reports (Group, Peer, Self)
  - Interviews
- Contract

Teacher Responsibility
- Observational Checklists
- Anecdotal records
- Group evaluation
- Interview
- Performance-based assessment
- Narrative summary

Whatever assessment approaches are used, arts educators must publicize and use results to improve both the effectiveness and the status of the arts programs.

Sample Outcomes

To illustrate how the design-down format might work with local curriculum development based on state department of education guidelines, the five Illinois State Goals for Learning in the Fine Arts are used as **Program Outcomes** in the following examples. (The discipline-based components: aesthetics, criticism, history, and production are embodied in the state goals.) Examples are provided for specified arts areas.

Sample One

Program Outcome (State Goal One): Students will be able to understand the principal sensory, formal, technical, and expressive qualities of each of the arts.

Third Grade Outcome (Visual Arts, Criticism): Students will describe the primary and secondary colors in a given selected image.

Learning Activity; Given a selected image (e.g., *Still Life with Apples and Peaches* by Paul Cezanne, *Sketch I for "Composition VII"* by Wassily Kandinsky, *Past Pastures* by Emilio Cruz) students working in cooperative learning groups will describe each artist's use of primary and secondary colors and how the colors used contribute to the expressive qualities of the painting.

Assessment Procedure: Students point out and describe the primary and secondary colors used in similar works to those discussed in class. Teacher records observations and notes anecdotal statements.

Sample Two

Program Outcome (State Goal Two): Students will be able to identify processes and tools required to produce visual art, music, dance, and drama.

Sixth Grade Outcome (Music, <u>Criticism and Production</u>): Students will recognize processes used to create solo, ensemble, choral, instrumental, and electronic music.

Learning Activity: Students will present a piece of music to others as a solo or in an ensemble (e.g., *It's a Small World* by Richard M. Sherman and Robert M. Sherman, **vocal:** solo, duet, group; **instrumental:** bell, autoharp. *Sarakatsani Song* [Greek Folk Song], **vocal:** boys, girls alternate; **instrumental:** finger cymbals, tamborine, drums).

Assessment Procedure: Student observers analyze processes used and interview the performers.

Sample Three

Program Outcome (State Goal Three): Students will demonstrate basic skills necessary to participate in the creation and/or performance of one of the arts.

Eighth Grade Outcome (Dance, <u>Production and Criticism</u>): Students will choreograph a short study incorporating basic principles of dance form.

Learning Activity: For a predetermined amount of time, students listen and prepare a movement study which reflects the mood of the piece (e.g., *Ballet Melodies* by Montovani and Orchestra; *Patterns in Jazz* by Robin Hector; *Good Morning Blues* by Heddy Ledbetter; *pia nio chao fing [Hundred Birds Courting the Phoenix]* - North China Folk Song) and incorporates some basic principles of dance form: repetition, contrast, transition.

Assessment Procedure: After viewing videos of students' choreographed performances, peers prepare evaluations considering predetermined criteria. Responses will be placed in each student's comprehensive portfolio. Individual performers journal their own comments and perceptions of the performance and evaluation.

Sample Four

Program Outcome: (State Goal Four): Students will be able to identify significant works in the arts from major historical periods and how they reflect societies, cultures, and civilizations, past and present.

Eleventh Grade Outcome (Drama, <u>Production and History</u>): Students will analyze ways in which drama reflects society.

Learning Activity: Students compare the themes from *Antigone* by Sophocles and *St. Joan* by George Bernard Shaw, or *Othello* by Shakespeare and *Joe Turner's Come and Gone* by August Wilson, as they relate to the historical period in which they were written. Groups of students perform scenes as written, then update to a contemporary time period.

Assessment Procedure: After viewing students' performances, peers prepare evaluations considering predetermined criteria. Written responses will be placed in students' portfolios. Teacher prepares summative evaluation, checking analysis, evaluative thinking, and use of atypical strategies and solutions.

Sample Five

Program Outcome (State Goal Five): Students will be able to describe the unique characteristics of each of the arts.

Tenth-Twelfth Grade Outcome (Dance, Drama, Music, Visual Art, <u>Production, Aesthetics and Criticism</u>): Students identify and describe the composite nature of a theatrical production.

Learning Activity: Students view a musical production (e.g., *Oklahoma, Grease, Chorus Line*) and discuss how the music, visual art, and dance contribute to the total production.

Assessment Procedure: Groups select an individual arts area and analyze components. Each group presents written and verbal descriptions of the expressive qualities of its selected art form used in the production. All students evaluate the effective usage of the art form. Personal written responses are placed in individual portfolios.

Fine Arts Basics:

- A comprehensive arts curriculum is basic to education and plays a vital part in preparing students to be responsible citizens of the 21st century.

- An arts education program that draws from the disciplines of aesthetics, criticism, history, and production offers fundamental training that expands students' capabilities and builds critical thinking skills, decision-making and problem-solving skills; increases the ability to make informed judgments and evaluations; provides opportunities to work cooperatively; encourages the appreciation of different cultures and points of view; and promotes self-esteem, imagination and creativity.

- Implementing any new curriculum is a long-term process, with no quick fixes. Time and patience, cooperation and positive attitudes are essential. Shifting from a studio/performance-based focus to a comprehensive approach in an arts curriculum is a complex endeavor.

- Design-down concepts help curriculum developers focus on basic reasons why the subject is taught and offers a structure for preparing a substantive, sequential curriculum. The result will be a quality arts education program which provides challenging learning experiences for students to develop knowledge, skills and affects necessary for their future success.

PLANNING FOR TECHNOLOGY

The special resource person for this section is Dan Lumley, Spring Hill Public Schools, Spring Hill, Kansas.

Futurists agree the world is in the midst of an information revolution that will rival the industrial revolution in terms of impact and importance. Emerging technologies such as the computer, telecommunications, CD ROM, and videodisc are primary examples of tools that have powered this revolution.

Educational planners tell us that our society and educational institutions will be transformed radically in the next few decades. Schools will continue to be a significant part of this period of rapid change well into the 21st century.

In the near future the global classroom will be a reality. Students of all ages will be able to tap into vast intercontinental computer networks that give students and teachers the power to create, access, and share data, text, pictures, and sound in a very motivational fashion. Students will have access to notebook sized computers which will contain a cellular phone, radio, television, and compact disc (CD) player. Entire curricula will be available on CDs for these computers, causing less reliance on the school building as the main locus of instruction. Learning will occur anyplace and anytime.

Schools Have Not Yet Joined the Revolution

Unfortunately, schools have yet to join this information revolution. Schools are in a precarious position because they have not kept pace with technology. While the military, business, medicine and science worlds have been going through a technological metamorphosis, education is just beginning to leave 19th century patterns for designing and implementing curriculum and instruction. If Horace Mann were to walk the halls of a twentieth century school he would feel at home among the paper, pencils, chalkboards, and textbooks. He would quickly recognize bored students recalling facts from short-term memory, a curriculum segregated into separate subjects, standardized tests, and teachers being "a sage on the stage," pouring facts into empty vessels. On the other hand, if Horace Mann were to visit a modern factory or hospital he would feel lost. In short, education is not "plugged in" to the Information Age. With respect to technology, schools are creeping along in a Model T Ford while other institutions in America are speeding along in a supersonic jet.

Why Hasn't Technology Been Fully Integrated Into Education?

Lack of planning is the major stumbling block in the impending technology revolution in education. One technology expert has described educational technology planning in the United states as "... a massive and confusing sea of information." Few well-written technology plans exist in American schools. School leaders often fail to develop a district plan for technology because they lack knowledge of technology and its relationship to student learning, budgeting, facilities, curriculum, and staff development. The lack of strategic and long range planning for technology often results in district technology programs which cost large sums of money but do not meet the district's teaching and learning goals. It is common for school districts throughout the nation to have (a) no clear purpose or focus for technology, (b) a wide range of technology abilities among the staff, (c) ill-defined processes for hardware and software acquisition, (d) no centralized procedures for storing and cataloging electronic technology, (e) no alignment or coordination of curriculum applications, and (f) limited staff development activities and programs that focus on technology.

This lack of planning can be compared to sailing a rudderless ship into the 21st century. If school districts continue to navigate without a technology rudder in the 1990s, our educational programs will either run aground or float aimlessly into the future.

Long-Range Planning for Technology

This section is designed to help school leaders take control of a rudderless technology ship by long-range planning for technology integration. The notions that careful planning is crucial to technology integration, and that there are no short cuts to planning, are central to this issue. Careful planning is especially necessary in the technology area because of its complexity and the large investments involved.

What follows is a step-by-step model for developing a long-range technology plan.

Select & Train the Technology Planning Committee

Selecting and training a technology planning committee is the *first step* curriculum leaders, specifically the curriculum coordinating council, must take when developing a technology plan. Committee members must be selected with care because they will become emissaries of technological change in the district. The establishment of a planning committee insures maximum participation by those most involved with the everyday operation of the schools, and will establish an organizational scaffolding which is needed for developing the district's long-range technology plan. Planning for technology integration is complicated. It may take two to three years to develop and implement an effective long range technology plan.

Since a number of instructional and administrative issues will be dealt with, it is recommended that a broad cross section of people be represented on the planning committee. While teachers and administrators will hold a majority of the positions, others from the community and district organization can be valuable members, especially in communicating the committee's work and progress to the rest of the staff and interested patrons. Successful integration of technology in a school district is dependent on all players understanding what others will be doing during the planning and implementation process. All stakeholders must feel that they are part of the process, and details regarding committee purposes, functions, and members should be written into the bylaws of the curriculum coordinating council.

Planning committee membership should include representatives from the following groups:

1. teachers from elementary, middle and high school levels,
2. building and central office administrators,
3. library media specialists,
4. school board,
5. community at large, and,
6. district support staff.

The actual number on the committee will depend largely on the size of the school district. A general rule of thumb is to select a planning team of 15 or fewer members. A group larger than 15 becomes unwieldy for consensus building and decision making.

Before the committee has been identified, a chairperson should be selected by the curriculum coordinating council. This person should provide structure for the tasks of the group within the framework of desired program outcomes.

Prior to the first meeting of the committee, the chairperson should address the following questions:

1. What resources (human and financial) are *currently* available and requested by district personnel?
2. What is the curriculum coordinating council's thinking about the relationship of technology planning to existing documents that guide district governance (e.g. mission statement, bylaws, curriculum documents, and board goals)?
3. What provision should be made for record keeping (e.g. minutes, public relations, data collection)?
4. How can exemplary school districts be identified, and what technology planning documents could be obtained from them for examination?
5. Will there be a need for outside consultants?
6. Has the curriculum coordinating council prepared a clear "charge" to the committee that includes a suggested plan of action?
7. What are the latest trends in technology?
8. What does recent research in technology say?
9. What should be the frequency of meetings? What provisions should be made for creature comforts (e.g. food, drink, and rest breaks)?
10. How will the agenda be developed by team members?
11. Where will the meetings take place?
12. What is a realistic timetable for completing the study?

After the chairperson has had time to give attention to these questions, he or she should meet with the curriculum coordinating council to report findings, and then to begin the selection process for committee members. The committee members, in turn, will need some time to think through and discuss the task before them. Planning for technology integration in the schools is different than planning for other school-related issues. Among the short and long-range issues the committee should consider before beginning to write the plan are:

1. Additional hardware will be necessary.
2. Additional software will be necessary.
3. Teacher involvement in all aspects of technology will be essential.
4. Current curriculum patterns will need to be realigned.
5. Current and future facilities will need to be modified for technology.
6. Technology budgets will need to be established.
7. To prepare for obsolescence and the rapidly changing nature of technology, the committee will need to set up a procedure whereby the curriculum coor-

dinating council annually considers recent trends in hardware and software in its long-range plan.

8. After the district has been organized for the integration of technology, comprehensive planning for staff development and curriculum applications must be prepared by the curriculum coordinating council.
9. A timeline of implementation will need to be closely monitored.
10. The committee needs to think <u>technology</u> — not just computers.
11. Planning must not be too narrow in focus. The emphasis will be K-12 and embrace all curriculum areas.
12. Planning must focus on curriculum, budgeting, facilities, and staff development.
13. The committee must be sensitive to equity issues. All students regardless of gender, socioeconomic status or special needs must be given the same opportunities to learn with technology.
14. The committee needs to plan for teacher access to technology.

While these issues seem overwhelming, the committee should be reminded that its work will be spread over a long period of time, and that the prioritizing of tasks will make the work manageable.

Preparing the Committee for the Study

Preparing the committee for development of a long-range technology plan is the *second major step* for the chairperson. Committee members should receive orientation to (1) committee member responsibilities and roles, (2) emerging technologies, (3) implications of the Information Age for education, and (4) the need for systematic planning for technology. The purpose of the orientation sessions is to provide the committee with important information which can be used to make knowledgeable recommendations to other stakeholders and ultimately to the board of education. In addition, this orientation will enable committee members to gain an overall picture of technology and the planning process.

While the orientation sessions are primarily for committee members, other stakeholders should be welcomed and encouraged to attend. Public notices and open letters of invitation to faculty, administrators, and selected community and student leaders should precede orientation sessions.

The orientation sessions should be co-chaired by the curriculum coordinator and committee chairperson. These people are key individuals who must demonstrate the need for technology planning.

At the first committee meeting, all members should be given a general overview of responsibilities and roles which include the following:

1. Review missions and long-range goals for technology as established by the curriculum coordinating council.

2. Determine current resources and requests for technology.
3. Project a technology budget.
4. Draft, implement, and institutionalize a long-range technology plan that aligns with the curriculum coordinating council's action plan.
5. Attend all committee meetings.
6. Maintain communication between committee and building faculties, and act as resource persons to the district.
7. Become familiar with emerging technology research, trends, and developments, and disseminate such information to fellow committee members.
8. Participate in all discussions, planning, and decision making.
9. Make specific recommendations and map strategies for technology implementation.
10. Develop a well-crafted blueprint for action that clearly outlines specific action steps, identify who will carry them out, and define a timeline for implementation. The timeline will keep the committee on task and may take some of the mystery out of the planning process.
11. Prepare a list of recommendations for the curriculum coordinating council.

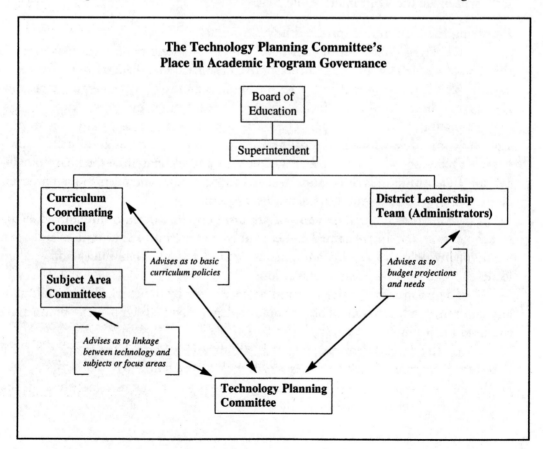

The Technology Planning Committee's
Place in Academic Program Governance

12. Orient all stakeholders to the district's technology mission and goals (see schematic).
13. Think technology and education rather than merely computers.
14. Base long-range plan on realistic assessment of funding, staff, time, and facilities.
15. Understand that real change takes three to five years or longer.

At the second and third meetings of the committee, all members should receive orientation to the broad range of emerging technologies which can revolutionize teaching and learning. Orientation sessions should be designed to capture the interest of committee members and help them grasp the potential impact of emerging technology as a tool in improving and revitalizing teaching and learning. Members need to understand that technologies will continue to emerge since 90% of the technological practices we will use in the year 2000 are either not yet available or have not been invented.

The sessions must be conducted by someone who is knowledgeable in the area of emerging technologies. If no one in the district qualifies, then a visiting expert should be employed.

It is very important that the new technologies not only be identified, but demonstrated. If possible, committee members should be allowed "hands-on" time. For many, these sessions will be the first introduction to emerging technologies. Therefore, it is critical that this orientation be professionally presented and "risk free" to all stakeholders.

Emerging Technologies

Emerging technologies can be defined as evolving and sophisticated communication devices which create, capture, transfer, and use words, music, sound, numbers, and images. Four major classifications of emerging technologies are:

1. *Computer* — microcomputers, laptops, mainframe, and networking
2. *Telecommunications* — online data bases, facsimile transmission, modems, electronic bulletin boards, and distance learning
3. *Instructional & Management* — electronic card catalog, computerized circulation, Hypermedia/Multimedia, and Integrated Learning Systems
4. *Laser Disc* — laser video disc and CD-ROM

It is suggested that the committee, in cooperation with the curriculum coordinating council, select the newest and most promising emerging technologies, which include networking, distance learning, hypermedia/multimedia, integrated learning systems (ILS), and compact disk read only memory (CD-ROM) to be demonstrated at committee meetings. Descriptions of these prominent technologies follow.

• Networking is a technology system whereby individual computer workstations are linked together by a file server (high powered personal computer [PC] with a hard disk). The file server directs and monitors the flow of information to and from other computers. Networking facilitates the communication and sharing of software among a large number of computers in a laboratory, school or district.

- Distance Learning is an electronic interactive technology that uses computers, fiber optics, television, microwaves, cable, telephone, and videodisc to connect classrooms across district, state and even national boundaries. Simply stated, it is electronic delivery of information over vast distances. With this technology students will be able to take courses via satellite, provided they have a television screen and telephone. Distance learning provides students with the opportunity to ask questions and make comments during the presentations. In the not too distant future, entire libraries and art galleries will be available to students on distance learning. This technology opens windows onto the world of learning.

- Hypermedia/Multimedia are systems that use optical discs to access still images, film footage, sound and speech in non-linear fashion. Most instructional materials force the learner to receive information in linear fashion. Using software called Hypertext, students can quickly move from one subject to another through interconnected, weblike representation of symbols such as text, graphics, images, and software codes. The learner using intuition, memory and interests can follow this web along alternative paths through links. With this technology, a true integrated curriculum is possible. For example, using Hypermedia technology, a social studies "electronic book" would contain links to mathematics, science, language arts, and other appropriate content areas. Textbook publishers are rapidly moving into the Hypermedia arena. The newest textual materials are aligned with various videodisc segments. Using existing bar code technology, teachers can wave a bar code reader over a bar code in the textbook or lesson plan, which triggers the videodisc to play an appropriate segment on the videodisc player. With this technology, teachers have a huge "grab bag" of related materials (e.g. essays, photographs, songs, text, film, and voice) to enhance their presentations.

- Integrated Learning Systems (ILS) is a comprehensive package of computer-based instruction in basic skills such as mathematics, reading and writing. Newer systems also include adult learning, English as a second language, GED, and science. The courseware is delivered on a networked system of microcomputers linked to a file server. Using the special features of the computer, these systems: (1) generate problems in a random fashion, (2) adjust the difficulty and sequence of problems based upon student performance, (3) provide appropriate and immediate feedback, (4) utilize color graphics and sound, and (5) maintain detailed records of student performance. In an ILS package, instructional objectives are specified with individual lessons tied to the objectives. Instruction is individualized and personalized with these systems. In other words, teachers know exactly where students are having difficulties and how long it took for each student to answer each question on a test; thus, it enables teachers to identify and individualize extended learning opportunities. One of the most important features on an ILS package is that the feedback students receive in the laboratory is private. Students do not risk public criticism and embarrassment when they attempt to answer a problem with a computer, which fosters greater motivation to learn.

- Compact Disc-Read Only Memory (CD-ROM) is an optical disc technology that is used to store large data bases such as reference books and library catalogs. The laser discs that are used in a CD player are capable of storing 250,000 pages of text, 2,000 pictures or 74 minutes of sound or a combination of all three. Placed in a school library media center, CD-ROM provides students with the capability of rapidly finding reference information, magazines, newspapers and journals. For example, with CD-ROM technology students can look up information on Beethoven by using an optical disc, hear his music, view the musical score and conduct a search on how this music influenced other composers. The use of CD-ROM technology for satisfying information needs across the curriculum are almost limitless.

After receiving an orientation to emerging technologies, the committee should be exposed to the notion that America has undergone a shift from an industrial society to an information society. Futurists have identified three major changes that will dominate the next century: (1) global interdependence, (2) knowledge proliferation, and (3) information processing. A common thread that has run through all the predicted changes is electronic technology. These major changes will alter the knowledge and skills that students need to become competent workers and will profoundly influence how they work, where they work, and how they communicate.

In order to provide a philosophical foundation to the study, the committee must work closely with the curriculum coordinating council in addressing three fundamental questions:

1. What education will students need to prepare them for the Information Age future? What kinds of skills are needed to meet the challenges of a rapidly changing world?
2. How can technology better prepare students for the future (e.g. knowing how and where to access information)?
3. How can the new technology tools aid teachers in providing a better education for their students?

Both the committee and curriculum coordinating council must recognize that planning for technology is essential if schools are to fully participate in the

Information Age. Technology must become a part of the school's culture because it is no longer a luxury — it is a necessity.

Systematic Planning and Drafting the Long-range Plan

Step three is the actual development of a written technology plan. This is the major task of the committee in terms of effort and time. The plan identifies what must be done to prepare the district for a technological and changing future, and must be fully integrated with all other efforts to modify curriculum. Generally speaking, the final plan will facilitate the organization of the district's human, material, time, physical, and financial resources and provide a focus and direction for all stakeholders in the school.

The actual long-range plan for organizing the school district for technology should focus on five critical areas: budgeting, facilities, staff development, leadership, and the library media center.

Area #1: Budgeting

Funding is a major barrier to technology integration in American schools. Technology costs large amounts of money and these high costs are a big hurdle for most schools. For example, achieving a ratio of one computer to every three students in the United States would require an extra $4 billion annually for many years into the future. The high cost of technology requires school districts to explore different and broader funding avenues such as business partnerships, collaborations and other joint efforts. All funding sources, whether they are local, state, or federal, should be tapped. When developing budget plans for technology, the committee should do the following:

1. Determine who should have purchasing authority in the area of technology — district office, building, or both.
2. Determine who should decide which technology systems to purchase.
3. Identify district bidding requirements and purchasing procedures.
4. Consider business partnerships in technology. Increasingly there are opportunities to network with and receive free technologies from businesses.
5. Discuss the drafting of written statements that identify the roles, rights, and responsibilities of each partner in business partnerships.
6. Discuss the notion that technology integration requires a continuing investment — not a one time shot.
7. Consider "bundling costs" (e.g. hardware, software, maintenance, security, furniture and staff development costs in one bundle).
8. Explore establishing a purchase and/or leasing plan.
9. Establish baseline standards for each school (e.g. one ILS system in every middle school mathematics program).

The committee, working with the curriculum coordinating council, will need to draft budget plans in the following five general areas:

1. *Capital costs* — include actual amounts for equipment and facilities.
2. *Development costs* — start- up expenses such as:
   • hardware acquisition
   • staffing
   • software acquisition
   • space and furniture
   • facilities created or modified
3. *Operating costs* — include such things as service and repair, maintenance, expendable materials, salaries, utilities, administration, and security.
4. *Expansion costs* — deal with future expansion of programs, facilities, equipment and materials.
5. *Curriculum and staff development costs* — cover:
   • substitute pay
   • training costs
   • visits to exemplary schools
   • consultant wages
   • extra duty pay for teachers
   • college tuition

School districts often rush to buy technology without budgeting for the kind of curriculum and staff development which is the key ingredient to successful integration of technology.

Area # 2: Facilities and Location

A major computer company recently stated that, in the past, companies advocated one computer for every student. Now they are saying one computer for every teacher. The idea is that if every teacher has a computer, then students will come to the conclusion that technology is an acceptable tool and resource. If every teacher is to have access to technology in the future, then the committee should begin drafting facility recommendations for any new schools that will be added to the district. At the same time, the committee must recognize that older and outmoded buildings will need remodeling in order to accommodate tomorrow's technology. The committee should consult architects and building engineers who have had experience with technology in schools.

Experts suggest planning for schools with a technology systems hub which houses all controlling equipment. The hub should be the library media center, which is linked by fiber optic cable to wall boxes in each classroom. Schools of the future will provide teachers and students with immediate access from the classroom to an electronic card catalog, compact disc information, telephone, and video, through the media center, local cable networks, and satellites.

When the committee works on facility design, there are technology requirements that must be addressed. They include:

1. Electrical power
2. Network access
3. Appropriate furniture
4. Good lighting
5. Electronic cables with simple plug-in connections to carry voice, data, and video communications to and from the library media center
6. Cable trays or raised floor to carry cables
7. Student seating for all work areas
8. Communication and power outlets for teacher stations
9. Security and storage
10. Climate control (sunlight, light, dust, dry markers, static)
11. Floor strength
12. Telephone capacity

In addition to facility issues, the committee should address technology location issues such as:

1. Portable laboratories (e.g. vans and buses)
2. Stationary laboratories
3. Single or multiple units in classrooms
4. Library media center
5. Classroom needs
6. Labs and/or decentralized locations
7. Take home programs (overnight, weekends and vacations)
8. Teacher access in lounges

The committee should be told that electronic learning does not have to take place in the classroom, or even in the school building for that matter. In other words, school is where the learner is because students can "plug in at home."

Area # 3: Staff Development

Teacher training in the area of technology assumes a pivotal role. People are the most valuable resource when planning for technology — it is important to invest in them. Teachers must not be passive spectators of technology integration. They are the key players in the development and implementation of a technology plan and program, and they must be encouraged to learn and grow in this area.

The problem is that technophobia afflicts a large number of American teachers, a condition which is a significant barrier to successful integration of technology in the schools. Moreover, skilled teachers in the area of technology are in short supply.

Prior to reviewing what the experts say about staff development in technology, the committee should be made aware that change is gradual, difficult and process-oriented — not a one time shot. The committee should work with the curriculum coordinating council in addressing the change process in schools and developing strategies for managing it.

Critical staff development elements the committee should plan for are access, training, and time. Training has to be practical, hands-on, and regular. Experts have provided a number of suggestions in teacher training for technology:

1. Teacher empowerment is the appropriate approach to technology training.
2. Teachers must be able to choose training — mandates don't work.
3. Participants must be motivated by various forms of incentives.
4. The administration must provide moral and financial support for training.
5. Staff development programs must be flexible and on-going.
6. Hands-on activities and training should be linked to actual curriculum, lesson plans, and classroom activities. Teachers must see a direct connection to their world.
7. Follow-up training must be offered.
8. Opportunities for peer interaction must be present, as teaching is too often an isolated profession.
9. Training needs expressed by faculty are better than those imposed in a top-down fashion.

In the past, teacher training focused on programming and technical operations. Today the focus is on how technology is merged with the curriculum, and how student learning in the classroom can be influenced by the new technologies. Experts caution that teachers should not receive training before equipment arrives. Train them on the equipment/technology they will use in the classroom.

Characteristics of effective staff development practices can be applied to technology. These practices include:

1. Training conducted in school settings — as part of the curriculum development process.
2. Linking staff development activities and programs to other district-wide efforts.
3. Teachers and administrators planning together.
4. A focus on *all* teachers, not just on a small cadre of technology enthusiasts who have dominated the field.
5. Emphasis on self-instruction with differentiated opportunities.
6. Planning for awareness, demonstration, practice, feedback, and coaching activities.
7. Training that is concrete, hands-on and ongoing. (Don't spend all of the time on presentation and demonstration.)

8. Support that's available upon request.
9. Budgeting for staff development (e.g. released time, extra duty pay).
10. Recognizing and planning for the fact that teachers will be at different levels of sophistication.
11. Planning for different scheduling options — after school, weekends, released time, inservice days, summer workshops, and evenings.
12. Putting the hardware and software in locations where teachers have ready access to them.

Area # 4: Leadership

One of the committee's most important tasks is to work with the curriculum coordinating council in developing long-range plans for leadership in technology integration. If technology is going to be successfully integrated in the school district, then strong leadership must be evident at both the district and school levels. Teachers play an important role in technology integration, but the leadership, organization, and funding need to come from a supportive and visionary curriculum coordinating council and district leadership team. Experts suggest the following general guidelines for school technology leaders:

1. Visionary leadership should be the focus as opposed to management based on expediency.
2. Technology should be viewed as a method of transformation, not improvement. *It should be integrated into regular district curriculum patterns.*
3. Curriculum technology leaders must be visionaries who involve teachers in all phases of technology implementation.
4. Leaders should think technology, not just computers.

Area # 5: Library Media Center

Experts tell us that the library media center should be the hub of the school's technology program and the locus of electronic technology. Technology currently exists which enables the library media specialist to automate circulation, acquisition, cataloging, serials control, interlibrary loan, and film/TV booking. Existing technology also assists the library media specialist with tasks such as overdue notices, purchasing orders, catalog card production, periodical holdings, budgets, and bibliographies.

Media center staff must be trained in the use of all technology tools and how to develop policies and procedures to insure that the various technology tools are available to staff and students alike. The traditional role of the library media specialist has to change to meet the increasing demands of technology.

Library Media Specialists Should -
1. become more involved in curriculum and facility design.

2. be managers of information resources.
3. be facilitators and trainers in technology.
4. provide software collection, selection, organization, maintenance and dissemination services.

Library Media Centers Should -
1. be the technology and information hubs of the schools.
2. have computer controlled library circulations.
3. offer computer terminal searches which give students a focused bibliography on selected topics.
4. provide laser disc technology (CD ROMs and Videodisc) so that students can access numerous electronic resource tools (e.g. electronic encyclopedias).
5. allow students to access on-line information data bases on modems and computers.
6. link library collections, catalogs, and CD-ROM resources through search stations in each classroom.

Presenting the Plan to the Curriculum Coordinating Council, District Leadership Team and Board of Education

Building political coalitions is important for institutionalizing the plan. Change requires alliances for support, and visions must have champions. Communication with stakeholders is essential. Everyone must understand what changes will occur and whom they will affect. Technology that suddenly appears in the classroom or school media center one day, unheralded and unexpected, will be resisted and its impact diminished.

After the long-range plan has been finalized, it is suggested that the committee meet with the curriculum coordinating council in a study session leading to a presentation of the completed long-range plan to the board of education. During this meeting committee members should emphasize the benefits of technology and explain how the long-range plan is linked to the district's mission and curriculum patterns.

The following items should be addressed during the study session with the curriculum coordinating council:
1. The potential of emerging technologies for school improvement.
2. The condition of the district's current technology program.
3. The new long-range plans developed by the planning team which include -
   • hardware and software purchases,
   • staffing,
   • staff development,
   • budgeting,
   • facilities,
   • library media centers,

- leadership,
- implementation,
- monitoring and evaluation, and
- business/school partnerships.

4. The notion that implementation of the plan should be flexible and dictated by careful monitoring and evaluation.

The curriculum coordinating council needs to exercise rigorous oversight of the long-range technology plan as an inherent part of the curriculum development process. The district leadership team and board of education should support and fund that comprehensive plan. Every effort should be made to avoid implementing district technology in a piecemeal fashion. Among the overarching technology issues the curriculum coordinating council, district leadership team, and board of education should address through policy and practices are: access, staff development, equipment and software purchases, copyright protection, facility renovation, and new construction.

Progress highlights and benchmarks of the long-range plan should be publicized. Teacher feedback is critical to the implementation process.

Technology Plan Basics

- **Technology will play an increasingly more important role in the schools, so school districts need a long-range plan for technology that is integrated into general curriculum development.**

- **The *technology planning committee*, appointed by the *curriculum coordinating council*, plays a key role in studying, creating, and implementing a long-range technology plan.**

- **Committee members should be carefully selected and well trained. They should understand district needs and maintain a continuing familiarity with emerging technologies.**

- **It is important that the committee follow specific implementation steps. Considerable attention should be given to budgeting, facilities and location, staff development, leadership, and the library media center.**

- **Attention to detail is also important in preparing reports and presentations to the curriculum coordinating council and board of education.**

- **Institutionalizing a technology plan requires the building of alliances and good communication with the educators who will use it most — the teachers. Therefore, their on-going involvement from "day one" is considered to be of critical importance.**

COOPERATIVE LEARNING IN A RESULTS BASED SYSTEM

The special resource person for this section is Toni Bowling, Burlington Public Schools, Burlington, Kansas.

Districts implementing the Accountability-Based Curriculum Model must utilize instructional strategies that are most effective in attaining mastery learning and higher level thinking skills among all students. If applied correctly by a competent and well-prepared teacher, cooperative learning shows extraordinary success in both areas. This method of instruction can effectively be used in conjunction with direct instruction, student modeling, guided practice, and such student assistance components as correctives and enrichments.

Cooperative learning is an old idea in a new light. Recent research has again proven what teachers in one-room schools knew from the beginning: peer instruction is extremely effective in achieving student learning. Just as the one-room teacher placed older students into the role of teacher, cooperative learning gives this role to classroom peers. Students are more actively involved in the learning process and, as a result, build critical thinking skills and reinforce the thinking skills of others.

The primary objective of the outcome based model is that every student succeed academically, and effective use of cooperative learning strategies can aid in achieving this goal. Individual accountability is an essential component of an effective cooperative learning program. With teamwork and cooperation, students have more opportunities to experience academic success both as team members and as individuals. This success has a positive effect on self-esteem. Success and self-esteem nurture a sense of competence in every student's ability to achieve. Once this sense of competence is developed, the student feels more comfortable about taking risks in order to succeed academically.

Teamwork is an Appropriate Curricular Outcome

Students need to learn skills that are important for the real world, and today many employers say our high school graduates are lacking in communication and cooperation skills. In the early part of this book, we talked about the theories and management practices of William Edwards Deming, who revitalized Japanese industry. One of his primary complaints about American industry was that it's lacking teamwork. At a seminar in Springfield, Massachusetts, Dr. Deming stated:

"Did you every stop to think of the power of teamwork? You (American industries) don't have it. We don't have it in this country. It is every man for himself. Everybody is an individual business man, looking out for himself. Call it rugged

individualism. Better stop to think, when everybody is an individual businessman, there cannot be teamwork."

Traditionally, schools have been partially responsible for this lack of cooperation, because students get the message that they must be number one. According to Deming, certain forces in our schools "create fear, self-defense, competition, and humiliation. Competition is for the highest grade in school." Our educational standards have cultured a competitiveness among children that discourages cooperation. Sharing and communicating with other classmates may lessen the chance of being "on top" academically. However, in order to be a success in the job market, a person must be able to cooperate and communicate with fellow employees. As Deming states, industry does not need the individual to earn a "bigger piece of the pie." Industry needs the teamwork that will make the pie bigger.

Cooperative learning methods are instrumental in developing a cooperative attitude because they create an atmosphere of sharing, communication, support, and responsibility. Students learn to trust and respect one another as they learn to work together, values that are vital to our society.

Children of all ages have a strong need to socialize because peers play a significant part in their lives. Friends know and are willing to talk about things that parents and teachers are not. Too many times teachers incorrectly remind students that they are not in school to socialize. On the contrary, one of the major purposes of school is to provide opportunities for socialization, because students must be socially as well as academically prepared for adulthood. Socialization in schools should not be limited to the halls and lunchroom. Cooperative learning is a strategy that will help teachers meet the social needs of students in the classroom under supervision and guidance. Well-planned cooperative learning activities will encourage positive interaction and group acceptance.

Quality of life as an adult depends greatly on social skills. For example, higher paying and more interesting jobs require such skills as being an effective leader, getting others to cooperate, coping with problems of power and influence, and helping people to solve problems. In 1982, the Center for Public Resources conducted a survey of individuals who had been fired from various jobs. Ninety percent of the individuals were fired because of poor attitude, poor interpersonal relationships, and inappropriate behavior. Few were fired because of lack of technical skills. The report concluded that the ability to work effectively and communicate with other personnel is as essential for employability and job success as a college degree or vocational training.

Components of Effective Cooperative Learning Activities

Cooperative learning, sometimes called team learning, is the result of a teaching strategy in which students are involved in small-group learning activities. There are six components that are essential for maximum effectiveness of a cooperative learning activity.

1. Heterogeneous Grouping
2. Group Goal
3. Individual Accountability
4. Face-to-face Interaction
5. Positive Interdependence
6. Collaborative Skills

A seventh component, rewards, can add to the effectiveness of a cooperative learning activity, but some feel it is not essential.

Grouping is heterogeneous with equal distribution of high, middle, and low achievers in each group. The level of achievement is determined by previous academic performance. When assigning groups, the teacher also considers integrating sexes, races, and different ethnic backgrounds into each group.

Working with others to attain a common goal can be extremely rewarding for students, especially when the group experiences success in attaining that goal. There is a sweet satisfaction in being part of a successful team and helping others to succeed. Respect for oneself and one another is a direct result. Under traditional schooling, this type of cooperative activity is limited to athletics and seldom used in regular classrooms. While working in cooperative groups, students are encouraged to make a collaborative effort to meet a common group goal. The goal could be completing a worksheet, writing an essay, or solving a problem. The goal could also be that everyone in the group master a certain concept, unit of information, or process. It is stressed that the students "learn" something as a team as opposed to simply "doing" something as a team.

Once the goal is met, all members of the group should receive recognition for their efforts. This recognition could be in the form of verbal feedback, certificates, grades, rewards, or any other type of indicator that the team has been successful. In order to fully succeed in achieving the **group** goals, **individuals** within the teams must set goals. These goals may be to master the material or to show a certain amount of improvement in performance. Using improvement goals is a means of giving low-achieving students the opportunity to contribute to the success of the team. Improvement goals also provide motivation for high-achieving students to continue to challenge themselves and perform at high levels.

In order to have effective cooperation, the students must be able to interact face-to-face. Students going off in separate directions to complete their part of an assignment are not participating in an effective cooperative learning activity.

Students must feel a certain amount of dependence upon one another. They must know that the success of the group depends upon the success of each individual team member.   All members must also realize that each person is held accountable for learning the material.

Collaborative skills must be taught to the students. A teacher cannot simply tell the students to "work together" and expect quality teamwork. If the class has not had any previous experience with cooperative learning, it would be wise to teach a prerequisite unit on working together effectively.

Does Cooperative Learning Really Work?

Cooperative learning has been proven to be effective in many aspects of learning and social development. In thirty-five studies of team learning methods, twenty-nine (83%) of these studies found that students in team learning situations gained significantly more in academic achievement than did students in traditionally taught classes. None found differences favoring control groups. The quality of these studies is quite high as the researchers made use of a wide range of conditions and random assignment to experimental and control groups. Standardized achievement scores were used as assessments in order to ensure objectivity and reliability. As a result, the research indicated that the effect of student team learning is equally strong for students at all grade levels in urban, rural and suburban schools and for students who are high, average, and low in achievement level. Studies show that students involved with cooperative learning also do better on questions requiring higher level thinking skills.

Research also shows that traditional instruction better stimulates competitiveness among students while team learning increases cooperation, mutual understanding, and positive social interaction among students. Teachers who have successfully integrated cooperative learning into the classroom are extremely enthusiastic about the results. Some of the benefits stated by teachers are:
1.   Higher academic achievement
2.   Higher self-esteem
3.   Increased social skills
4.   Improved behavior
5.   Better attendance
6.   Better classroom management
7.   More success for all students
8.   Quality time on task
9.   Immediate feedback

Cooperative Learning Models

There are many cooperative learning methods that offer guidance and structure. This section will discuss models developed by Robert Slavin of Johns Hopkins University, David and Roger Johnson of the University of Minnesota, Spencer Kagan of the University of California, and Elliott Aronson of the University of California.

One model developed at Johns Hopkins University that is fairly simple to implement in a classroom is Student Team Achievement Divisions (STAD). In STAD, students are assigned to teams of three or four. The teams are heterogeneously mixed in ability, sexes, and ethnicity. Base scores are established from each student's past performance. A lesson is taught to the whole class. The students work in their teams to make sure every member knows the material. Then the students take a quiz individually. Awards are given to the teams whose members show individual improvement over past performance.

The following is a synopsis of a second grade teacher using **STAD** to teach science. *The outcome is that students will group a variety of given objects according to common characteristics. The teacher spends approximately thirty minutes per day for science. Base scores have already been determined by an average of previous scores on science assessments.*

On the first day the teacher begins by showing the whole class several objects , passing them around so all students can touch the objects, and then asking them to make observations about each one. Their observations are recorded on the board; the teacher then guides the students to recognize a common observation (characteristic) for two or more objects. After several common characteristics have been identified, the students are instructed to work together to find as many commonalities as they can.

On the second day, the group task is to examine a new set of objects and cooperatively describe characteristics for each one. The second group task is to identify the common characteristics of their objects and prepare a large poster board illustration showing which objects were arranged together and why. This activity may take a couple of class sessions. As the groups begin to complete the illustrations, the teacher reminds them that their work is not done until everyone in the group can name a characteristic and correctly identify all the objects that share that characteristic.

As a final test, students individually, without help, sort a new set of given objects. Each set must be sorted into at least two groups. The students illustrate their groupings and while they work on their illustrations, the teacher approaches each child and asks him or her to describe the common characteistics that were used for the groupings. The individual test scores are compared with the base scores to determine improvement points for the teams. Teams meeting the criteria for super team, great team, and good team are recognized on the bulletin board.

Another method developed at Johns Hopkins University is Teams - Games - Tournaments (**TGT**). In TGT, the same procedure is followed as in STAD, but instead of taking quizzes, the students compete in tournaments against students of equal ability from other teams. Team points are determined by how well each member does in his or her tournament.

A sixth grade teacher uses TGT to check mastery of states and capitals. After the teams have the opportunity to work together and study the material in groups, the teacher assigns the students to tournament tables. Students are matched in ability at each tournament table so that low achievers play with low achievers and high achievers play with high achievers. Each table has a stack of cards with the names of the states on the top side of each card and the capital on the underneath side. The first player reads the state on the top card and names the capital. After the answer is given, the card is turned over to check the answer. If the answer is correct the player may keep the card. If the answer is incorrect, the card is placed on the bottom of the deck and the games goes on to the next player. The order of the players rotates counter clockwise around the table.

Before the card is turned over to check the answer, the person on the right has the opportunity to challenge if he thinks the answer given is incorrect. The challenger then gives an answer. If the challenger is correct, he keeps the card. If he is incorrect, he must give a card to the player. The game continues until there are no more cards in the stack. Points are awarded to each player according to his or her place in the game. The teacher figures team scores by averaging the points earned by each member on the team. Teams meeting the criteria for super team, great team, and good team are awarded certificates.

A method called **Jigsaw** was developed by Elliott Aronson at the University of California. Jigsaw places students in groups of four to six members. Each student is given a specific item of information to study. Then the student presents information to the rest of the group. Individual tests are given over the material presented by each of the team members. Robert Slavin modified Jigsaw so that the students meet in groups with members from other teams studying the same material. Team scores are figured as a result of individual quizzes. The Jigsaw method can be used quite successfully at all grade levels, even primary. The following is an example of how Jigsaw can be used to teach the letters of the alphabet in kindergarten or first grade.

Using A, B, C, and D as examples of the letters to be mastered, the lessons could go like this. One child in each group is assigned each of the letters. All the children assigned the letter A are placed at the same table. After receiving instruction from the teacher, the group practices reading and writing the letter. At the same time, the other students are working in groups on their own letters. By the end of the session, the children become "experts" at reading and writing the letter that they have been working on. During the next session, the "A experts" go through pictures beginning with the letter A. They may draw their own pictures and make models of the letter. During this time the other children are working in expert groups on the other letters B, C, and D. Finally, the "experts" return to their teams ready to teach teammates about their letter. The "A experts" begin by showing and modeling the letter A. Then they give examples and show pictures of words beginning with the letter A. When the students practice writing the letter, the experts keep watch to make sure everyone is writing the letter correctly. The team will repeat the activity until all the experts have presented a letter. After all four letters have been practiced, the group cooperatively completes a worksheet that checks for understanding of all four letters. As an assessment, the students individually complete a similar worksheet. Awards are given to the teams in which all members demonstrate mastery of all four letters.

Learning Together was designed by David and Roger Johnson at the University of Minnesota.   Students work together to complete a single task for which the group receives praise and recognition. Johnson and Johnson recommend assigning team members specific roles or jobs to perform within the group. For example, a captain may do the reading for the group, the recorder may do the writing, the encourager may keep everyone on task by praising and encouraging cooperation, and the checker may report back to the teacher on how well the group worked together. These are only a few examples of the various roles which can be assigned to members of a team. The possibilities are limited only by the imagination of the teacher.

A seventh-grade math teacher uses Learning Together roles to add structure to the teams. The roles assigned are the captain, the writer, the checker, and the encourager. When working on a group task, each person contributes to the effectiveness of the activity. The captain reads the problem and asks teammates for suggestions on how to solve the problem. This person is the only team member who may ask the teacher for help, which makes it necessary for the team members to discuss questions before going to the teacher. Many times the question is answered in the group without the aid of the teacher.

The checker keeps an eye on the work of other teammates as they go through an assignment. One important job is to check that all agree on answers and the processes used to solve each problem. The checker also keeps a calculator to use when needed to check computations or to assist with tedious calculations.

When the group finishes an assignment, everyone signs the writer's paper to indicate that they agree with the answers and the work on that paper. Then the papers are stapled together with the writer's paper on top. The teacher checks the writer's paper carefully for answers and processes. The other papers are spot-checked to make sure that everyone participated and completed the work. Credit is given to each person completing the assignment.

The job of the encourager is to keep everyone on task. The encourager must be positive at all times. Another responsibility of the encourager is to fill out a check sheet reporting on how well each team member cooperated.

The chart on the following page is used to assign daily roles. Everyone sits on the same side of the table each day. The dial is rotated daily to change roles. For example, today the captain is the student on the north, the writer is on the east, the checker is on the south, and the encourager is on the west. Tomorrow the dial will rotate and the captain will be on the west. The writer will be on the north, the checker on the east, and the encourager on the south. If a person from the team is absent, the encourager takes the job of the missing person.

As the children become more experienced in teamwork, assigned roles become less important because the students begin to develop the collaborative skills needed for effective teamwork.

Spencer Kagan of the University of California uses a method called **Numbered Heads Together.** In Numbered Heads Together the students sit in heterogeneous teams with (as nearly as possible) one high, two middle, and one low achieving student. Each student is assigned a number of one, two, three, or four. When a question is asked of the whole class, the teams put their heads together and make sure everyone knows the answer. After all have had a chance to confer and settle on an answer, the teacher calls on a number for the answer. Another student in the group is then called upon to explain the answer or how the answer was determined. This assures that all group members really understand the information.

A high school science teacher uses "Numbered Heads Together" to provide guided practice in his Chemistry classes. Each student is assigned a number for identification. The teacher presents a problem or question to the class. Each individual is to solve the problem or answer the question alone. After a given time, the students are to put their heads together, compare answers, check each other's work, and come to a consensus. It is mandatory that each student understand how or why the group agreed upon a particular answer. After the discussion is completed, the teacher randomly selects a number to indicate which student must answer the question. The teacher then selects another student from the same group to explain how or why the group agreed on that particular answer. Students from other groups are called upon to check for agreement or disagreement to the answer. Each individual student must be prepared to state how or why the group arrived at any answer.

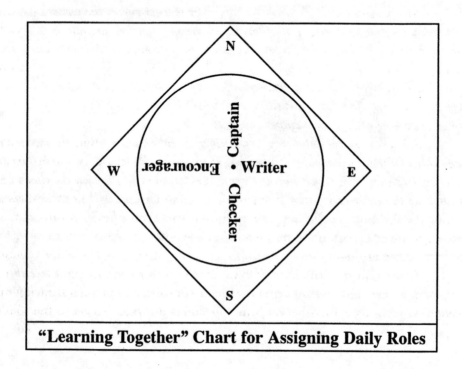

"Learning Together" Chart for Assigning Daily Roles

Direct Instruction

The teacher using cooperative learning techniques has unlimited resources to enrich instruction. These resources walk into the classroom everyday. Children are or can be extremely effective instructors to their peers. By combining the expertise of the teacher and the insight of fellow students, the direct instruction phase of an outcome-based model can be carried out with maximum effectiveness.

This is not to say that the teacher should turn over all instruction to the students. Direct teacher instruction will always be vital to student learning. But in many situations it is quite effective for the teacher to step away from the center of attention and let the students take on some responsibility for their own learning and the learning of others. When teachers give up some of their control over the learning situation, students will utilize and better understand learning strategies.

Modeling is another aspect of direct instruction that is a constant in cooperative learning situations. Effective student modeling adds to the success of any learning unit. For example, after explaining the concept of finding a fractional part of a number, the teacher models how to go through the computation. In checking for understanding, it is evident that some understand and some do not understand the process. The teacher may instruct students within each team to model the process while teammates follow along. It is of utmost importance that the teacher closely monitors the groups to ensure that the modeling is correct. After a few examples, more of the students will understand the process. The teacher may call on others in the group to do the modeling. This is also a good way to check for understanding within the group.

In learning teams, student modeling is automatic and continuous. Students who do not quite understand a concept can observe fellow teammates successfully go through the processes. High achievers are able to explain material to low achievers in a small group setting without the stress for either type of student to have to perform in front of an entire class.

Guided Practice

Students working together allows guided practice time to be much more meaningful. When team members encourage others to stay with the group and participate, time on task is increased. Students are able to check each other's responses and understanding instantly, which helps to eliminate practicing misunderstanding. This often happens in traditional instruction because it is physically impossible for the teacher to be at every student's side all of the time.

When students are continually checking each other, quality practice time results. The quality of time is not only improved for the low achievers but for the high achievers as well. By checking for quality of work and helping students make the needed corrections, a higher level thinking skill is utilized. To get to the root of misunderstanding, students must analyze the situation. They must search for different ways to explain the material so that their teammates will understand. This process will provide even better understanding for all.

An eighth grade mathematics teacher uses the "Bidding Game" as a guided practice activity. Each team is given ten points at the beginning of the game. Five problems are assigned at a time. A time limit is set for completing the problems. The teams are allowed to work through the problems together and come to an agreement on the solution. Each member of the team must write down the process and the solution in order to participate in the game. After time is called the team members may no longer confer with each other. The teacher randomly selects a student to give the answer to the first problem. The student must bid on how sure she is that the answer is correct. The range of acceptable bids is from two to ten.

For example, a student who is reasonably sure of the answer will bid a nine or ten. If the answer is correct, the bid is added to the team score. If the answer is incorrect, the bid is subtracted and a student from another team is given the opportunity to bid for the answer. Once the correct answer is given, the teacher calls on someone for the second problem and so on. At times, the teacher will ask questions about the processes of the solution. Again, the student must bid on her answer to the question. This ensures individual accountability of understanding each problem and encourages the teams to work through the processes together instead of simply giving each other the answers. The game continues through three or four sets of problems as time allows.

Peer Tutoring: A Strategy for Effective Correctives and Enrichment

Once group processes are learned, the teacher can use those skills that apply to peer tutoring for correctives and enrichments. Peer tutoring gives the teacher a great deal of flexibility for managing correctives and enrichments after an assessment of mastery has been conducted. Peer tutoring can serve as an enrichment for the students who have already mastered the concept. For a student to assist another student in learning, a higher level thinking skill is utilized and developed. Extended learning occurs when a student must review, clarify, and invent new ways to explain material to peers. The tutor must focus upon discussion and think critically to highlight key information. Then the information must be summarized in a way that the tutee will be able to understand. Analysis is needed to identify the ideas that are not clear or may be confusing to the tutee. Explaining a concept to another student reinforces the learning of the tutor and increases the chances of long term retention. When tutoring, students gain a deeper understanding by teaching the content from their own perspective and using metacognition.

Peer tutoring has a great impact on correcting misunderstanding and improving student achievement. Tutors should be encouraged to teach others from their special, unique perspectives. For example, visual learners can teach well by presenting information with a picture or chart. Auditory learners may explain the information in their own words. Tutors can explain how they conceptualize the information and help classmates develop the ability to do the same. If a student in need of correctives is exposed to a number of tutors with different perspectives, the chances of finding a personal learning style is increased, thus increasing the chances of learning.

In order for peer tutoring to be successful, the teacher must model instructional strategies and questioning techniques. Tutors must be aware that it is necessary to tell the tutee what they are to learn and why. Peer tutoring groups must be monitored closely in order to assess the effectiveness of the tutor and identify any misinformation that the tutor may be passing on. Short quizzes are a good way to determine both the tutor's and the tutee's grasp of the lesson content. The tutor must be given enough control to feel responsible for the learning of the tutee. The realization of this responsibility will increase the potential for achievement and the development of thinking skills.

The roles of peer tutor and tutee should change depending on outcomes of each assessment. Some students will be tutors in one unit and tutees in the next. All students should be given the chance to tutor, not just the brightest students. A student-tutor only needs to be a little ahead of tutees in a particular concept. The effective teacher will find some situation in which each child can demonstrate leadership. It can be a tremendous self-esteem boost to become a tutor.

A well-planned single activity can provide both enrichment and correctives to individual students within a group. As enrichment, students may design diagrams and charts that illustrate a concept. They may plan ways to demonstrate a concept using manipulatives. Those students in need of correctives may participate by keeping notes of the activity or helping with the construction of the project. This gives the student another way to look at the concept and perhaps develop a better understanding.

Implementing Cooperative Learning into the Classroom

Using cooperative learning teams does not mean that teachers have to change their entire classroom management systems. The following are practical strategies that one can use to structure cooperative learning activities in the classroom.

1. Prepare the classroom for cooperative learning activities. The classroom must be organized in such a way that groups may interact freely. Desks should be pushed together facing each other, rather than in rows facing the front of the room. Tables are ideal for face to face interaction. Wall and bulletin board space should be allotted to team charts, posters, and certificates.

2. Develop a system of assigning students to teams. Teams are usually made up of

three to five students who represent a cross section of the class in past performance, ethnic background, and gender. The size of the teams is determined by the teacher. When in doubt, start small.

Teams are assigned by the teacher. Students are not allowed to choose team members because they tend to choose others like themselves.

While selecting teams, assign a base score to each student according to past performance. This can be done by considering test scores, grades, or simply using teacher judgment. Rank the students from highest to lowest using the base scores. Base scores may also be used later to calculate improvement points.

A team of four people is a good size to manage when you begin. Decide how many teams are needed by dividing the number of students in the class by four. This quotient is the number of teams needed. The remainder tells how many five member teams there will be. For example, a class of twenty-six students will have six teams. Two of the teams will have five members. If the teacher feels that teams of five are too large, the class could be placed into teams of three and four members. For example, a class of twenty-six students could have five teams consisting of four members and two teams of three.

Renumber the list of students according to the number of teams desired. For example, if six teams are needed, use the numbers one through six, then six through one. Alternating the order of the numbers will give a good mix of abilities in the final groups. The following is an example of how a teacher ranks her students and assigns groups.

Base Score	Name	Team Assignment
95	Sue	1
93	John	2
89	Chris	3
88	Kelsey	4
83	Liz	5
80	Mary	6
80	Darin	6
78	Craig	5
78	Stacy	4
77	Julie	3
77	James	2
77	Stephanie	1
75	Kirk	1
74	Troy	2
74	Amber	3

73	Sara	4
73	Jamie	5
72	Brett	6
71	Matt	6
71	Andy	5
70	Hardy	4
69	Josh	3
68	Justin	2
68	Missy	1
61	Patricia	1
55	Kristin	2

This assignment resulted in the following teams:

Team 1	Team 2
Sue	John
Stephanie	James
Kirk	Troy
Missy	Justin
Patricia	Kristin

Team 3	Team 4
Chris	Kelsey
Julie	Stacy
Amber	Sara
Josh	Hardy

Team 5	Team 6
Liz	Mary
Craig	Darin
Jamie	Brett
Andy	Matt

Notice that Teams 1, 2, and 6 do not have a balance of boys and girls. The teacher can switch students who are close in ranking to correct this imbalance. Stephanie and James can be switched to eliminate the imbalance on Teams 1 and 2. Sara and Brett can be switched on Teams 4 and 6. The final team assignments now look like this:

Team 1	Team 2
Sue	John
James	**Stephanie**
Kirk	Troy

| Missy | Justin |
| Patricia | Kristin |

Team 3	Team 4
Chris	Kelsey
Julie	Stacie
Amber	**Brett**
Josh	Hardy

Team 5	Team 6
Liz	Mary
Craig	Darin
Jamie	**Sara**
Andy	Matt

3. Decide how long teams should stay together. This also is determined by the teacher. Most teachers have students stay in groups for about four to six weeks, depending on the lengths of units covered. This seems to work very well for middle-elementary through secondary classes. Primary and special education teachers usually keep the teams together for shorter periods of time, sometimes for only one lesson.

4. Set up a record keeping system for improvement points. The improvement point scoring system allows each student to work toward individual improvement. It also encourages teammates to pull together and make sure that every member of the team understands the material. This system gets students to be supportive of each other instead of competing with one another. Initially, students think that only the "smart kids" will earn team points, but the improvement points soon demonstrate that it is very difficult for the students with high averages to earn points. Since the average and low achievers have more room to improve, they can be the greatest contributors to the team. (See Figure A.)

   Two kinds of worksheets are needed for record-keeping: a "Quiz Score Sheet" and a "Team Summary Sheet." This may seem like a lot of record keeping, but it soon becomes routine and easy to do. The "Team Summary Sheets" on which students can record points can be posted on the wall or bulletin board. (See Figures B and C.)

5. Plan for appropriate team recognition. The teacher should set criteria for team recognition. The following is an example of how the criteria are set for STAD.

Team Rankings

15-19 pts.	Good Team
20-24 pts.	Great Team
25-30 pts.	Super Team

Figure A

Calculating Improvement Points (STAD and TGT)

Score	Improvement Points
More than 10 pts above base	30
100%	30
0 - 10 pts. above base	20
1 - 10 pts. below base	10
More than 10 pts. below base	0

Figure B

Quiz Score Sheet

	Date: Quiz:			Date: Quiz:		
Name	Base Score	Quiz Score	Improvement Points	Base Score	Quiz Score	Improvement Points

---

Figure C

Example Team Scoresheet

Team name: The Brainy Bunch	Base Score	Quiz Score	Improvement Points
Joey	76	90	30
Sam	93	100	30
Julie	97	95	10
Terri	60	60	20
			Total 90

(The teamscore is the average of the team's improvement points.)   Teamscore 23

Recognition may be provided for the teams which meet the criteria for "Good Team," "Great Team," and "Super Team." Many teachers recognize them verbally and encourage them to work a little harder for a higher team ranking. Others put displays of names on the bulletin boards or walls or display pictures of "Super Teams" on the wall. Newsletters are a terrific way to recognize the accomplishments of teams, especially if they are mailed home to the parents. "Good Teams," "Great Teams," and "Super Teams" may be given certificates, stickers, or buttons for their efforts. Most students love getting extra privileges, such as free time or homework passes. Whatever the award is, the student will be excited if the teacher is excited about the accomplishments of the students. Use lots of imagination and creativity to vary the rewards.

6. Introduce Team Learning to the students. **This is one of the most crucial steps in implementing cooperative learning.** Few students walk into the classroom with the collaborative skills required to be effective group members. If the students are not trained to work together, the group work will not be as effective as it could be. The teachers, as well as students, may become frustrated and give up. Certain behaviors must be taught, and the teacher must believe that all students can learn these behaviors.

When introducing team learning, have students list ways they can be cooperative, such as sharing ideas, accepting ideas, listening well, and encouraging others to participate. Discuss appropriate ways of dealing with disagreements. Initiate discussions with the class about the differences between cooperation, competition, and independent work. Once the concept of cooperation is established, teach the class specific language that will aide each one of the students as a team member. For example, give the class a list of comments and/or gestures that will illustrate encouragement. (See Figure D.)

Figure D	
Signs of Encouragement	
Comments	Gestures
"Good Job!"	Thumbs up
"Nice Work!"	A pat on the back
"I like that idea!"	A smile
"We need your opinion about this."	Eye contact
"_____, what do you think?"	Handshakes
"Let's try this way."	High five
"Thanks for your suggestion."	

These are only a few of the many things that students can be taught about encouragement.

Give the students opportunities to practice behavior skills. Role playing is an excellent way to do this. Concentrate on only one or two skills with each lesson. Plan cooperation activities that do not require new academic learning. Puzzles and fun sheets make excellent team builder activities. Provide feedback on how well each student is performing as a member of the team. Allow the students to provide feedback as to how they feel they are performing as a team member.

Some children tend to be much more honest and open if given the opportunity to fill out these evaluations anonymously. (See Figures E and F.)

Figure E

Self Evaluation

Rate yourself according to the following scale:

4 = always	1 = very seldom
3 = most of the time	0 = never
2 = some of the time	

_____ I contributed to the success of my group.

_____ I was interested in the work of my group.

_____ I learned from working with this group.

_____ I communicated with others in the group.

_____ I pulled my fair share of the load.

_____ I offered ideas that others could build upon.

_____ I gave extra effort for the success of the group.

_____ I was personally involved with the group work.

Figure F

Group Evaluation

Rate your team according to the following scale:

4 = always	1 = very seldom
3 = most of the time	0 = never
2 = some of the time	

_____ All members of my group participate.

_____ Ideas come out freely from my group.

_____ There seems to be trust among group members.

_____ My group is accepting of members' ideas.

_____ My group demonstrates a positive attitude.

_____ All members of my group are encouraging to others.

Comments: _____

7. Set up rules and guidelines which must be followed during cooperative learning activities. When students are motivated and actively involved in learning activities, they are usually well-behaved. However, it is good practice to take steps to ensure that students will use class time effectively. Behavior expectations should be defined clearly in advance for successful classroom management. Many teachers keep team rules posted with classroom rules.

8. Develop team spirit and cohesiveness among the groups. This can be done by providing activities that will allow both individuals and teams to experience success and to realize that success is the result of the efforts of working together. These activities should instill positive feelings among team members and encourage team efforts. Assigning the task of creating good positive team names, slogans, and logos that reflect personalities within the teams is an excellent way to start. During these activities, team members should begin to develop an appreciation for the individual differences within the group and realize that the contribution of each and every member is vital for the success of the group.

9. Listen to the comments and suggestions of your students. As your classes become more and more involved and experienced in teamwork, the students become excellent resources for updating a program. Now that they are taking a more active part in the learning process, they have insights that may, at times, be helpful to you as the coordinator. On the following page is a survey used by a mathematics teacher at the end of the first grading period (Figure G).

10. Keep a file or notebook of ideas that prove successful for future use. Activities, team builders, certificates, coupons, surveys, suggestions, etc. can be organized and kept for references in future years. Form a group with other teachers using cooperative learning and share these ideas. Besides providing fresh ideas, such networking fosters teacher support, confidence, and enthusiasm.

Problems and Solutions

There are certain problems that may arise when using cooperative learning methods, but they need not be barriers to continuing these strategies. The section that begins below addresses some of the pitfalls experienced by teachers using cooperative learning and offers a few remedies for overcoming these difficulties.

Personality conflicts within teams

This is a common problem mainly because of the heterogeneous grouping. Conflicts usually diminish as students become more experienced at working in groups because they realize that they must cooperate in order to be successful. Students must understand that they will be working together for a long time and will not be allowed to change teams. Some students will have to be reminded constantly that cooperation is

---

Figure G

Congratulations! You have just completed nine weeks of cooperative learning in math. Whether you realize it or not, you have had a lot of success with teamwork. In order to make the teams even more successful, I need some input from you. Please answer the following questions as best you can. Your answers will help me plan team activities for the next nine weeks.

1. Name   2.   Hour

3. Explain three things that you like about working in math teams.

    1.
    2.
    3.

4. Explain three things you do not like about working in math teams.

    1.
    2.
    3.

5. List any students who have been on your team more than once.

6. List three students you feel you would work with best on a team.

    1.
    2.
    3.

7. List up to three students (if any) you feel you could not work as well with on a team.

    1.
    2.
    3.

8. Would you like to work alone a day or two each week and still maintain the teams?

9. Which role on the team do you like the best?

10. Which role do you do the best?

11. Which role do you like the least?

12. Which role do you do the worst?

Comments: (Any suggestions you have to make teamwork more successful and enjoyable.)

mandatory and that putdowns or making fun of teammates is not acceptable behavior.

Providing rewards for cooperative teams is sometimes helpful. Some students may not care how well the team is working together until they realize that cooperative teams can earn free time, bonus points, assignment coupons, etc.

If a teacher is having several problems with team members not getting along, it may be advisable to change all of the teams after a short time. The new team assignments can be made in a way to avoid the same problems encountered before.

Removing a student from a group because of misbehavior is an option, but often these are the very students who need the team experiences the most. However, students must not be allowed to sabotage the success of the group. If it does become necessary to remove a student from a group, place the student temporarily at a desk to work alone, with the understanding that certain behaviors will earn back the privilege of working with the team.

Noise level too high

This problem can usually be dealt with easily. Many times when students become involved in a task, it is natural for them to become too noisy. The teacher can remedy this by using a signal to get the classroom completely quiet. The signal must tell the students to stop talking and give their attention to the teacher. Teachers may flip the lights off and on or ring a bell. Another method is for the teacher's hand to be raised. It is important that the students respect and follow the signal every time it is used. Giving points and recognizing teams that are quick to become quiet may be helpful.

Students visiting rather than staying on task

Providing structure for practice sessions will usually assure that the time is used well. When students are assigned specific roles to perform, they tend to be able to use time more wisely. Sometimes it is necessary to instruct the students on how to keep the group work flowing smoothly.

Some teachers give bonus points to teams that stay on task. If this is done, the teacher should move from team to team pointing out good teamwork. The students should know in advance that they can earn points for staying on task.

If there is a particular team having difficulty staying on task, proximity usually helps.

Getting the shy student to contribute

Again, assigning roles within the groups can help eliminate this problem. The captain of a team can go around the table and call on one student at a time to explain an answer or problem. The encourager can use positive comments that will give the shy student confidence to share and participate.

Absences

This can be a problem when using teams because students depend upon one another. When a student is absent for a test, do not penalize the team. Simply divide the team score by the number of team members present. If there are students who are habitually absent, spread them out among the teams. Emphasize that good attendance is an asset to every team. Many times working in teams will motivate the habitual absentee to improve attendance.

Implementing Cooperative Learning into the District

An increasing number of elementary and secondary schools have begun to apply cooperative principles at the school level. These principles involve teachers in cooperative planning, peer coaching, and team teaching. Many districts are encouraging staff to implement cooperative learning into the classroom.

A district that is currently using the Accountability Based Curriculum restructuring model will initiate training as part of the implementation phase for a particular curriculum. Although the curriculum coordinating council should conduct "overview" inservice sessions, it is a subject area committee — working with building principals — that has the greatest responsibility for training faculty. A subject area committee develops its strategy for providing training in (1) methods for teaching high achievement outcomes, (2) techniques for cooperative learning and teaching, and (3) processes that account for differing learning styles.

Whether a district is using the ABC model or not, it is important that an awareness session that provides an overview of the cooperative learning concepts be provided before asking teachers to jump into an extensive "how to do it" training program. Staff should be made aware of the benefits of such a program and be given the opportunity to experience practical, hands-on use of the strategies.

A district using the ABC model will work with key teachers on the use of cooperative teaching and learning techniques. While participation is strongly encouraged, it should remain optional. Initially there may be only a small group showing interest. Those teachers and/or administrators can be given extensive training and later used as resources for training in pairs or groups in order to share plans, ideas, problems, and successes. Cooperation among teachers will complement the introduction of cooperative learning.

Training and support for participating teachers should be provided at regular intervals during the school year. Teachers will need release time and compensation for time spent outside the work day. District support (funds, coaching, encouragement, etc.) should be continuous throughout the training and implementation.

As teachers witness the success of the program, interest will grow and more staff will be willing to become involved. At this time, training opportunities will need to be expanded, making use of experienced teachers within the district as trainers.

Follow-up support will increase the probability of continued success for teachers using cooperative learning. Periodic networking sessions for teachers to share ideas and discuss problems are valuable. Teachers need to visit classrooms to observe cooperative learning in action. Once teachers implement the program, they can provide follow-up support by visiting each other's classes to observe and give feedback.

Cooperative Learning Basics:

- Cooperative learning is a valuable strategy in an outcome-based program because it is effective in achieving mastery learning. The nature of this method of instruction complements components of the outcome-based model.

- Cooperative learning is a teaching strategy in which students are involved in small group learning activities. There are various models of cooperative learning ranging from highly structured teams to simply putting students into groups.   Components that are basic to most cooperative learning methods are common goals, team rewards, individual accountability, and equal opportunities for success. Keeping these components in mind when planning activities will better ensure success for any program.

- The theory that people working together toward a common goal can accomplish more than people working alone has been thoroughly researched in relation to student achievement.   Use of practical cooperative learning strategies in the classroom has been found to be instructionally effective in attaining mastery across the curriculum at all levels of education. Research proves that students working together in small cooperative groups can master material presented by the teacher better than students working on their own.

- Practical suggestions to follow when implementing cooperative learning into the classroom are:
  1.   Prepare the classroom for cooperative learning.
  2.   Assign students to heterogeneous teams.
  3.   Determine how long teams should stay together.
  4.   Develop a system of determining team points.
  5.   Plan for appropriate team recognition.
  6.   Teach team learning to the students.
  7.   Set up rules and guidelines.
  8.   Develop cohesiveness among the groups.
  9.   Get feedback from students.
  10. Keep a file or notebook of ideas.
  11. Form a network group with other teachers.

- Districts which are considering implementing cooperative learning along with outcome-based strategies should start slowly. Volunteers should be recruited rather than the district mandating participation. As the effectiveness and success of the program become evident, additional staff will accept the concept and become ready to implement the program into more classrooms.

LEARNING STYLES IN A RESULTS BASED CURRICULUM

The special resource persons for this section are Clarice Faltus and Jeannine Schaull, the Catholic Diocese of Wichita, Kansas.

Everyone recognizes the importance of student learning styles, but many teachers find it difficult to identify the proper theoretical approach and apply it in day-to-day circumstances. Moreover, some find it challenging to associate learning styles with other educational perspectives and teaching strategies. The purpose of this section is to help resolve those dilemmas, and to show why it is important to consider student learning styles at every stage in the development of a results based program.

A Definition

Since there are many researchers now in the field who concentrate their attention on learning styles, it is important to identify the interpretation that best fits our needs. To do that, we must work with a few basic definitions. First, *style* is defined by Webster as being a *distinctive manner of behavior and expression.* The key word is "distinctive," and that word implies something all educators know intuitively....that each human being is unique. While we all have something in common, our physiological and psychological differences cause us to interact with the world in highly individual ways. Consequently, in helping individuals understand one another teachers must accept the idea that human work styles, intelligence, and methods of interaction are difficult to classify, and that efforts to classify such characteristics in the last 100 years have been frustrating to educators. For example, the definition of human intelligence isn't as clear to us in the 1990s as it was to researchers, psychologists, and educators of 50 years ago. There are simply too many exceptions to the earlier-established rules, and misuse of pencil and paper tests leading to such numerical indicators as "intelligence quotients" has sometimes been scandalous.

Even achievement tests, many of which are produced by the Educational Testing Service, are criticized as being invalid and even irresponsible. Although new versions are being prepared and administered, earlier tests used a single evaluative method and tended to assess dimensions of learning that are narrow and exclusive of real-life applications. Over-reliance on intelligence and achievement tests, some say, has led many former students to the conclusion that they have little or nothing to offer society... simply because a "scientific" assessment of their intellectual level indicated below normal ability. That conclusion has led to a cultural self-fulfilling prophesy that causes us to miss the potential contributions such people could have otherwise provided.

While classification of human beings is risky business, those of us who are educators must use some organizational construct through which we can interact with and influence student learning behavior. Unlike E.S. Neill in *Summerhill,* we can't just accept the idea that there are so many individual kinds of ability in our classes that efforts to plan, instruct, and evaluate students are in vain. We teachers must devise useful ways to think about student needs or we will experience the worst kind of pedagogical overload, the kind that forces us to revert to the easiest way out. And the easiest way out is to plan for the student who fits traditional school cultures by paying attention to instruction, reading assignments, memorizing factual material, passing pencil and paper tests, and behaving quietly and purposefully in class. Students who have difficulty subscribing to the "easiest way out" are slowly eliminated from the educational scene. Those students fail, and their teachers justify that failure by strongly suggesting that failure is a real life condition. The problem with such a rationale is that failure, instead of being helpful and instructive to the student, leads to a long-term and perhaps permanent diminishing of the student's self esteem and power to make future contributions. It is just as bad as intelligence and achievement tests in its power to convince individuals with potential ability that they have little or nothing to contribute.

The "easiest way out" syndrome can be avoided by accepting the idea that good instruction involves using a variety of strategies, understanding the importance of a few learning style classifications, and realizing the usefulness of learning style classifications to plan, conduct and evaluate instruction. Research, practice, and common sense have long proven the effectiveness of using variety in an instructional program. However, clear and appropriate classifications of learning styles eluded us for many years.

The "Proper" Theoretical Approach

In 1971 David Kolb was able to isolate and describe four distinct learning styles which he classified as follows; (1) the sensory/feeling dimension...*concrete experience,* (2) the watching dimension...*reflective observation,* (3) the thinking dimension...*abstract conceptualization,* and (4) the doing dimension...*active experimentation.* He concluded that every human being carries around aspects of all four learning styles, but tends to be dominated by one or two of them. If each style is considered in its pure form, a person's behavior could be described as shown below:

1. **Concrete Experience:**
    These persons perceive information concretely and process it actively. These are the *sensors, feelers and doers.* They do not begin with an idea but with what their senses tell them. Then they take the plunge and get into action.
2. **Reflective Observation:**
    These persons perceive information concretely and process it reflectively. They

are the *sensors, feelers and watchers*.   They study life as it is lived, reflect on their observations, and move toward generalizations.

3.   **Abstract Conceptualization:**
These persons perceive information abstractly and process it reflectively.
These are the *thinkers and watchers*. They begin with an idea, reflect upon it, and watch it evolve.

4   **Active Experimentation:**
These persons perceive information abstractly and process it actively. They are the *thinkers and doers*.   They begin with an idea, try it out, and test it.   They must be personally involved.

As we look at the classifications, we begin to recognize people that possess the described characteristics, and those individuals can be students, teachers, administrators, parents, and others who live and work in our professional world.   The challenge, then, is to understand and appreciate the characteristics of those persons not fully like us, and to adopt a curriculum model that allows students in all categories to easily achieve success in their "home" style.   In addition, persons in all four categories must be expected to do some stretching in order to achieve success when functioning in learning styles areas that do not specifically address their home style.

Choosing the *proper* theoretical approach for learning styles is no easy task for those using the Accountability Based Curriculum model, because the model is focused primarily on academic programs.   While we recognize its value in a broad sense, we believe the approach advocated by Dunn, Dunn and Price is not fully compatible with the model because it focuses on educational conditions more than the academic program.   Categories in that learning styles research are environmental, emotional, sociological, and physical.   *Environmental preferences* include sound, light, temperature, and the need for either a formal or informal instructional design. Motivation, persistence, responsibility, and the need for either structure or options are *emotional preferences*. *Sociological preferences*   include self, pair, peer, team, adult, or varied groupings. And *physical preferences*   are perceptual strengths, need for intake, time of day or night, energy levels, and the need for mobility.   Again, we do not dispute the value of this approach in a generic sense, but find it to be less useful when applied to our academic model.

David Hunt is another researcher who focuses a great deal on educational conditions, and he suggests that student learning styles are those educational circumstances within which people are most likely to learn.   He essentially describes the amount of structure individuals require.

Readers of this book are encouraged to examine numerous learning styles theories and critique them according to their usefulness in designing and implementing curriculum.   As a sample, we will use Kolb's research as a springboard to show some meaningful categories for learning styles. Those categories are stated in simple terms so they can be remembered and used easily. The following chart serves as a cross-reference for Kolb's terminology and practical interpretations.

KOLB'S THEORIES	INTERPRETATIONS
CONCRETE EXPERIENCE	STYLES OF LEARNING THAT ARE ASSOCIATED WITH TANGIBLE CONCEPTS, PROCESSES OR THINGS
REFLECTIVE OBSERVATION	STYLES OF LEARNING BY STUDENTS WHO ARE RECEPTIVE TO STANDARD CLASSWORK
ABSTRACT CONCEPTUALIZATION	STYLES OF LEARNING BY STUDENTS WHO ARE BUSY THINKING THROUGH COMPLEX PROBLEMS
ACTIVE EXPERIMENTATION	STYLES OF LEARNING BY STUDENTS WHO FREQUENTLY ASK "WHAT IF" QUESTIONS AND WANT TO TEST IDEAS

Concrete styles are seen in students who learn better if they can manipulate the pieces of a puzzle. As shown in the chart above, they like to work with tangibles, and to put the world in order. *Reflective styles* of learning are found in students who learn by associating the familiar with the unfamiliar. These students are "empty vessels to be filled," and they like the concrete yet segmented teaching methods ordinarily used in schools today. They observe something new and reflect upon it in terms of what they know in order to draw conclusions. *Abstract styles* of learning are shown by students who look at things from more than one perspective. They enjoy thinking through complex ideas and ways problems might be solved. *Active styles* are apparent in those who want to jump ahead and figure out alternate possibilities; they ask "what if?" and then do something to answer their own questions.

Development and Planning Applications in a Results Based Curriculum

Learning styles must first be considered by a subject area committee when it develops the high achievement outcomes for each grade level and course. After that it is the responsibility of each teacher, in breaking down those high achievement outcomes into instructional units and lessons, to consider learning styles in planning methods, activities, assessments, and extensions. It almost goes without saying that a consideration of varied learning styles will never show up in the teacher's task analysis planning if inadequate attention is given to them in the development of the outcomes themselves.

We prepared a list of activities appropriate for various learning styles and — using that list — created a technique for analyzing an outcome and its critical elements. The concept map below shows basic points to be considered by subject area committees as they develop each high achievement outcome. It can also be used by teachers as they plan to teach to each of those high achievement outcomes.

Elements within each of the activity categories are those which: (1) include pretests, direct instruction, homework, review questions, and post-tests; (2) involve observation and demonstration; (3) can be experiments and other hands-on processes; (4) include research, exploratory processes, or different points of view.

CONCEPT MAP: LEARNING STYLES PLANNING

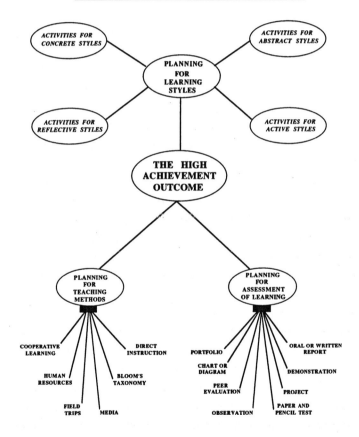

Remember, a consideration of learning styles must begin with the development of high achievement outcomes. When the subject area committee members have participated in the design-down process, and used appropriate phrasing and word use to develop high achievement outcomes, they are ready to analyze each outcome for its sensitivity to learning styles differences. Only then is it possible for teachers to plan appropriate lessons. Here is a brief checklist that might help the subject area committee:

____1. Write high achievement outcome.
____2. Analyze outcome for its potential in creating a variety of activities in terms of concrete, reflective, abstract, and active styles.
____3. Determine student learning tasks, instructional methods, activities, assessments, and extensions with the above four categories in mind (see the section on task analysis).

It is possible for a teacher to limit the consideration of learning styles to the planning stage, making the assumption that an instructional program that has taken into account the four categories shown in number (2) above will meet the needs of all students. If teachers are certain that each unit and lesson contains a variety of instructional approaches and student activities, then they have made major accomplishments in providing for all students.

Incorporating Learning Styles in the Instructional Process

In the example we provide, the subject is fifth grade science and the outcome is that "Students will contrast elements, compounds, solutions and suspensions by collecting, organizing, and analyzing data and drawing conclusions." Under activities for concrete styles, the teacher uses common items found in a kitchen — baking soda, salt, and pepper — to demonstrate substances and the physical and chemical properties of solutions. Food coloring is used for a concentration/dilution demonstration. All of these substances are familiar to students, hence, they can be used in the demonstration. Some students could even demonstrate the use of these substances at home to their parents.

Under activities for reflective styles the teacher assures that students understand basic properties and formulas by using standard pencil and paper tests, which can also assess some higher level knowledge. Learning does not stop once knowledge is gained, but continues in the form of practical applications.

Activities for abstract styles have students performing their own experiments on solutions and suspensions. And for active styles, students may choose one of three activities: 1) students compare the taste of different sweeteners by making solutions and rating sweetness; 2) students conduct a dilution/concentration experiment to decide at which point or threshold a difference in taste is noticed; or 3) students use a CHEM kit to explain chemical and physical reactions.

For extension activities students can do one or both of the following. "Observing Chemical Change" uses a combination of magnesium sulfate and water, and calcium chloride and water. Students pour the contents of both into one test tube and then observe the results. "Mystery Spill" (CHEM kit) is a test of six different substances; a seventh substance is tested and the students match it with one of the other six substances. These activities can be either corrective or enrichment; in fact, students might be paired — one "enrichment student" working with a "corrective student" to conduct these activities. As the students work on the assignment together, the students with the lower degree of understanding can see how their peers work through the problem.

Learning Styles Basics:

- Students learn in a variety of ways generally called styles. Traditionally schools have instructed students by primarily using knowledge level activities. As a result of this, educators have seen many students never reach maximum potential.

- If we truly believe that all students can learn, we must also believe they do not all learn in the same way, thus the need for teachers to gear instructional methods to all styles of learning.

- Consideration of learning styles must begin with the subject area committee's development of high achievement outcomes, and continue with the individual teacher's planning of lessons.

- Educators should examine various learning styles theories to determine which one best suits their needs for planning and implementing curriculum.

DEFINING AND APPLYING MASTERY IN A RESULTS BASED CURRICULUM

One of the biggest concerns of educators involved in school improvement efforts today is the whole issue of mastery. They know that they must help their students achieve mastery of expected learning outcomes, but no one knows for sure exactly what that means, let alone how they should go about accomplishing it. The following scenario illustrates some of the confusion that reigns.

At a recent faculty meeting in Example High School, the task for the day was to begin drafting a statement about mastery. That issue had become increasingly important as the school district moved from traditional to outcome-based curriculum, instruction, and student assessment. It had become clear to many teachers that old-style criterion ref-

erenced tests, with their emphasis on content coverage and memorization of facts, were not appropriate for declaring mastery of high achievement outcomes. Consequently, the district's curriculum coordinating council had asked faculty members in each school to discuss the subjects of authentic assessment and mastery. The only premise council members wanted each school's faculty to accept was that authentic assessment should be defined as "assessments that parallel real life and evaluate student learning in terms of stated outcomes." The council has also expressed interest in developing a portfolio system for recording and managing student progress, a system that necessitates a clear perspective on mastery.

Soon after Example High's faculty meeting started, discussion focused on two key questions: "Just what is mastery?" and "How is mastery defined or determined?" After a short but thoughtful silence, the following responses were offered.

Pete: Well, mastery means that students really learned what I wanted them to learn.

Sue: Yes, but how do you know they really learned it?

Pete: The same way we've always decided if learning has really happened — through tests. I think the issue is how well do students have to do on a test for us to say they've mastered it? I've been reading about this lately, and it seems like most schools are requiring at least 80% — some 85 % — to declare that a student has met mastery.

Max: That 80% bothers me. In my last geography unit there were ten things I thought were absolutely essential for students to know. Are you telling me that if they know eight of those things, but don't have a clue about the other two, they've reached mastery? Or are they supposed to know each of the ten things at an 80% level? I'm not sure I know how to put that kind of value on each part.

Gerri: I have another kind of problem with it. I have students in every one of my math classes who have scored 100% on a major test. Yet a month or so later, when I surprise them with a few review problems, the very same kids who scored 100% are lucky to get half of them right. Obviously their learning was short-term and not permanent. There's no way you would call that mastery.

Robert: Besides that, you all are talking about written tests. My art classes are strictly performance-based. How do you decide on an 80% for a piece of pottery?

Sue: Don't you evaluate against a set of performance criteria? I'd think it would depend on whether the student met 80% of your criteria.

Robert: Yes I do. But I'm like Max. Are you saying that students just have to meet eight of my ten criteria, or do they have to meet each criterion at an 80% level? I can tell you I'm not going to accept two of those criteria being ignored, so the first interpretation doesn't work. And as for the second one, I don't know how you can put a percentage on something like "student's design was original." It either was or wasn't; there's no 80% to it.

James: (chuckling) Well, there's something else at stake here that no one has brought up yet. I teach driver's education. Is it okay with all of you if I send these kids out on the road in real-life vehicles if they only know 80% of what they need to know about safe driving?

Amy: I think it's obvious that we've all seen — or are beginning to see — some problems with the percentage factor. James said a couple of key words that have been on my mind recently: real-life. I've been really pleased with the effort put forth by my government students this year. Studying the Constitution and amendments can be really tedious. But they have worked hard! They've read everything I've asked; they can answer the usual questions, and they've all — well, most of them — have done really well on their tests. And yet, when something comes up in the morning paper, and I ask them how that issue applies to what we've been learning — I get a lot of blank stares. They just aren't transferring learning from the textbook and the classroom to the real world.

Angela: I have something that's similar, yet different. I have a student in my English class who almost always does well on paper — whether it's a daily assignment or a test or whatever — and yet when we have our class discussions I'm appalled at how poorly she expresses herself. I know she hasn't mastered some of the basics that I'm teaching this year, and yet how can I justify that opinion? What can I show her parents if they come in for a conference? I know what I know, but it's only based on my observations and opinions!

Joe: Because I serve on our district's curriculum coordinating council, I know how difficult it is to resolve some of the issues you've introduced. The council's debate focused on "authentic" assessment, and we decided that it pertains to everything that has been said here today — and more. We temporarily decided that authentic assessment must be based on the stated outcome and — as Amy has pointed out — must reflect real-life situations; that's the reason for the premise we gave you. That reasoning is compatible with Pete's comment about teacher expectation, because teachers must have a great deal to do with outcome development. But there is no doubt that teachers must also come up with more specific criteria, and more flexible, comprehensive, and long-range methods of assessment. Giving only one test, one time, for units of instruction just isn't a sufficient measure of real learning, especially when most of those tests are paper and pencil varieties.

If the discussion going on at Example High School sounds familiar, it's because your school or district has reached a very critical moment in the evolution of an outcome-based system. Even if you aren't yet at the point of discussing mastery-related issues, it should be obvious that the time will certainly come when someone asks, "Just what is mastery? How is it defined? And beyond that, how do we apply the definition in day-to-day classroom situations?"

In this section we attempt to define mastery in a generic way, something that a curriculum coordinating council must do during the first or second year of implementing this model. A generic definition is important as a guide to subject area committees as they strive to clarify the concept of "authentic" mastery within their specific areas of study. Second, we discuss the tools used to measure and label mastery, and offer alternatives to the more rigid processes currently applied by some teachers. Third is a discussion of teacher professionalism and its relationship to the qualitative judgment of student performance. Fourth, you are given suggestions on criteria development and use (based on example high achievement outcomes), and how a teacher can produce both quantitative and qualitative evidence for use in a portfolio system. Finally, we offer a glossary of terms so that your associates can better understand the jargon developing around the topic of results-based assessment.

Mastery in a Results-Based System

A generic definition for mastery is an important contribution of the curriculum coordinating council because it clarifies in the minds of subject area committee members, teachers, administrators, and professional support persons what the district or school stands for in terms of excellence. That definition cannot be simplistic, nor can it be reduced to numbers or percentages. It must be expressed in complete sentences and phrases — in the kind of language which is carefully considered and reviewed in dynamic faculty dialogue. It is written in good narrative form because mastery is as much a function of faculty scholarship as of measurable student achievement. In other words, the scholarship of students is only as good as the individual and collective scholarship demonstrated by their mentors.

The kind of scholarship discussed in the previous paragraph may make some teachers uncomfortable, but it is pointless to accept anything less. Academic growth is an all-encompassing condition, so everyone in a school or district, including students in the lower elementary grades and special education, should recognize its importance. If that point is understood, then it is much easier to accept the idea that mastery can be assessed both qualitatively and quantitatively, because the professional staff understands and continuously works with academic depth.

The following generic statement was produced by a district associated with the Curriculum Leadership Institute. It works as a guide in the district that produced it, but should be used only as an example for other curriculum coordinating councils. As with all CLI-related processes, the best products and actions are those created at the local level.

Mastery

Mastery is the point in a student's learning at which there is a clear, observable and consistent demonstration of skills, knowledge, and their applications, measured according to criteria taken from the district's essential learning outcomes.

Teaching to Mastery

Teaching to mastery involves the use of clearly stated and challenging outcomes, varied instructional methods, focused student learning tasks, and forms of assessment that are aligned with essential learning outcomes. The final determination of mastery is based on the individual and collective decisions of teachers.

Assessments

Assessments used to determine the extent of mastery require the development of outcome-based criteria and the accumulation of qualitative and quantitative evidence. A combination of the following assessment tools provides evidence that supports teacher decisions: (1) formative and summative criterion-referenced tests, (2) written and oral assignments, (3) developmental projects, and (4) observable student performance.

Other Assumptions About Mastery

An outcome-based curriculum in each subject discipline is the product of a workable district mission statement. That statement clearly delineates the educational purpose of the schools in regard to student preparation for advanced education or entry-level employment. Each teacher must subscribe to the idea that all students can learn the content and skills associated with a challenging and prescribed curriculum. This is possible when there is student readiness, sufficient student learning time, diversity of instructional methods, and institutional/community support and assistance. Administrators and teachers, with the assistance of parents and students, develop programs to maintain conditions that insure quality student learning.

Linking Mastery to High Achievement Outcomes

Teachers will utilize high-achievement outcomes when determining mastery. A high achievement outcome is one that meets the following criteria:

it contains a positive statement
it tells what the students themselves will do
it uses a verb that describes specific action
it contains an end result, and that result relates directly to our intention
it requires a high cognitive level of thinking
it requires dynamic student involvement
it is relevant to the students' lives
it can be authentically assessed

Measuring and Labeling Mastery: Going Beyond the Number Game
        In the scenario described in the beginning of this section, Pete said he had
been reading about mastery and that it seems most schools require 80% or 85% proficiency to declare that a student has met mastery of a particular outcome. CLI personnel have worked with educators from every region of the country, and we find this
to be a common perception. Most likely this comes from the fact that Thomas
Guskey, recognized as an expert in the mastery learning process, originally recommended between 80% and 90% as the standard for determining mastery. Guskey has
had several books and many articles published, and has been on the national circuit
as a presenter for a number of years now, so it's not surprising that from coast to coast
we hear people talking about that magic 80%. However, applying that formula just
didn't work in the real world, and those who have heard Guskey recently will find that
he, too, is now talking about standards other than percentages of right and wrong
answers.
        Why doesn't that 80% indicator work in circumstances where curriculum is
based on real world needs, and where high achievement outcomes are regularly
applied? It doesn't work for the reasons given by Max, Gerri, and the other teachers
in our earlier scenario. Let's look at some of those problems in detail.

TOTAL NUMBER OR QUALITY?

        In some cases, figuring 80% is simple. It is easy to compute the percentage
correct of any kind of test that has distinct right or wrong answers. Examples include
objective tests that have true-false or matching kinds of questions, math tests where
students must compute sums, differences, or other single-answer problems, or any
kind of test that asks for a specific response, such as "Who is the author of *To Kill a
Mockingbird?*" However, in many instances the task is more complex. In trying to
decide if a student has achieved 80% of what is expected, the first question that comes
to mind for many teachers is the one Max raised: Do we mean that a student must
achieve 80% of the total number of expectations, or that each expectation must be
met an an 80% level?
        For example, in Eric's biology class one outcome requires students to perform
and record a particular experiment. The written record is the "test" that Eric evaluates. There is a set *number of items* that Eric looks for: the hypothesis, four necessary steps to be conducted, and the conclusion. If he had only to evaluate whether
each of these items was included in the written report, he could easily figure whether
the student had met the 80% standard. Instead, Eric must also judge the quality of
some of the items in the student's report. The student may indeed reach a conclusion,
but that conclusion may be faulty. Or the student may list the completed steps in
such an abbreviated form as not to explain them fully. The fact that the student

included all six items in the report is just not enough to indicate mastery. Therefore, if Eric were to use the 80% standard, he would have to evaluate not only whether each of the six items had been included, but whether <u>each one</u> was described at an 80% level as well. And trying to decide whether the student described each item "80% well enough" is complicated, to say the least.

PUTTING QUALITY INTO PERCENTAGE CATEGORIES

Proponents of the 80% rule often look at the information above and still claim there is no problem. Their answer is to use the 80% either way — if your test requires right or wrong answers, expect 80% of the total; in all other cases, evaluate each item according to an 80% level of quality. However, the teachers who use the latter means of evaluation know this suggestion is not so easy as it sounds, nor is it practical in many situations.

It is true that when we try to evaluate the quality of something, we should establish the criteria for quality ahead of time. We set the criteria, communicate those criteria to the students, and then determine whether each criterion has or has not been met. But this puts the teacher right back into the same situation described above. The fact that a student achieved 80% of the criteria does not necessarily mean that the student has mastered that which was intended. The remaining 20% of the criteria — the ones that were not achieved — may be crucial to the expected outcome. So once again the teacher's only solution, when forced to apply the 80% rule, is to try to decide whether each criterion has been met at an 80% level. And some criteria just cannot be put into percentage categories.

Marsha teaches a drama class and she must evaluate the quality of each student's stage performance. One criterion of a quality performance is voice projection. The students must project well enough that the audience can hear them. Marsha says, "Let's suppose I have five criteria, and projecting the voice so that the audience can hear is only one of them. I suppose if a student met the other four criteria, but not this one, I could say the student met four of my five criteria, so that's 80%. But that means the student would have "mastered" the outcome for stage performance, and I do not agree that such mastery has occurred if the audience can't hear him. So next, I'm supposed to decide if he met the voice criterion at an 80% level. Tell me, how do you do that? Should I poll the audience to see if 80% of them could hear the student? Come on!"

What Marsha does instead is explain to the student that the outcome has not yet been achieved because the student's voice projection is weak. She then provides some corrective activities that the student can do to improve projection. She continues to reassess, pointing out when and how the student is improving and identifying performances that are not YET good enough. The student continues with corrective activities until Marsha, in her professional opinion, is satisfied with progress. But at no point does she try to say, "Your voice projection is now at a 65% (or 80%....90%....etc.) level."

DETERMINING PERCENTAGES FOR THE AFFECTIVE DOMAIN

Another problem with the 80% factor occurs when outcomes relate to the affective domain. Some educators believe that the outcome-based philosophy can only be applied to the "academic" areas — that we cannot identify an end result for teaching to and assessing affective qualities. This is simply not true. It is true that you cannot accurately measure what a student is thinking or feeling. This is why when we write outcomes we avoid using such terms as *understand, appreciate, respect,* or *value.* However, the affective domain is very much a part of our curricular goals. We would not be producing the kind of graduates we want if we were to ignore such things as acceptance of responsibility, working cooperatively with others, or responding to the rights of others. What we can do is teach specific lessons and look for specific behaviors that demonstrate application of the principles we have taught.

For example, idealistically we would like students to appreciate, or respect, the rights of others. Realistically, we cannot read a student's mind to know whether she does or does not actually "appreciate" the fact that her rights do not supersede the rights of other people. In actual fact, she may disbelieve or resent this concept. However, we can observe her behavior in the classroom and determine whether she is — at least in these circumstances — applying the rules that protect the rights of others. We can only hope then that continued application of appropriate classroom behavior will become a "habit" and transfer to out-of-classroom experiences. The outcome we write would not say the student will appreciate the rights of others; instead it would require students to recognize the relationship between personal rights and the rights of others, and to demonstrate appropriate behavior or to modify personal behavior, when necessary, to comply with the rights of others.

There are specific lessons that can be taught — and assessed — regarding student behavior and attitudes. There are all kinds of materials and suggested activities available through local, state, and national law-related education projects. The "Boys' Town" curriculum from the original Boys' Town home and school in Omaha, Nebraska, also provides practical, step-by-step procedures for teaching such things as social behavior and responsibility. A lack of materials, programs, and activities is not the problem. The point is, assessing these kinds of outcomes on a percentage basis is ludicrous. When a particular behavior is expected, teachers watch for that behavior and of course notice when it is not exhibited, and they particularly notice when it is violated repeatedly. But the only way they could determine if a student has met the outcome at an 80% level is to document each student's behavior every day, and then figure whether a student has behaved appropriately 80% of the time. Not only is this record-keeping task ridiculous, so is the notion that 80% appropriate behavior is acceptable.

FIGURING A PERCENTAGE FOR LONG-TERM GOALS AND OUTCOMES

Similar to the problem of determining a percentage basis for mastery of affective outcomes is one dealing with long-term goals and outcomes. There are some outcomes that cannot be accomplished in a single unit of instruction; they may take months or even the entire school year to accomplish. For example, a second grade science outcome that has been described earlier in this book says that students will demonstrate proper care and treatment of classroom pets. A seventh grade English outcome states that students will read a variety of kinds of books in addition to assigned readings, will select books appropriate to their reading levels, and will demonstrate comprehension of each. A high school physical education outcome says that students will assess their levels of strength, stamina, and flexibility, set personal goals for improvement, and evaluate accomplishments.

In each of these cases there are too many variables to make the percentage factor a reasonable one. The situation of the classroom pets is much like the one described above for behavior. The teacher creates and maintains documents for each child assigned the responsibility of pet care. If, throughout the year, a child demonstrates proper care and treatment, then the outcome has been met. But if a child mishandles an animal or forgets to care for it, does a percentage of occurrences determine mastery? More likely the teacher evaluates the seriousness of mistreatment, when (early or late in the school year) problems occur, and whether by the end of the year the student is demonstrating correct and responsible care and treatment.

A student who performs correctly 80% of the time still may not have mastered the outcome if the 20% includes serious infractions. Conversely, a child who "forgot" 40% of the time during the year may have done all of her forgetting during the early months but was performing perfectly through the whole second semester. Wouldn't common sense tell us she had mastered the outcome?

In the seventh grade English example, must the teacher decide if by the end of the year 80% of the student's selections were on his reading level and then if each selection was "80% comprehended"? And in the physical education example, if setting and meeting goals is evaluated according to a percentage factor, wouldn't students focus on that aspect rather than on realistic personal goals and a sense of accomplishment?

The explanations of these four categories may seem to indicate that percentages should never be used to determine mastery. That is not the case. A percentage factor is very appropriate for particular outcomes. The point is that a district's definition of mastery cannot be based on percentage alone.

Long-Term Goals and Transfer

Gerri, Amy, and Angela raised some other points that are crucial to the determination of mastery. Gerri talked about the students who score as high as 100% on a test, but do very poorly when checked on the same skills or concepts at a later date. Not only have we all seen this happen with the students in our classes, but we've probably all experienced this as students ourselves. Surely you can recall one (or many) examples of times that you "crammed" for a test. You may have received a good grade for that test, but you knew even then that as soon as the test was over, all that "learning" would be gone. Obviously, you did not **master** that which was intended.

So what can we now learn from our experiences? We should know that mastery is not determined by a "one shot" evaluation. In determining mastery we must evaluate whether the student can demonstrate this knowledge / skill / behavior next week, next month, or next year. As we progress from outcome #1 to outcomes #2... #10... and so forth, we must include spiraling assessments. Throughout the year we implement small spot-checks as well as major repeat demonstrations to assure ourselves, as well as the students, that previous outcomes really have been met (mastered).

Equally important to the long-term is the transfer factor. It is a fact that many students who perform superbly in textbook, paper-and-pencil kinds of activities and assessments never see the relationship in terms of real-world applications. This has been the source of one of the greatest criticisms of our educational system. Parents and people in the business world tell us that we have not prepared our students for life after high school. Yet when we ask for specific examples of problems, we are often bewildered. We say to ourselves, "But we taught that and they learned it!" In most such instances, the problem has been lack of transfer from the paper world to the real world. If you want to know if your students have mastered an outcome, determine how they might use this knowledge or skill in the real world and then *have the students demonstrate accordingly.* Sometimes the actual "real world" application is possible; other times simulations, role-plays, or creative methods may need to be implemented. But do not assume that your students have mastered an outcome unless you have in some way evaluated their transfer of knowledge to a new or different situation.

Teacher Professionalism, Qualitative Judgments, and Mastery

It was said earlier that *mastery is as much a function of faculty scholarship as of measurable student achievement. In other words, the scholarship of students is only as good as the individual and collective scholarship demonstrated by their mentors.* That viewpoint shouldn't be remarkable, but we've encountered educators who are intimidated by the concept of faculty scholarship. Perhaps the problem lies in how the word "scholarship" is interpreted, that it is somehow laden with images of stodgy research and boring academic musings. Actually, nothing could be further from the truth.

The practice of intellectual investigation, or research, must be at the heart of every educational enterprise... not because it is a tedious obligation, but because it is exciting, stimulating, and worthwhile in terms of student learning outcomes.

We go so far as to declare that teachers who do not consider themselves active scholars are not fully professional educators. The essence of professional practice is the teacher's ability to interact effectively with the subjects being taught, and to share that love of learning with students in a well organized and managed environment. Professionalism has little to do with the teacher's punctuality, dress, and willingness to comply with administrative directives; those areas of concern are more pertinent to employee competence and loyalty. Both professionalism and employee competence are important, but we should never confuse one with the other.

So what does teacher scholarship and professionalism have to do with student mastery? It has everything to do with it when teachers teach to high achievement outcomes and expect students to meet attendant criteria. That approach to instruction and learning makes it imperative for teachers to think deeply about the meaning and applications of learning, which puts them in a better intellectual position to *qualitatively* assess student growth.

For decades there was fear that the qualitative judgments of teachers were tantamount to shallow subjectivity; that public school teachers needed fool-proof textbooks and professionally prepared assessments to be effective. That fear was present in students, parents, patrons, and in teachers themselves. In fact, it has become so pervasive in the minds of the American public that it has diminished the stature of the education profession. In excruciatingly plain English, teachers have too often been seen as people with average intellects, mediocre organizational ability, and excessively soft hearts. There has also been a notion that teachers are little more than "baby sitters with a training agenda."

To overcome those perspectives of teachers and schools, we must give a booster-shot to our own professional self-esteem. We must prove that we are intellectually astute as shown by an interest in dynamic scholasticism; that we can organize our curriculum and instruction so that it has focus and meaning; and that we care so much for students that we create and maintain a no-nonsense set of expectations. Our schools must be certain in their claim that mediocrity and failure are not acceptable, and spend whatever energy, time and money are required to make that claim a reality.

Mastery is a state-of-mind as much as it is the result of tests, performance assessments, and other demonstrations of ability. Anyone who has been a teacher more than a year or two knows that condition to be true. The modus operandi must be that teachers perform in an atmosphere in which inquiry and high expectations are part of a personal credo, and that students should share that level of performance. Students from dysfunctional families or those with serious learning disabilities will always loom large in our thinking, but they too must be made aware of what the school stands for... and what it won't stand for. Likewise, teachers must stop trying to put these students into the rigid molds of traditional learning styles. They must recognize that there are many different ways for students to learn and demonstrate learning, and then *use their professional judgement as to the actual learning progress of a particular student. Too often teachers view mastery as an inflexible accountability measure of their teaching rather than as a determination of student learning and a map for getting students to the desired end results.*

Professionalism of the kind described above will allow teachers, in communicating with students or parents, to say something like this: "In my professional judgment, based on criteria and accumulated evaluative evidence shown in this progress portfolio, you (your child) have mastered (or not mastered) these learning outcomes." It also will allow teachers to plan, in concert with students and parents, the direction the student's learning should take in the days/weeks ahead.

Criteria Development, Evidence, and Decision-Making

Schools and districts with which we work are particularly interested in specifics with regard to the identification of mastery. At this point it may be useful for you to re-examine the section of the book on *The Task Analysis Process.* Pages 176 through 181 of that section show examples of task analysis forms in grade 1 science, grade 3 mathematics, grade 7 English, and high school American Government. Each task analysis form contains six columns titled *Tasks to Accomplish, Teaching Methods, Student Activities, Means of Assessment, Mastery Criteria and Evidence,* and *Extensions.* The column for **mastery criteria and evidence** lists the teacher's expectations for each task; it helps the teacher decide whether students are ready to move on to the next task or whether additional instruction is needed. This same information can be the basis for an individual student's report to be placed in a portfolio. Let's look at how that might be accomplished.

The Portfolio Management Form

The next section of this book covers portfolio assessment, so it isn't our intention to delve into that subject at length here. But we do want to point out the importance for teachers to understand the necessity of maintaining good records on each student....and one way to accomplish that task is to use some sort of portfolio management process. Using the examples shown in the *Task Analysis* section, we have prepared a few scenarios that might help teachers grasp the idea of guiding students toward, and making decisions about mastery... using a portfolio system.

SCENARIO A - CHECKING FOR MASTERY

Mrs. Jones teaches first grade. She maintains a portfolio for each student in each academic discipline (subject). In a prominent place on that portfolio is the subject area committee's designated course purpose for that subject in first grade, and each outcome under that purpose is clearly shown....perhaps in a format that looks very much like a grade card. Here is an example:

Science Outcome #1 for: <u>*Andrea Jackson*</u>

STUDENTS WILL RESEARCH AND DEVELOP HYPOTHESES ON THE CAUSES OF SHADOWS AND THE CAUSES OF CHANGES IN SHADOWS.

First task: RESEARCH THE CAUSES OF SHADOWS.

Assessment:
Students participate in research project — using various light sources, and experimenting to see that they make shadows and how they make shadows.

Criteria and evidence:
Each student must actually manipulate the materials provided (not just be an observer). Students must continue to experiment with materials until they successfully make shadows with at least two different sources, and they must be able to successfully repeat those procedures.

Dates assessed: _____
Extensions used (if any):

Dates mastery level demonstrated: _____

Second task: DEVELOP HYPOTHESIS FOR CAUSES OF SHADOWS.

Assessments:
  1. Students state the hypothesis.
  2. Given a set of pictures, students circle items that could cause shadows.
  3. Students demonstrate causing a shadow.

Criteria and evidence:
  Assessment #1.   Students explain in their own words that light shining on an object casts a shadow of that object.
  Assessment #2.   Students must achieve 80% proficiency.
  Assessment #3.   Students must consider a set of materials provided, tell the

teacher which items can make shadows, and demonstrate making a shadow with one or more of those light sources.

Dates assessed: _____
Extensions used (if any):

Dates mastery level demonstrated: _____

Third task: RESEARCH CAUSES OF CHANGES IN SHADOWS.

Assessment:
Cooperative group experiments, and illustrations or sentences recording experiments.

Criteria and evidence:
Students must actively participate in the experiments. Using the written or illustrated records, each student must explain at least one thing that was tried by the group and the results of that trial.

Dates assessed: _____
Extensions used (if any):

Dates mastery level demonstrated: _____

Fourth task: DEVELOP HYPOTHESIS FOR CAUSES OF CHANGES IN SHADOWS.

Assessments:
  1. Students must name at least one variable that affects size/shape of shadow.
  2. Students must explain to the teacher — orally, or through illustrations or demonstration — how the shadow is affected by the above variable.
  3. Given a list of variables, students indicate those that affect changes in shadows.

Criteria and evidence:
  Assessment #1.   Students must correctly identify a variable that affects

size/shape of shadow.

Assessment #2.   Explanation must be confident and include a correct conclusion.

Assessment #3.   Students must achieve 80% proficiency.

Dates assessed: _____

Extensions used (if any):

Dates mastery level demonstrated: _____

If we assume that there are six outcomes for first grade science, then it is easy to see how this form could be used for all six of them. Papers students might complete, such as illustrations or written documents, could be stapled to this form.

Notice that the form calls for *dates assessed* and *dates mastery level demonstrated.* Recall the point made by Gerri in our sample faculty discussion at the beginning of this section: that students may score 100% on an original assessment but do very poorly when the same skills are assessed at a later date. As we have pointed out repeatedly in this book, a single assessment does not denote mastery; the spiraling technique must be used to check for continual retention of learning throughout the year. Therefore, this form allows the teacher to record not just a single assessment, but all of the dates that specific learning was assessed, and whether mastery level performance was demonstrated each time.

SCENARIO B - CHECKING FOR MASTERY

Mr. Abbott teaches seventh grade English in the communications department. He maintains a portfolio for each student. In a prominent place on that portfolio is the subject area committee's designated course purpose for seventh grade English communications, and each outcome under that purpose is clearly shown....perhaps in a format that looks very much like a grade card. Here is an example:

Communications Outcome #1 for: *Bill Patterson*

STUDENTS WILL READ A SELECTION OF THEIR CHOICE FROM THE REQUIRED 7TH GRADE READING LIST; PLAN AND PARTICIPATE IN GROUP PRESENTATIONS ABOUT THE STORIES; COMPARE PROBLEMS OR DILEMMAS OF MAIN CHARACTERS OR ACTIONS TAKEN; AND WRITE SHORT EVALUATIVE ESSAYS ABOUT THE CHARACTER BEHAV-

IORS USING CORRECT GRAMMAR, SPELLING AND PUNCTUATION.

First task: REVIEW BASIC PUNCTUATION AND GRAMMAR.

Assessment:
       Written quiz.

Criteria and evidence:
       Students must achieve 80% proficiency.

Dates assessed: _____
Extensions used (if any):

Dates mastery level demonstrated: _____

Second task: SELECT AND READ STORIES.

Assessment:
       Individual conferences.

Criteria and evidence:
       Reading must progress at acceptable rate — so that book will be conclud-
ed in one week's time. Student reponds correctly to teacher questions, and gives
short summaries to demonstrate comprehension.

Dates assessed: _____
Extensions used (if any):

Dates mastery level demonstrated: _____

Third task: MAKE VOCABULARY LISTS AND CREATE DICTIONARIES.

Assessments:
    1. Vocabulary list is submitted for evaluation.
    2. Students participate in vocabulary - Jeopardy game.
    3. Students are given spot quizzes during individual conferences.

Criteria and evidence:

Assessment #1.   Words must be spelled correctly, and definitions provided appropriate to the way the words are used in the story being read.

Assessment #2.   All students must participate in the game. Since speed is involved, no percentage of correct answers is required; however, incorrect answers will be noted for corrective needs.

Assessment #3.   Students must achieve 80% proficiency.

Dates assessed: _____

Extensions used (if any):

Dates mastery level demonstrated: _____

Fourth task: COOPERATIVE LEARNING PRESENTATION.

Assessment:

Evaluation of group products and perfomances.

Criteria and evidence:

Each group must prepare a skit, panel discussion, puppet show, collage, or other project or activity. Students must actively participate in both the preparation and presentation of the group activitiy. Clarity and detail in the project or performance must be such that students in the audience can summarize the story's plot.

Dates assessed: _____

Extensions used (if any):

Dates mastery level demonstrated: _____

Fifth task: COMPARISONS OF CHARACTERS AND ACTIONS IN THE SELECTED STORY WITH CHARACTERS AND ACTIONS IN PREVIOUS-LY READ STORIES.

Assessment:

Evaluation of group bulletin board project.

Criteria and evidence:

Students will be evaluated according to active participation in graphically illustrating comparisons using bulletin board materials. Comparisons must be logical and defended by oral or graphic presentations.

Dates assessed: _____

Extensions used (if any):

Dates mastery level demonstrated: _____

Sixth task: WRITE ESSAYS; PEER CRITIQUE; MAKE CORRECTIONS.

Assessment:
    Peer evaluations.

Criteria and evidence:
    Students evaluate partner's essay for clarity, detail, correct spelling, grammar, and punctuation. Teacher facilitates process and evlauates effort and cooperation; teacher also spot-checks essays and offers suggestions. Completed essays are added to portfolios.

Dates assessed: _____

Extensions used (if any):

Dates mastery level demonstrated: _____

Summative assessment:
    Students are given a short story to read. They write in-class essays on character behavior, analyzing and comparing short story characters to those in previously read books.

Criteria and evidence:
    Students must demonstrate analysis and evaluative thinking by making logical comparisons in their essays. Comparisons must be supported by specific examples. Students must use correct grammar, spelling, and punctuation. Points are assigned for logical conclusions, supporting detail, descriptive language, grammar, spelling, and punctuation. Students must achieve at least 80% of the total number of points possible.

As in Mrs. Jones' class, we can assume that there are a number of outcomes for seventh grade English, and that this form can be used for all of them. Papers students complete could be fastened to the form; the portfolio might also include a snapshot of the bulletin board display, and the student's self-evaluation of the group presentation or project.

While the processes shown in these scenarios might appear to be complex functions, they actually work very smoothly once the initial forms are completed. The district's curriculum coordinating council and subject area committees may ask for specific criteria and evidence for summative assessments. Individual teachers may also want to vary the form or type of recording device, as approved by the subject area committee, if their classes or courses make this process difficult to apply. However, in all cases these aspects must be in place:

1. Criteria and evidence are clear enough for the teacher to make a justifiable quantitative or qualitative decision about student progress and attainment of mastery.
2. There are definite "benchmarks" to which teachers can refer when discussing student . progress and mastery with parents, other teachers, and the students themselves.
3. There must be ways for the students to overcome deficiencies in a timely and efficient manner.
4. There must never be the appearance of arbitrary judgments on the part of teachers; qualitative assessments are accepted by everyone if those assessments are obviously the product of intelligent and thoughtful reflection.

Glossary of Terms Pertaining to Mastery

There is considerable confusion about certain terms associated with assessment and mastery, so it may be useful to identify some of the more commonly used words and phrases, and provide definitions that are sensible and practical. We sometimes start with dictionary definitions, and will add professional interpretations as necessary.

All Students Can Learn

Some educators find this idea hard to swallow. Our interpretation is that a statement such as "all students can learn" is a much better impetus for the self-fulfilling philosophy than the more typical statement, that "students can learn to the extent of their ability." The worrisome aspect of the latter, more commonly accepted perspective is that somehow we as educators have a lock on the nature of student ability... and that simply isn't true. The history of the world is rife with examples of people who made marvelous contributions as adults, who were nothing better than mediocre in school. On the other hand, no one suggests that we have entered a

Pollyanna world in which all human beings perform at truly excellent levels. What we suggest is that schools should create conditions in which students with various kinds of intelligence and potential are given repeated opportunities to grow, using a wide variety of teaching methods and assessments. And every effort must be made to insure that every student performs at a level of expectation that will allow that person, as an adult, to make good contributions to the society in which he or she is a member. Those few who can't, or won't meet expectations, will not be recognized for having fulfilled requirements. Though retentions are rarely recommended, promotions are not made strictly for social reasons. And as students are promoted to a new grade level, portfolios, checklists and reports indicate outcomes that still have not been met and need attention. Likewise, students are not socially promoted out of school into the adult world... no fraudulent graduations. Students may need to stay in school longer to continue to work on specific outcomes for specific courses before being granted diplomas. Certificates instead of diplomas, or alternative programs (similar to a G.E.D.) may need to be provided for some students.

Authentic Assessment

Webster's New World Dictionary, Third College Edition says that "authentic" pertains to trustworthiness, reliability, genuineness, or that which is authoritative. The definition that most closely fits our use of the term is "genuineness"... ..that mastery is meaningful to the extent assessment is based on intended student learning outcomes which focus on real-world applications.

Correctives

This one word can give educational practitioners problems because it suggests remediation for the student, usually within the context of an existing classroom program. Teachers tend to say, "here we go again, being asked to shoulder problems associated with recalcitrant, maladjusted, slow, or intellectually inferior students." While we are not in the business of letting teachers totally off the hook with this, we strongly suggest that the district's board of education and administration have a firm responsibility to find the money, personnel, and other resources to help teachers give students the guidance, assistance, and encouragement they need. Correctives need to be specific to intended outcomes, and should be applied first within the classroom, and then when necessary, outside the existing classroom in evening/Saturday tutorials, outcome-specific summer school, or within extended academic year configurations. The first place to begin with the concept of correctives is the local board of education; the board must be willing to say that "all students will learn in this district... we not only insist on it, but we give *tangible* support to parents and educators to make certain it happens!"

Criterion-Referenced Tests

In the minds of some people the only true *criterion-referenced* test is one that is pencil and paper, and preferably multiple-choice, true-false, fill-in-the-blank, matching, or some other "objective" assessment of student knowledge. That definition is wholly inadequate, since any assessment that uses specific criteria taken from intended student learning outcomes is criterion-referenced. Such a test could be teacher observation of student demonstrations or performance, or the creation of an object or piece of writing. It could pertain to the adequacy of student participation in small groups, or the ability of students to perform certain mathematical or scientific functions within an experimental setting. Criterion-referenced testing should go on virtually all the time, with evidence accumulated on a regular basis to make certain students are learning and performing as intended. The point we wish to underscore here is that no externally or internally developed criterion-referenced test should be used to develop curriculum; curriculum is first, then test development.

Electives and Enrichments

A really tough "sell" for advocates of outcome-based education and mastery learning is the idea that a smaller published curriculum is in fact the better one. It is a hard idea to establish because the American public has held the conviction that a bigger curriculum is synonymous with a better education. But educational researchers and practitioners have discovered that the curriculum which is a "mile wide and an inch deep," or a cafeteria smorgasbord of offerings, propagates the trivializing of learning. Every curriculum council needs to review all elective courses at the secondary level, and analyze the "enrichment" philosophy of elementary teachers responsible for self-contained classrooms. If electives and enrichments do not focus on declared outcomes in relatively specific ways, then justifications for their continued existence might be in order. We hasten to add that there very well may be justifications, but teachers need to consciously state what they are and follow though by helping students understand the reasons why they are studying those subjects.

Extensions

This word is usually applied to student activities that might now be called "extra credit" for those who accomplish a task sooner, or more competently than their peers. Those working with the ABC model use the term *extensions* to include both enrichment and corrective activitites, because both experiences extend the original instruction process. Students and teachers alike have often placed such tasks in the busy-work category, something to keep gifted students from being a problem while slower students continue to work. The "busy-work" label is all too appropriate when teachers do not give careful prior thought to what should constitute a logical, meaningful, and outcome-appropriate extension. Earlier sections of this book, as well as a detailed section that follows, show how this process should be integrated into a classroom program, and it is a topic that merits considerable discussion among those serving on curriculum councils and subject area committees.

Formative Assessment

The standard definition for "formative" suggests the practice of helping to shape, develop, or mold. In schools the term applies to a kind of *mastery in the making,* that students become better little by little, and that the acquisition of each new skill or area of knowledge makes more possible the kind of high achievement outcome intended by the teacher. Formative assessments are the every-day, or every-task kinds of assessments; they are the means used to evaluate the skills or areas of knowledge that eventually are synthesized into a more complex result. In a "total quality management" atmosphere, we seek the assurance of ultimate quality through giving attention to detail and making sure every aspect of the developmental process is done well.

Heterogeneous Ability Grouping

Ability grouping is another difficult issue, especially among those who teach mathematics and other so-called *hard* courses, or courses that are designed for college preparation. Segregating students according to academic ability is almost inherent to the way American educators function, and the reasons for it are abundantly clear. Nevertheless, research has shown repeatedly that previously mediocre or slow students will rise to the level of expectation once they truly understand what the teacher wants, and that the teacher will not accept poor work. Some students may need the kind of pressure and genuine caring that comes from more than just one teacher.... the pressure and caring that can come from groups of peers, groups of teachers, administrators, or board members. As seen in the section on cooperative learning, heterogeneous ability grouping is possible for all students if the outcomes are stated and implemented properly, and if the expectations are such that every student understands that mediocre and failing work will not be tolerated.

"J" Curve

This term is usually explained as being the mastery learning alternative to the bell-shaped curve in which some students receive As and Bs on the one end, Ds and Fs on the other, and in which a large portion receive Cs where the bell's bulge is. The "J" concept merely suggests that all students must learn; that all must learn in the *A* or *B* (and sometimes *C*) categories, and that no one receives a *D* or *F*. Students who do not meet intended learning outcomes are "in progress" or "incomplete."

Mastery Learning

Although mastery has been discussed earlier in detail, a short definition may be useful. For our purposes, *learner mastery is the satisfactory accomplishment of pre-scribed student learning outcomes.* Nothing more needs to be said if the outcomes are written so that high achievement is inherent to student tasks.

Norm-Referenced Tests

A norm-referenced test is usually an assessment of general achievement, apti-tude, attitude, psychological outlook, or some other student characteristic considered important by educators or professional persons interested in student development. It is rarely linked with a taught curriculum (though could be), and the scores derived are "normed" in accordance with how the entire population of test-takers performed. Student performance is usually reported in terms of percentile ranking, with scores disaggregated according to certain student characteristics or subject areas. Although most educators agree that norm-referenced tests have a use, it is obvious that the achievement type of test that is not linked to a taught curriculum, and measures only factual and comprehension kinds of knowledge is not a valid indicator of student growth. It is also obvious that such tests have been, and continue to be over-used in this country to offer so-called conclusive evidence of the quality of student learning and the quality of schools in general. Our position is that any *exclusive* use of those assessments to determine mastery is ludicrous.

Summative Assessment

This term is pure education jargon, but it is useful in that it describes an act which pulls everything together. The dictionary, while not recognizing *summative* as being a real word, does indicate that a *sum* constitutes the whole amount...the aggre-gate. As professional jargon, it is merely a kind of final examination. In our work with high achievement outcomes, it is an activity that allows students to demonstrate a comprehensive understanding of the skill or knowledge that is inherent to those out-comes. Increasingly we hear the term "capstone," meaning a kind of summative assess-ment that determines whether or not the student has achieved at some ultimate level of proficiency. Even elementary schools are using capstone concepts that look a little like graduate-level theses, dissertations, or culminating projects. Another example of a "capstone" is the "Eagle Project" used by the Boy Scouts of America....a project de-signed to pull together all skills necessary to achieve lower ranks and merit badges.

Teaching to Mastery

Students won't master learning if teachers don't teach to it. While that may seem patently obvious, there is more to the issue than what first meets the eye. Many teachers are not clear as to what they want students to become in any way that is focused, relevant to real world needs, and scholastically challenging. The accumula-tion of trivial pieces of knowledge has nothing to do with real mastery. Real mastery occurs only when teachers know where they wish to lead students, and that the destination they have in mind is worth traveling toward.

Mastery Basics:

- Mastery must be defined as more than just a percentage factor; it involves qualitative as well as quantitative judgements of teachers.

- The curriculum coordinating council should prepare a generic definition of mastery that serves as a guide to subject area committees as they develop a curriculum and to teachers as they implement that curriculum.

- Mastery is a state of mind as much as it is the results of tests and performances; it is also as much a function of faculty scholarship as of measurable student achievement.

- Criteria and evidence are necessary for teachers to determine if students are performing at mastery level.

- A task analysis includes criteria and evidence for mastery of tasks and the final outcome; a portfolio record can show that criteria and evidence — and the timeline and extensions included — for an individual student's achievement of mastery.

THE PORTFOLIO ASSESSMENT SYSTEM

The special resource person for this section is Kaye Tague, Emporia Public Schools, Emporia, Kansas.

Use of a portfolio assessment system involves issues that should be considered at the district level by the curriculum coordinating council. The council should develop one kind of portfolio system, with a moderate amount of "individualizing," which we will discuss later in this section. Portfolio assessment is strongly encouraged for an outcome or performance-based curriculum that seeks student learning mastery in prescribed curricular areas.

You've probably read numerous articles about authentic assessment of students and found that many of those encourage the use of portfolios. If so, you probably have the same questions other educators have raised, such as...

- What is authentic assessment?
- Is authentic assessment really "good" assessment?
- What is a portfolio and what is its purpose?
- What are the benefits of portfolio assessment?
- What is student self-reflection and how does it work?
- How could our district use portfolios?
- How could we implement a portfolio system?
- What are some possible pitfalls?
- What should a portfolio include?
- What about time and physical management?
- Are there maintenance hints that would be helpful?
- How can portfolios be shared with parents?
- What else should we consider before starting?
- What should be included in a final checklist?

This section provides answers for those questions and concerns, as well as a checklist to help you get started.

WHAT IS AUTHENTIC ASSESSMENT?

This question was addressed in our last section, so you may recall we said that *authentic* means the assessment is based on intended student learning outcomes which focus on real-world applications.   But what about the meaning of the word *assess?* Turning again to the dictionary, we find that the word assess means to "sit beside," to "assist the judge."   For our purpose, assessment is defined as a process of collecting and organizing student work in ways that make it possible for people — teachers, parents, and students — to judge or evaluate student work.

Recent criticism and dissatisfaction with existing tests has given rise to developing new assessment alternatives, which is why so much attention is now being given to authentic assessment.   This type of evaluation causes students to use prior knowledge, recent learning and relative skills to actively accomplish complex and significant tasks.   In other words, in authentic assessment, students must perform, create, produce, or do something.   They must use problem-solving and other higher-level thinking skills.   They apply skills and knowledge to work with real-life situations, and they generate rather than choose a response.

Authentic assessment should grow out of authentic tasks.   The following list provides some examples of authentic assessment.
- Write a letter to a friend, relative, pen pal, or favorite author.
- Read a book to younger students or other members of the class.
- Write a book, story, or play for younger students.
- Design and carry out a scientific experiment.
- Compare cost of grocery items from several grocery advertisements.

- Determine the number of calories in a recipe or meal.
- Complete an application for a job.
- Cut in half or double a recipe.
- Graph the results of a survey.

WHAT IS *GOOD* ASSESSMENT?

There are all kinds of assessments, but some are considered to be better quality than others. There are a number of characteristics to look for when evaluating your assessment instruments. First of all, good assessment provides data which are indicators — or which provide evidence — of learning. It measures and reveals more than just what students know and understand; it shows what they can do with this knowledge and these skills that they've learned. Good assessment communicates what we value. It assesses those things that are valued and thus considered important, rather than those things that can easily be graded.

Good assessment promotes further learning or instruction, and has the potential to integrate instruction, learning, and assessment. It allows for transfer of learning. It assesses not only the outcome of learning, but the process of learning as well. Good assessment reflects goals for students and measures how students perform on the knowledge and skills stated in those goals. It allows students to evaluate themselves.

Perhaps the main characteristic to look for is that good assessment is a process that facilitates appropriate instructional decision-making by providing information on two fundamental questions: (1) How are we doing? and (2) How can we do it better? And the best way to answer these questions is to sit beside the learner and evaluate the student's work together.

The **tasks** that make good assessment are ones that resemble real-life challenges rather than busywork that is fragmented and easy to grade. The tasks are known to the students well in advance and point them toward higher levels of thinking. The tasks selected for assessment must give a clear enough picture of what the student knows and can do that they cause the teacher to view them as "worth the trouble."

Authentic assessment is "good" assessment because it meets the above criteria. Students are asked to perform tasks that they are likely to encounter in real life. The tasks measure more than just what the students know; they allow for transfer of learning. Authentic assessment involves higher levels of thinking. And because the assessment tasks are relevant to the students, motivation is increased, which leads to further learning and greater degrees of transfer and application.

WHAT IS A *PORTFOLIO?*

You can accomplish the tasks listed above by using a portfolio system. You may have heard or read several definitions of portfolio and you should consider them in terms of what is most appropriate for your district. The following is a list of the most common definitions. You may find that one definition is exactly what you had in mind, or — more likely — that a combination of these definitions suits your district's needs.

- A student portfolio is a purposeful collection of student work that tells the story of the student's efforts, progress, or achievement in a given area.
- A portfolio is an edited collection of materials that provides a framework for demonstrating knowledge, understanding, experiences, and processes for learning.
- A portfolio is a systematic and organized collection of student work samples used by the teacher, student, and parent to monitor growth of the student's knowledge, skills, and attitudes in a specific subject area.
- A portfolio is more than an activity record of experiences; it also indicates whether and how goals have been achieved by the student.
- A portfolio is a vehicle for ongoing assessment of the student.
- A portfolio provides evidence of the mastery of learning outcomes.
- A portfolio includes any work that helps to tell the story of the student's learning. Think of the portfolio as a picture album of the student that shows the growth of the student.
- A portfolio provides the student with a tool for reflecting upon skills, knowledge, and understandings and includes evidence of this self-reflection. This is a key element of a portfolio and sets it apart from the "collection of student work" which your teachers may have been using with students for many years. (More information is provided about student self-reflection later.)

As you can see, all of the definitions of a portfolio do have some common statements. The particular definition, or combination of definitions to be used may vary among teachers, depending on the age of their students, the subject area targeted, and their purpose for using portfolios.

WHAT MAKES IT A *PORTFOLIO?*

As mentioned above, the portfolio contains student self-reflection. This allows the students to tell who they are as learners. The students help select the pieces for inclusion in their portfolios. This practice gives the students the opportunity to tell what is valued in their work. Students often choose to include a piece that is not their "best" work because the piece is important to them.

In a portfolio the collection of student work has a purpose and is not just a random selection; therefore, not all of the student's work is collected for the portfolio. If too many assignments are put in the portfolio it becomes messy and less important to the student. The teacher selects specific assignments to be included in the portfolio as well as the student-selected pieces of work. These assignments should be taken from regular classroom activities rather than special projects which are not related to daily activities.

BENEFITS OF PORTFOLIO ASSESSMENT

School districts that have implemented portfolio assessment cite a number of benefits derived. Some frequently listed ones tell us that a portfolio...

- Respects the student's and teacher's individuality. Key words in the relationship between teachers and students are mutual respect and trust. Everyone's individuality is encouraged, and taking a risk is okay.
- Documents the student's growth and progress over a period of time. The growth is "right in front of you."
- Allows teachers to evaluate more than one draft of work.
- Links instruction, learning, and assessment in a cycle. It supports and guides instruction because the teacher and student can decide what should come next. It helps them answer the question, "What does the student need to know or do next?"
- Through ownership, helps students to value the work and progress they make. Students have a vested interest in the work that will be included in the portfolio.
- Encourages students to be self-reflective. How am I doing? What am I learning? How do I feel about what I am learning? This opportunity to reflect is essential to learning.
- Promotes lifelong learning which is a goal that all students should have for themselves and that educators should have for them.
- Supports a student's chance for success and feelings of self worth. The focus is on student accomplishments and strengths rather than mistakes.
- Requires the student to be an active learner because it is not passive assessment. Students are involved in self-evaluation and self-reflection.
- Allows teachers to assess the learning process, not only the coverage of facts.
- Serves as a vehicle for communicating with parents, who are engaged in seeing first-hand what students are achieving. Student progress and growth are evident because parents have concrete examples of that growth.
- Allows assessment to become collaborative rather than foster competition among students.
- Provides the opportunity for teachers to obtain a richer, clearer view of their students' progress over time.
- Allows teachers to get to know their students — as readers, writers, thinkers, and human beings — and to view student work from these perspectives rather

than base their judgment on test scores alone.

This impressive list of benefits should help convince teachers that portfolios would be worth the effort they take to implement, even if the teachers had to work in isolation — if there were no district-wide curriculum efforts. *However, one of the most important benefits of a portfolio system is its role in a district-wide curriculum development process that uses the design down approach, working from the district mission statement to mastery of student outcomes.* Remember that the Curriculum Coordinating Council develops a generic definition of mastery, the Subject Area Committees apply that definition when they prepare high-achievement outcomes, and individual teachers determine criteria and evidence necessary to evaluate whether those outcomes have been mastered.

As pointed out previously, teachers must assess student learning both quantitatively and qualitatively, and they need to maintain good records on each student for these assessments. Keeping records of quantitative assessments is not difficult, because such assessments deal with numbers such as scores and percentages. Qualitative assessment, however, is another matter. It deals more with the **way** students approach learning — the processes used, their inquiry, their reflections on learning, and the general "state of mind" necessary for an atmosphere of high expectations and mastery. Teachers have always been influenced by qualitative judgements when they assess student learning, but more often than not, they have been hesitant to use those judgements as a part of the actual evaluation report *because there was no way to gather evidence to support their opinions!* Portfolio assessment, with its inclusion of student reflections as well as teacher observations and anecdotal records, provides the means for accumulating criteria and evidence of qualitative assessment. The portfolio goes way beyond simply recording scores or letters (A, B, C) in a grade book. It provides evidence of specifically what and how a student is learning in a particular course or grade level of a subject, as well as evidence that the student is learning in accordance with the district mission.

So how does the portfolio help us provide this evidence? Are there specific things to be included, as well as things to avoid? Are there things we need to know about management for the system? These questions and others need to be considered before you actually implement a portfolio system.

STUDENT SELF-REFLECTION

Remember that the teacher and students select what the portfolio should contain. However, when a piece of work is placed in the portfolio the next step is a big one and probably is the major difference between a portfolio and a collection of student work. That next step is self-reflection and it is not easy. Many students have not been asked to think about an assignment after it has been completed. The teacher's guidance is very necessary as students begin to think about what they have done. Consider some of the following questions for stimulating the student to think about or reflect upon a piece of work.

- What makes this your best piece?
- What did you like about this piece?
- Why did you select this piece?
- How did you go about writing it?
- What were you thinking about when you wrote this?
- What have you learned?
- What would you like to know more about?
- If you worked further on this piece, what would you do?
- Tell me about the story that you wrote.
- If you hadn't written this yet and were just now starting, would you change the story? How? Why?
- What problem(s) did you encounter?
- How did you go about solving the problem(s)?
- Find your best opening sentence. Why is that the best one?
- Find an example of a sentence that you think is really powerful. Explain your choice.
- Find a paper that you enjoyed writing. Why did you enjoy this one?
- What do you think your strengths are in writing?
- How is your work at the end of the year different from your work at the beginning?
- How does this project compare with other pieces of work you have done this year?
- Where did your thinking go wrong?
- Why did you miss this problem?
- What would you like to work on improving in your next piece of writing or your next project?
- What will you do next?

Notice that many of the questions were "why" questions; asking students to tell "why" helps them get started in self-reflection. Individual teachers develop a list of questions relevant to particular assignments and suited to their groups of students. As they conduct conferences with students about their portfolios, teachers also need to develop the art of getting the students to talk about their work. And they need to listen — really listen — to what students have to say.

Student evaluation of the total collection of work at the end of the school year has also been very successful in some classes. This ensures that students see their growth and progress. What if the growth or progress is not very noticeable? This could happen, and with those students teachers need to have conferences directed toward specific growth indicators and strengths. Teachers must be aware during the year when progress is slow and give special attention to the work of those students, building on the student's strengths and helping guide self-reflection toward using those strengths.

INSTRUCTIONAL PITFALLS AND CONCERNS .

Is the portfolio system of student assessment perfect? Will it solve all of your assessment problems? The answer to both questions is NO. There is no single port-folio model that is right for everyone at every grade level and in every subject area. That fact may bother you if you insist on having one right way to do everything. But the purpose for the portfolio makes each system different. Accept that fact and move ahead. Each classroom will reflect a unique approach to portfolio assessment and each student's collection of work will differ. If an individual teacher's portfolio system answers the criteria for good assessment and it works for that teacher and his students, it is right. At the same time, you should be aware of some pitfalls and concerns about the use of portfolios because they can be avoided once you know what they are. Consider the following examples.

The portfolio should not become a catch-all. Students cannot keep all of their products, and portfolios are not merely storage areas for student work. The teacher and students must be selective and remember the purpose of the portfolio when deciding what to keep.

The link to instruction must be maintained. A collection of special projects done just for the portfolio does not provide that cycle of assessment, instruction, and learning. Regular classroom assignments or projects are the best pieces of work to keep. Also, the control of the portfolio should not be rigid. The teacher and student both have ownership and control over what pieces go into the portfolio.

Resist the temptation to include "worksheet" types of assignments. The student-centered and student-created pieces are more apt to help paint the real picture of the student as a learner. Emphasis on self-reflection should be obvious. The teacher must allow time for this activity and encourage as well as guide the students to reflect. The sample questions provided earlier can be used as a guide for teachers to make lists of their own. The time students spend on self-reflection is time well spent.

WHAT A PORTFOLIO SHOULD INCLUDE

By this time you may be asking yourself what students *should* or *could* put in their portfolios. You might share the following list of possibilities with teachers to get their imaginations started; then they can make their own decisions about what to include.

- jokes/riddles/poems/comic strips

- art work
- pictures of projects
- personal stories
- book reports
- reviews of news articles
- computer work
- letters to pen pals or job inquiries
- stories — fiction or nonfiction
- assignments from math, science, social studies classes
- audio tapes of reading, speaking or singing or videotapes of performances
- projects, surveys, reports, or experiments
- record of books read and impressions of the books
- notes from individual reading and writing conferences with the teacher

The list of possible items that could be included is endless. Individual teachers must ask themselves, "What is the purpose of my portfolio?" The pieces of work in the portfolio must reflect that purpose. Most portfolios are kept in order to show student growth over a period of time. Including the same assignment or the same type of assignment over the school year can easily show that growth and improvement. For example, if you ask a young student to draw a tree at various times during the first grade, you can see the changes as the student shows more details, colors, or form.

The student's work is the most important element in the portfolio; however, the portfolio should also contain a cover letter. Students write or dictate a letter that explains why certain pieces were selected and includes thoughts on how they feel about themselves as a reader/writer/producer. Students also include a self assessment. They list their individual goals and recognize their growth. Attitude and interest surveys may be included as well.

Portfolios should also contain teacher observations and anecdotal records. The teacher monitors a student's use of learning strategies and thinking skills and includes copies of notes taken. Notes and records should include a variety of information that will be helpful to students, parents, and successive teachers.

A portfolio should include a student's reading log, which is a list of books the student has read. The list should include free reading choices as well as assigned instructional reading materials. Writing samples are also an important part of a portfolio. The student chooses pieces that reflect success in different types of writing, e.g. poems, original stories, problem-solving strategies, essays, or research reports. Writing samples should be a part of the portfolio for any subject area — not just language arts courses.

Remember that one definition of portfolio is a document that tells a story of the student's growth and learning. If that is the selected purpose for developing a portfolio system, then the pieces in each portfolio should tell that story. Evidence of growth should be apparent to anyone who reads the pieces.

TIME AND PHYSICAL MANAGEMENT

Several decisions must be made before implementing the use of portfolios. The time taken for student-teacher conferences about the work to be included in the portfolio must be taken from another scheduled block of time. What can be eliminated? Where will teachers find the time in an already full day? How much time is needed?

Conferring with students about pieces to be placed in the portfolio can be done while others are working in small groups or individually. Some teachers set aside time for two or three portfolio conferences per day. If class time includes a study period or chance to start homework, that time can be used to meet with a student or two. Once a routine is established the students will look forward to this private time of discussion.

Where will the portfolios be kept? Do you need a "safe" place for storage? Will students have access to their portfolios any time? Some teachers who have been successful users of portfolios use two containers. One container serves as the student's working folder, and it is just that — a manila folder. The student uses that folder for work that is ongoing or for the various drafts of a written assignment. The working folder is stored in a basket or plastic crate to which the student has easy access. The other container is the "final" portfolio. It is usually an expandable file folder, which can easily hold snapshots of projects and audio or video tapes along with the written portions of the portfolio.

If budget is an issue, folded colored construction paper can be used for the working folder. Also, several publishing companies use plastic crates for packaging the instructional materials they send to teachers. If your school is involved in textbook adoption, check out the possibility of free crates. Ask your teachers to be on the lookout for items that could be used as portolios or portfoilio storage; most teachers are experts at finding the few extra materials needed to make a project successful.

The storage for the final pieces that are selected and placed in the expanded file folder should probably be a secure place like a file cabinet. Students should not "get into" someone else's portfolio. The teacher is responsible for taking out a portfolio and giving it to the owner.

HELPFUL MAINTENANCE HINTS

Everyone who uses a portfolio system will eventually develop a list of maintenance ideas. However, teachers will find it helpful to have the following "get started" hints.

- Date all pieces of work before they are placed in the portfolio. If you want to show growth or progress over a period of time, the date becomes important.
- Inform the reader of the assignment. This can be accomplished by stapling the assignment to the piece, or by having the student write a brief description of his or her perception of the assignment.
- If the piece is one selected by the student, that could be noted.
- Inform the reader of the writing process used. Is this a pre-writing exercise, a second draft, or a polished piece? If the piece represents multiple drafts, the drafts could be numbered and clipped together to help the reader see the student's thinking process.
- Inform the reader of any collaboration. If a student has completed this piece or project in a group or with another student, that should be noted.
- Monitor the frequency with which you examine portfolios by including in the folder a sheet which you initial and date upon each viewing.
- Include checklists, rating scales, conference notes, anecdotal records, and/or any other assessment information that you have collected that will help tell the growth or progress of that student.
- Ask students to select one piece of work with which they were satisfied and one piece with which they were dissatisfied. Hold conferences or use small group discussions to help students analyze what it is that caused them to rate each piece the way they did. Help students determine what they can do differently on a future assignment to improve the piece they rated low.
- Consider selecting (jointly with students) several pieces from each student's portfolio that can be passed along to the next year's teachers. Pertinent comments can be attached to each piece. Many schools routinely send student portfolios to the next teacher(s). Talk to the teachers in your building and see what they think about this idea.
- Organize the final portfolio. The readers of other portfolios have found it helpful to have the following items in this order: (1) table of contents, (2) student's work, and (3) student's self-reflection (clip or staple the self-reflection to the piece).

Maintenance also includes the need to establish some rules about using portfolios:
- A portfolio never leaves the classroom. Only single papers from the portfolio may be taken home.
- Students are not allowed to "get into" another student's portfolio.
- Should students want to take a specific piece of work home, copy it for the portfolio.

Other maintenance ideas or helpful rules will come to mind as the year progresses and their necessity becomes evident. In fact, sometimes the students themselves will come up with the best suggestions as they become involved with the portfolio process.

CHECKLISTS, ANECDOTAL RECORDS, AND RATING SCALES

Information about checklists and rating scales was provided in the section about evaluation of student learning. These evaluation instruments are frequently used in portfolios, as are anecdotal records.

Checklists

Decide what you want to assess. Use a limited number of items to be assessed. For example, if you want students to write a letter to a pen pal in Spanish, maybe you will look only at the grammar and syntax. Your list might include subject and verb agreement, proper use of verb inflections, and correct use of negatives. Develop a form and complete it for each student, simply making a checkmark to indicate whether the criterion is or is not met. Clip the form to the piece that is placed in the portfolio.

Rating Scales

Follow the same steps as with the checklists; however, instead of checking whether each item is present, use a *continuum* for rating performance. For a writing assignment, you might rate such items as organization and sentence structure or any of the six traits used by many teachers to score student writing.

A continuum for organization might state:
- no beginning or ending; poor transitions (a rating of 1), or
- logical ordering of ideas; good beginning and ending (a rating of 5).

A continuum rating sentence structure might show:
- all simple sentences, run-on sentences, sentence fragments (a rating of 1), or
- complex sentences, varied sentence patterns, parallelism (a rating of 5).

Anecdotal Records

Observe students' performances when they are normally involved in instructional activities. Record both atypical and routine behaviors that you notice. Use index cards so that you can keep a file box that is easy to reach and use. Circulate around the room and see what is happening. Use a class roster to check off names to ensure that you observe every student.

HOW TO SHARE PORTFOLIOS WITH PARENTS

One of the major purposes for having a portfolio system of assessment is to share with parents the student's work and self reflections. The student's record of growth or progress and his or her thoughts about what has been accomplished provide an ideal way to show parents what their child is actually doing. Yes, it does take some planning and extra effort, but teachers who have successfully used the portfolio system report that the extra time and effort are worth it. As one teacher put it, "The pay-off is worth the work."

In making plans to share portfolios with parents, consider these ideas that have worked with other teachers at various grade levels. Teachers can choose one that they think will work best for them and their students and parents.

The Parent Lunch

A lunch meeting is not often practical on the secondary level because of scheduling problems, but it does work well for elementary teachers. The teacher selects a week and invites parents to have lunch with their child. Five or so parents come at one time. Parents and students eat in the classroom. The teacher roams around the room while students tell their parents about the pieces in their portfolios. The teacher is there to answer questions. Students have already conferred with the teacher, written their self-reflections, and know what they want to show their parents. This may take an extended lunch period. The teacher can work out details with the building principal. The principal might even want to be part of the welcome team that greets parents at the door.

The Parent Evening

The same idea can take place over three or four evenings, and can be used by any elementary teacher or by secondary teachers in small districts. The teacher sets up after school or evening sessions, inviting a few parents each time. Teacher responsibilities and those of the students would be the same as for the lunch meetings. The teacher monitors the conversations and answers questions. Evening meetings require extra time spent at school and some teachers find that to be a problem. Those teachers would need to weigh the benefits of the communication that would be accomplished against the loss of their personal time. Both lunch and evening parent-student meetings also require that additional time be spent conferring with the students. They must understand in advance what needs to be explained to the parents.

Scheduling and Arranging for Parent Lunches or Evenings

Another decision that needs to be made, and one that will affect how teachers meet with parents, is the number of times they wish to have parents view the portfolios. Four times a year is the recommended number if they really want parents to be part of the student's learning process. If their school regularly schedules parent-teacher conferences during the year — say at the end of the first and third quarters — then parents could view portfolios during these scheduled sessions. The lunch or evening meetings could then be arranged during the second and fourth quarters.

Teachers who decide to have parents view the portfolios at parent/teacher conference time should ask the parents to arrive ten or fifteen minutes before the scheduled meeting. A desk, paper, and pencil should be provided along with their student's portfolio. Parents are encouraged to read the pieces and the self-reflections, and then write their own reactions to what they read. This can become the basis for a very important portion of the conference. Parents are often amazed at what they find in a portfolio.

The Secondary Teacher In A Large District

Secondary teachers can, and certainly do, successfully use portfolio assessments in their classes. However, with the exception of those in very small districts, secondary teachers often have so many students assigned to them that the parent lunch or evening meetings described above are not feasible. Some secondary teachers solve the problem by dividing their students into four groups, then meeting with the parents from only one group each quarter. Other secondary teachers use the portfolio primarily for the benefit of themselves and their students, but do also use it when parents request a conference or question their students' progress or grades. In districts that schedule regular parent-teacher conferences on the secondary level, teachers usually have the portfolios available; as in the elementary example, parents are encouraged to look at their student's portfolio while waiting to talk to a teacher.

Some secondary schools also have a cross-curriculum portfolio: teachers and students from each class select one or two items; the student's portfolio then shows a selection of work from each of the student's classes. Parents are asked to come to the school at a scheduled time to look at their child's portfolio. In some cases this precedes the regularly scheduled parent-teacher conferences. In other places, there is no scheduled conference to follow, but parents may then request a conference with particular teachers if they wish to discuss their child's work after viewing the portfolio.

Other districts choose not to have the parents come to the school, but instead periodically send the portfolios home with the students to discuss with their parents. A form is included for the parents to sign to indicate they've seen the portfolio; there is also space for the parents to make comments. Keep in mind that if you do use this process, you may want to keep copies of the contents.

Better Than a Report Card

Report cards with letter grades merely give parents an indication as to how well their child is doing, but tell nothing about what the child is learning. The portfolio gives parents the opportunity to see both: the samples of their child's work show what and how the child is learning; the self-reflections and teacher comments tell how well the child is meeting goals.

If students are guilty of not taking home their school assignments, parents have not had the opportunity to see their work. Even those who do regularly examine papers and products rarely sit down beside their child to talk about what an assignment was about and what it meant to the child. The student's self-reflection will be extremely enlightening for almost all parents. In addition to the self-reflection, the selections of items can provide much insight as well. For example, if a portfolio includes the entire process for one writing assignment, the parents get to see the first draft and all the other steps leading up to the final draft. They can better appreciate the final draft after seeing all the work done to achieve the finished product.

However teachers decide to share student portfolios with parents, they will need to take their plan to the building principal. The principal and other staff resource persons may be able to offer assistance or advice to help put the plan into action. Parents, students, and teachers will all benefit from this sharing experience.

WHAT ELSE SHOULD TEACHERS CONSIDER BEFORE STARTING?

Does your school or district have teachers who are currently using portfolios as part of their plan for student assessment? If so, plan for other interested teachers to visit with them and see if they can be of help in getting them started. The visiting teacher should have a list of questions prepared. She should visit the classrooms to see where and how portfolios are stored. She should talk to students and determine what they think of self-reflection and the sharing of portfolio contents with parents.

If no teacher in your district can help, check with neighboring districts to see if they have teachers using portfolio assessment. Seeing the process in action may be important to teachers who are not comfortable in doing some experimenting on their own. Share this section of the book with interested teachers, and look for other published articles that may be helpful. Check the programs of workshops to see if this topic is being presented in the near future. You don't have to find nationally recognized speakers; an area teacher who is using the process can be even more effective in helping a teacher get started.

One more word of advice... *start small.* You can always do more later. If teachers and their students experience success and feel good about using portfolios, they can increase what they're doing. Ask them to start out by having one purpose and sticking with it. They should think big and start small, keeping only a limited number of pieces. Perhaps the best way to start in the elementary classroom is for the teacher to select only one curriculum area. On the secondary level, the teacher could choose one skill that is on-going, that shows up in multiple outcomes, or concentrate on only one part of the course. They should think success in one area at a time.

SUMMARY....A FINAL CHECKLIST

You may want to use these checklists to help teachers plan for implementing the use of portfolios.

The Decision-Making Process

Check	Points to Consider
_____	I really want to implement a portfolio assessment.
_____	I believe that the extra time will be worth the effort.
_____	I feel comfortable designing a plan.

Questions to Ask After the Decision to Use Portfolios Has Been Made

Check	Questions to Ask
_____	What subject area(s) or part(s) of a course will be the focus for my portfolio?
_____	Will my (elementary) students work across the curriculum and include more than one subject area? If so, what areas?
_____	Where will the folders be stored?
_____	Will my students have a working folder and a final product folder?
_____	Will audio/video tapes be included?
_____	Do I have camera equipment to allow pictures of projects?
_____	What will be the purpose of my portfolio system?
_____	If the purpose is to show student growth or progress over a period of time, how will I accomplish that?
_____	Which definition(s) of a portfolio did I choose?
_____	Is my definition of a portfolio system compatible with my purpose for using portfolios?
_____	How will I introduce portfolios to my students?
_____	Will the portfolios be shared with parents? If so, how and how often?
_____	How often, when, and how will I schedule portfolio conferences with the students?
_____	Have I developed a list of age-appropriate questions to assist students with their self-reflections?
_____	How often will I allow time for student self-

reflection?

_____ What will happen to the portfolios at the end of the year?

_____ How many and which assignments will I include in the portfolio?

_____ How many assignments will I allow the students to select for inclusion in the portfolio?

_____ Who in the building/district can I call on for support?

_____ Is my building principal in agreement with and supportive of my plans?

_____ Do I have the manila folders, expandable folders, crates, or other materials that I need?

_____ Who will have access to the portfolios?

You will certainly think of other questions that should be answered prior to taking the plunge into portfolio assessment. No checklist is ever complete. But remember, a portfolio system strongly supports the implementation of the district's mission and its intended student learning outcomes. It should be a system that works in conjunction with the published curriculum and its high achievement outcomes, as well as with the individual needs of students.

EXTENSIONS: CORRECTIVES AND ENRICHMENTS IN AN ACCOUNTABILITY BASED SYSTEM

The question of extensions has been addressed briefly in previous sections of this book, particularly those concerning the task analysis process and the subject of mastery. In school districts that are committed to an outcome or performance-based system, it is often this question of extensions that is most troublesome. Educators adopt the belief that all students can learn, and they understand that to turn the belief into reality requires extended opportunity for some students. The problem is determining what those extended opportunities should be, and how to manage them. Teachers ask questions such as...

• What kinds of things should I have the students do?

• What do I do with the other students while some are working on correctives?

- How long should I allow students to keep working on something before we move on?
- What happens if we have to move on and some students still haven't mastered the outcome (or the task)?
- Won't our high-achievers be held back by having always to wait for the other students to catch up?
- How can you keep students on task if they're all working at different levels, and on different things at the same time?
- If students retake tests a number of times, how do we determine their scores or grades?
- How do we manage all the record keeping?
- Surely the classroom teacher can't do all of this alone! Who's going to help? How will we pay for it?

These questions are not just smoke screens for an I-don't-want-to-change attitude; they are valid questions that pertain to how we put our beliefs into actual practice. The curriculum coordinating council needs to begin addressing these concerns in the early stages of the curriculum development process — definitely no later than when the first subject area committee begins to meet. According to the long-range plan, it is during the following year that the new, outcome-based curriculum will be implemented and validated. If teachers still have these questions and no one has any answers, implementation is going to be difficult, teachers are going to be frustrated, and students will end up getting little — if any — extended opportunities for learning.

Defining Extensions

Let's do a little review to be sure we all have the same understanding of the topic at hand. Webster offers numerous definitions of "extensions," primarily: *the processes of stretching, expanding, enlarging, continuing.* Extensions in the curriculum can be enrichment or corrective, but in either case, they abide by the definitions. They do not merely repeat; instead they continue, enlarge, expand or stretch the original learning tasks. Too often these extensions are either not provided at all, or they are offered only in the forms of drill, repetition and busywork.

Correctives are exercises, activities or assignments designed to bring certain students to mastery of a task or outcome when regular class exercises, activities and assignments have failed to achieve that goal. Enrichments are exercises, activities or assignments designed to give certain students an opportunity to enrich their learning when the students have demonstrated mastery of the original task or outcome. These students may have mastered the outcome through participation in the class instructional processes, or they may have had previous knowledge or natural talent that enabled them to demonstrate mastery with little or no instruction.

The decision of whether a student has or has not achieved mastery should be based on formative assessments (checks for student learning of <u>each task</u>, or each <u>step</u> of the learning process) as well as summative assessments (evaluation providing evidence that the student can do that which is stated in the <u>entire outcome</u>). Teacher judgments during the assessment processes should be both qualitative and quantitative.

When the teacher administers formative assessments, the results usually show that some students have mastered this particular step (task/learning strand) of the outcome, and others still need instruction or practice time. The latter students definitely need corrective activities. Teachers need help in knowing what to do with these students. Let's look at some suggestions that can be shared through faculty meetings and staff development sessions. Later, under the "Enrichment" heading, we'll address concerns regarding students who need additional challenge.

Note: Some curriculum leaders hold full-time administrative positions while others have some classroom responsibilities. In guiding teachers through a discussion of extensions, the curriculum leader must assume the role of a teaching colleague. Teachers need to feel that administrators are working with them, and that the dilemma of extensions is not their problem alone. Therefore discussions need to be from the point of view of "we educators," not "you teachers."

Correctives

If you started a new job and your supervisor showed you how to do your tasks on the first day but you didn't really understand, what would you want to happen next? How would you want it to happen? Probably the most important thing that subject area committees and individual teachers can do is keep this in mind when planning correctives for students who do not successfully complete (master) a task through the original instructional procedures. Most of us would want a supervisor to be — above all other things — patient with us. Kids want and need the same thing.

Often students will start out really trying to do well and will ask questions or ask for help when they don't understand. But after only one or two requests, most of them will stop asking. Why is that? Classroom observers have found that most often it is because the teacher — knowingly or unknowingly — begins to lose patience after explaining something a second or third time. The students don't want to be the object of the teacher's anger nor do they want to be embarrassed in front of their peers because they still "don't get it."

What we as educators need to recognize is that too often the student still isn't catching on because <u>we</u> are not tuning in to the actual problem. We give the same information in the same way, and yes — we lose our patience when the student then keeps asking the same question! We often conclude that the student is just not listening, but that may or may not be the case. What we have to do, at any point in the instructional process where a student is not performing correctly, is analyze the situation to determine exactly what the problem is so we know how to go about correcting it.

Analyze the Problem

Most likely the student's learning problem will fit into one of the following categories:

- The student is not developmentally ready for this task.
- The student simply needs more practice.
- The student needs more processing time.
- The student has a different learning style than that used for the original instruction.
- The selected activity is ineffective.
- The task is too complicated.
- The student wasn't paying attention.
- The student doesn't care.

Let's look at each of these problems individually and consider some suggestions for their solution.

Student is not developmentally ready. This is a problem that is most pronounced in the primary grades, particularly in kindergarten or first grade. We all know that children do not grow in size at the same rate; they enter school in a wide variety of heights and weights. Likewise, children do not grow *developmentally* at the same rate. They don't all crawl or walk or talk at the same ages. Their attention spans, motor skills, and thinking processes are not all at the same developmental level when they begin school.

All students can be included in the original instruction activities for particular outcomes. Young children are naturally curious and adventuresome, and will attempt all kinds of new learning situations. But if a child is not developmentally ready to perform certain mental or physical tasks, then continuing with instruction in those tasks will bring nothing but frustration to student and teacher alike. Instead the teacher should postpone further instruction for those students and try again at one or more times later in the year.

Some students are not ready for certain tasks even by the end of the school year. Here is another example of how helpful portfolios can be. Samples of a child's first attempts at a task, and anecdotal records about a student's readiness can be slipped into a portfolio, which is given to the next year's teacher.

Student needs more practice. There are certain tasks that we can only become proficient in through practice. This is the only category for which "more of the same thing" is acceptable. However, extended repetitions of anything become boring, and boredom causes lack of interest, so practice is no longer productive. Two things can help: 1) space practice sessions over a longer period of time, with other kinds of instruction and activity in between; and 2) vary the way practice is conducted — use a different kind of worksheet, a game or puzzle, a contest, simulation, or have students practice with a partner or team/group.

The student needs more processing time. We don't all learn or work at the same rate of speed. Sometimes students simply need more time to think something through, figure it out, or apply it. Confer with the students to let them know you understand and to set — together — a realistic, but·extended time period for completing the task. If the task is complex, set a time frame for each step so the students don't get too far behind and so you can check for understanding as they progress. Time frames may need to be adjusted more than once in order for the student to achieve the desired results.

The student has a different learning style than that used for the original instruction. Research has been conducted for decades that verifies human beings have different styles of learning. It has also shown we tend to teach the way we learn best ourselves. (Refer to the earlier section on learning styles.) The most common styles of learning are by visual means, auditory means, a combination of visual and auditory means, or hands-on experiences. If instruction was given primarily through only one style, try one or more of the others. If the students are still having problems, ask yourself: how else could this be approached? Perhaps another student could explain how he/she does the task; perhaps the students themselves can give suggestions for specific ways they need help.

The selected methods/activities are ineffective. This problem is very similar to the one above, and yet differs slightly. Sometimes we do match a student's learning style, and yet he still doesn't "catch on" — the particular method or activity used just doesn't work for this student. For example, a teacher who **demonstrates** a procedure is providing for visual learners, yet for some students — even though they are visual learners — the demonstration may happen too quickly or may be too complex. They may not be able to notice all the details or even to focus on the important component of a given step. These students would probably be much more successful if provided a chart or a series of close-up photos showing each step to be performed.

In this situation, like the one on learning styles, the best thing we can do is ask ourselves, How else could this be approached? What else could we try that involves the same information or skill?

The task is too complicated. A task that has multiple steps may be too much for some students to handle all at once. Break the task into smaller pieces. Check for mastery of each step before having the student move on; check that the student can combine two steps before adding a third, and so forth.

The student wasn't paying attention. The traditional approach to this problem has been, "Too bad you weren't paying attention; it was your fault, so now you'll just have to accept a failing grade." The problem with that approach is that the student still hasn't learned — hasn't reached the outcome which we've deemed so important. In addition, if this outcome lays the foundation for others that will follow, the student will never be able to catch up.

Students who weren't trying to pay attention need to know that they will still be held accountable for their learning, that they can't just accept a poor grade and be done. For most of these students, having to come in on their own time for the repeat instruction will "cure the problem."

Some students can't really help themselves. A really creative child may start out paying attention until something in the lesson really captures her interest and then she starts mentally exploring that concept instead of paying attention to the rest of the instruction. Another student may have a short attention span that causes her to be incapable of "tuning in" to long periods of instruction. Other students may be easily distracted by people or things around them.

These students have to be taught how to pay attention, just as they're taught the academic content and skills required for an outcome. Like the students for whom a task is too complicated, they usually benefit from having tasks broken down into shorter, more manageable pieces. The following are additional strategies that often work.

1) Tell the student he will have to teach this information or skill to another student when you are finished.

2) Have the student take notes as you are instructing; move about during instruction, looking over her shoulder frequently to be sure she's still taking notes and she's still "with you."

3) Ask the student to repeat your instructions or to paraphrase the information you've just given.

4) Make a list of pay-attention techniques such as maintaining eye contact, using good posture, having supplies ready, and getting rid of distractions (gum or candy, gadgets, photos, etc.). When a student is not paying attention, point out what — in particular — is not being done correctly. Have the student tell and show you how to correct the behavior.

<u>The student doesn't care.</u> Indubitably, this is the hardest job we have —
teaching the students who don't want to learn and don't care whether they pass or fail.
Too often they are deemed just not worth the trouble — because it is indeed a lot of
trouble and it takes a lot of time to get them to learn. **However, in most cases, the
reason these students don't care is that they have not been successful in the past;**
they tried and failed so many times that they finally gave up — probably a long time
ago. Additionally, **we have allowed them to fail!** When they've not paid attention or
not done their assignments, we've just given them a failing grade and moved on.

These students also must be held accountable for their learning, but they will
need to be "led by the hand" to get started. They have to know that we intend for
them to learn, and we're not going to let up on them until they do.

A Pollyanna approach is not being suggested here; it is certainly unrealistic to
think that we will turn every noncaring student into a prized pupil. What we have to
remember is the outcome-based education belief that *success breeds success.* The key
here is to **do whatever is in our power** to cause these students to have some success.
These students must be convinced that we care enough about them not to let them
fail.

Two of the points that were made previously stand out when designing correctives. The first is the advice to be patient: think how you would want to be treated if you didn't understand or couldn't perform the tasks for a new job. The second
is the admonition not just to do drills or more of the same thing (whatever it was).
We, as individual teachers, have just been presented with a problem; how can we solve
it? What different approach could be used; what new thing could we try; what other
materials are available; who else could help?

Enrichments

Now let's go back to the problem mentioned earlier: students who have
already mastered a task or outcome do not need to participate in the corrective activities designed for those who still need help. Instead, we need to plan for these students
a <u>meaningful</u> type of enrichment — something that will stretch their thinking or
expand their opportunities to apply learning. Enrichments should do just what the
word implies — <u>enrich</u> the original task or outcome. In other words, they should <u>not</u>
be tasks that...

- are simply more of the same thing. (If you can do two of these in the time given
  so far, surely you can do six more in the time left.)
- are unrelated to the original task or outcome. (Now that you've completed your
  electromagnet, why don't you make a model of the human skeleton.)
- are nothing more than busywork. (There's a box of puzzles and cryptographs on

the second shelf; choose one of those to work.)
- are reward systems for getting done quickly. (Since you're finished, you may try the new computer game we've been wanting to open.)

When thinking about enrichment, one of the first things we have to consider is whether the students have mastered only a specific task related to the outcome or whether they've mastered the entire outcome. Equally important is whether the tasks are hierarchical. This information makes a tremendous difference in the types and numbers of activities we select.

Naturally, if each task is essential to accomplishing the outcome, then we want all students to be able to perform all tasks. Assume that an outcome has four essential tasks. If those tasks are hierarchical, that is if students <u>must</u> be able to do the first task before they can do the second, then correctives and enrichments need to be planned for each task — to be implemented at those points of the instructional process.

On the other hand, if all four tasks are essential but can stand alone, then all students can continue instruction on all four tasks. At the end of the instructional process, those who've demonstrated mastery of all tasks can participate in enrichment, while the others do correctives for whichever task(s) they were unable to perform. In this case we would not need to plan as many enrichments as correctives, and the enrichment would be related to the entire outcome, not just to a specific task as would the correctives.

Occasionally we also find one or more students who can already do the entire outcome before instruction even begins, or perhaps shortly after it's started. These students should also be guided directly into an enrichment activity that relates to the entire outcome. Forcing them to participate in "discovery" and practice of something they can already do well is boring and nonproductive. If continued practice can make them better at what they're doing (such as a physical skill) then it is justified. But practice that is required just because we have nothing else for these students to do means we're limiting their potential and we're not doing our jobs well.

How do we plan meaningful kinds of enrichment activities? We answer the following kinds of questions:
1) What else would I like to have the students do with this if only we had more time?
2) How might the students use this knowledge or skill in real life? Is there some way we could do that?
3) Are there other resources (print, media, or human) available that the students could work with to expand their knowledge or skill?
4) How might they share this knowledge or skill (with peers, younger students, family, senior citizens, other sections of the community)?

The table that follows provides some examples of enrichment activities. Refer also to the sample task analyses provided earlier in this book.

SAMPLE ENRICHMENT ACTIVITIES

Original Topic	Enrichment
creative writing	Investigate what it would take to get the story/poem/article published.
Constitution/law/ government	Prepare/conduct a mock trial. Talk to an attorney or legislator about real-life examples of the current topic.
physical education activities	Design a game that requires the same skills, that a teacher could use with younger children. Propose a way to improve the skill, or determine how the skill/activity could be used/enjoyed/improved on your own (no gym).
map skills	Plan a real or "dream" vacation; prepare maps of your itinerary (country, city, area, activity, routes). Prepare a map for a treasure hunt in which the class could participate.
mathematical computations	Plan a budget for a class party or field trip. Propose a fund raiser and figure necessary amounts for overhead and profits.
human body systems	Interview a health-care professional about the particular system (issues, recent research, disease, preventive care, treatments).

Management and Time Allotments

We need to realize that *extensions are an important part of the instructional process!* Although students may do portions of their extension work outside of class, a majority of it should be done during class time. For many teachers, this causes a number of concerns — particularly one regarding the <u>time</u> needed for such instruction. It is for this reason that subject area committees need to pay particular attention to the concept of *selective abandonment* during the decision-making process of curriculum design, as well as when writing outcomes.

Our education system has a history of "covering" a wide range of material without getting depth in any of it. In fact, there's an analogy that says we have a "3-4" curriculum — one that is **34 miles** long, but only **3/4 inch** deep. If the subject area committee includes in the curriculum all of the topics currently being covered, then indeed the teachers will not have the time necessary for extensions. Instead, the committee must selectively abandon those topics not considered **essential** for all students to learn.

As pointed out previously, a single class or grade level of a subject should have only five to fifteen high-achievement outcomes for the entire year. Since these outcomes are cumulative, they do often combine or "bundle" several topics together. But the committee must be careful not to put too much into any one such bundle; the outcome should not just be a clever disguise for keeping every little thing still in the curriculum.

If the curriculum is effectively narrowed to only the essential outcomes, time for extensions is then made available. However, teachers still have questions such as, What about the students who are really struggling? How much time should I allow them to work on something before we move on? The answer to this problem varies, depending on the circumstances. Obviously we cannot keep the majority of the class working on extensions for weeks at a time while we continue to guide one or two students through correctives. There comes a point when we must move the class, as a whole, on to the next outcome. Teachers should use their professional judgment to determine what is a *reasonable* amount of time, and then move on.

In the meantime, what do we do about the students who are not ready to proceed? In some cases, mastery of an outcome (or task) is absolutely necessary before the additional outcomes can be approached; this is very often the case in math and frequently occurs in other subjects as well. If this is the case with the students in question, then expecting them to move on is pointless! If outcome number two <u>requires</u> knowledge/skill of outcome number one, and we know for a fact the students can't do outcome number one, then why would we expect them to be able to accomplish the second outcome? The only result we will get is a more confused and thoroughly frustrated student.

When situations like this occur, the decision has to be based on the individual and the particular circumstances. Perhaps a teacher will have to work with a student on an individual basis while the rest of the class is moving ahead. Perhaps a tutor could be found to provide the individual help. Other suggestions include before and after school sessions, Saturday classes, attention from a special-services teacher, assistance from the principal, the use of paraprofessionals or volunteers, and peer tutoring. Or, it may turn out to be in the student's best interest to be transferred to a prerequisite or different class. The point to keep in mind is that we don't just shrug our shoulders. Once again we do everything we possibly can to help the student achieve success.

Outcomes or tasks that are not hierarchical are less difficult to manage. For example, in a particular science class, the first outcome deals with magnetism and electricity, while outcomes number two and three involve planets and space. The student who can not master the first outcome could, nevertheless, move on with the rest of the class to outcome number two. The fact that the student did not master the first outcome must not be ignored; some of the suggestions offered above might be applied here as well.

Another suggestion is for the student to participate in outcome-specific summer school. Most school districts do provide summer school programs, offering both enrichment and remedial courses. The problem is that, traditionally, the remedial classes *require the student to repeat the entire course!* Suppose a student demonstrates mastery of eight out of twelve possible course outcomes. Why should the student have to take the entire course over again, repeating all twelve outcomes? Not only would that be nonproductive for the student, but it would cause the summer school teachers to spend time on unnecessary repetition that they could be using to help additional students, and that in turn is a waste of district money.

Districts can usually find additional ways to help students with extensions. Many districts recruit parent and community volunteers. Retired persons can be a tremendous source of assistance — *particularly retired teachers!* The important thing, as stated previously, is that the curriculum council needs to start early to determine ways that extensions will be provided. A good brainstorming session will get the ball rolling. But once suggestions are on the board, don't just let them sit there, saying that they'll "never work because...." Determine which ones are the best, identify the obstacles, apply more brainstorming as well as problem-solving techniques for overcoming the obstacles, and make an action plan for when and how the ideas will be implemented.

Obstacles and Strategies

Suppose the curriculum council has narrowed its list of solutions to three of the suggestions given above: outcome-specific summer school, parent and community volunteers, and Saturday classes. What are the obstacles they would most likely encounter, and what strategies have been successfully implemented in other districts?

Summer School Classes

The summer school and Saturday programs have much in common, both in problems and solutions. One of the first problems that will surface is the cost, because both programs require hiring one or more people to provide the instruction. Two related problems that will come to mind immediately are, how many people do we need to hire, and from what subject areas/grade levels? Obviously the answer to the second question affects that of the first.

A summer-school program is actually easier to plan for than the Saturday sessions, both financially and administratively. As mentioned before, most districts have a summer school program of some kind already in place; therefore much of the budgeting and logistics are likewise in place. What needs to change is the structure of the "remedial" classes that are offered — to the outcome-specific format described earlier.

The numbers of teachers needed and the courses/grade levels to be included depend on the needs of students and can be determined by late spring. Throughout the year, teachers can fill out simple forms regarding students who will need some summer help to complete one or more outcomes; the forms list the specific outcome(s) that need to be completed. These forms are submitted to the curriculum council or to a designated person in charge of the record-keeping. Teachers also send follow-up notices when students who were originally identified for extra help end up completing their outcomes before the year is over. Because these records are sent throughout the year and not just the end of May, the council has a pretty good idea of the numbers of students who will need help, as well as which subject areas and grade levels are required, and they can plan personnel and space needs accordingly.

It is not necessary to have a separate teacher for each grade level in the summer school program. Classes can be divided into levels, such as primary, intermediate, middle, and high school. On the elementary level, since most teachers teach all of the subjects anyway, the students and teachers would not necessarily need to be separated by subject area unless the numbers of students so dictate. For example, if the students identified include many who need help with math and just a few who will work in science and reading, two teachers might be employed: one for the math students only, and one for the combined group of science and reading. The same general format can be used with middle and high school students as long as the teachers assigned are qualified to teach the subjects needed.

The summer school classes are taught in an individualized format. Although a few students may be working on the same outcome(s), there will be as many or more instances where each student is working on something different. Frequently the technique used is much like that of the contract system, which has been around for many years. Each student meets with the teacher to discuss and outline the outcome(s) to be completed, how each will be accomplished, and the criteria and evidence needed to demonstrate a successful conclusion. The outline becomes the "contract" between the teacher and student; both know (and agree on) precisely what is expected for all phases of this learning experience.

Because of the individualized approach, teacher-pupil ratios need to be small — probably not more than a half dozen, or ten at the most, students per teacher. However, not all students need to be assigned to the program at the same time. Some students may need to work for a month or six weeks to complete their outcomes, while others — particularly those who have only one outcome to accomplish — may be successful by the end of one week. Amazingly accurate estimates can be made on the length of time needed for each student, based on teacher recommendations of the child's work habits, particular difficulties, and so forth. Therefore, while no student should be *limited* to a particular time period, the **starting dates** for students can be staggered if necessary to accommodate large numbers of students.

Saturdays Are Different

Saturday classes pose a couple of different problems. First of all, few districts already have such a program in place, so extra funding will be necessary for implementation. Curriculum council and board of education members need to start early to determine ways to provide such monies. Grants can be applied for, and sometimes local businesses can be persuaded to subsidize such programs. But in most cases, what is required is a hard look at the district's priorities. Administrators and members of the board of education need to look at each item on the budget and weigh its relationship to accomplishing the district's mission. Many items, while deemed important, will be less so than accomplishing the core outcomes of the curriculum; therefore those in charge must "bite the bullet" and eliminate or cut down on those lower-priority items in order to provide for corrective instruction.

The second difference from the summer school program is that students in Saturday classes may be working not only on outcomes, but on individual tasks that lead up to an outcome. The advantage to this program is that students can be helped along the way and thus avoid getting so far behind in accomplishing their outcomes. (This is especially important for tasks and outcomes that are hierarchical!) It also cuts down on the numbers of students who will need to participate in the summer school program. The disadvantage is that in this situation it's much more difficult to anticipate needs and make advanced plans.

The solution used by many districts is to limit the number of teachers employed, and once again to assign students according to levels. In other words, there is one primary and one intermediate teacher available each Saturday morning, and usually two middle and two high school teachers — one at each level for math and science, and one each for language arts and social studies (or whatever combinations for which the identified teachers are qualified). Teachers must submit request forms for student services a week in advance; the classes are filled on a first-come, first-served basis. If no students are identified for any given week, then obviously no classes need to be held at that time. In most districts, teachers are paid on an hourly basis for actual time worked; in some districts a yearly or semester salary is negotiated and thus is paid regardless of whether services are needed.

Both the summer and Saturday programs will require advanced, thorough communication with parents. A student's participation in these additional instructional periods will not likely occur without parental support. Some parents will welcome the individualized attention and extended opportunities being offered their children. Others, particularly those who view the programs as an infringement upon personal or family time, will refuse to allow their children to participate.

While in most instances the participation cannot be forced, these parents and students must be held accountable for their role in the learning process; if not willing to participate in the programs offered, they may have to spend extra time on homework, arrange for tutoring, or in some way assure that the student is achieving that which is expected. The curriculum council and board of education members must anticipate any such problems and decide their expectations — what the district will and will not stand for — and be prepared to stand behind them fully, including the possibility of a student not being allowed promotion or graduation.

Community Volunteers

Parent and community volunteers are a terrific source of assistance during the school year. The biggest advantage in this source is that little or no funding is needed. The biggest disadvantage is in management. Questions that surface include: what specifically do we want the volunteers to do; how do we find them; what kind of training and supervision of volunteers will be required; and when and how can training and supervision be provided?

The answers to most of these questions depend on the qualifications of the people available. Those not trained in teacher education will naturally be more limited in what they can do, and will require more training and supervision. However, don't write them off because of these restraints. Many districts have found non-teacher trained parent and community volunteers to be of tremendous assistance for both corrective and enrichment activities. Sometimes these volunteers work right alongside the teacher in the classroom, especially when the teacher is working with both corrective and enrichment activities at the same time. The teacher gives instruction to one group of students who are then supervised by the volunteer while the teacher works with the second group.

In other words, volunteers can do much the same kind of work that paid paraprofessionals do. And both sets of people (volunteers and paraprofessionals) can often be utilized more effectively than current practices dictate. Instead of simply grading papers, copying worksheets, and supervising recess, these assistants could — under the teacher's supervision — be helping individual or small groups of students accomplish their learning tasks. The training and supervision are simplified when adult assistants meet with teachers regularly for planning sessions, and then are present during the initial instruction, which guides them for the follow-up services they will provide. With such assistance readily available, students receive needed help sooner, their work is checked as they progress, and thus feedback and correction are immediate. This type of assistance usually ends up being as much — or more — of a time-saver for the teacher than help with paperwork and administrative tasks.

Community members can also be called upon when a specific topic/activity relates to their careers, e.g. an attorney works with students on a mock trial; a health-care professional guides activities related to nutrition, first aid, or science lab work; a business owner conducts a simulation of retail practices or marketing strategies; a local librarian assists students with techniques for locating resources. Some districts have a read-to-me program for elementary students in which volunteers are assigned a particular student who needs reading and comprehension practice. The volunteer comes to school weekly at a prearranged time to listen to the child read and to discuss the story or book.

While all of these volunteer services can be extremely helpful, they do take organization and time for planning and arrangements. In no instance should a volunteer be asked to "just show up and help out." In the read-to-me program volunteers are gathered together at the beginning of the year and given a training session that includes what to listen for, when and how to prompt or correct, kinds of questions to ask, and instructions on how to report progress to the teacher.

Volunteers can be used to help tutor students in any number of situations and subject areas, but in each case would need training on specifically what they are to do and how they and the teacher(s) will communicate about the students' work. Business persons asked to conduct a particular activity need to know specifically what outcome the teacher expects, the amount of time available, what students already know or can do, how many students will be involved, and what space and materials are available. Former or retired teachers would not need as much training as other community members, but would still need to know the information just described before beginning any assignment.

A curriculum council considering the use of volunteers would need to decide the "who, when, and how" of the training sessions necessary. Teachers themselves would need a training session on how to contact and work with volunteers to assure that the assistance given is effective rather than haphazard or just a "babysitting" task while the teacher is involved in another activity.

When all of the details have been considered and decisions made about the kinds of volunteer services sought, management, and training, **then** the council is ready to solicit the volunteers themselves. This can be done through parent organizations and school newsletters, presentations to service organizations and senior citizen groups, and articles in the local paper. Planning and organization are equally important in this phase of the program. Prospective volunteers will be reluctant to make a commitment if expectations and details are vague. Council members need to carefully plan announcements and presentations, and even to rehearse their presentations to check for clarity and consistency in information provided.

More Answers

So far we've addressed the first four questions that appeared at the beginning of this section. Now let's look at the remaining questions, for which the responses are less complicated.

- *Won't high-achievers be held back having to wait for other students to catch up?*
  Not if we're using appropriate enrichments as described earlier.

- *How do you keep students on task if they're working on different things at different levels?*
  This is not really anything new to elementary teachers — they've been doing it for years with reading groups, math groups, interest centers, and so forth. On the secondary level, there may be a period of adjustment for teachers and students alike. Procedures are eased considerably when teachers let students know **precisely** what is expected, in terms of both academic accomplishment and behavior. A positive attitude of teachers is essential. Those beginning the process with the thought that "this will never work" will find their predictions coming true even as those around them succeed.

  Most teachers find that they can successfully handle at least two kinds of activities by themselves if the tasks are not too complicated. For more extensive projects, they use techniques such as: team teaching (I'll take the correctives and you do the enrichment); tutoring, teaching, coaching, or supervision by outside resource persons; assistance from special services teachers; or peer tutoring and cooperative learning activities.

- *If students take tests a number of times, how do we determine their grades?*
  Grades should be determined by <u>whether</u> a student masters the task/outcome, not by how long it takes him to do so. Averaging scores punishes the student for not already knowing what you are trying to teach him. Refer to the section on evaluation of student learning, page 223: "And Then Comes the Question of Grading...."

- *How do we manage all the record-keeping?*
  Keep reading... evaluation of student learning, page 224: "Keeping Track"; mastery, page 330: "Criteria Development, Evidence, and Decision-Making"; and all of the section about the portfolio system.

- *Surely the classroom teacher can't do this alone; who's going to help and how will we pay for it?*
  The question of who's going to help has already been addressed — parents, community members, special services teachers, the principal, colleagues, and even the students themselves. The only thing that needs to be added is that **students who are not learning are not the problem of only the teacher to whom they've been assigned!** Remember our mission, and that we're all working together to accomplish it.

Everyone in the district has a responsibility to see to it that all students learn. Small group discussions and even full faculty meetings can and should be used to address problems and try to solve them.

As for "who's going to pay for it" — many of the suggestions that have been given, such as the use of community volunteers, team teaching and peer tutoring, will not require additional funds. However, to be completely successful, it is probable that money will need to be allocated, particularly for such things as Saturday or summer school programs. As mentioned before, the curriculum council, administrators and board of education will need to work together and to take a serious look at their priorities. Once again we remind you to take a look at your mission statement; whatever it takes to accomplish that mission takes priority over everything else.

Extension Basics:

- **Extensions include both corrective and enrichment instruction and activities.**

- **The curriculum coordinating council needs to begin addressing the question of extensions early in the curriculum development process so that strategies and programs can be in place when the first subject area committee is ready to implement new curriculum documents.**

- **Extensions are an important part of the instructional process and should be provided both in and out of the regularly scheduled class periods. Some in-class time will be procured if the subject area committee selectively abandons the curriculum to only those essential outcomes that all students must achieve.**

- **Extensions can be provided by the teachers, administrators, parents or community members, and even by the students themselves.**

- **Problem-solving techniques and the setting of priorities need to be employed to assure that meaningful and effective extensions are an integral part of the curriculum. Without such extensions it would be difficult to accomplish the**

THEMATIC INSTRUCTION, INTERDISCIPLINARY APPROACHES, AND OUTCOME BASED EDUCATION

One of the most persistent school renewal concepts is that we must change the appearance of the curriculum by merging its components under what curriculum specialists used to call "broad fields" categories. The theory is simple, that most curriculums do not match real life situations, so schools should become what John Dewey called a "microcosm of the community." In other words, we should combine classical studies known as mathematics, science, language arts, social studies, and other discrete subjects under broad (umbrella) themes that are based on how students will actually use those knowledge areas.

There is a good possibility you have heard about such interdisciplinary theories, and — especially if you are a middle school teacher or administrator — you may have actually done some curriculum work in that area. Elementary teachers frequently combine discrete subjects, especially in the lower grades, as part of their instructional program. This is especially true now that "whole language" concepts have become so prevalent. Many teachers are combining reading and writing under a different teaching format, and incorporate those skills into other subjects taught in the elementary grades. Primary grade teachers frequently use themes to incorporate not only the four core academic areas, but the fine arts components as well.

We in the Curriculum Leadership Institute believe that middle level interdisciplinary programs and instructional combinations for various subjects are excellent practices, and advocate them whole-heartedly. But, as you might imagine, there are some cautions which must be considered. In this section we will review the background of interdisciplinary curriculum and instruction, indicate the advantages it offers for student learning, discuss the logistical problems inherent to its practice, and show how an outcome based curriculum will actually promote the development of "broad theme" approaches.

Interdisciplinary Curriculum and Instruction: A Background

There is no need to bore you with a treatise on educational foundations, but everyone should know that interdisciplinary forms of curriculum and instruction are certainly nothing new. In American education its practice is as old as the schools themselves; in the European Renaissance period it became a sacred maxim to anyone claiming to be a scholar. The political leaders who started our country were practitioners of that kind of scholarship, and doubtless you've read about those known as "Renaissance Men" — Thomas Jefferson and Benjamin Franklin, to name just two.

But while some early American colleges promoted that kind of scholarship, most were designed to provide more specialized education....primarily for the ministry and college teaching. Initially, public schools provided a general curriculum aimed at preparation for citizenship, agriculture and commerce... usually terminating after grade eight. Advanced education other than formal training for the ministry and college teaching was usually a matter of apprenticeships.

Although the professions developed more formal training programs within university settings, usually connected to apprenticeships and internships, public K - 8 schools maintained basic skills curriculums focused on citizenship, agriculture, and commerce until World War II.

High schools had been formed in the late 19th Century as preparatory schools for college, so their curriculums looked very much like college programs. The high school's cloning of college programs was assured by the development of the Carnegie Unit, a technique similar enough to the semester or quarter hour method of measuring academic progress that record keeping could be systematic and measurable.

The trickle-down process from colleges to high schools not only influenced *academic bookkeeping,* it made high school curriculums look more and more like those used at colleges... with their strong emphasis on major fields, academic disciplines, and concentrated research. And because high schools were often attached to elementary school districts, their very stringent forms of approaching curriculum and instruction strongly influenced the educational processes used in all lower grades. Therefore, for nearly a century now we've seen K-12 education become increasingly influenced by higher education through its *programmatic goals and design.*

While higher education's programs were a strong influence, an even greater impact on the public schools was created when teacher preparation schools were either annexed by the larger college or university, or became transformed into the kinds of colleges considered more prestigious....those with a liberal arts and sciences mission. Teacher education became segmented in the same way other disciplines on campus were segmented, so methods classes focused on traditional subjects. Moreover, convenience dictated that there be an almost absolute division between elementary and secondary preparation programs. *Antiquated teacher and administrator education programs* continue to cause difficulty when school districts attempt to develop and implement a truly coherent or interdisciplinary curriculum.

Possibly the most vexing difficulty is that K - 12 *textbooks are frequently authored by college professors* who believe public schools are little more than prep schools for higher education; that students who succeed in mastering the curriculum presented in texts are those best suited for a liberal arts college. It is of little consequence to those authors or the companies that sponsor them that there are other students in the public schools who need a curriculum that is broader than mere preparation for entrance into a liberal arts college.

The chance that public schools can easily move to a more interdisciplinary curriculum is meager, because higher education has so long controlled K - 12 curriculum through its *academic bookkeeping techniques, program design, teacher education,* and *control of textbook authorship.* Now there is a movement on the part of higher education administrators to create a "seamless curriculum" from grades kindergarten through grade 16, a notion that could have merit if liberal arts colleges are willing to modify their curriculums to meet the evolving goals of public and private schools. Since that is unlikely, it would be better for public schools to break away from the grip of higher education. One way to do that is to examine all of post-secondary education, including that offered by industry, community colleges, and vocational/technical schools, and to slowly rethink curricular offerings in light of what is discovered.

The Advantages of an Interdisciplinary Curriculum for Student Learning

We've already mentioned some advantages of an interdisciplinary curriculum, especially if one believes in the efficacy of Dewey's admonition that schools should become microcosms of the community they serve. But there are other advantages more closely akin to the act of learning itself, and the intellectual and academic needs of students.

Students benefit from an interdisciplinary curriculum because it seems more authentic in terms of their own needs. That's because interdisciplinary approaches are based on multi-faceted themes, and those themes are usually created out of conditions that have potential for motivating students. For example, middle level themes like "The Future," "Exploration," and "Success" are terrific for linking all major disciplines and stimulating student imagination. If organized well, a theme with that kind of title is ready-made for dealing with questions students may already have. All students have questions about their own future, and the future of the society in which they are a part. Exploration comes from an innate curiosity that young children and middle level students have in abundance. And success is an abstract concept in the minds of many students, a concept they would like to understand in more tangible and personal terms.

In the case of whole language instruction, related skills support each other... skills such as reading, writing, and speaking are so mutually supportive that both teachers and students are almost forced into thematic instructional programs and projects. And frequently those themes match real-world activities. Technology has been a catalyst for more thoroughly integrating mathematics and science, and language arts and social studies have always been more than academic cousins. And there are a few curricular areas (often put in the category of *elective* or *enrichment)* that are in some ways more important than those in which we have traditionally put so much value, such as health and physical fitness, family living, human sexuality education, and economics. If it isn't possible to teach such areas as required courses, then they certainly need to be thoroughly integrated into those subjects that are required. The same holds true for the fine arts, a curricular category which always seems to struggle for funding and other forms of recognition.

Importance of Thematic Units in Curriculum and Instruction

If you ask a second grade student about math the answer might be "that is something you do in the morning." Young students look at the arbitrary divisions of math, reading, social studies, science, art, music and physical education, and begin to define the subject areas as separate bodies of knowledge with little relationship to one another. Today, as students move into the middle and senior high schools, the subject matter delineations will become more entrenched as the academic areas are focused into time blocks taught by individual specialists. No wonder many secondary school students complain that school is irrelevant to the larger world.

Over the past few years the interest in and need for curriculum integration has intensified throughout the country for several reasons:

- *Knowledge is growing rapidly. Each area of the curriculum has the blessing and burden of growth. Subjects like human sexuality education and family life are now a part of the public school program in many states. They add pressure to an already crowded schedule. Knowledge will not stop growing. We must find ways to integrate the curriculum.*

- *The school day is fragmented. Elementary teachers complain that they never have all of their students for a prolonged period of time. Unfortunately, the secondary school's need to meet Carnegie Unit stipulations, usually associated with 50 to 55 minute time blocks, not only prevents secondary teachers from more flexible programs, it also has influenced elementary teachers in the way they organize their day. They hesitate to use alternative techniques.*

- *Students consider course work to be irrelevant to their lives outside school. Only in school do we have math, then English, and then science. Outside of school we deal with problems and concerns in a flow of time that is not divided into discrete knowledge fields.*

- *Training in specializations does not help people later cope with the multi-faceted nature of their work. The renewed trend in the schools toward interdisciplinary curriculums will help students transfer strategies from their studies into the larger world.*

So what is a themes unit? It is an in-depth study of a particular topic, and can easily be found in any good high achievement outcome. Work on this topic should extend over a period of days or weeks, depending on the students' ages and nature of the topic. A thematic unit on weather is appropriate for students at many grade levels. Weather surrounds all of us and can be studied for a lifetime. Examples of activities to be developed might include weather forecasters, temperature and wind studies, sayings and myths, and seasons.

The idea of teaching interdisciplinary units can begin small, with just one or two teachers, all grade level teachers, or a department. The success and enthusiasm of these teachers can capture the interest of the entire school faculty. In a particular elementary school where that happened, 80 percent of their year is now spent in interdisciplinary work.

An interdisciplinary unit should be prepared to stimulate high student interest, correlate with the existing outcome based curriculum, and align with the availability of materials. Teachers should follow those principles in planning and implementing the unit. A suggested model contains three basic components:

1. brainstorming ideas for activities,
2. sequencing the activities, and
3. mapping the activities according to subject areas, skills and processes that are practiced.

A group of primary teachers using this model estimated that in the beginning approximately 160 hours of time is needed to develop, teach, monitor student progress, and evaluate the successes and near successes of the unit. As teachers gain experience, planning is less time-consuming because the philosophy behind interdisciplinary teaching makes minute-to-minute planning unnecessary. As teachers begin to explore a theme or unit to include all disciplines, they may use a device such as the six-spoked wheel. The center or hub is the theme. Each of the spokes is a discipline area.

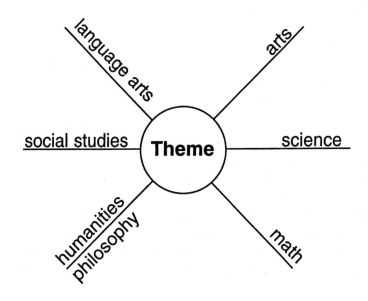

Several positive outcomes have been noted in classes/schools at the completion of a thematic unit:

- significant drop in absenteeism

- better student and teacher attitudes toward learning and school

- more cooperation among participating teachers

- student development of lifelong learning skills such as responsibility and self-direction, independent study, research, and time management

- increase in homework completion

- increased use of teaching strategies like cooperative learning

- improvement in work habits (time on task)

When considering whether or not the time for planning and implementing thematic units is worth the effort, think about these points:

- all content areas overflow their boundaries

- things have to connect to make sense

- working alone has severe limitations both for students and adults

- curriculum integration makes sense

- the curriculum and the day are too full not to integrate subjects

Cautions to be Noted for Using Themes

All of the points made above might lead the reader to believe that we are suggesting the use of themes for — at the very least — the majority of subject matter to be taught in the elementary grades. School districts where we've served as consultants can tell you otherwise. While thematic instruction can be a positive tool, for all the reasons cited above, it can also be a problem when we are striving for particular results in our curriculums, especially when districts are just beginning a results-based program. The problem arises because teachers get so caught up in the theme, that the *theme itself* becomes the focus rather than the specific results students should achieve in the various disciplines.

For example, let's say a group of third grade teachers chooses the theme of transportation. Virtually every subject can be addressed through this theme. Students can **read** fiction and nonfiction, poetry, and biographies of people associated with transportation. They can **write** factual reports, creative stories, and their own poetry about the topic. They can practice **speaking** and **listening** skills as they share what they've read and written. All kinds of **science** research and experimentation can center around how vehicles work. **Math** concepts abound in terms of weight, mass, movement, speed, inclines, forces, and various other measurements. Elementary **music** books are full of songs about cars, planes, boats, trains, and bicycles; **visual art** includes many famous paintings and drawings about modes of transportation, and there are multitudes of projects students could do to create their own transportation-centered art. **Social studies** concepts are inherent in the ways transportation expanded our country geographically, as well as the economic and social impacts. Even **physical education** lessons could center around ambulatory and cycling skills, as well as various games with vehicle themes.

Sounds great... but keep in mind that the Subject Area Committees have spent much time and effort trying to eliminate *gaps and redundancies* in the curriculums. By concentrating so on the transportation theme, these third grade teachers have created some new gaps and redundancies. For example, they spent a great deal of time on how the railroad contributed to westward expansion, which is the area of focus for fifth grade, and thus caused a redundancy. They did some wonderful research and experiments on how machines work (a fourth grade outcome — thus another redundancy) but spent so much time in that endeavor that they were unable to complete the third grade science outcomes, thus creating a huge gap.

Similarly, although students were doing lots of listening to reports and stories, they were not ever getting to the *particular end result* called for in the third grade listening outcome. The outcome stated that students would demonstrate listening comprehension by summarizing what has been orally reported or read to them. Obviously, the transportation unit was not the only time during the year that students were listening to oral reports and readings. From one thematic unit to the next, teachers had students listening to oral presentations and stories; consequently they sincerely believed they were having students demonstrate real mastery of that outcome because of the repeated and consistent demonstrations. The problem is, they would allow students to ask questions after an oral presentation, they themselves would ask questions of the students, they would occasionally have students draw an illustration about one part of a story... but nowhere did they have students demonstrate comprehension by *summarizing* what they'd heard. A similar problem occurred with a math outcome about measurement. Most of the outcome was completed when students measured real or simulated vehicles, distances, and areas, but the outcome stated not only that such data was to be collected, it was also to be interpreted and used for *predictions* — a strand that was overlooked through the transportation focus.

The bottom line is, thematic instruction is a wonderful way to make learning authentic and is a highly recommended practice — *if* teachers can show the direct links to their own outcomes and that they are indeed achieving the expected results stated in those outcomes.

There are a few other cautions that should be considered when teachers first start planning to teach according to themes:

Once teachers are involved in the excitement of a new idea, they might voluntarily bite off more extra work than they can really manage. Remind them that "Rome was not built in a day."

Creating a new and better learning environment for students is a long, trial and error process. Let teachers have the opportunity to try these new ideas and strategies without fear of being punished.

Teachers should not think of thematic units as a quick fix which must be totally implemented immediately. They should start small and let it grow.

Thematic units must be aligned with the curriculum <u>as it is developed at the district level,</u> and should be focused on student learning outcomes.

Unless there is only one teacher for a given grade level, time must be made available for teachers to work and plan together. Success and enthusiasm depend on this element being in place.

Logistical Problems Associated With Practicing an Interdisciplinary Curriculum
We've already described some of the foundational problems that mitigate against the success of a public school interdisciplinary curriculum: *academic bookkeeping, the influence of higher education's program design, segmented teacher education,* and *textbook authorship by those most closely associated with college-level liberal arts and sciences.* Those are problems that originate outside the public school structure, but there are a few that exist within the organization itself. One of the most significant is the creative thinking required to amalgamate subject areas under coherent themes. While there are many experts (especially those associated with textbook companies) who are willing to offer materials based on interdisciplinary curricular configurations, it takes considerable time, intellectual energy, and professional flexibility to actually implement those programs in the classroom. Even when the intellectual energy is present, almost always there is a problem with time and professional flexibility. Finding the time to work on such projects, and loosening a hold on the status quo, are daunting challenges. Yes, we've worked in many schools where those challenges have been successfully met, but rarely are we convinced that the new academic approaches will persist as an inherent part of the school's regular curriculum. Those projects are simply too dependent on powerful building leadership and a particularly dedicated faculty.
Another problem usually associated with interdisciplinary or thematic

instruction pertains to teacher teams. *Intra* disciplinary (same traditional subject) team teaching is difficult enough, primarily because it takes extensive planning time and human compatibility, but adding the interdisciplinary variable is sometimes an insurmountable challenge. Individual elementary teachers who work in self-contained classrooms and are not bound by rigid schedules are able to merge subject themes on their own. Conversely, interdisciplinary teaching is almost impossible for those teachers prepared for secondary instruction, who have long worked in a departmental setting. Again, we find interdisciplinary team teaching in a few buildings, but are not convinced that those projects will continue after the current leadership and cadre of dedicated teachers leave the scene. This condition is a flaw in the Re-Learning Project sponsored by the Coalition of Essential Schools; sponsors of that project do not have internal governance mechanisms which insure that their otherwise avant garde, thematic, and scholastically oriented curriculums will last over time.

Another commonly mentioned difficulty with interdisciplinary curriculums is the lack of appropriate textbooks and other resource materials. We see this problem diminishing so rapidly as to be nearly non-existent, mainly because *information age* advances offer us an almost unlimited reservoir of publications and computer software. Nevertheless, it is a challenge that needs to be addressed in specific ways when the curriculum is drawn together under thematic or broad-fields concepts.

Creative thinking, time, intellectual energy, professional flexibility, team teaching, and (to a lesser degree) *lack of resources,* are all internal logistical problems associated with interdisciplinary or thematic teaching. And, while those challenges can be met successfully by good leaders and dedicated teachers, the most pervasive difficulty has to do with insuring that changes made to the system become part of its long-lasting culture. That is the toughest challenge of all.

How an Outcome/Performance Based System Can Develop Interdisciplinary Approaches That Continue Over Time

There are many descriptors for interdisciplinary teaching and learning, and one of the best is a term introduced as "broad fields." While it is used synonymously with "thematic," it tends to suggest that many concepts and skills can be brought together to form something larger, yet coherent. Analogous examples are certain monumental human endeavors, such as the building of the Panama Canal or development of the space program. In the case of the Panama Canal there was an almost unbelievable mix of historical and cultural influences, political intrigue, governmental decision-making problems, complex financial arrangements, scientific and technological challenges, and health-related concerns. An intensive study of the building of the Panama Canal, all by itself, could offer a coherent examination of history, geography, government, sociology, psychology, economics, business, literature, communication, science, mathematics, technology, industrial education, health, vocational home economics, and even elements of the fine arts. That one study could easily serve as a thematic or broad fields catalyst for many subject areas. More contemporary events, such as the space program would work just as well.

Let's assume that an eighth grade course purpose for social studies is that students will isolate no fewer than eight interactions between world events and key American activities between 1875 and 1925, and analyze those interactions in terms of how they influenced the cultural, political, economic, scientific and technological growth of the United States during that period. And let's also assume that we use those eight interactions as the foundation for eight high achievement outcomes that, when translated into units of instruction, will constitute the course. One high achievement outcome could be that students will identify the key events leading up to, during, and after the building of the Panama Canal, and evaluate the extent to which that effort influenced the cultural, political, economic, scientific and technological growth of the United States during that period.

Once that kind of outcome based academic program is initiated in the social studies, it takes little more to devise similar course purposes and high achievement outcomes in the other subjects taught in the eighth grade. The scientific, technological, and mathematical problems associated with building the Panama Canal are mind-boggling....dams built, cubic yards of earth removed, volumes of water rechanneled, locks installed, width and depth calculated in terms of ship size, and more. And from a literary and arts point of view, the human drama was reported in hundreds of books, paintings, photographs, journal articles, and newspapers.

The main point of this discussion is that a well-developed performance and outcome based curriculum will move teachers toward using interdisciplinary processes without any other kind of tinkering with the academic program. There wouldn't be a need to develop other kinds of subject area themes, because the themes would already be found in the course/grade level purposes and high achievement outcomes. There wouldn't be a need to attempt staff restructuring around team planning and team teaching, because the result of the outcome system will automatically create more faculty interaction and horizontal/vertical coordination. If educators in the district are also successful in clarifying mastery, with attendant benchmarks and capstone events, then even assessment processes will lead to interdisciplinary results.

As always, we don't want to sound overly Utopian about any of our recommendations. Everyone who reads our publications should know that installing an outcome/performance system such as the one we've been describing in this book is no easy matter... and results aren't always immediate or Utopian. On the other hand, it is easy to see improvement in teacher and student scholasticism when high achievement outcomes are used. And real scholasticism is certainly nothing less than a broadening of the intellectual perspective and the merging of crucial elements in any knowledge base.

Thematic and Interdisciplinary Basics:

- Interdisciplinary and thematic curriculum and instruction are often presented as means to improve learning effectiveness and there is plenty of historical justification and research to support it.

- Trying to implement it in the public schools has been very difficult because of the influence of college curriculums, and certain logistical and personnel problems in the schools themselves.

- As difficult as implementation is, it remains important for educators to continue the effort because student learning improves when they view their studies as being relevant and authentic to real life situations.

- Because thematic instruction makes learning authentic, it is a highly recommended practice — *provided* teachers can show the direct links to their own outcomes and that they are indeed achieving the expected results stated in those outcomes.

- A well developed performance/outcome based curriculum will automatically institute interdisciplinary considerations, because course purposes and the high achievement outcomes subsumed under them have a tendency to become more focused on student scholasticism... by definition a *broad fields* kind of thinking.

- It is <u>not</u> recommended that additional tinkering with the curriculum occur in terms of organizing teams of teachers, or developing other subject area themes.

PERSONALIZATION OF TEACHING AND LEARNING

It's true that any curriculum containing intended student learning outcomes must be taught with individual students in mind. That's because — while curricular content and standards must be fairly uniform — each student needs different instructional approaches, learning time, and assessment techniques.

But it isn't true that we must now discard direct instruction to classes, or avoid other instructional processes traditionally used with groups of students. And it isn't true that schools must individualize to the point of creating non-graded class organizations.

Those of us who have been in education 30 years or more can remember the experiments that influenced public schools between roughly 1960 and 1980. Among those projects were Individually Guided Education (IGE) for elementary schools, the Trump Model Schools Plan for high schools, and various techniques used in middle schools (advisor base, school within a school) to help teachers work more closely with individual students. The flood of federal grant money available in those years supported many such individualization projects either directly or indirectly, and a number of schools participated. Even the high school mini-course program was a way to make academic studies more interesting to individual students (to help reduce the dropout rate), yet it has been attacked repeatedly as being a "smorgasbord" (aimless) curriculum.

If nothing else, those experimental years taught us that any project which seeks to individualize teaching and learning must not be based on Pollyanna notions or logistically complicated arrangements. Research has invariably shown that individualized (personalized) instruction suffers when:

(1)   curriculum is too broad and imprecise,
(2)   student learning goals are vague,
(3)   instructional techniques are too simplistic and repetitive, and
(4)   enrollment numbers exceed classroom management possibilities.

One purpose of this section is to review those difficulties, and *identify ways to avoid them.* Then recommendations are offered on *how to increase personalization of teaching and learning so goals of an outcome based system are realistically achieved.* Specific suggestions are offered with regard to the *teacher/student contract...* a simplified version of the individualized education plan (IEP) with which special education teachers are acquainted. Finally, linkages between contracts, portfolios, mastery benchmarks, and assessments are made clear.

Avoiding Broad and Imprecise Curriculums — The Academic Imperative

Lack of focus was one reason why individualized instructional programs used in the past were not successful. Teachers used existing textbooks and other materials, but did not always clarify intended student learning outcomes in their minds and the minds of students. As special education teachers know, for an individualized education plan to be successful there must be considerable clarity as to: curricular content, reasons why a subject is studied, instructional strategies, and assessment procedures. Those points must be firmly understood and accepted by teachers, not just viewed by them as something recommended in an instructor's guide or other published curriculum documents.

Without a clear perception and acceptance of what *must* constitute learning, teachers are unable to convince individual students that there is a real and meaning-ful academic imperative. An academic imperative is an intended student learning out-come that is non-negotiable, which means that the curriculum is written in such a way that tolerance for mediocrity and failure does not exist.

Much of our own research has verified this, that individualized programs are considered by students to be annoying busy work when neither teacher nor student can find an academic imperative in the curriculum. An outcome based curriculum overcomes that problem because the curricular rationale is clear to both student and teacher, and that rationale is *authentic to real life* and *scholastically credible.*

Curriculum that is created and delivered by people who teach it is more like-ly to convey a sense of the imperative, because those teachers are committed to its importance. The imperative becomes even stronger when the school's professional support persons and parents share that commitment.

Avoiding Vagueness in Student Learning Goals

A clearly written curriculum that contains identifiable imperatives for learn-ing will help teachers avoid vagueness in specific student learning goals. However, as pointed out in earlier sections of this book, well stated high achievement outcomes found in curriculum documents aren't always easy to break down into focused and authentic instructional elements. Our work with teachers has shown that "designing down" is sometimes easier said than done, but that a little practice helps teachers align intended student learning outcomes, instructional tasks (subordinate outcomes), instructional methods, activities, and assessments.

Returning to a high achievement outcome that we've used previously as an example, we can see the importance of clarity and specificity as a teacher begins to individualize instruction. Our example is taken from high school social studies: "Students will analyze the causes of the Civil War and interpret the moral and eco-nomic arguments that prevailed during its conduct."

Although the outcome is clearly stated, there are components of it that might be vague to both teacher and students. In this case, the teacher decides that no stu-dent can "analyze" in a vacuum, and that analyzing requires small group work, which she accepts as a form of individualization. Small groups can promote individual accomplishment because they are interactively dynamic; a carefully organized group can promote completion of individually assigned tasks (see the previous section on *cooperative learning).*

Each group organized by the teacher must research the causes of the Civil War before those causes can be analyzed, and once the most commonly accepted causes are identified they are studied according to certain criteria: Which of the causes seemed most significant and why? Who were the key players behind the start of the war, and would conditions have been different if one or two of those individuals hadn't been present? Are there any causes of the war that might have played a greater role than usually reported by historians... such as personal ambitions or philosophical convictions?

After causes have been analyzed in small group settings, each individual student must prepare an interpretation of the moral and economic arguments that prevailed during the war. First, each of the mainstream moral arguments would need to be isolated... slavery, racial and cultural dominance, racial and cultural feelings of superiority and inferiority, philosophical and religious convictions of the time, and others. Second, each of the economic arguments must be identified... industrial dominance, agrarian dominance, management of interstate and international trade, role of the territories, and more. The teacher decides that each student will prepare a paper which covers those interpretive points, and explains to students that merging the moral and economic arguments in some coherent way would cause their papers to be especially good. Again, examples would need to be offered so students would know what is expected. An agrarian way of life might be a strong influence on certain philosophical and religious convictions, and a student who could justify that point of view would certainly have thought deeply about those relationships.

By clearly defining and working with the two verbs in the outcome (analyze and interpret), teachers and students overcome vague communication about learning goals. The academic imperative in the curriculum must become an explicit set of learning expectations for it to have any real meaning, and the person most responsible for that function is the teacher.

Avoiding Simplistic and Repetitive Instructional Techniques

Simplistic and repetitive instructional techniques were used ad nauseam in the 1960s and 70s, with everything from national curricular projects to the use of mechanical or computerized "teaching machines." At that time there were educational theorists who believed that "learning by doing" was a matter of having students participate in repetitive exercises that were fragmented and academically trivial. They eventually learned that students get bored when the instructional techniques aren't varied, or when the content is shallow. That is one reason why so many Apple computers are sitting in closets today; they were purchased to stimulate learning but their technology was too simplistic (and operating procedures too complex) to positively challenge the human brain for more than a few hours of drill. Even today's more complex computer programs can get boring once the technological "gee whiz" factor disappears, *if* the human instructor working with the activity isn't creative, curious, and intellectually stimulating.

Hard copy worksheets, learning activity packets, and textbook exercises are also poor substitutes for authentically challenging, and intellectually demanding scholastic interactions. A rule of thumb is to create a classroom climate in which simplistic and repetitive drills are used at a minimum, and only when the kind of learning they elicit is required for the satisfactory fulfillment of a high achievement outcome. Avoid circumstances in which activities are used to fill time, or academic challenges are eliminated because certain students appear to be too slow to meet them. Even those so-called slow students need to see their learning in the context of a larger picture, and keeping them in that picture is essential to their academic growth... no matter how long it takes.

Avoiding Excessive Class Size

Hundreds of research studies have shown us that excessive class size is detrimental to quality teaching and learning. It is particularly detrimental to classes that use high achievement outcomes which are taught to mastery through use of individualized approaches. Even common sense tells us that.

As true as those points are, there is a financial and logistical reality that can mitigate against optimum conditions. Compromises are usually structured under "this is a temporary condition," or "we'll employ a paraprofessional to help with this excessively large class." Those kinds of compromises rarely work, because *temporary* has a way of becoming *permanent,* and additional adults in a classroom are helpful only when they are well trained members of the instructional team.

Point #9 of the Coalition of Essential Schools' *Nine Principles* says that high schools should not exceed a ratio of 80 students per teacher. In a five period day such a formula would set individual class size at 16. That same formula could be applied to departmentalized middle schools, and elementary self-contained classrooms should probably have no more than 20 students. The Coalition suggests that these conditions be made financially possible by reducing or eliminating other services on a phased basis. Our interpretation of that recommendation is that mission-focused schools are in a better position to reduce curricula and services peripheral to stated purposes. That's easier said than done, we know, but no aspect of true school reform is simple. It takes making hard decisions about valued components of the traditional school program to achieve real change.

Small schools may not have a problem with class size, but at the middle and high school levels there are difficulties associated with coaching and multiple preparations. The Coalition of Essential Schools rarely works with small schools and districts, *but we do.* Therefore, we are aware of concerns on the opposite end of the scale. It is possible for a teacher in a small high school to have five preparations or more, and two or three coaching responsibilities. That is why the Curriculum Leadership Institute has become a strong advocate of multi-district *curriculum consortia* in circumstances where administrative consolidation of districts is out of the question. We also advocate supplementing coaching staffs with carefully selected and professionally trained coaches who are not necessarily certified teachers, thereby allowing teachers to spend more time focusing on classroom instruction and assisting individual students.

The main point here is that giving in to expediency when it comes to class size and teacher load is a sure way to destroy the kind of individualization required to make an outcome based instructional program work. Decisions about class size and teacher load must be made at the board level, and included in district policies. And those policies should not allow future options or contingencies related to administrative expediency or temporary compromises.

Increasing Personalization of Teaching and Learning

Let's say your district now features *a better focused curriculum, more precise student learning goals, instructional techniques appropriate to the teaching of high achievement outcomes,* and *manageable class sizes.* It is now necessary for every teacher to organize lessons and classroom activities around individualized instructional processes.

As we consider specific recommendations, it might be helpful for you to review several earlier sections of this book. Refer again to the <u>task analysis</u> process, which is a means for breaking down outcomes into teachable elements. Some examples shown under *teaching methods* and *student activities* strongly suggest individualized approaches. <u>Cooperative learning</u> is an important technique for individualizing instruction. As mentioned earlier in this section, no student really learns in a sociological or psychological vacuum. In the section on <u>learning styles</u>, you will find specific techniques for individualizing instruction according to the learning style of each student. We have given much attention to the topic of <u>mastery</u>, which requires individualized instruction and assessment. The section addressing that issue discusses tools used to measure and label mastery for each student. And finally, the section on <u>portfolios</u> is particularly compatible with all points pertaining to individualization. Please read that section carefully.

We have found that one of the best ways to actually create a climate for individualization is to use a student learning contract in concert with a portfolio for tracking progress. A contract is simply an agreement between two people to do something, in this case between teacher and student. Contract conditions are clear enough for each party to understand what is to be done, and who is to do it. To be sure no one misunderstands the agreement, it is written down and signed by each party.

Many teachers already use a form of contract, and include parents in the agreement... especially for younger children. Student learning contracts can be prepared in accordance with high achievement outcomes, and include:

- the high achievement outcome itself.
- a description of each task required to accomplish the high achievement outcome (taken from the teacher's task analysis sheets).

- a statement which indicates agreement that the teacher will arrange activities designed to help the student learn, and that the student will take advantage of those activities in accomplishing the outcome. Some teachers also address parents or guardians in this statement.
- a review of formative and summative assessments, *criteria* the teacher established for satisfactory demonstration of knowledge and skills, and *evidence* students must provide to prove satisfactory progress toward the accomplishment of tasks and outcomes.

Using one of our sample task analyses and the elements shown above, a sample contract might look like the one shown below. An easy and nice looking way to develop the contract is to use a computer program which prepares and saves each student's document. Formats can be essentially the same, saved, and tracked as students progress through the learning tasks. If students have their own discs and access to computers, they can help with the tracking; otherwise they would have hard copies in contract notebooks.

This contract is very comprehensive, but once the basic format is developed the document is easy to manage within the student's portfolio. The seventh grade English teacher whose contract is shown as our sample will probably create ten to fifteen of these contracts, save the basic format in a computer program, change student names and other incidental information each year, and use them to guide and track student progress. Contracts are also a good way to communicate with parents and, in this era of full inclusion, they are useful to special education teachers. Finally, library media specialists love contracts because they provide considerable information as to the teacher's requirements for supplemental study and learning resources.

Contract

It is agreed that the teacher will arrange activities to help the student learn, and that the student will participate in those activities for the purpose of meeting the intended learning outcome. The criteria used by the teacher to *formatively* check student learning are these:

- The student will *read* required stories.
  Evidence & Criteria: The student can demonstrate a thorough understanding of the stories by explaining plot, characters, and apparent meanings of the author.

- The student will *create* a vocabulary list and dictionary.
  Evidence & Criteria: The student submits a written list of vocabulary words self-selected during reading, as well as a software created dictionary of the select-

ed words. Through game participation and spot quiz, the student can define and provide usage examples of words included in the dictionary.

- The student will *plan* group presentations about the stories.
  Evidence & Criteria: The student participates in an assigned cooperative learning activity, and presents a written or oral summary of personal tasks performed and group plans formulated.

- The student will *participate* in group presentations about the stories.
  Evidence & Criteria: The student fulfills agreed-upon tasks for the group presentation, and does so in a way that supports group goals.

- The student will *compare* problems or dilemmas of main characters or actions taken.
  Evidence & Criteria: The student prepares a paper or graphic to show the similarities and differences between characters and behaviors of the selected reading to those of previous readings outlined on the bulletin board.

- The task for the <u>summative</u> assessment is that the student will read a given new selection and *write* a short evaluative essay comparing character behaviors to those of previous selections.
  Evidence & Criteria: The student demonstrates analysis and evaluative thinking by describing the similarities and differences of behaviors among the various characters, and stating an opinion (supported by detail) about the appropriateness of those behaviors. The student uses correct grammar, spelling and punctuation.

I agree to satisfactorily complete this contract on or before February 23, _____

I agree to provide instruction and create activities and a classroom environment that helps the student meet the outcome.

_____

      (student)

_____

      (teacher)

Linking Contracts, Portfolios, Mastery Benchmarks, and Assessments

A *contract* is an agreement between teacher and student that a learning outcome will be met through the teacher's organization of learning and the student's active participation in that learning activity. A *portfolio* is a folder that contains contracts

LEARNING CONTRACT #1 BETWEEN DUANE JENKINS AND MRS. JOHNSON IN SEVENTH GRADE ENGLISH

Outcome: Students will read a selection of their choice from the required 7th grade reading list, plan and participate in group presentations about the stories, compare problems or dilemmas of main characters or actions taken, and write short evaluative essays about the character behaviors using correct grammar, spelling and punctuation.

Date instruction started: February 2, 19_____

Learning Tasks	Activities	Assessment	Date Completed
REVIEW BASIC PUNCTUATION AND GRAMMAR	SMALL GROUP WORK; PREPARE PRACTICE SHEETS; TRADE, WORK, AND CORRECT.	WRITTEN QUIZ.	_____
SELECT AND READ STORIES	READ; CONFERENCE WITH TEACHER; OUTLINE HIGHLIGHTS TO SHARE LATER WITH GROUP.	INDIVIDUAL CONFERENCES TO CHECK: ACCEPTABLE RATE OF PROGRESS IN READING; COMPREHENSION; OUTLINES.	_____
MAKE VOCABULARY LISTS; CREATE DICTIONARIES	MAKE VOCABULARY LIST AS STORY IS READ. USE SOFTWARE TO CREATE DICTIONARIES. PLAY JEOPARDY-TYPE GAME TO PRACTICE USE OF VOCABULARY AND SPELLING.	VOCABULARY LIST IS EVALUATED. PARTICIPATION AND SUCCESS IN GAME. SPOT QUIZZES AS CONFERENCES CONTINUE.	_____
GROUPS OF SAME STORY PLAN AND MAKE PRESENTATION	DISCUSSION, DECISION-MAKING AND ACTION FOR SKIT, PANEL DISCUSSION, PUPPET SHOW, COLLAGE PRESENTATION, RAP, ETC.	PRODUCTS AND PERFORMANCES: BY TOTAL GROUP PARTICIPATION, CLARITY, DETAIL.	_____
MAKE COMPARISONS	GROUP WORK TO PREPARE BULLETIN BOARD THAT LISTS AND COMPARES CHARACTERS AND ACTIONS.	COMPARE MAIN CHARACTERS OF EARLIER-READ STORIES TO BULLETIN BOARD INFORMATION (APPLICATION).	_____
WRITE ESSAYS; PEER CRITIQUE; MAKE CORRECTIONS	WRITE ESSAYS TO EVALUATE ACTIONS OF MAIN CHARACTERS. USE PERSONAL DICTIONARIES FOR VOCABULARY/SPELLING. PARTNER CRITIQUE ROUGH DRAFT; MAKE CORRECTIONS.	SUMMATIVE: READ ASSIGNED SHORT STORY AND STUDENTS WRITE SHORT ESSAY ON CHARACTER BEHAVIOR...ANALYSIS AND COMPARISON TO UNIT'S CHARACTERS. NO PEER CRITIQUE. TEACHER CHECKS CONTENT (ANALYSIS, EVALUATIVE THINKING) AND WRITING SKILLS (GRAMMAR, SPELLING, PUNCTUATION).	_____

and examples of student work, and is used to track a student's progress through all the outcomes subsumed under the course or grade level purpose. A *mastery benchmark* is that element of a high achievement outcome which clearly denotes student learning, such as the evidence and criteria shown in the summative assessment in the sample contract above. An *assessment* is a means of determining whether or not students have achieved the mastery benchmark, and is usually a formative or summative criterion referenced test (which may or may not be pencil and paper).

Each outcome-focused contract becomes part of the portfolio for the course or grade level subject. Mastery benchmarks are found in the contract itself, and assessments are designed to focus on those benchmarks. Assessments may or may not be kept in the portfolio, depending on their importance as formative and summative documentation of learning progress.

The linkages among those four elements for tracking student learning are important in an outcome based system. And once the system is in place, classroom paperwork is easier than ever before to manage... especially if teachers make good use of computers and available software.

Personalization Basics:

- Individualization (or personalization) of instruction is certainly not a new concept, but its use in regular K - 12 classrooms has been only marginally successful. The reasons for that spotty record are that *curriculum is too broad and imprecise, student learning goals are vague, instructional techniques are too simplistic and repetitive,* and *enrollment numbers exceed classroom management possibilities.*

- Those problems can be remedied by creating and implementing an authentic and outcome based curriculum, teaching to those essential outcomes in highly specific ways (using a design down format), using instructional techniques that are interactive and intellectually stimulating, and keeping class size at a level research shows as optimum.

- Contracts are useful in an individualized system because they clarify outcomes and the elements used in teaching to those outcomes. They are also a good way to present outcomes and learning requirements to students, parents and other interested parties.

- A contract contains the high achievement outcome, a description of learning tasks, a statement which establishes agreements, and a review of criteria and evidence required for assessing student learning progress.

- It is important that the contract be linked to the portfolio system, and the use of mastery benchmarks and assessment instruments/procedures. All four of those considerations are necessary in an effective outcome based program.

GRADE REPORTING

You've just received your daughter's high school report card. You see that she has an "A" in algebra, "B" in English and physical education, a "C" in Spanish and a "D" in geography. Now which of the following are true?

A. She's naturally talented in mathematics.

B. She's not naturally talented in math, but all the tests have been multiple choice and she's a good guesser.

C. She is able to understand abstract concepts.

D. Her English class focused on literature this past nine weeks.

E. She uses appropriate grammar, punctuation, and sentence structure when she writes.

F. She understands plot, but not character development.

G. She can perform fitness activities quite well, but is a little lazy about doing so.

H. She participates in all physical education activities and demonstrates good sportsmanship.

I. She doesn't have a "good ear" for linguistic sounds.

J. She can read Spanish well, but not speak it.

K. She hasn't been studying her geography.

L. She has been studying her geography, but the teacher doesn't know how to explain things.

M. She's not good at memorizing.

N. All of the above.

O. None of the above.

P. Who knows?

Most of us think we know our children pretty well, so we may make assumptions or guess at what's going on when we read their report cards. But assumptions and guesswork rarely result in accuracies, and the fact is, reading a report card like the one above does little to enlighten us. In fact, based on the report card described above, the only answer we could accurately choose for the "which of these is true?" question is "P."

When you stop and think about it, what does a letter grade really tell us? Whether a student has worked hard and studied a lot? Not necessarily. Some students do have natural talents, interests, or previous knowledge that allow them to breeze through a class making "A"s with little or no effort. Conversely, some students pay attention, do their assignments, and devote many extra hours each day to a subject, only to barely pass or even to fail the subject's requirements. And frankly, is "how much a student studied" important? The main issues are whether and what the student is learning. What does the student know, what can he do, and what are the specific problems he's encountering? A letter grade does not impart that information. Parents and teachers alike are often frustrated by the lack of communication that the traditional report card allows.

Outcomes: The Communicators

Interestingly, one of the things about outcome based education that educators most often question is also one of the most simple, clear cut, and desirable components. Educators ask, If we switch to an outcome based system, what do we do about report cards? The answer is to print a "report card" that lists the outcomes, or perhaps even the separate tasks (learning strands), with space to mark whether or not the student has accomplished each.

In the report card described above, we know that the student is not doing well in geography. That's really the only thing the report tells us. Consider how much better informed we would be if we received the report shown in the box.

GEOGRAPHY

Outcome 1: Students will interpret an atlas and selected maps.

	Dates Assessed	Dates Mastery Demonstrated
Students will demonstrate the use of longitude and latitude.	9-6, 9-9, 10-15	9-9, 10-15
Students will use maps to classify land and water formations.	9-13, 9-17, 9-23	9-23
Students will use an atlas to analyze a country's population, resources, and geography.	9-30, 10-8	(not yet)
Students will locate countries and cities in the major regions of the world.	10-15	(not yet)
Students will analyze proximity of countries to the U.S. and evaluate consequent impact on U.S.	(in progress)	

In this case we see precisely what the students are supposed to know and be able to do. We also see that this particular student has never mastered a task through the original instructional process (by the time of the first assessment) and still has two tasks that have been assessed but not yet mastered. Hopefully a parent whose child is having this much difficulty in a subject would still want to visit with the teacher to see examples of work and to talk about how to provide the help needed. But how much better informed the parents would be when heading into a conference, than had only a "D" been reported.

The same would be true for parents whose children were not having so much difficulty. For example, if Sharon is doing well on all of the tasks except the one about longitude and latitude, her parents can see precisely where a problem exists and they'll know whether that's something they can help her with at home. In the meantime, Amy's report shows that she demonstrated mastery of each of the tasks during the first assessment. Obviously she's doing well and doesn't need help, but at least her parents know what she's been learning. Many parents who are interested and try to talk with their children each day about what they're learning in school get responses so vague as to be useless, and trying to get more information out of them is as difficult as the cliche about pulling teeth. There's no doubt that those parents would appreciate an outcome based report like the geography one in the box!

Letter Grades or Other Indicators

Districts that change to an outcome based reporting system may or may not choose to eliminate letter grades. The important thing is to report what is expected and whether that has been accomplished. Reporting "what is expected" is done by simply listing the outcomes or tasks. Reporting "whether that has been accomplished" may be done in several ways, and the most common are described here.

- *The checkmark approach.* When an outcome has been accomplished, it is "checked off." A simple checkmark is made in the blank next to the outcome; no checkmark indicates it has not yet been accomplished.
- *The date method.* This is the method used in the geography report above. It is similar to the check mark method in that an outcome is "checked off" when it has been accomplished, but a date is written in the blank instead of a checkmark. This provides additional information because it tells not only that an outcome has been met, but when it was accomplished.
- *The letter grade marking.* When mastery of an outcome has been demonstrated, a letter grade is assigned and that letter is placed in the blank next to the outcome.

As these methods are described above, it is clear when an outcome has been met. What is not clear is whether an outcome has been attempted, but not yet accomplished, and this is indeed important information about the student's learning progress. For example, if all twelve course outcomes for the year are listed, and only two of them have indicators of accomplishment, does this mean that only two of them have been taught so far, or could it be that the student has attempted three or four of them but demonstrated mastery of only two? If an outcome has been attempted but not yet mastered, some type of indicator or code must convey that information. Most districts use a letter code: either an "N," which means "Not Yet," or an "I," which stands for "In Progress." A blank next to an outcome that has nothing written on it indicates future work that the student will encounter as the year progresses. Anything that has already been undertaken will have some type of indicator in the blank.

Districts that continue using letter grades may or may not average the grades to obtain one indicator for the grading period. Most districts give a letter grade for each outcome ... period. No averaging is done, and this makes the process much less complicated for teachers to implement. Students and parents can see the grade that was assigned for each outcome, and once again this says so much more than a single indicator. For example, a student who receives a "B" for three outcomes and an "A" for two of them sees exactly that... three "B"s and two "A"s rather than the "B" that would result from averaging.

However, some districts still prefer to arrive at one indicator for the grading period. This can be accomplished in the same way it always has been done with traditional grade averaging. Traditionally, teachers averaged the grades for all assignments and test scores to determine one final letter grade. The same thing is done with outcomes, except that the teacher averages the grades for all tasks and outcomes. The big difference here is that students who have one or more outcomes still "in progress," receive an "I" for this marking period, regardless of the grades assigned to other outcomes. The "I" says the student has not yet accomplished all that was expected, therefore the grades can not yet be averaged. That "I" remains on the report card itself, but when the outcome is eventually completed, the date and assigned grade are written next to the "I," and the grade can then be computed in future averages, such as a semester summary.

There is another major difference to be noted when using letter grades in an outcome reporting system, and that is that no "D"s or "F"s are reported; in fact, in many districts no "C"s are reported! The reason for this is one of common sense: if a student has performed only "D" or "F" quality of work, then obviously the student has not mastered the outcome! In this system we are reporting whether and when the outcome has been met. And in a true outcome based, mastery learning district, *we are not allowing students to be lazy or to do substandard work;* we offer correctives and support and insist they continue to work until they accomplish that which is expected. Therefore they either receive an acceptable grade ("A", "B", or perhaps "C") or their work is still in progress.

A final recommendation: including dates of assessment provides additional important information. Once again, consider the geography report provided above. If the report gave only the dates that mastery was demonstrated, this student's parents might think that the first two outcomes were easily completed; they would not realize that their child had actually continued to work on those outcomes for some time …through two and three assessments… before being successful. But because the report does include assessment dates as well as mastery dates, the parents have a much better understanding of their child's progress (or lack thereof).

It should also be noted that the second column says *Dates Mastery Demonstrated* (rather than Date Mastered). You may recall from your earlier reading in the sections on mastery and evaluation of student learning that *one* assessment is not enough to denote true mastery. Teachers must check periodically to see that students are retaining learning… that they still know or can do a task throughout the instruction of an outcome, and that they still can demonstrate that outcome throughout the school year.

Predetermined Criteria Are Essential

Obviously, in order to declare that a student has or has not demonstrated mastery of an outcome, the teacher must have a set of criteria and specific evidence against which to measure the student's achievement. (Refer once more to the section on mastery.) The criteria that will be used for evaluation and the evidence required should be conveyed to the students at the beginning of the instructional process. The teacher should not only tell the students what he or she is expecting, but should provide this information in writing as well; the contract described in the last section is an excellent way to be sure that each student has a clear understanding of those expectations. This written documentation is invaluable during parent-teacher conferences. The report card shows the outcomes or tasks and whether the student has mastered them; the contract or other documentation shows how the teacher determined that mastery.

If the district chooses to continue to use letter grades on the report card, then a rubric (criteria for those grades) must also be determined and put in writing. This was not so difficult to do when student achievement was determined almost exclusively through written objective tests that had specific right or wrong answers and thus percentages could easily be figured. But as pointed out previously, teaching to high achievement outcomes often requires qualitative as well as quantitative judgments, so a simple percentage cannot be identified as the measure of success. Therefore, while teachers definitely can and do say, "This is what you must know and do to earn an 'A' and this is what is required for a 'B'," their descriptions are usually several sentences or paragraphs rather than just "90% and above is an 'A' and 80-89% is a 'B'."

You may recall this sample rubric that was provided earlier for evaluating a student's science experiment:

Category: Logical progression
Rating of "1" = haphazard or disjointed progression
  • leaves out steps
  • performs steps out of order
  • inserts irrelevant steps
Rating of "2" = Acceptable progression
  • completes all necessary steps
  • steps are progressive, logical
  • errors may occur, but are corrected in subsequent attempts
Rating of "3" = Effective progression
  • completes all necessary steps
  • steps are progressive, logical
  • steps are performed correctly — no repeats needed
  • steps are clearly defined & described by student as performed

Category: Conclusion
Rating of "1" = improper conclusion
  • no conclusion formed
  • conclusion is faulty — not supported by findings
  • conclusion not stated clearly
Rating of "2" = acceptable conclusion
  • conclusion aligns with hypothesis
  • conclusion supported by 2 or more findings in any order
  • conclusion recognized and clearly stated
Rating of "3" = clear & logical conclusion
  • conclusion aligns with hypothesis
  • conclusion supported by 3 or more findings
  • findings are sequential
  • conclusion recognized and clearly stated

In addition to making the above information available to students, the teacher explains that in order to receive an "A" for this project, the student must get a "3" rating on both the progression and conclusion categories. If they get ratings of "2" in both categories, or a "2" in one category and "3" in the other, they earn a "B." If they get a rating of "1" in either category, they receive an IP (in progress) and must continue to work on the project until they can demonstrate the skills more proficiently.

Problems You May Encounter
Eliminating "D"s and "F"s. You would think that parents would be happy to know that no more failing or below average grades were going to be given at their

children's school, but this is not always the case. A good percentage of parents are reluctant to give up the grade of "D" because they say, "That's the only way my child will ever make it through some of the courses that are required." The point here is that students who do only "D" work have not really learned that which was intended. If they had "learned" it, they would meet our expectations and thus they would have a higher grade. Educators in districts and individual schools faced with this opposition must seriously ask themselves what they stand for and thus what they will accept and do. They must ask themselves these questions: Do we consciously and willingly accept failure in this school? Do we consciously and willingly accept mediocre (or worse) performance in this school? If the answer to either of these questions is yes, then these educators have not accepted the basic premises of outcome based education and mastery learning; they might as well stick with the status quo and quit giving lip service to anything different. However, if the educators answer no to those questions, then they must be prepared to follow through; this means that students will not be allowed to "slip by" with substandard performances.

Honor rolls. Parents and teachers alike often ask what happens to honor rolls in an outcome based system. Those schools that still use letter grades, even if they've eliminated "D"s and "F"s (or even "C"s), may still decide to have honor rolls; they use the same criteria they've always used, such as the "All 'A's Honor Roll," or the "3.5 Honor Roll," and so forth. Districts that eliminate letter grades also do away with honor rolls in the traditional sense. The rationale is that all students are expected to meet high academic standards; therefore, there's no need to distinguish among those who do and those who do not. However, in most cases, these schools do still recognize outstanding student achievement. The difference is that they use a wider range of criteria and those criteria are more qualitative than quantitative. In other words, "honor" is not determined by just a number, such as a grade point average. Students who are recognized are those who have done well academically and have also exhibited qualities of leadership, school spirit, and citizenship, or who have shown particular talents or dedication in individual curricular or extra-curricular areas.

Eliminating letter grades means no grade point averages for resumes and applications. A similar concern is raised about providing grade point averages for potential employers or ...more commonly... colleges and universities. Again, if the school has not completely eliminated letter grades, then nothing really changes; a student's cumulative grade point average can be computed and provided.

The concern has more validity in schools that have completely eliminated letter grades, although it's not really the problem that most people envision. While it's true that students are still asked to provide their grade point averages on virtually every college application, it must be noted that such information is only peripheral.

This is especially true for the exclusive private colleges and universities that so many parents and teachers are worried about. The concern is that a student must have an outstanding grade point average to qualify for admission to these schools. On the other hand, the fact is that 99.9% of all students who apply to these schools have outstanding grade point averages. So this information alone does nothing to help school officials decide who should be admitted and who should not. If an admissions committee is looking at thousands of candidates, all of whom have perfect 4.0 academic records, how can they choose whom to admit?

This is why such colleges and universities have traditionally not only looked at ACT and SAT scores, but have also required such things as student essays, letters of recommendation from teachers, counselors, and administrators, and often even personal interviews of students. They also want to know what classes students have completed, because they'd rather have a "B" student who has taken challenging courses than an "A" student who has enrolled in all of the easiest classes offered. Additionally, many of these colleges and universities are now accepting, or even requesting, portfolios or lists of outcomes that students have completed! This information tells admissions committees much more about the student's past performance and potential than any grade point average or test score.

Eligibility for athletics and other activities. Outcome based districts need to view these activities from a slightly different perspective than in the past. The first step is to examine the district mission statement to determine if the provision of these experiences in the schools aligns with that mission. If no justification can be found in the district mission statement, then such activities should be eliminated. However, in most cases, athletics and other extra-curricular activities are found to be valid... and valuable... because they help accomplish goals and exit outcomes such as leadership, citizenship, working cooperatively with others, developing and maintaining self-esteem, or being physically fit. If such a determination has been made, then traditional kinds of eligibility requirements should be eliminated. In other words, if the curriculum council and other educators have determined that these activities are vital to accomplishing the mission, then everything should be done to encourage and support student participation in them, rather than use them as the motivation for academic performance.

This is not to say that there should be no rules regarding student participation in activities, but that questions regarding participation should be dealt with first at the local level, in accordance with the district mission, and based on more than just "a passing grade" in a minimal number of courses. Beyond that, schools must of course adhere to any state requirements for participation. However, in many states, these rulings are also in a period of transition, particularly in regard to outcome based schools. State education agencies and departments are understandably struggling with all kinds of questions related to outcome based education... from accreditation requirements and procedures, to mandated outcomes and performances, to activities eligibility. And, just as understandably, they often look to the districts themselves for input on changes that need to be made. Once again, a district that can justify its decisions through the district mission statement, a long-range plan, and systematic implementation and validation procedures will usually have no difficulty meeting state requirements.

Grade Reporting Basics:

- Letter grades alone impart little information about student learning. Conversely, reports that include specific outcomes or tasks, and dates of assessment and mastery demonstration tell students and parents precisely what is expected and what has been accomplished.

- Outcome-based reports are especially important when progress reports are sent to the students' homes and thus there is no parent-teacher conversation in which to explain the report or elaborate on particular components. However, an outcome based report is equally valuable during parent-teacher conferences since it   provides focus to both teacher and parents as they converse about the student's learning progress.

- Mastery of each outcome or task can be indicated with a checkmark, a date, a letter grade, or ...preferably... a combination of date/checkmark or date/grade.

- A one-time demonstration of mastery does not denote true mastery. Some tasks, and all outcomes should be assessed in more than one way, and over an extended time period.

- Indication of mastery requires predetermined criteria and specific evidence against which a student's achievement is measured. These criteria and evidence should be revealed to students at the beginning of the instructional process; they are also extremely beneficial when explaining evaluations to parents.

- Outcome based reports are not that different from report forms that have traditionally been used by many elementary schools (particularly in the primary grades). The differences are noticed most at the secondary level, and it is here that educators also run into questions about such things as honor rolls, grade point averages, and eligibility for athletics and other extra-curricular activities. These questions need to be dealt with first by the curriculum coordinating council, and then with all other stakeholders in the schools, but they are not as much an obstacle as they might seem. As in all other aspects of converting to an outcome based system, the district mission statement should be the guiding force in decisions that are made.

PARENT CONFERENCES AND DAY-TO-DAY RELATIONSHIPS

Most educators agree that once parents understand and begin working with an outcome based system, parent-teacher conferences and day-to-day relations are better than ever. Parents generally want what is best for their children, so it stands to reason that an optimum condition can be attained if parents, teachers and students work together within a curriculum that clearly specifies expected student learning outcomes.

In an outcome based system, teachers report student progress to parents in terms of clear expectations, well-defined methods for achieving those expectations, and specific criteria for determining the point at which mastery has been demonstrated. With that information in hand, parents are better equipped to help their child by creating home conditions that support school goals.

Day-to-Day Relationships

Promoting parent involvement, and consequently a better understanding of an outcome based system, requires that teachers make mothers and fathers feel welcome to observe, volunteer assistance, and share materials and talent. Parents should also feel welcome to offer recommendations on how intended learning outcomes can be improved, as another means of internally validating the curriculum. All of that can be initiated by a letter sent to parents early in the school year, hense beginning the continuous flow of communication between school and home. Frequent, positive, and constructive communication is also achieved through:

- initiating phone calls
- sending home completed student work
- requesting parent signatures on homework assignments
- sending student prepared letters to parents
- sending home regular notes such as a weekly "teacher gram"
- supporting and contributing to a weekly or monthly newsletter from the school

Phone calls of a positive and friendly nature that focus on specifically mastered outcomes may be made on a weekly rotation so that every child's parent is contacted at least once during a school quarter. When a student's completed work is sent home, a form is attached which describes the intended lesson or unit outcome to which the work applies. Homework that is to have a parental signature includes a check-list based on expected outcomes. Students write letters to their parents once or twice weekly, explaining a particular learning activity. Frequent letters help parents understand what is being taught. Weekly "teacher grams" or "classroom grams" are used to communicate progress toward meeting expected outcomes. Building or district newsletters sent monthly to parents give an overview of the entire outcome based system used by all teachers, and provide details as to how the K - 12 curriculum is coordinated and sequenced so that student progress is constantly reinforced.

In addition to regular verbal and written communication, having parents participate in activities on-site gives them the opportunity to see the outcome based system in operation. Involving parents on the school site can include the following:

- open houses
- room or department meeting
- small group meetings
- coffee hours
- activity events (arts fairs, concerts, exhibits)
- parent days at school

District or school open houses are appropriate for telling parents how the outcome based program works. Specifically, parents may be helped to understand ways the new system differs from past programs, what an outcome actually is and how it was created, what role outcomes play in the total curriculum, how lessons are organized with outcomes in mind, and kinds of assessment techniques teachers use. Follow-up room or department meetings with small groups of ten to twelve give parents an opportunity to examine curriculum lessons, and assessment procedures used in their child's classroom. Informal coffee hours are useful for question-answer sessions.

Verbal and written information about expected outcomes found in the performance based curriculum can be shared at such activity events as arts and technology fairs, concerts and exhibits. This information will help parents and community members who come to look, listen and enjoy to also see what specific student learning is taking place.

To find out how the school's outcome based system works in the classroom, parents may wish to attend school with (or instead of) their children. Some schools offer a "switch" day — giving the student a day off if one parent attends school for a day. Active involvement in the process provides a better understanding than simple observation, so parents should expect to participate in all class activities and discussions.

Parents may not realize the difference between an outcome based approach and the more traditional approach to assessment. Providing parents with experience of an assessment procedure used in the classroom helps them understand the use of a scoring rubric. During a school orientation session, provide parents with an example of their own student's work and a scoring guide. Assist the parents with the assessment so that they can see the differences in meeting or not meeting the outcomes. Parents who actually complete a scoring sheet used to assess a science experiment or a writing assignment will have a better understanding of the assessment procedure.

Parental awareness of an outcome based system will be significant if teachers make mothers, fathers, and guardians feel welcome in the classroom. Parents should be encouraged to observe, serve as instructional assistants, and share materials and special talents.

Parent Conferences

The major purpose of parent conferences is to provide mothers, fathers and guardians with a better understanding of a child's progress. The conference can be used as a tool to communicate intended learner outcomes of a particular lesson or unit, and how they are associated with course or grade level purposes. When outcomes and specific expectations are evident, parents are much better able to identify a child's strengths as well as necessary areas of improvement.

When and how often should parent conferences be held? Three or four individual conferences throughout the year are recommended. Prior to individual conferences, a room, grade level or department meeting could be arranged with parents of all the children at once; or meetings of small groups of parents might be arranged at different times. Those kinds of meetings are good opportunities to present and explain grade level or course outcomes, and to demonstrate how instruction and assessment procedures work. One or two conferences scheduled after grading periods can highlight individual student progress, as it relates to outcomes that are preset at the beginning of the year. During a final conference at the end of the year, teachers can accurately tell parents which intended outcomes were met and which are yet to be mastered. Teachers and parents can confer about materials that will remain in a portfolio as part of the student's permanent record.

What should be shared at the parent-teacher conference? Parents want to know about their child's progress. Since letter grades alone do not adequately report student achievement, teachers can share evidence of the student's learning that is more than test/project scores. When shown actual examples, the parent is more aware of what is taught, and what constitutes expected outcomes for the child. The parent sees specifically what the child can do by examining evidence of progress and rates of scholastic development. Parents acquainted with expected outcomes are in a better position to offer help at home, to extend learning and to off-set deficiencies.

The amount of student learning is determined through various assessment procedures that provide more than paper and pencil evidence. These procedures include:

- rubrics
- skills checklist
- portfolios containing examples of student work
- performance and/or production documentation
- video and audio tapes and computer disks of presentations or special projects
- interviews
- anecdotal records

Portfolios containing examples of in-progress and completed student work provide parents with an overview of student learning. Parental examination of student products is better than the teacher attempting to describe how well a pupil is achieving. This category includes projects and assignments in which students keep representative stages of the work including those that are in progress, preliminary work and all variations of the final product.

Documentation of performance or production (exhibits) is an acceptable method for assessing student learning. After establishing criteria related to the problem, and identifying parameters within which students are expected to perform, several types of data could be collected for evaluation. These include teacher written notes, written or oral self-reports, preliminary works including models and/or sketches, interviews of students completing their tasks and, of course, any finished product. A computer disk can contain the evidence of a student's development of language skills, perhaps as they are applied in a whole language domain that weaves in social studies, health, science and virtually all other subjects. Tangible application of mathematics skills can also be displayed on computer disk and hard copy projects. Tapes of vocal or instrumental music, as well as oral readings, can be produced at intervals throughout the year and periodically shared with parents. Video taping a student's drama, dance or musical performance, and experiments, reports, or presentations provides the parent with actual documentation of a student's success, rather than just a teacher's description.

Pencil and paper tests, projects and papers do not accurately reflect a student's ability to interpret, define, apply or evaluate ideas and established principles. Recorded interviews between students, or between a student and teacher, help students value the contributions of others and gives parents a chance to "listen in." Parents can then determine the level of involvement and insight shown by their child in interactive settings, and provide home assistance to improve performance.

Anecdotal records can also be kept of student behavior when working individually or cooperatively. After making careful observations, teachers should record exactly what was observed. A representative sample of each student's performance, recorded throughout the year, shows the level of progress for students of all ages. Evidence of student learning obtained from these assessment procedures is shared with parents so they better understand that the scope of curriculum, instruction and learning is broader (and perhaps more intellectually demanding) than their own student experiences of twenty to forty years ago.

Sharing Evidence of Learning From Qualitative Assessment Procedures

Assessment processes are used to systematically gather student performance data that validly reflect what students know and do. Wayne Erickson and others, in *Outcome Based Education: A Minnesota Vision,* suggest that appropriate reporting of student achievement includes formative data which students and teachers need on an ongoing, often daily, basis, as well as summative data that parents, students, and teachers need periodically throughout the school year.

Teachers often avoid talking with parents about student behaviors that have been evaluated in nonquantifiable terms. In other words, they are not sure how far they can assert their own professional judgment when evaluative criteria and evidence of student work can not result in the assignment of numerical scores or accepted "grade" categories. The Minnesota writers suggest two primary considerations in the development and adoption of assessment procedures. The first, content validity, is defined as the extent to which assessment procedures match outcomes statements. This involves a judgment process rather than statistics. One must ask, "Does this item adequately reflect the outcome?"

The second consideration is measurement flexibility. Measurement approaches available to teachers go far beyond paper and pencil objective tests. They can also include teacher observation, performance/production and documentation. Qualitative assessment procedures can be more comfortable for teachers, when talking with parents, if they take into consideration points made by Audrey M. Kleinsasser and Elizabeth A. Horsch in *Teaching, Assessment and Learning: Invitation to a Discussion.* They suggest that meaningful assessment:

- is based on a clearly articulated consensus of what the learner must know or be able to do.
- demands that the learner construct meaning as well as respond to questions.
- probes the process used to answer the question.
- assigns tasks that are both meaningful to the learner and accurate measures of the instructional program.
- allows for more than one acceptable answer.
- probes understanding of the big picture.
- allows for alternative ways for demonstrating achievement.
- includes the use of appropriate tools.
- allows for individual and group performance.
- includes self and peer evaluation and student-teacher collaboration in designing the assessment process.
- is an ongoing process which measures growth.
- is a celebration of success rather than proof of failure.

Student Participation in Conferences

Opinion on whether or not students should be involved in teacher-parent conferences varies. Students should be involved as much as possible, a situation that works well if surprises and uncomfortable discussions are kept to a minimum. Students should have a relatively clear understanding of the agenda of the planned conference, and know that the focus of the conversation will be on the intended student learning outcomes all students are expected to accomplish. Joint conferences with parents work especially well if teacher-student conferencing in the classroom is a common occurrence. Students who are in the habit of using portfolio samples in explaining their work to teachers and peers should have little or no difficulty doing the same with parents in a joint conference. Student explanations of portfolio work can help all participants in the conference agree on what should be retained as representative samples of student knowledge and skill.

Riverton Elementary School in Wyoming involves students, parents, and teachers in monitoring student achievement. Once or twice a week the student is asked to write a letter home, explaining a particular learning activity. Those letters help teachers know if students understand what is being taught. That kind of ongoing communication makes a subsequent joint conference easy to conduct.

Parent Conferencing Basics:

- Parent conference and day-to-day relationships are shown to be more effective in an outcome based system. All three parties to the teaching-learning program receive clear benefits.

- Parents have a precise understanding of intended learner outcomes, and can get a better sense of how their child is progressing toward mastery of those outcomes.

- Since letter grades are less important, parents know what to look for in their child's work and have a better idea of how to provide home assistance.

- Involving parents in assessment allows them to view their own children as learners from a more objective and broader perspective. They also have an increased understanding of what their youngsters experience at school.

- Teachers are better able to take the initiative in maintaining communication with the student's home in an outcome system, because learning goals are clear and explainable.

- No less important is that collecting and sharing evidence of learning demonstrates a real concern for promoting student success, a fact not overlooked by today's parents. Clear and explainable goals, and an ongoing effort to include parents and guardians, reduces disagreements and conflicts.

- Students will naturally achieve better if parents are given opportunities to be involved in the teaching-learning act, the knowledge of intended student learning outcomes, and the chance to help make decisions about the management of student produced materials.

- Research, educational tradition and good old common sense tell us that boys and girls (and men and women) will do better work and become more effective human beings if they acknowledge the importance of being part of a team or community. The most important team in our schools is the one formed by parents, students and teachers, thereby making scholastic and personal growth a 24 hour a day enterprise.

PART V:
SCHOOL IMPROVEMENT AND PUBLIC POLICY

DISTINGUISHING BETWEEN SCHOOL IMPROVEMENT AND ACCREDITATION STANDARDS

Accreditation standards and procedures sponsored by government or officially sanctioned regional associations are designed to insure that public institutions maintain quality programs year after year. Virtually all public agencies are examined regularly for the purpose of keeping administrators and other personnel operating at acceptable levels of proficiency. Colleges, prisons, hospitals, and many public schools regularly undergo a systematic self study, culminating in examination by a visiting team to verify that conditions are as expected and reported. Until the 1980s, most states accredited their public schools to insure they:

- employed properly certified professional educators.
- met minimum curriculum standards.
- conducted instructional programs a minimum number of days and hours.
- sponsored appropriate governance and support functions.
- maintained other conditions pertaining to library size, personnel, facilities, food service, and sanitation.

Traditionally, most state boards of education assumed that public school accreditation which went beyond checking minimum standards was the responsibility of regional accrediting associations. Membership in regional accrediting associations is often voluntary, and meeting their standards was usually a matter of conducting a self study in various aspects of the school program, and undergoing examination by a visiting team of outside educators. Standards and conditions were developed by the applicant institution in certain prescribed categories (e.g., administration, counseling, and curriculum), internal tests were made to be sure those standards and conditions were met, results of those assessments were written in a self study document, and external evaluation was provided by a visiting team. That visiting team evaluated the school in terms of *whether or not it was actually doing what the self study said it was doing.*

It may be fair to say that until the late 1980s public schools rarely ran into trouble with state accreditation offices, and had little or no difficulty with regional accrediting groups. Regional (voluntary) groups were usually designed to evaluate high schools, and then only those schools willing to provide time and money for faculty meetings, report writing, document preparation, and meetings with visiting team members. The cost and effort associated with voluntary accreditation was considered good for both student learning and public relations.

Today the situation is dramatically different. States, while continuing to check for logistical considerations, are increasingly interested in the quantity and quality of student learning. Some states, such as Kentucky and Michigan, are highly prescriptive about curricular content and what students should learn. Those states tend to use state prepared criterion referenced tests, minimum cut scores, and the threat of reducing or eliminating state funding to force public school compliance. Other states have prepared less restrictive mandates that are designed to encourage district level curricular restructuring.

Voluntary accrediting groups are moving away from their emphasis on high school programs, structured self-studies, and external examinations that compare stated goals to actual practice. They are expanding to include all grades (K - 12), the conduct of self-studies that emphasize equity and student learning outcomes, and external examinations that focus primarily on improvements in learning among all students.

The purpose of this section is to help educational leaders deal with two very important issues pertaining to school improvement and accreditation:

1. Distinctions that should be made between school improvement and school accreditation.
2. How the Accountability Based Curriculum improvement model can be made compatible with evolving accreditation standards.

We will point out that there are dramatic differences between systematic school improvement which is conducted over a long period of time, and reactions to state accreditation mandates that create unwarranted fear and trivialized curriculums. There will also be a set of specific recommendations on how the ABC model for school improvement "fits" most of the evolving accreditation standards and processes.

School Improvement as Distinct From School Accreditation

Unfortunately, many policy makers and school leaders think that radical school improvement is a function of tough accreditation standards and processes. While we don't argue that schools might improve in some key aspects as a consequence of meeting rigorous accreditation requirements, it isn't reasonable to assume that the essence of good teaching and student learning will be affected in any positive way. School bureaucracies which respond well to accreditation standards on the surface, are often less able to influence *real* changes in the classroom. For example, a district can hire a resource (research) specialist to gather and disaggregate data on students, and prepare a school profile; the data collection process may be excellent, and the interpretation of those disaggregated data might be insightful. But invariably the main sticking point in the process is making those data influence changes in curriculum, instruction, and student learning. If the curriculum actually taught in the classroom is not clear to school or district policy makers, and processes are not in place for systematically changing it, then all the data in the world won't make an iota's worth of difference.

An even greater problem is the fact that most data currently available to educators aren't compatible with curriculum and instruction that use high achievement outcomes. A data base that is filled with nothing more than scores from norm referenced standardized tests is of little value in a district interested in helping students "use their minds well." Even criterion referenced tests written outside the district, and based on an imposed core curriculum, are only partial and marginal indicators of student academic growth. While some of today's criterion referenced tests created by states and testing companies are more sophisticated than in the past, they continue to test for "trivial pursuit" skills in isolation from real life applications.

Using data on student learning to determine the quality of the curriculum is definitely important. But the curriculum must be under control at the most fundamental levels before anyone can claim that "school improvement is data driven."

Getting the curriculum under control is only possible when districts receive positive assistance through use of a workable improvement model. Once they have received that *assistance,* and created a better focused and more manageable "real" curriculum, they are better able to be in compliance with accreditation standards that recognize the efficacy of that improvement model.

The "assistance, then compliance" principle works in ways that many regional accreditation associations are beginning to advocate. First, there must be a governance component that has authority and decision making processes in place to make necessary changes. Second, there must be a clear linkage between that governance system and the development and maintenance of curriculum. Third, there must be a clear linkage between what is written in the curriculum and what is actually taught *and* learned in classrooms.

Since many districts do not have adequate academic program governance systems, accrediting associations try to help develop them through an assistance component. They do that by assigning a trained visiting team chair to serve as a kind of quasi-consultant, a person who has some insight as to what the district should do to better develop and manage curriculum and instruction. A first team visit is scheduled only after the district has met the team chair's expectations in developing a workable governance strategy.

Unfortunately, that is where the process gets fuzzy. Accrediting groups tend to suggest development of "goals" targeted for implementation, and recommend that committees be developed for each of the targeted goals. Committee members are to be representatives of various district constituencies, so that changes they recommend can be implemented in their constituent buildings and classrooms. Those committees rarely have authority to create and implement broad new curricula, and absolutely no power to make fundamental changes in classroom instruction. And although strategies for maintaining those "in-between" linkages are weak, regional accrediting associations spend much time building assessments for student learning.

So what we have are (1) systems for establishing academic program governance that are marginally effective, (2) methods for linking governance, curriculum, instruction and student learning that are weak, and (3) processes for measuring student learning outcomes that may not align with the evolving curriculum. The assistance component provided by accreditation groups may feature untrained leaders, inadequate resources, and a questionable governance and implementation mode... any one of which can make the process an exercise in frustration for local educational leaders interested in making substantive changes.

It is important to say again that we see considerable value in external accreditation... as <u>accreditation and not school improvement</u>. So in our opinion no schools or districts should seek accreditation from a regional association (or even a state) until after they have spent two to three years in a school improvement process that, while compatible with accreditation standards, are not driven by them. This reduces the fear factor, and allows the school or district an opportunity to build systemic approaches to getting better.

The Accountability Based Curriculum Improvement Model and Outcomes Accreditation

The Curriculum Leadership Institute's school improvement process starts with academic program governance, which includes: adoption of a change model, appointment of a curriculum coordinator, creation of a curriculum coordinating council, development and adoption of academic program governance bylaws, development and adoption of a working mission statement, development and adoption of a curricular long range plan, and training of the first subject area committees. In the box below are how those improvement components correlate with the recommendations of most outcomes accreditation policies. Accrediting organizations are usually impressed with the CLI's change model and accept it as a satisfactory method for

Improvement Model	Accreditation Requirements
ADOPTION OF CHANGE MODEL	EVIDENCE MUST BE PRESENT THAT THE SCHOOL OR DISTRICT IS COMMITTED TO CHANGE
APPOINTMENT OF CURRICU-LUM COORDINATOR	AN INDIVIDUAL IS ASSIGNED THE RESPONSIBILITY FOR COORDINATING THE CHANGE EFFORT
CREATION OF CURRICULUM COORDINATING COUNCIL	A SCHOOL IMPROVEMENT STEERING COMMITTEE IS APPOINTED
CREATION OF BYLAWS	EVIDENCE MUST BE PRESENT THAT PROCESSES ARE IN PLACE WHICH INSURE ON-GOING IMPROVEMENT
CREATION OF WORKING MISSION STATEMENT	EVIDENCE MUST BE PRESENT THAT THE SCHOOL OR DISTRICT HAS A CLEAR MISSION STATEMENT, AND THAT STUDENT LEARNING EXIT OUTCOMES EXIST
CREATION OF A LONG-RANGE PLAN	EVIDENCE MUST BE OF-FERED THAT THE SCHOOL DISTRICT HAS A LONG RANGE IMPROVEMENT PLAN
IDENTIFICATION AND TRAIN-ING OF SUBJECT AREA COMMITTEES	THE SCHOOL OR DISTRICT MUST IDENTIFY "TARGET AREA GOALS" FROM MISSION STATEMENT AND EXISTING DATA ON STUDENT POPULA-TIONS

improving the schools. When fault is found, it usually pertains to the fact our model focuses on curriculum and instruction... and only peripherally on issues relevant to administration, support services, facilities, budget, and other logistical matters. It isn't difficult to add those aspects if the school or district remains focused on improving the academic program.

Accrediting groups are very interested in identifying "change agents with authority" in the district, and a strong curriculum coordinator usually fills the bill. Again, accrediting groups want verification that the leader in charge of change is looked upon with respect and administrative credibility.

Our model's curriculum coordinating council, with its highly representative membership and strongly worded bylaws, is usually a much more powerful group than the steering committee suggested by accrediting associations. Steering committees may have bylaws, and most associations recommend them, but steering committees can also be ad hoc (temporary) groups. The temporary nature of ad hoc steering committees can make them weak, so our council structure is usually well accepted. So are the bylaws we recommend. Our working mission statement, with the inclusion of student learning "core" outcomes, is always considered appropriate... primarily because target area goals are clearly identifiable.

The Institute's long range plan, with its focus on academic program development, is well accepted with the caveat that another plan be created to guide the continued strengthening of administrative and support functions. That is certainly reasonable, and easy to accomplish inasmuch as there is so much clarity with regard to intended academic program improvements.

It is the last point where the two systems are not fully compatible. As said before, accrediting groups recommend the use of target areas and target area committees. Also mentioned before, we believe those target area committees are ineffective because they do not have a systematic way to change or even influence curriculum, and are certainly ineffectual in changing teaching and learning behaviors. Our system uses the subject area committee (SAC) method, since those committees do have authority and processes to influence both curriculum and instruction in substantive ways. A SAC may take a little longer to accomplish its assignment, and the total curriculum may not be fully influenced for as much as seven years, but the results will be much more thorough and comprehensive. The best metaphor for this distinction may be that target area committees put "band aids on problems associated with curriculum and instruction," while a subject area committee "provides a model for the on-going strengthening of outcome based curriculum and instruction."

Data Collection and the Resource (Research) Specialist

One function the Curriculum Leadership Institute does not work with directly is data collection about student populations, and the use of those data in modifying programs. However, most accrediting organizations use that process extensively. Because they emphasize gaining information about students, and how that information can be used to improve curriculum and instruction, accreditation groups may require schools or districts to select a research or "resource" specialist. To do a good job, that specialist must have certain skills, and be able to:

- align data currently available in district records with targeted goals.
- identify other data collection instruments appropriate to targeted goals.
- create data collection instruments and/or processes in situations where they do not exist.
- distinguish between student populations so that equity issues can be isolated and resolved.
- treat the data using appropriate measurement tools, such as statistical analysis.
- display the data so that results are clear to all district stakeholders (especially a steering committee).
- interpret the data so that district stakeholders (steering committee, administrators, board of education) can make decisions about how the information can be used in modifying programs.
- assist with the development of a school or district "profile."

As you may have concluded while reading that list of functions, the research or resource specialist must be a very talented individual. In addition to the points made above, the specialist is likely to be a person who enjoys working with computers... . because the amount of data to be treated could be enormous. Also, correlating relationships between the characteristics of student populations and diverse forms of data will certainly require use of sophisticated software programs.

Our position with regard to data collection is that it definitely should be undertaken, but after the curriculum development process is initiated, and after one or two subject area committees are actively functioning. That short delay will allow a curriculum coordinating council time to get control of the academic program, and to make significant and real modifications in accordance with research findings. There is a good chance that accrediting organizations will authorize that kind of delay once they understand the improvement model being used.

Assessment of Student Learning

Most accreditation groups emphasize the assessment of student learning, and we do too. The differences involve timing and method... or when and how assessments should be applied. As we've stated before, the Curriculum Leadership Institute advocates the systematic development of curriculum before examinations are developed, and the incorporation of those examinations in a portfolio assessment process. It is difficult for us to accept any other method, especially one that advocates curriculums generated by tests. Most accrediting organizations accept the principle that curriculum development and implementation should precede the creation of assessments, and that assessments are multi-faceted pieces of evidence... not simply the score on one criterion referenced test.

Hints for Working With Accrediting Groups

There are a few perspectives you might find helpful as you work with state departments of education and regional accrediting associations. These perspectives are offered in light of the very *fluid situation* now existing in most states, and in the policies set forth by associations. Nothing is absolute or concrete, but there are definite trends which give clues about the future. Here are some of those trends:

- Accreditation will focus more on the *quality of student learning* than it ever has in the past.
- Accreditation will make greater use of organizational and student *performance standards*.
- Accreditation will emphasize the concept of *learning equity*, and will follow the tenet that "all students can learn." This will cause virtually all academic programs to be *outcome based*.
- Accreditation will be a matter of focusing on both *assistance and compliance issues*, especially during the transition period in which schools are changing their administrative and academic "cultures."
- Accreditation will be a *continuous activity*, not a situation in which self study reports are written and team visitations are conducted every five to seven years. External review will likely be an annual event, but will require much less staff meeting time and expense.
- Accreditation *visiting teams will be much smaller and better trained*. Teams of 15 to 25 members will be a thing of the past, as most teams will probably range in size from three to seven.

An over-riding principle all school leaders should recognize is that both state and regional accrediting agencies are really interested in one thing: that your school or district is committed to quality student learning, and that you are employing a logical and systematic process for accomplishing that end. Especially now, accreditation groups can be very flexible if they are convinced that honest convictions are connected to workable procedures.

Schools and districts using the model advocated by the Curriculum Leadership Institute have never had problems with accreditation agencies. The reason is that use of the model demonstrates a commitment, and that the model itself is a logical approach to school improvement. Moreover, even though the model is very specific in its structure, it allows considerable decision-making latitude within that structure. That latitude allows many opportunities to meet state and regional accreditation standards.

School Improvement/Accreditation Basics:

- All public institutions are accredited to insure they comply with certain standards.

- Public schools have traditionally been accredited by state boards to determine if required conditions exist, especially in the areas of teacher certification, curricular offerings, amounts of time allotted to instruction, and support functions.

- In the past, regional accreditation associations accepted responsibility for checking more than minimum standards, usually by guiding high schools through a self study process. Accreditation was granted if a visiting team determined that the school was actually doing what it said it was doing.

- Conditions are different today. Most states and regional accrediting associations are much more interested in conditions that promote quality student learning. Because conditions are changing rapidly, schools and districts need considerable *assistance* before *compliance* is possible.

- At this time the assistance component is usually inadequate, given the challenges associated with outcomes accreditation. The Accountability Based Curriculum model developed and used by the Curriculum Leadership Institute fits nicely with most outcomes accreditation processes, with modifications required in the use of target area goals (subject area) committees. The timing of resource collection is also somewhat different, as is the application of student learning assessments.

- Perspectives on working with accrediting agencies include more emphasis on: quality student learning, performance standards, learning equity, the distinction between assistance and compliance components, accreditation as a continuous activity, and smaller and better trained visiting teams.

- Schools and districts should understand that most accreditation agencies are flexible if there is commitment and a logical improvement process in place. Schools and districts that use the model advocated by the Curriculum Leadership Institute do not have problems meeting new and evolving accreditation standards because the model allows considerable decision-making latitude.

APPENDIX

GLOSSARY

core outcomes: the outcomes expected of <u>all</u> students in the school system. Elective courses have essential outcomes, but those outcomes are not *core* because not all students in the system will take the elective course. In required courses and grade level subjects, essential outcomes are also core outcomes because every student must achieve them.

correctives: an additional set of student activities for a particular essential or core outcome, to be used with students who did not master the outcome through completion of the first instructional experience. These activities should help the students achieve the same end result, but approach the learning process from a different perspective.

course or grade level purpose: a statement of focus for a particular course or grade level of a given subject area. The focus narrows the curriculum to essential learning of related topics. When students have completed this course or grade level, what should they know or be able to do? The statement must align with the subject area mission; when all course and grade level purposes have been accomplished, then the subject area mission will have been accomplished.

Curriculum Coordinating Council (CCC): a governing body that has extensive authority over the district's academic program. Its membership is representative of the district's primary components (faculty, administration, support staff, board of education). Its first role is to initiate the action agenda for the district's school improvement model; later it serves as "keeper of the vision" for that model, as well as a conduit and think tank for keeping the academic program on the cutting edge of educational practice.

deliver-up: when teaching the intended curriculum, the teacher starts with the most **specific** outcomes (an individual lesson) and checks for mastery before proceeding; mastery of the specific leads to mastery of the broad, or general outcomes. If students master the outcomes for each lesson or unit, they will have mastered the core or essential outcomes; if they master all the core/essential outcomes, they will have mastered the course or grade level purpose.

design-down: the process of designing the curriculum that starts with the **broadest** (exit) outcomes, and ends up with the most **specific** outcomes (what should the students know and be able to do at the end of this lesson?). The outcomes must align with one another: district mission dictates the subject mission, which dictates the purpose of each course or grade level in that subject, which dictates the core or essential outcomes for that course or grade level, which dictate the unit or individual lesson outcomes.

district mission statement: a written document that is used as the guide for all district decision-making. It is a point of focus that incorporates four components: the purpose of the district; goals for student learning, including the exit outcomes; the means of accomplishing the curriculum; and statements of accountability.

essential outcomes: the outcomes for a particular course that all students in that course must master. What things do we still want students to know and be able to do long after they have left this course?

exit outcomes —usually listed in the district mission statement: the things we want students to know or be able to do, or the characteristics we want them to exhibit (affective), when they exit the school system. What are the end results that we want for all students when they have completed their K-12 experiences?

enrichments: (1.) a set of student activities, related to a particular core or essential outcome, to be used with students who have mastered the outcome and are ready for opportunities to reinforce or expand that learning. (2.) additional outcomes, not directly related to the core or essential outcomes for a particular course or grade level subject. They may be used as expanded opportunities for some students while others are still working on the core/essential outcomes, **or** they may be taught to all students after all of the core/essential outcomes have been completed (mastered by all students).

extensions: corrective **or** enrichment activities and outcomes. They do not merely repeat what has been done before; instead, they continue, enlarge, expand, or stretch the core/essential outcomes.

formative assessment: a short, frequently administered form of assessment; one should be administered for each step of the learning process. Formative assessments help the teacher see where learning problems are occurring before they are compounded. They also help the students focus on what's important and see the relationships of prior learning to new information.

high-achievement outcome: an outcome that meets the following criteria:

(1) contains a positive statement; (2) tells what the students themselves will do; (3) uses a verb that describes specific action; (4) contains an end result that relates directly to our intention; (5) requires a high cognitive level; (6) requires dynamic student involvement; (7) is relevant to the student's present or future life; and, (8) can be authentically assessed. Essential outcomes and core outcomes should also be high-achievement outcomes.

long-range plan: a timeline developed by the Curriculum Coordinating Council for development, implementation, validation, and evaluation of curriculum in all subjects and grade levels.

mastery: the point in a student's learning progress at which there is a <u>clear and observable</u> demonstration of the desired knowledge, skill, or behavior. The observations should be qualitative as well as quantitative; written tests, projects, and various performances need to be supported by the observations and professional judgments of the teacher. The teacher must be convinced that the learning is long-term: a one-time demonstration does not denote mastery. Will the student be able to demonstrate the knowledge/skill/behavior next week, next month, next year?

outcome: the <u>end</u> <u>result</u> of the teaching/learning process. What should the students know or be able to do as a direct result of their participation in a particular set of learning activities? Outcomes describe what the <u>student</u> will do (not what the teacher will do or what is in the textbook).

outcome-based education: a philosophy in which all of the district's academic programs and instructional efforts are focused around clearly defined outcomes that all students must master before exiting the system. OBE is based on three premises: all students can learn, success breeds success, and schools control the conditions of success.

Resource Advisory Committee (RAC): a permanent, on-going committee appointed by the Curriculum Coordinating Council to research products and services related to educational resources. It serves as the communication link between the district and companies and agencies that supply the products and services.

Subject Area Committee (SAC): an ad hoc task force appointed by the Curriculum Coordinating Council in accordance with that body's long range plan for curriculum development. The primary responsibility of the SAC is to formulate an outcome based curriculum by following an action agenda prescribed by the CCC.

steering committee: an ad hoc committee, appointed by the superintendent, that includes representation of teachers, professional support persons, administrators, and one or more board members. Its primary purpose is to write the bylaws that guide the academic program's decision making process. The group may also critique the district's action plan and/or initiate procedures for establishing the Curriculum Coordinating Council.

subject area mission statement: a statement of purpose that tells why this subject is taught. It may be a general statement only, or it may also include subject exit outcomes. When students have completed all of the required courses in this subject area, what should they know or be able to do? The statement must align with the district mission statement; it shows how learning in this subject is necessary to accomplish the exit outcomes.

summative assessment: a cumulative assessment that is administered at the end of the teaching/learning process for a particular outcome. The summative assessment includes (separately or combined) all skills and concepts that were evaluated in the formative assessments. It measures whether the student can indeed do that which is stated in the outcome.

task analysis: a process of analyzing an outcome to determine the separate teaching and learning components necessary for achieving the outcome. Those components ordinarily include: tasks (learning strands), teaching methods, student activities, assessments, mastery criteria and evidence, and extensions.

Technology Resource Advisory Committee (TRAC): a permanent, ongoing committee appointed by the Curriculum Coordinating Council to research, formulate, and implement a long-range plan for the addition of technology in the district. The CCC coordinates the plan with the work of the Subject Area Committees and the Resource Advisory Committee.

Unified School District
#119

Sample City, Kansas

Curriculum Action Plan

1995

**Presented to the Sample City Superintendent
and Board of Education**

Prepared by Susan Smith, Sample City Curriculum Coordinator

INTRODUCTION

The foundation of a school system is its curriculum. Curriculum is the content and process by which learners gain knowledge and understanding and develop skills. Sample City is made up of a staff who are talented and dedicated. All of the teachers have developed instructional programs for their students, and should be admired and respected for their individual efforts. However, our district can be even more effective by planning and implementing a curriculum on a district-wide basis. Without such a plan, there is a likelihood that there are areas in our curriculum that are not being properly addressed. There may be overlaps where the same topics are covered in consecutive grade levels or gaps where important topics are being omitted.

In order to move our district from where we are now to where we want to be — from our present eclectic curriculum to an accountable, outcome-based and focused curriculum — we need a long range plan of curriculum development. We recommend the Accountability-Based Curriculum (ABC) Model as the means to meet the needs of our students. The ABC Model is a systematic process of developing, implementing, and maintaining curriculum through a governance structure established within the school district. It was developed by correlating background, research, trial and error, and "what works" practices. Ideas which support the basic premise of the ABC Model, that all students can learn given the right conditions and opportunities, are systematically arranged into a governance plan that may be implemented by any school district. In addition, the model outlines the specific steps involved in curriculum development and implementation.

This model has been proven to be very effective in school districts across the country and in districts close to home, such as Neighbor City, Kansas. Educational leaders in school districts that have used this model appreciate it because it gives direction to the academic curriculum and causes everyone to feel greater ownership and accountability to their programs. The process promotes an increase in professional conviction and leadership among their faculty members. It also gives a clearer sense of what schooling is for among educators, students, parents, and patrons in their districts.

You are probably aware that this is not a quick-fix process. It is complicated and time-consuming. Using the Accountability Based Curriculum Model will require organization, time, effort, and money. **Included in this Action Plan are a First Year Timeline and First Year Budget.** We are requesting that you carefully study this plan, approve the project, and provide necessary funding and support. The results will be measurable and effective, benefiting all participants of the educational process.

> **"If you don't know where you're going, any road will take you there."**

TABLE OF CONTENTS

GLOSSARY OF TERMS

core outcomes: the outcomes expected of <u>all</u> students in the school system. Elective courses have essential outcomes, but those outcomes are not *core* because not all students in the system will take the elective course. In required courses and grade level subjects, essential outcomes are also core outcomes because every student must achieve them.

Curriculum Coordinating Council (CCC): a governing body that has extensive authority over the district's academic program. Its membership is representative of the district's primary components (faculty, administration, support staff, board of education). Its first role is to initiate the action agenda for the district's school improvement model; later it serves as "keeper of the vision" for that model, as well as a conduit and think tank for keeping the academic program on the cutting edge of educational practice.

district mission statement: a written document that is used as the guide for all district decision-making. It is a point of focus that incorporates four components: the purpose of the district; goals for student learning, including the exit outcomes; the means of accomplishing the curriculum; and statements of accountability.

essential outcomes: the outcomes for a particular course that all students in that course must master. What things do we still want students to know and be able to do long after they have left this course?

exit outcomes —usually listed in the district mission statement: the things we want students to know or be able to do, or the characteristics we want them to exhibit (affective), when they <u>exit</u> the school system. What are the end results that we want for all students when they have completed their K-12 experiences?

extensions: corrective **or** enrichment activities and outcomes. They do not merely repeat what has been done before; instead, they continue, enlarge, expand, or stretch the core/essential outcomes.

high-achievement outcome: an outcome that meets the following criteria: (1) contains a positive statement; (2) tells what the students themselves will do; (3) uses a verb that describes specific action; (4) contains an end result that relates directly to our intention; (5) requires a high cognitive level; (6) requires dynamic student involvement; (7) is relevant to the student's present or future life; and, (8) can be authentically assessed. Essential outcomes and core outcomes should also be high-achievement outcomes.

long-range plan: a timeline developed by the Curriculum Coordinating Council for development, implementation, validation, and evaluation of curriculum in all subjects and grade levels.

outcome: the <u>end</u> <u>result</u> of the teaching/learning process. What should the students know or be able to do as a direct result of their participation in a particular set of learning activities? Outcomes describe what the <u>student</u> will do (not what the teacher will do or what is in the textbook).

outcome-based education: a philosophy in which all of the district's academic programs and instructional efforts are focused around clearly defined outcomes that all students must master before exiting the system. OBE is based on three premises: all students can learn, success breeds success, and schools control the conditions of success.

Resource Advisory Committee (RAC): a permanent, on-going committee appointed by the Curriculum Coordinating Council to research products and services related to educational resources. It serves as the communication link between the district and companies and agencies that supply the products and services.

Subject Area Committee (SAC): an ad hoc task force appointed by the Curriculum Coordinating Council in accordance with that body's long range plan for curriculum development. The primary responsibility of the SAC is to formulate an outcome based curriculum by following an action agenda prescribed by the CCC.

steering committee: an ad hoc committee, appointed by the superintendent, that includes representation of teachers, professional support persons, administrators, and one or more board members. Its primary purpose is to write the bylaws that guide the academic program's decision making process. The group may also critique the district's action plan and/or initiate procedures for establishing the Curriculum Coordinating Council.

Technology Resource Advisory Committee (TRAC): a permanent, on-going committee appointed by the Curriculum Coordinating Council to research, formulate, and implement a long-range plan for the addition of technology in the district. The CCC coordinates the plan with the work of the Subject Area Committees and the Resource Advisory Committee.

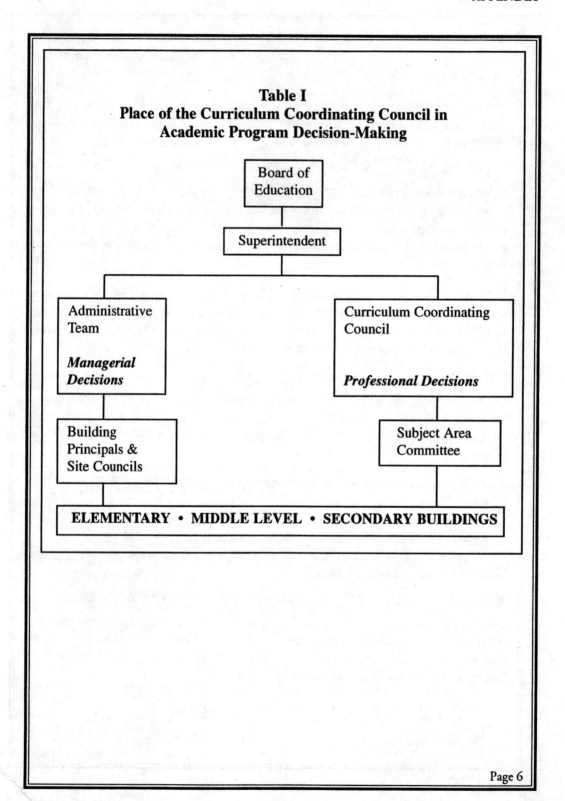

Table I
Place of the Curriculum Coordinating Council in
Academic Program Decision-Making

Board of
Education

Superintendent

Administrative
Team

*Managerial
Decisions*

Curriculum Coordinating
Council

Professional Decisions

Building
Principals &
Site Councils

Subject Area
Committee

ELEMENTARY • MIDDLE LEVEL • SECONDARY BUILDINGS

COMMITTEE ORGANIZATION AND FUNCTIONS

The two basic committees in our curriculum process will be the Curriculum Coordinating Council (CCC) and the Subject Area Committee (SAC). The basic difference between the two groups is: the CCC is for *policy making and program management,* and the SAC performs the challenging task of *assembling the new curriculum and putting it into motion.*

The CCC is a representative group that advises the Board of Education, through the Superintendent, in matters concerning curriculum development and instructional planning. The CCC will serve as a sounding board for certified personnel in curriculum matters. The CCC **may** be organized as follows:

Primary (K-2)	1 member
Intermediate (3-5)	1
Middle (6-8)	2
High School	2
Support Services	1
Administration	3
Superintendent	1
Board of Education	2
Patron	1
Coordinator	1
Total Membership	15

The major functions of the CCC will be to establish and coordinate a systematic, on-going process for creating and evaluating K-12 curricula. This includes the coordination of subject area and resource advisory committees, as well as the promotion of communication among buildings and levels within the district.

A SAC is a task force established by the CCC. A SAC will be formed for each subject area that is to be analyzed. The primary responsibility of each SAC is to develop, implement, and evaluate a results based curriculum document by following the model format and the direction of the CCC.

Two additional committees will also be formed: the Resource Advisory Committee and the Technology Resource Advisory Committee. These two groups will also follow guidelines of the model and direction of the CCC to study, plan, and advise regarding expenditures for instructional resources and technology acquisitions.

TRAINING

Once the Curriculum Coordinating Council and the Subject Area Committees are selected according to the guidelines of the model and the provisions of this Action Plan, intense training is necessary. While many of these individuals have had previous training pertaining to curriculum, a more in-depth study of results based education would be beneficial.

The CCC will be the first committee to be trained. The Curriculum Coordinator will train the CCC with the help of a consultant when needed. The most abundant training for this committee will occur in the first two years. Additional training at this time will provide a good foundation for the model. If our CCC has a solid foundation of knowledge it will be easier to train other district members.

Second, the first SACs will be trained by the CCC and a consultant The CCC members will also be a part of the various Subject Area Committees. The SAC will have more in-depth training than the CCC as their functions require direct use of results based procedures.

The training needed for this model will be an on-going process for the committees as well as the other staff members in the district, as they eventually implement and validate the curriculum. Consultant services will be needed until training has been received in all steps of the model; after that, the curriculum coordinator and the CCC will be able to provide the on-going training.

TRAINING NEEDED FOR THE FIRST YEAR

- The CCC and the first SAC will need training from a consultant before they can begin to assemble a new curriculum document and implement the Long-Range plan.

- Consulting in the curriculum model and its process will be given to the CCC through the Coordinator, as needed, by the Curriculum Leadership Institute and by the Area Service Agency.

- In-service meetings will be needed to train the teachers and other staff members in this model... how it works, how it will benefit them, and how it will be implemented.

MISSION STATEMENT

Last year our district established the statement of purpose to our Mission Statement. It is as follows:

THE MISSION OF THE SAMPLE CITY SCHOOLS IS TO PROVIDE A POSITIVE AND APPROPRIATE EDUCATIONAL EXPERIENCE FOR EACH STUDENT. WE WILL PROVIDE A SAFE, CARING, AND CONSISTENT ATMOSPHERE WHICH WILL ENABLE EACH STUDENT TO SUCCEED ACADEMICALLY AND TO CONTRIBUTE AS A RESPONSIBLE MEMBER OF SOCIETY.

This purpose is the beginning of a *comprehensive* district mission statement that our staff will generate this year. The comprehensive mission statement will express what our district does and will do to *carry out* our mission. For example, it will include the exit outcomes for our students, recommended instructional techniques, and statements of accountability.

Exit outcomes are clearly defined and publicly derived. The entire staff, as well as the community, will have input for these outcomes. Exit outcomes directly reflect the knowledge, competencies, and orientations needed by positive contributing adults in an increasingly complex, changing world, and are what all students successfully demonstrate before they leave school.

The staff will need time together as a district and some background information before this can be accomplished.

SUBJECT AREA COMMITTEE'S
ACTION AGENDA

The action agenda for the Subject Area Committees outlines what the SACs do in order to assemble a new curriculum in each subject area and put it into motion in the classroom. It is a standard approach and will save wasted time and money by providing a systematic process for each SAC to use. The steps of the action agenda are as follows:

1) establish the action agenda, with timeline
2) gather information
3) analyze information and make decisions
4) create focus areas and indicators
5) create a subject mission statement
6) convert focus areas to course and grade level purposes
7) convert indicators to high achievement outcomes
8) create task analysis guides
9) prepare the curriculum document
10) solicit document approval from the CCC and Board of Education
11) train the faculty
12) validate the curriculum internally
13) validate the curriculum externally
14) make adjustments to the curriculum document
15) identify appropriate resources
16) prepare an on-going evaluation process

This process will require training for our CCC and first SAC but will be used over and over as each area of our curriculum "comes up" to be reviewed and written. One or two curriculum documents will be produced each year and will be thorough, accepted, and effectively used. This process will continue indefinitely as we put a Long-Range Plan into effect.

LONG-RANGE PLAN

> **Those who wish to establish true educational accountability and implement effective reform must recognize that long-range planning is as important in the academics as it is in the "Three Fs": Fiscal control, Facility maintenance, and Faculty management.**

The Long-Range Plan will modify what we have traditionally called our "textbook cycle." For the most part, textbooks have *been* the curriculum in our district. Textbook adoption, therefore, has been what drove the entire curriculum. Our district will now be using textbooks as *resources* to support the teacher-developed curriculum and quality classroom instruction. The procedure for textbook adoption will be conducted in such a way that resources will be selected for their value in supporting the district's curriculum, not to *be* the curriculum.

Curriculum work takes time. For our district, each cycle in our Long-Range Plan would be five to seven years in length. Remember, this is not a quick-fix process. A quick-fix is just what the term implies — a quick fix — not an effective or lasting accomplishment. You must give the process enough time for thoroughness. This will prevent the teachers from being pushed too hard and too quickly. Remember that while the teachers are actively involved in implementing the improvement process, they also have a primary commitment to the present education of their students. When too much is pushed too fast, something will suffer: the improvement program itself, the current quality of education of the students, or the general energy, enthusiasm, and degree of commitment of the teachers.

The Long-Range Plan will include the following steps for **each subject area:**

1) Development of curriculum documents

2) Implementation and validation (internal and external) of the new curriculum

3) Resource selection and evaluation

An example of one district's Long-Range Plan is on the following page, and should provide a clearer picture of the process.

LONG RANGE PLAN
Pleasant Valley Public Schools

<u>Abbreviations:</u>

        C....Development of curriculum documents
        I.....Initial Implementation of the new curriculum
        V....Validation (internal and external)
        R....Resource selection
        E....Evaluation

Subjects	96/97	97/98	98/99	99/00	00/01	01/02	02/03
Social Studies	C	I/V	R/E				
Science		C	I/V	R/E			
Mathematics			C	I/V	R/E		
Communications			C	C	I/V	R/E	
Foreign Language					C	I/V	R/E
Business		C	I/V	R/E			
Home Economics		C	I/V	R/E			
Industrial Education		C	I/V	R/E			
Speech/Theater				C	I/V	R/E	
Art				C	I/V	R/E	
Music				C	I/V	R/E	
Health			C	I/V	R/E		
Physical Education				C	I/V	R/E	

FIRST YEAR PROJECTED TIMELINE
1996-97

bold:CCC
italics: *SAC*
<u>underlined:</u>   <u>District In-Service</u>

SEPTEMBER   • Steering Committee created by Coordinator and Superintendent
                 • Action plan studied, revised, accepted

OCTOBER   • Action plan presented to Board and approved or revised
             • By-laws developed

NOVEMBER   • By-laws completed, presented to Board and approved or revised
              • Plan in-service session

DECEMBER   • <u>In-service session explains model, by-laws and CCC application</u>
               <u>process</u>
              • CCC selected
              • Secretary appointed

JANUARY   • **CCC trained in the model**
            • **Begin mission statement process**

FEBRUARY   • **Long-Range Plan developed**
             • **Continue mission statement process; plan in-service**
               and community presentations

MARCH   • <u>In-service session for mission statement</u>
          • **Conduct meetings or presentations for community**
            input for mission statement

APRIL   • **Long-Range Plan implemented: SACs appointed**
        • **Discuss feedback from faculty and community;**
           revise mission statement

MAY   • Mission statement adopted by Board and published
       • *Training* for CCC and first SAC

SECOND YEAR GENERAL TIMELINE
1997-98

During the second year, the CCC will direct the work of the first Subject Area Committee and coordinate staff development efforts with the curriculum and instruction processes. They will participate in research, discussion, and decision-making processes related to issues that are vital to accomplishing the mission of the district. They will work with accreditation processes. At the end of the school year they will train the new SACs.

The first Subject Area Committee will establish and begin implementing their Action Agenda. They will complete the first ten steps of that agenda: 1) establish the agenda with timeline, 2) gather information, 3) analyze information and make decisions, 4) create focus areas and indicators, 5) create a subject mission statement, 6) convert focus areas to course and grade level purposes, 7) convert indicators to high achievement outcomes, 8) create task analysis guides, 9) prepare the curriculum document, and 10) solicit document approval from the CCC and Board of Education. They will begin the 11th step, training of the faculty.

THIRD YEAR GENERAL TIMELINE
1998-99

The CCC continues to serve as "keepers of the vision." This includes implementation of the model through training and directing the Subject Area Committees, and making decisions and taking actions to accomplish the mission. They will insure internal communication and work with accreditation processes.

The first SAC implements the new curriculum and continues to work with faculty development for teaching that curriculum. They validate the curriculum internally and externally, and make adjustments to the curriculum document.

New SACs follow the same processes that the first SAC completed during the second year.

PROPOSED FIRST YEAR BUDGET

Steering Committee:

    6 members: three meetings X $30.00 substitute pay $ 540

Curriculum Coordinating Council:

    Substitutes will be needed only for those with classroom responsibilities, e.g. the representatives of the various grade level categories, support personnel and the part-time curriculum coordinator.

    8 members: six meetings X $30.00 substitute pay $ 1440

    Stipends $ 2400

Secretary for CCC and SAC $ 1200

Materials (supplies, postage, printing) $ 600

Refreshments $ 500

Consultant fees $ 1500

Total. $8180

INDEX